LIBRARY OF NEW TESTAMENT STUDIES

688

formerly the Journal for the Study of the New Testament Supplement series

Editor
Chris Keith

Editorial Board
Dale C. Allison, Lynn H. Cohick, Kylie Crabbe, R. Alan Culpepper, Craig A. Evans,
Jennifer Eyl, Robert Fowler, Juan Hernández Jr., John S. Kloppenborg,
Michael Labahn, Matthew V. Novenson, Love L. Sechrest, Robert Wall,
Catrin H. Williams, Brittany E. Wilson

The Gospel of the Son of God:

Psalm 2 and Mark's Narrative Christology

By
James M. Neumann

t&tclark

LONDON • NEW YORK • OXFORD • NEW DELHI • SYDNEY

T&T CLARK

Bloomsbury Publishing Plc, 50 Bedford Square, London, WC1B 3DP, UK
Bloomsbury Publishing Inc, 1385 Broadway, New York, NY 10018, USA
Bloomsbury Publishing Ireland, 29 Earlsfort Terrace, Dublin 2, D02 AY28, Ireland

BLOOMSBURY, T&T CLARK and the T&T Clark logo are trademarks of
Bloomsbury Publishing Plc

First published in Great Britain 2024
Paperback edition published 2025

Copyright © James M. Neumann, 2024

James M. Neumann has asserted his right under the Copyright, Designs and Patents Act, 1988, to be identified as Author of this work.

For legal purposes the Acknowledgments on p. vii constitute an extension
of this copyright page.

All rights reserved. No part of this publication may be: i) reproduced or transmitted in any form, electronic or mechanical, including photocopying, recording or by means of any information storage or retrieval system without prior permission in writing from the publishers; or ii) used or reproduced in any way for the training, development or operation of artificial intelligence (AI) technologies, including generative AI technologies. The rights holders expressly reserve this publication from the text and data mining exception as per Article 4(3) of the Digital Single Market Directive (EU) 2019/790.

Bloomsbury Publishing Plc does not have any control over, or responsibility for, any third-party websites referred to or in this book. All internet addresses given in this book were correct at the time of going to press. The author and publisher regret any inconvenience caused if addresses have changed or sites have ceased to exist, but can accept no responsibility for any such changes.

A catalogue record for this book is available from the British Library.

Library of Congress Cataloging-in-Publication Data

ISBN: HB: 978-0-5677-1148-9
PB: 978-0-5677-1152-6
ePDF: 978-0-5677-1149-6
ePUB: 978-0-5677-1151-9

Series: Library of New Testament Studies, volume 688
ISSN 2513-8790

Typeset by RefineCatch Limited, Bungay, Suffolk

For product safety related questions contact productsafety@bloomsbury.com.

To find out more about our authors and books visit www.bloomsbury.com
and sign up for our newsletters.

Contents

Acknowledgments		vii
List of Abbreviations		viii
1	Introduction	1
	1.1 Justification for this Study	2
	1.2 Methodology and Presuppositions	10
	1.3 Clarifications	18
	1.4 The Argument	19
2	The Son of God and the Story of Psalm 2	23
	2.1 The Story within Psalm 2	23
	2.2 Psalm 2 in Early Judaism	27
	2.3 Psalm 2 in the New Testament and Early Christianity	36
	2.4 Summary: The Story of Psalm 2	52
3	The Beginning of The Gospel	53
	3.1 Mark's Incipit: The Son of God in the Beginning	54
	3.2 Preparing the Way (Mark 1:4-8)	58
	3.3 Introducing God's Son (Mark 1:9-11)	60
	3.4 Excursus: Mark 1:11 in Twentieth-Century Interpretation	66
	3.5 A Storied Metalepsis: Psalm 2 in Mark's Prologue	70
	3.6 Looking Ahead: Mark 1:11 and the Rest of the Story	78
4	The Son of God in Conflict	83
	4.1 An Unlikely Chorus: God's Word and the Demons' Words about Jesus	83
	4.2 Plundering Satan's Kingdom: Jesus's Exorcisms in the Gospel of Mark	84
	4.3 Mark 1:21-28: "I Know Who You Are"	87
	4.4 Mark 3:6-11: "You Are the Son of God"	90
	4.5 Mark 5:1-20: "You Are the Son of the Most-High God"	98
	4.6 Summary and Conclusions	104
5	The Son On The Mountain	105
	5.1 Climbing the Mountain with Mark: Mark 9:7 in Narrative Perspective	106
	5.2 The Mountain Remembered: Echoes of Sinai in Mark 9:2-8	109
	5.3 Apocalyptic Topography and Radiant Garments: The Reinterpretation of Sinai in Mark 9:2-8	113
	5.4 Jesus in the Throne Room	116

	5.5	Jesus's Transfiguration and Daniel's Vision (7:9-14)	118
	5.6	Conclusion: Psalm 2 and the Son's Enthronement in Mark 9:2-8	125
6	The Son In The Parable		129
	6.1	The Parable at a Glance: An Allegory Rooted in Israel's Scriptures	129
	6.2	The "Beloved Son" and Psalm 2	133
	6.3	A Story within a Story: Mark's Parable as *Mise en Abyme*	137
	6.4	Summary: The Death of God's Son Foreshadowed	142
7	Part 1: The Son of God On The Cross		143
	7.1	Are You the Messiah the Son of God? (Mark 14:61-62)	144
	7.2	Are You the King of the Jews? (Mark 15:1-15)	148
	7.3	Irony and Parodic Enthronement in Mark 15:16-32	152
	7.4	Part 1 Summary	157
	Part 2: The Centurion'S Confession (Mark 15:39)		158
	7.5	The Problem(s) of a Centurion's Confession	159
	7.6	The Son of God in the Roman World	162
	7.7	Excursus: A History of Irony	170
	7.8	The Centurion's Confession and the Fulfillment of Psalm 2	172
	7.9	Conclusions	174

Conclusions	177
Bibliography	181
Index of References	215
Index of Modern Authors	237

Acknowledgments

This book is a revised version of my Ph.D. dissertation, the completion of which carries with it an enormous debt of gratitude to those who helped make it possible: both those who contributed to this project directly and those who have done so indirectly by their investment in me over the years. First and foremost, I wish to thank the members of my committee: Professors Dale Allison (who supervised this project), Clifton Black, and George Parsenios for their careful reading and engagement with this work at various stages, as well as their instruction over the past five years. One could scarcely ask for a more dedicated advisor than Dale Allison, who promptly read every chapter along the way and provided countless insights and suggestsions for improvement, as well as much enouragement. I am better scholar thanks to him.

Among my earlier teachers, I am grateful to the faculty at Gordon-Conwell Theological Seminary, who taught me exegetical rigor and consistently modeled the integration of scholarship with one's life of worship. I mention especially Mark Jennings who supervised the Th.M. thesis that served as a precursor to the present project. From my days at Mississippi College, I also owe special thanks to Roger Greene ("Big G"), who first sparked my interest in Mark and "Son of God," in particular.

Among the greatest blessings of my time in Princeton have been my dear friends, Alex and Annie Kato, Peter and Alyssa Evans, and the many other members of our family at Stone Hill Church of Princeton. Their friendship, encouragement, prayers, and mutual commitment to Christ have not only sustained me during the past several years, but filled them with joy. Most of all, I give thanks to and for my beloved wife, Amelia. As I was finishing this project, we were only beginning to discover our love for one another. First as a friend and now as my wife, she has been God's greatest gift to me during this project.

Finally, I wish to thank my parents, Jim and Anita Neumann, who have loved encouraged, supported, and inspired me all my life. The best of what I am is because of them. I dedicate this book to my grandmother, Louise Allensworth, who first taught me that Jesus is the Son of God.

Abbreviations

AB	Anchor Bible
ABD	David Noel Freedman (ed.), *The Anchor Bible Dictionary* (New York: Doubleday, 1992)
AGJU	Arbeiten zur Geschichte des antiken Judentums und des Urchristentums
AJEC	Ancient Judaism and Early Christianity
AnBib	Analecta biblica
ANF	Anti-Nicene Fathers
ANRW	Hildegard Temporini and Wolfgang Haase (eds), *Aufstieg und Niedergang der römischen Welt: Geschichte und Kultur Roms im Spiegel der neueren Forschung* (Berlin: W. de Gruyter, 1972–)
ANTC	Abingdon New Testament Commentary
AOTC	Abingdon Old Testament Commentary
AOAT	Alter Orient und Altes Testament
ArBib	The Aramaic Bible
ATANT	Abhandlungen zur Theologie des Alten und Neuen Testaments
AUSS	*Andrews University Seminary Studies*
BBB	Bonner biblische Beiträge
BDAG	Danker, Frederick W., Walter Bauer, William F. Arndt, and F. Wilbur Gingrich. *Greek-English Lexicon of the New Testament and Other Early Christian Literature.* 3rd ed. Chicago: University of Chicago Press, 2000.
BDB	Francis Brown, S.R. Driver and Charles A. Briggs, *A Hebrew and English Lexicon of the Old Testament* (Oxford: Clarendon Press, 1907)
BDF	Friedrich Blass, A. Debrunner and Robert W. Funk, *A Greek Grammar of the New Testament and Other Early Christian Literature* (Cambridge: Cambridge University Press, 1961)
BETL	Bibliotheca Ephemeridum Theologicarum Lovaniensium
Bib	*Biblica*
BibInt	*Biblical Interpretation: A Journal of Contemporary Approaches*
BNP	*Brill's New Pauly: Encyclopedia of the Ancient World.* Edited by Hubert Cancik. 22 vols Leiden: Brill, 2002–2011.
BNTC	Black's New Testament Commentaries
BBR	*Bulletin for Biblical Research*
BR	*Bible Review*
BSac	*Bibliotheca Sacra*
BT	*The Bible Translator*
BTB	*Biblical Theology Bulletin*
BWA(N)T	Beiträge zur Wissenschaft vom Alten (und Neuen) Testament
BZ	*Biblische Zeitschrift*
BZAW	Beihefte zur *ZAW*
BZNW	Beihefte zur *ZNW*
CahRB	Cahiers de la Revue biblique

CBC	Cambridge Bible Commentary
CBQ	*Catholic Biblical Quarterly*
CBQMS	*Catholic Biblical Quarterly*, Monograph Series
CChr	Corpus Christianorum
ClQ	*Classical Quarterly*
CNT	Commentaire du Nouveau Testament
CNTUOT	*Commentary on the New Testament Use of the Old Testament*
ConBNT	Coniectanea biblica, New Testament
ConBOT	Coniectanea biblica, Old Testament
CRBS	*Currents in Research: Biblical Studies*
CRINT	Compendia rerum iudaicarum ad Novum Testamentum
CSEL	Corpus scriptorum ecclesiasticorum latinorum
CTR	*Criswell Theological Review*
DDD	Toorn, K. van der, Bob Becking, and Pieter Willem van der Horst, eds. *Dictionary of Deities and Demons in the Bible*. 2nd ed. (Leiden/Boston: Brill; Grand Rapids: Eerdmans, 1999)
DJD	Discoveries in the Judaean Desert
EBib	Etudes bibliques
EKKNT	Evangelisch-Katholischer Kommentar zum Neuen Testament
ETL	*Ephemerides Theologicae Lovanienses*
EvT	*Evangelische Theologie*
ExpTim	*Expository Times*
FRLANT	Forschungen zur Religion und Literatur des Alten und Neuen Testaments
FTS	Frankfurter theologische Studien
HALOT	Ludwig Koehler, Water Baumgartner, and Johann J. Stamm. *The Hebrew and Aramaic Lexicon of the Old Testament*. 3rd ed. (Leiden: Brill, 1995, 2004)
HBM	Hebrew Bible Monographs
HBT	*Horizons in Biblical Theology*
HNT	Handbuch zum Neuen Testament
HTR	*Harvard Theological Review*
ICC	International Critical Commentary
Int	*Interpretation*
ISFCJ	International Studies in Formative Christianity and Judaism
JAAR	*Journal of the American Academy of Religion*
JBL	*Journal of Biblical Literature*
JCTCRSS	Jewish and Christian Texts in Contexts and Related Studies Series
JES	*Journal of Ecumenical Studies*
JETS	*Journal of the Evangelical Theological Society*
JHC	*Journal of Higher Criticism*
JQR	*Jewish Quarterly Review*
JR	*Journal of Religion*
JRS	*Journal of Roman Studies*
JSHS	*Journal for the Study of the Historical Jesus*
JSJ	*Journal for the Study of Judaism in the Persian, Hellenistic and Roman Period*
JSNT	*Journal for the Study of the New Testament*
JSNTSup	*Journal for the Study of the New Testament*, Supplement Series
JSOT	*Journal for the Study of the Old Testament*
JSP	*Journal for the Study of the Pseudepigrapha*
JSPSup	*Journal for the Study of the Pseudepigrapha*, Supplement Series

JT	*Journal of Theology*
JTI	*Journal of Theological Interpretation*
JTS	*Journal of Theological Studies*
KEK	Kritisch-exegetischer Kommentar über das Neue Testament
LB	*Linguistica biblica*
LCL	Loeb Classical Library
LD	Lectio divina
LNTS	Library of New Testament Studies
LQ	*Lutheran Quarterly*
LSJ	H.G. Liddell, Robert Scott and H. Stuart Jones, *Greek–English Lexicon* (Oxford: Clarendon Press, 9th ed, 1968)
MNTSS	McMaster New Testament Studies Series
NCBC	New Cambridge Bible Commentary
NechtB	Neue Echter Bibel
Neot	*Neotestamentica*
NIB	*The New Interpreter's Bible*. Edited by Leander E. Keck. 12 vols
NICNT	New International Commentary on the New Testament
NIGTC	The New International Greek Testament Commentary
NovT	*Novum Testamentum*
NovTSup	*Novum Testamentum*, Supplements
NPNF	Nicene and Post-Nicene Fathers
NTL	New Testament Library
NTS	*New Testament Studies*
NTSI	New Testament and the Scriptures of Israel
OBO	Orbis biblicus et orientalis
OCD	*Oxford Classical Dictionary*
OTL	Old Testament Library
OTP	James Charlesworth (ed.), *Old Testament Pseudepigrapha*
OTS	*Oudtestamentische Studiën*
PG	J.-P. Migne (ed.), *Patrologia cursus completa . . . Series graeca* (166 vols; Paris: Petit-Montrouge, 1857–83)
PL	J.-P. Migne (ed.), *Patrologia cursus completes Series prima [latina]* (221 vols; Paris: J.-P. Migne, 1844–65)
PNTC	Pillar New Testament Commentary
PTSDSSP	Princeton Theological Seminary Dead Sea Scrolls Project
RAC	*Reallexikon für Antike und Christentum*
RB	*Revue biblique*
RBS	Resources for Biblical Study
RCSOT	Reformation Commentary on Scripture Old Testament
RechBib	Recherches bibliques
RevQ	*Revue de Qumran*
RNT	Regensburger Neues Testament
RSR	*Recherches de Science Religieuse*
RTP	*Revue de théologie et de philosophie*
SBB	Stuttgarter biblische Beiträge
SBEC	Studies in the Bible and Early Christianity
SBJT	*Southern Baptist Journal of Theology*
SBL	Society of Biblical Literature
SBLDS	SBL Dissertation Series

SBLRBS	SBL Resources for Biblical Study
SBM	Stuttgarter biblische Monographien
SBS	Stuttgarter Bibelstudien
SBT	Studies in Biblical Theology
ScEs	*Science et esprit*
SEÅ	*Svensk exegetisk årsbok*
Sem	*Semitica*
SHBC	Smith & Helwys Bible Commentary
SJLA	Studies in Judaism in Late Antiquity
SNTSMS	Society for New Testament Studies Monograph Series
SP	Sacra Pagina
SPB	Studia Postbiblica
SSEJC	Studies in Scripture in Early Judaism and Christianity
ST	*Studia theologica*
STDJ	Studies on the Texts of the Desert of Judah
SUNT	Studien zur Umwelt des Neuen Testaments
SVTP	Studia in Veteris Testamenti pseudepigrapha
SwJT	*Southwestern Journal of Theology*
SymBU	Symbolae biblicae upsalienses
TDNT	Gerhard Kittel and Gerhard Friedrich (eds), *Theological Dictionary of the New Testament* (trans. Geoffrey W. Bromiley; 10 vols; Grand Rapids: Eerdmans, 1964–)
THKNT	Theologischer Handkommentar zum Neuen Testament
TLZ	*Theologische Literaturzeitung*
TZ	*Theologische Zeitschrift*
TNTC	Tyndale New Testament Commentaries
TynBul	*Tyndale Bulletin*
UNT	Untersuchungen zum Neuen Testament
USQR	*Union Seminary Quarterly Review*
VT	*Vetus Testamentum*
VTSup	*Vetus Testamentum*, Supplements
WBC	Word Biblical Commentary
WF	Wege der Forschung
WGRW	Writings from the Greco-Roman World
WMANT	Wissenschaftliche Monographien zum Alten und Neuen Testament
WUNT	Wissenschaftliche Untersuchungen zum Neuen Testament
YJS	Yale Judaica Series
ZAW	*Zeitschrift für die alttestamentliche Wissenschaft*
ZDPV	*Zeitschrift des deutschen Palästina-Vereins*
ZNW	*Zeitschrift für die neutestamentliche Wissenschaft*
ZTK	*Zeitschrift für Theologie und Kirche*

1

Introduction

Ἀρχὴ τοῦ εὐαγγελίου Ἰησοῦ Χριστοῦ [υἱοῦ θεοῦ].

Mark 1:1

It is not improper that the superscription in most manuscripts reads: "the Gospel of Jesus Christ, the Son of God."

Wilhelm Bousset[1]

It may seem odd to begin a book that one wishes to have read by noting a text-critical issue; yet one could hardly ask for a better introduction to a book about Mark's portrayal of Jesus as the Son of God than Mark's own, its textual questions included. The Gospel of Mark, as it has generally come down to us, announces itself as "the gospel of Jesus Christ Son of God," implying that these two epithets, "Christ" and "Son of God," are indispensable to the story that follows. Not all manuscripts contain the final words, υἱοῦ θεοῦ, of course.[2] Nevertheless, we are essentially left with two possibilities: either the evangelist himself claims that Jesus's identity as "Son of God" is central to the message of his Gospel, or else an early reader thought so and added the epithet to reflect the perceived character of the work.[3]

There are obvious reasons why one might have done so. Although [ὁ] υἱὸς [τοῦ] θεοῦ is not the most common title for Jesus in Mark, it occurs at pivotal moments, including the relative beginning, middle, and end of Jesus's story (1:11; 9:7; 15:39).[4]

---

[1] This author's translation of Wilhelm Bousset (*Kyrios Christos: Geschichte des Christusglaubens von den Anfängen des Christentums bis Irenaeus*, 2nd ed. [Göttingen: Vandenhoeck & Ruprecht, 1921], 53): "Nicht mit Unrecht steht in der Überschrift des Evangeliums in den meisten Handschriften: Evangelium von Jesus Christus, dem Sohne Gottes."

[2] Though the disputed words appear in most manuscripts, including ℵ¹ B D, they are notably lacking in ℵ* and Origen. See further the discussion in Chapter 2.

[3] In the latter event, the addition must have occurred early. Peter Head ("A Text-Critical Study of Mark 1.1: The Beginning of the Gospel of Jesus Christ," *NTS* 37 [1991]: 629) suggests around "AD 100"; Adela Yarbro Collins ("Establishing the Text: Mark 1:1," in *Texts and Contexts: Biblical Texts in Their Textual and Situational Contexts*, ed. Tord Fornberg and David Hellholm [Olso/Copenhagen/Stockholm/Boston: Scandinavian University Press, 1995], 125) suggests early in the second century.

[4] So already Ambrose, *Spir.*, 2.6.57 (*PL* 16:755b). Morna Hooker observes that these three acclamations correspond to the three climactic revelatory moments in the Gospel, which is to say that Jesus's sonship is the content of Mark's most pivotal revelatory moments; see *The Gospel According to St. Mark* (Peabody: Hendrickson, 1993), 175–76; and idem, "Good News about Jesus Christ, the Son of God," in *Mark as Story: Retrospect and Prospect*, ed. Kelly R. Iverson and Christopher W. Skinner, RBS 65 (Atlanta: SBL, 2011), 165–80. The most common title of Jesus in Mark, by comparison, is Son of Man, which occurs thirteen times in 2:10, 28; 8:31, 38; 9:9, 12, 31; 10:33, 45; 13:26; 14:41, 62.

Likewise, Jesus's earthly career is encapsulated between two declarations that he is God's Son: first by God himself, then by a Roman centurion, who is the first (and only) human character to recognize Jesus as such in Mark's Gospel (1:11; 15:39). In between, the demons identify Jesus as the Son of God (3:11; 5:7); Jesus himself nods toward his identity as God's "beloved Son" in an autobiographical parable foreshadowing his passion (12:6); and a variation of the title plays a critical role in his trial (14:61), leading to his death (15:37-39). It is not surprising, then, that ancient and modern interpreters alike have sometimes thought of Mark as "the gospel of the Son of God."[5]

Given the weight that Son of God bears for Mark, it is surprising that, to date, no monograph has traced its overall significance in the Gospel. Some readers may think of Carl Kazmierski's *Jesus, the Son of God* or Hans-Jörg Steichele's *Der leidende Sohn Gottes*, yet even these important studies limit their focus to particular aspects of Mark's Son of God (Mark's redaction and use of Scripture, respectively) rather than the meaning of Jesus's identity as Son of God *per se*.[6] Others may assume that the meaning of Son of God is obvious, or wonder whether such a study is necessary after the numerous titular christologies of the previous decades.[7] But to reconstruct the history of a title is not yet to comprehend what it signifies within the Gospel narrative.[8] And if the implicit claim in Mark's superscription is correct, then to miss the meaning of Jesus's identity as the Son of God is to miss an integral piece of the story itself. Indeed, for Mark, to call Jesus Son of God is not so much to assign to him an early christological title as to elaborate on the mission and accomplishments of the Christ: i.e., the gospel in shorthand.

1.1 Justification for this Study

In an essay on Markan Christology, Eugene Boring states:

> There is widespread but not universal agreement that [ὁ] υἱὸς [τοῦ] θεοῦ represents the key christological term for Mark, that the term had a broad spectrum of

---

[5] Theophylact, *Enarrat. Marc.* 1:1 (*PG* 123:493); cf. Albertus Magnus, *Enarrat. Marc*, in *Opera Omnia*, vol. 21, ed. Auguste Borgnet (Paris: Ludovicum Vives, 1894), 344. For modern interpreters, see below.

[6] See Carl R. Kazmierski, *Jesus, the Son of God: A Study of the Markan Tradition and Its Redaction by the Evangelist*, FB 33 (Würzburg: Echter, 1979); and Hans-Jörg Steichele, *Der leidende Sohn Gottes: eine Untersuchung einiger alttestamentlicher Motive in der Christologie des Markusevangeliums: zugleich ein Beitrag zur Erhellung des überlieferungsgeschichtlichen Zusammenhangs zwischen Altem und Neuem Testament*, Münchener Universitätsschriften 14 (Regensburg: Pustet, 1980).

[7] E.g., Oscar Cullmann, *The Christology of the New Testament*, Rev. ed., NTL (Philadelphia: Westminster Press, 1963); Ferdinand Hahn, *Christologische Hoheitstitel* (Göttingen: Vandenhoeck & Ruprecht, 1963 [5th ed., 2005]); C. F. D. Moule, *The Origin of Christology* (Cambridge/New York: Cambridge University Press, 1977); James D. G. Dunn, *Christology in the Making: A New Testament Inquiry into the Origins of the Doctrine of the Incarnation*, 2nd ed. (London: SCM, 1989).

[8] Leander Keck ("Toward the Renewal of New Testament Christology," *NTS* 32 [1987]: 362–77, here 368) captures this point nicely: "To reconstruct the history of titles as if this were the study of christology is like trying to understand the windows of Chartres cathedral by studying the history of coloured glass."

meanings in the Hellenistic world, some connoting 'divinity' and some not, and that Mark's meaning within this context must be determined by his own usage.⁹

Boring is correct on all accounts. In Jack Dean Kingsbury's estimation, Jesus's identity "as the royal Son of God is inextricably bound up with his destiny" in the Gospel.¹⁰ Like many before him, Brian Gamel argues in his recent study that the centurion's confession, "Truly this man was υἱὸς θεοῦ," is, in effect, the "punch line" of the entire Gospel.¹¹ From Theophylact (quoted above) to the present day, many others have voiced a similar conviction that "Son of God" is central to the Gospel Mark presents.¹² Despite this widely held belief, however, it is not clear that Markan scholarship as a whole has advanced much from Étienne Trocmé's position that "none of the titles applied to Jesus in the Gospel of Mark appears to be used by the evangelist as a vehicle for his own christology."¹³ Whatever the reasons for this seemingly paradoxical position—[ὁ] υἱὸς [τοῦ] θεοῦ is of key christological significance for Mark, but he does not thereby advance his own christology through it—the result is the same: the dynamics of Mark's narrative portrayal of Jesus as the Son of God have gone largely unnoticed.¹⁴

Michael Peppard begins his 2011 monograph, *Son of God in the Roman World*, by observing one reason why studies of "Son of God" in general have been lacking: "We think we know what it means."¹⁵ Peppard specifically has in mind the assumption from ancient times that the title refers directly to divine sonship *sensu metaphysico*. In the early centuries of the church, it became common to read "Son of God" as a statement of Jesus's divine nature in contrast to "Son of Man," which was thought to convey his human nature, without considering any further the connotations of son-of-God language in the ancient world.¹⁶

---

⁹ M. Eugene Boring, "Markan Christology: God-Language for Jesus?" *NTS* 45 (1999): 451–71, here 452.
¹⁰ Jack Dean Kingsbury, *Jesus Christ in Matthew, Mark, and Luke* (Philadelphia: Fortress, 1981), 34; cf. idem, *The Christology of Mark's Gospel* (Philadelphia: Fortress Press, 1989), *passim*.
¹¹ Brian K. Gamel, *Mark 15:39 as a Markan Theology of Revelation: The Centurion's Confession as Apocalyptic Unveiling*, LNTS 458 (London/New York: Bloomsbury T&T Clark, 2017), 3–4.
¹² E.g., Hooker, *Mark*, 175–76; idem, "Good News," 165–80; Simon Légasse, *L'Evangile de Marc*, 2 vols, *Lectio divina* 5 (Paris: Cerf, 1997), 1:53; Frank J. Matera, *New Testament Christology*, (Louisville: Westminster John Knox, 1999), 8; Edwin K. Broadhead, *Naming Jesus: Titular Christology in the Gospel of Mark*, JSNTSup 175 (Sheffield: Sheffield Academic, 1999), 123; William R. Telford, *The Theology of the Gospel of Mark*, New Testament Theology (Cambridge/New York: Cambridge University Press, 1999), 39; Adam Winn, *The Purpose of Mark's Gospel: An Early Christian Response to Roman Imperial Propaganda*, WUNT 2/245 (Tübingen: Mohr Siebeck, 2008), 19.
¹³ Étienne Trocmé, "Is There a Markan Christology?" in *Christ and Spirit in the New Testament*, eds. Barnabas Lindars and Stephen S. Smalley (Cambridge: Cambridge University Press, 1973), 3–14, here 8. Trocmé expresses this doubt just after affirming that Son of God is one of the most unambiguously positive christological titles in Mark—less ambiguous than Christ, Son of David, or King of the Jews.
¹⁴ At least one significant reason may be the once-prevalent view that Mark is relatively unsophisticated and lacks theological aims (see, e.g., Rudolf Bultmann, *The History of the Synoptic Tradition* [Peabody: Hendrickson, 1963], 350).
¹⁵ Michael Peppard, *The Son of God in the Roman World: Divine Sonship in Its Social and Political Context* (Oxford: Oxford University Press, 2011), 3.
¹⁶ For the first interpretation, see Ignatius, *Eph.* 20.2; *Barn.* 12.10; Irenaeus, *Ad. Haer.* 3.16.7, 17.1; Justin, *Dial.* 76.1; 100; *Odes Sol.* 36.3. For the second see Hippolytus, *The Discourse on the Holy Theophany*, 106 (ANF 5:236); Gregory Thaumaturgus, *The Fourth Homily, On the Holy Theophany* or *Of Christ's Baptism* (ANF 6:70-71); Ambrose, *Exposition of the Christian Faith* 1.10.67 (NPNF2 10:212); Augustine, *Letter 169, to Euodius* (FC 30:34-35); idem, *Questions*, 43 (FC 70:74-75). For a further discussion of the point above, see Dunn, *Christology*, 12–3.

By contrast, Hermann Samuel Reimarus took nearly the opposite approach in the eighteenth century. Although Reimarus was not the first to question whether "Son of God" should be understood as "God the Son" (i.e., the second person of the Trinity), he was the first to do so by appealing to the categories of Jewish messianism. Based largely on the Scriptural allusions in the *bath qol* at Jesus's baptism (Mark 1:11 par.), Reimarus argued that "to be called 'Son of God' and 'Christ, the Messiah' meant one and the same thing."[17] Reimarus did not explicitly discuss Ps 2:7, which identifies YHWH's משיח as his בן, but he may have had it in mind given that its presence in the baptismal voice had been recognized for centuries beforehand.[18]

Yet the critical response to Reimarus was mixed. As Max Botner explains:

On the one hand, many scholars, particularly those in the German-speaking world, followed his attempt to interpret christological categories within the framework of early Judaism, irrespective of doctrines and creeds. "Son of God" was thus routinely treated as a messianic epithet, cognate with "son of David" and "messiah." On the other hand, virtually no one was willing to follow Reimarus's assertion that the historical Jesus capitulated to the political expectations facing any would-be messiah. Instead, *Neutestamentler* lined up in droves to argue that Jesus eschewed the messianic spirit of his time."[19]

Hence William Wrede, while acknowledging the generative importance of Jesus's identity as Son of God in Mark's Gospel on a literary level, argued that this motif belongs not to the "history of Jesus" but rather to the "history of dogma," wherein Jesus becomes a "higher, supernatural being" through the reception of the Spirit at his baptism (1:9-11).[20] Rather than "Messiah" interpreting "Son of God," it is Jesus's

---

[17] Hermann Samuel Reimarus, *Fragments*, ed. Charles H. Talbert, trans. R. S. Fraser, Lives of Jesus Series (London: SCM, 1971), 81–3 (here 83).

[18] See, e.g., Justin, *Dial.* 88.8, 103.6 (*PG* 6:688, 717); Clement of Alexandria, *Paed.* 1.6.25 (*PG* 8:280); and others cited in Chapter 3.

[19] Max Botner, "What Has Mark's Christ to Do with David's Son? A History of Interpretation," *CRBS* 16 (2017): 50–70, here 51–2; idem, *Jesus Christ as the Son of David in the Gospel of Mark*, SNTSMS 174 (Cambridge: Cambridge University Press, 2019), 5. After Reimarus, Botner cites Bernhard Weiss, *Biblical Theology of the New Testament*. 2 vols, trans. David Easton and James E. Duguid (Edinburgh: T&T Clark, 1882–1883 [German 1873]), 1:78–81, 2:283–86; Ezra P. Gould, *A Critical and Exegetical Commentary on the Gospel according to St. Mark*, ICC 27 (Edinburgh: T&T Clark, 1896), 12; Julius Wellhausen, *Das Evangelium Marci* (Berlin: Georg Reimer, 1903), 6–7; Henrich Julius Hotlzmann, *Das messianische Bewusstein Jesu: Ein Beitrag zur Leben-Jesu-Forschung* (Tübingen: Mohr Siebeck, 1907), 100; idem, *Lehrbuch der neutestamentlichen Theologie*, 2 vols (Tübingen: Mohr Siebeck, 1911), 1:336–37, 340 352.

[20] William Wrede, *Das Messiasgeheimnis in den Evangelien. Zugleich ein Beitrag zum Verständnis des Markusevangeliums*. (Göttingen: Vandenhoeck & Ruprecht, 1901), 72–7, 131; ET: *The Messianic Secret*, trans. J. C. G. Grieg (Cambridge: J. Clarke, 1971), 72–7, 131. According to Wrede (131), Jesus's divine sonship belongs to those "motifs ... that give movement and determination to the Markan narrative." Wrede (74–6) believed that two passages in particular confirm the metaphysical sense of Jesus's sonship: the charge of blasphemy before the high priest (14:61-62) and the centurion's confession (15:39). In the first instance, Wrede reasons that the charge of blasphemy proves that Mark understood "Son of God" as a claim to equality with God; in the second, the centurion's confession is motivated by the sight of wonders accompanying Jesus's death, which persuade him that Jesus is a son of the gods or a divine hero.

supernatural sonship that interprets and even corrects Jewish messianism.[21] Building on Wrede's work, Wilhelm Bousset granted the "dominant role" played by Son of God in Mark, but believed that the title had "a much too mythical ring" to have arisen within the early Palestinian community—one "which stands in contradiction with the rigid monotheism of the Old Testament."[22]

One finds essentially the same position in Bultmann, whose endorsement of Bousset's *Kyrios Christos* ensured its influence for generations to come. Although Bultmann ostensibly acknowledged the possibility that Son of God could have functioned as a messianic title in Judaism derived from Psalm 2, he maintained that only the influence of Hellenistic mythology could account for its use in the New Testament.[23] Like Wrede before him, Bultmann argued that, in Mark, Jesus becomes a divine man (θεῖος ἀνήρ) by virtue of the Spirit's descent at his baptism.[24]

Throughout the first half of the twentieth century, then, it became commonplace to assert that "Son of God" was never used as a title for the Messiah.[25] With "Son of God" relegated to secondary dogma and/or Hellenistic mythology, so too the import of the Jewish Scriptures (such as Psalm 2) was effectively sidelined. The notion of "Son of God" as a messianic title once espoused by Reimarus would not return to Markan studies until the publication of Donald Juel's *Messiah and Temple* in 1977, when it would do so via an examination of Mark's use of Scripture.[26]

In the meantime, the θεῖος ἀνήρ concept was widely assumed by the *redaktionsgeschichtliche Schule*. Proponents of the "corrective christology" school, for instance, argued that the θεῖος ἀνήρ does not represent Mark's own christology, but rather that of his opponents, which he seeks to correct via his own *theologia crucis*. According to Johannes Schreiber, Mark does so by means of a competing Hellenistic concept of divine sonship.[27] Theodore Weeden argued that Mark wrote his Gospel to

---

[21] Wrede, *Secret*, 77.
[22] Bousset, *Kyrios Christos*, 93. Bousset (95–6) maintained that "it is still a long way from the form of address [at the baptism and in the transfiguration scene] to the title ὁ υἱὸς τοῦ θεοῦ" and doubted whether the title could have been formed "out of Old Testament beginnings (Ps 2:7)." Thus, he effectively restricts his investigation into the origins of the title to occurrences of the *title proper*, ignoring the title's place in a broader language game. Furthermore, Bousset suggests that the term παῖς θεοῦ (Isa 42:1) must have originally lied beneath υἱὸς θεοῦ, thereby negating the relevance of Psalm 2 (96).
[23] Rudolf Bultmann, *Theology of the New Testament*, trans. Kendrick Grobel, 2 vols (New York: Scribner's, 1955), 1:49–50.
[24] Bultmann, *Theology*, 1:130–31. Bultmann appropriates the hypothetical θεῖος ἀνήρ from Ludwig Bieler, *Theios Anēr: das Bild des "göttlichen Menschen" in Spätantike und Frühchristentum* (Wien: O. Höfels, 1935).
[25] So, explicitly, Bousset, *Kyrios Christos*, 53, 97; see also the summary by Cullmann, *Christology*, 274.
[26] See Donald H. Juel, *Messiah and Temple: The Trial of Jesus in the Gospel of Mark*, SBLDS 31 (Missoula: Scholars, 1977). Botner (*Son of David*, 8) helpfully observes that: "Reimarus opened up a Pandora's Box that continues to haunt New Testament studies to this day. Does the confession of Jesus as the messiah of early Judaism undermine the Christ of the church's creeds? Many have approached Reimarus's challenge that 'son of God' means 'messiah' rather than 'second person of the Trinity' as if it demands participation in a zero-sum game. This may explain why many conservative scholars, who were in fact much closer to Reimarus and Schweitzer on the question of the historical Jesus, eagerly embraced the Wredean premise that son-of-God language *in Mark* no longer has anything to do with the anointed king of the Jewish scriptures."
[27] Johannes Schreiber, "Die Christologie des Markusevangeliums: Beobachtungen zur Theologie und Komposition des zweiten Evangeliums," *ZTK* 58 (1961): 154–83.

refute the christology of certain "heretical" missionaries represented by 1:1–8:29 with his portrait of Jesus's suffering in 8:30–16:8.[28] Norman Perrin more or less agreed with Weeden but further suggested that Mark's theology of suffering is represented by *Son of Man*, which he uses to "interpret and give content to" the titles *Christ* and *Son of God*.[29] One by one, however, various studies began to question the legitimacy of the hypothetical θεῖος ἀνήρ, each concluding that it lacked any historical evidence whatsoever.[30] With the θεῖος ἀνήρ, so went corrective christology.[31]

In his 1977 dissertation, *Messiah and Temple*, and even more so in his 1988 monograph, *Messianic Exegesis*, Juel argued from the messianic interpretations of 2 Samuel 7 and Psalm 2 at Qumran that the earlier assertions that son-of-God language was never used to designate the Messiah were "unwarranted."[32] In Mark he finds clear evidence of the association of the Son and Messiah in the use of Ps 2:7 in the *bath qol* at Jesus's baptism.[33] In this respect, Juel lands more or less where Reimarus had landed two hundred years earlier: "'Son of God' is an epithet used of Jesus because he is Messiah."[34]

Around the same time, Hans-Jorg Steichele attempted to trace the theme of suffering across Mark's portrayal of Jesus as God's Son at three points: 1:11; 9:7; and 15:39. Like

---

[28] Theodore J. Weeden, "The Heresy That Necessitated Mark's Gospel," *ZNW* 59 (1979): 145–58; idem, *Mark: Traditions in Conflict* (Philadelphia: Fortress, 1979).

[29] Norman Perrin, "The Christology of Mark: A Study in Methodology," *JR* 51 (1971): 173–87. Other proponents of corrective christology in some form include Ulrich Luz, "Das Geheimnismotiv und die markinische Christologie," *ZNW* 56 (1965): 9–30; Leander E. Keck, "Mark 3:7-12 and Mark's Christology," *JBL* 84 (1965): 341–58; Paul J. Achtemeier, "The Origin and Function of the Pre-Marcan Miracle Catenae," *JBL* 91 (1972): 198–221; Dietrich-Alex Koch, *Die Bedeutung Der Wundererzählungen Für Die Christologie Des Markusevangeliums*, BZNW 42 (Berlin: De Gruyter, 1975), *passim*; Hans Dieter Betz, "Gottmensch II," *RAC* 12 (1982): 300–02; Ralph P. Martin, *Mark* (Atlanta: Knox, 1982), 156–62.

[30] See P. Wülfing-von Martitz, "υἱός" *TDNT* 8:338–40; Carl R. Holladay, *Theios Aner in Hellenistic-Judaism*, SBLDS 40 (Missoula: Scholars, 1977); Barry Blackburn, "*Theios Aner* and the Markan Miracle Traditions: A Critique of the "*Theios Aner*" Concept as an Interpretative Backround of the Miracle Traditions Used by Mark*, WUNT 2/40 (Tübingen: Mohr Siebeck, 1991). Morna D. Hooker ("'Who Can This Be?' The Christology of Mark's Gospel," in *Contours of Christology in the New Testament*, ed. Richard N. Longenecker [Grand Rapids: Eerdmans, 2005], 95) ultimately cites a complete "lack of evidence" for this former view.

[31] Besides the refutation of the θεῖος ἀνήρ concept, most scholars have since followed Kingsbury's argument that Jesus's identity as the Son of Man complements, rather than contradicts, his identity as the Son of God in Mark: see Kingsbury, *Christology*, 25–45, 174; idem, "The 'Divine Man' as the Key to Mark's Christology—The End of an Era?," *USQR* 35 (1981): 243–57. Kingsbury's argument is endorsed by Robert A. Guelich, *Mark 1:1-8:26*, WBC 34a (Dallas: Word, 1989), xl; Joel Marcus, *Mark 1–8: A New Translation with Introduction and Commentary*, AB 27a (New Haven: Yale University Press, 2000), 77; and Adela Yarbro Collins, *Mark: A Commentary*, Hermeneia (Minneapolis: Fortress, 2007), 117. Others have also observed the close identification of the Son of God with the Son of Man in Mark's Gospel and elsewhere: e.g., Seyoon Kim, *The "Son of Man" as the Son of God*, WUNT 30 (Tübingen: Mohr Siebeck, 1983), 1–3; and already Moule, *Christology*, 24–30.

[32] Donald Juel, *Messianic Exegesis: Christological Interpretation of the Old Testament in Early Christianity* (Philadelphia: Fortress, 1988), 61–82, here 78. Juel discusses 4QFlor and 1QSa II, 10-12 from Qumran and Luke 1:32-33; Heb 1:3-12; Mark 1:11; 14:61; and Rom 1:2-4 from the NT.

[33] Ibid., 79–80.

[34] Ibid., 81. Yet Juel is also more nuanced than Reimarus, who simply equated "Christ" and "Son of God": "The logic cannot be reversed. The confession of Jesus as Christ is not derivable from use of 'the Son' by Jesus. And the title Messiah is not subject to further development in the way Son of God is."

Juel, Steichele argues that Ps 2:7 provides the basis for Mark's son-of-God language in 1:11 and 9:7, though he does not suggest any further influence from the psalm, focusing instead on Mark's use of other Scriptures to convey the motif of suffering.[35]

Already, Martin Hengel's comprehensive examination of the primary sources for "Son of God" had concluded that the search for the title's origins in the pagan world yields an "entirely unsatisfactory result."[36] By contrast, Hengel traced various uses of son-of-God language through Jewish literature, including some messianic uses of the term, concluding (*contra* Bousset) that such language was not "completely alien to Palestinian Judaism."[37] Due in part to messianic interpretations of Psalm 2 found among the Dead Sea Scrolls, numerous scholars since Hengel have reinforced these conclusions, effectively reversing the "consensus" of earlier decades.[38]

Today, the messianic use of Ps 2:7 in Mark 1:11 and 9:7 is widely accepted.[39] In addition, various studies have highlighted Mark's christological[40] or programmatic[41] use of Scripture more broadly. Yet none of these studies consider the dynamics of

---

[35] Steichele, *Sohn Gottes*, 135–47, 184–85.

[36] Martin Hengel, *The Son of God: The Origin of Christology and the History of Jewish-Hellenistic Religion*, trans. John Bowden (Eugene, OR: Wipf & Stock, 2007), 41; originally printed as *Der Sohn Gottes: die Entstehung der Christologie und die jüdisch-hellenistische Religionsgeschichte* (Tübingen: J. C. B. Mohr, 1975). In addition to Hengel, Hahn (*Christologische*, 284); Cullmann (*Christology*, 272–75); Reginald H. Fuller (*The Foundations of New Testament Christology* [New York: Scribner, 1965], 31–3); and Moule (*Christology*, 28–30) all questioned the claim that "Son of God" never functioned as a messianic title in Judaism since the Davidic king is plainly called God's son in 2 Sam 7:14; Ps 2:7; and Ps 89:26–27. Whereas Bousset limited his investigations to the title proper, these scholars also took into account broader uses of son-of-God language.

[37] Hengel, *Son of God*, 45. Hengel demonstrates more cognizance than most of the term's polyvalence in antiquity, as well as the widespread encounter between Judaism and Hellenism that had begun even before Alexander (41–2). Nevertheless, "[t]he sources for early Christian thinking are to be sought primarily here, and not directly in the pagan sphere." Hengel (63) remains uncertain about the use of "Son of God" as a formal title in Judaism.

[38] See, *inter alia*, James H. Charlesworth, *Jesus within Judaism: New Light from Exciting Archaeological Discoveries* (New York: Doubleday, 1988), 150–51; Dunn, *Christology*, 33–64; R. H. Fuller ("Son of God," in *HCBD*, 1051–052), who states: "Yet in view of the discovery of Ps. 2:7 with a messianic interpretation in the Dead Sea Scrolls (4QFlor 10-14) it is probably safe to conclude that [Son of God] was just coming into use with this meaning during the period of Christian origins"; Adela Yarbro Collins and John J. Collins, *King and Messiah as Son of God: Divine, Human, and Angelic Messianic Figures in Biblical and Related Literature* (Grand Rapids: Eerdmans, 2008), *passim*; N. T. Wright, "Son of God and Christian Origins," in *Son of God: Divine Sonship in Jewish and Christian Antiquity*, ed. Garrick V. Allen et al. (University Park, PA: Eisenbrauns, 2019), 118–34; Menahem Kister, "Son(s) of God: Israel and Christ: A Study of Transformation, Adaptation, and Rivalry," in *Son of God: Divine Sonship in Jewish and Christian Antiquity*, 188–224.

[39] See, e.g., E.g., Joel Marcus, *The Way of the Lord: Christological Exegesis of the Old Testament in the Gospel of Mark* (Louisville: Westminster/John Knox Press, 1992), 48–79; Rikk E. Watts, "The Psalms in Mark's Gospel," in *The Psalms in the New Testament*, ed. Steve Moyise and Maarten J. J. Menken, New Testament and the Scriptures of Israel (London: T&T Clark, 2004), 25–45; idem, "Mark," in *Commentary on the New Testament Use of the Old Testament*, ed. G. K. Beale and D. A. Carson (Grand Rapids: Baker, 2007), 122–29; Richard B. Hays, *Echoes of Scripture in the Gospels* (Waco: Baylor University Press, 2016), 48.

[40] E.g., Marcus, *Way, passim*; and Hays, *Gospels*, 15–103.

[41] E.g., Rikk E. Watts, *Isaiah's New Exodus and Mark*, WUNT 2/88 (Tübingen: Mohr Siebeck, 1997); Robert D. Rowe, *God's Kingdom and God's Son: The Background to Mark's Christology from Concepts of Kingship in the Psalms*, AGJU 50 (Leiden /Boston: Brill, 2002).

Mark's use of Scripture in relation to his portrayal of Jesus as Son of God beyond the two instances just mentioned.

In recent decades, narrative approaches have, in principle, held a better promise of doing precisely that. Eugene Boring, for instance, has produced an entire commentary starting from the premise that Mark is a "story" that has "Christology" as its "generative and driving force."[42] Within this story, Boring recognizes that "Son of God" is initially interpreted by the heavenly voice in 1:11, which recalls the royal decree of Ps 2:7.[43] Without explanation, however, Boring harkens back to earlier scholarship's insistence that "Mark is heir not only to Jewish thought, but also Gentile thought wherein 'son of God' would denote a nonhuman being capable of superhuman feats," concluding that "for Mark 'son of God' cannot be reduced to the Israelite idea that the king was adopted as God's son."[44] As a result, Boring misses both the breadth of Mark's dependence on Scripture and the fundamental coherence of Jesus's sonship in the narrative.

Elizabeth Struthers Malbon's study, *Mark's Jesus*, deserves special recognition for its emphasis on the clear structure attending Mark's portrayal of Jesus as Son of God, displayed through the reverberation between God's only two statements in 1:11 and 9:7, as well as other formal agreements between the statements of Jesus's sonship throughout the Gospel, including the surprising inclusio formed by the *bath qol* in 1:11 and the centurion's words in 15:39.[45] Like Boring, Malbon recognizes the role of Ps 2:7 in defining Jesus's sonship early on and considers the context of the psalm more than most.[46] Nevertheless, she fails to consider the implications of the psalm for Jesus's sonship throughout the subsequent narrative, instead reducing the meaning of Mark's son-of-God language to its lowest common denominator: a metaphor connoting "obedience."[47]

An important pair of articles by Adela Collins seeks to combine the approaches of narrative and historical criticism by asking how Mark's first-century readers would have understood his son-of-God language.[48] Readers familiar with Jewish tradition, Collins argues, would have read Mark's "Son of God" as a title for the royal Messiah dependent on Ps 2:7.[49] On the other hand, readers "more familiar with Greek and Roman religious traditions" would likely think of the emperor's own title "son of god" (*divi filius*/θεοῦ υἱός) within the context of the imperial cult.[50] Though Collins does not examine Mark's portrayal of Jesus as Son of God across the Gospel as a whole, she rightly emphasizes reading the narrative according to the cultural encyclopedia of the first-century Mediterranean world, wherein it would have struck multiple chords at

---

[42] M. Eugene Boring, *Mark: A Commentary* (Louisville: Westminster John Knox, 2006), 1, 248.
[43] Ibid., 30–32, 45.
[44] Ibid., 251.
[45] Elizabeth Struthers Malbon, *Mark's Jesus: Characterization as Narrative Christology* (Waco: Baylor University Press, 2009), 78–82, 121–22.
[46] Ibid., 76–7.
[47] Ibid., 65–6, 76–7.
[48] Adela Yarbro Collins, "Mark and His Readers: The Son of God among Jews," *HTR* 92 (1999): 393–408; idem, "Son of God among Greeks and Romans," *HTR* 93 (2000): 85–101.
[49] Collins, "Son of God among Jews," 394.
[50] Collins, "Son of God among Greeks and Romans," 86.

once. Collins's articles also exemplify another important development in son-of-God scholarship: a renewed interest in the emperor's cult.

Whereas the *religionsgeschichtliche Schule* had originally treated the so-called imperial cult, or emperor's cult, as a facet of the larger category of Hellenistic divine-man language, more recent scholarship has recognized the emperor's designation as *divi filius*/θεοῦ υἱός as a significant category in its own right.[51] As Hengel and others since have shown, [ὁ] υἱὸς [τοῦ] θεοῦ does not appear to have existed as a generic designation for pagan demigods in the Hellenistic world, wherein such a title probably would have begged the question, "which god or goddess?"[52] By contrast, there was precisely one figure in the ancient world known as θεοῦ υἱός/υἱὸς θεοῦ: Rome's emperor. Indeed, "the most famous 'son of God' in the Roman world," Peppard reminds us, was the emperor.[53] Taking these facts into account, Bruce Winter argues that the emperor's claim to be the son of a god must have posed a serious challenge for Christians who proclaimed Jesus to be *the* Son of God.[54] Peppard similarly argues that Octavian's designation "son of a god" gave rise to an inevitable contrast for the early Christians between Jesus and the emperor.[55]

Both Craig Evans and Adam Winn go so far as to suggest that Mark intends to present Jesus as a counter-emperor to Vespasian.[56] In particular, Evans likens the language of Mark's incipit to the Priene Calendar Inscription honoring Augustus and further believes the centurion's acclamation in 15:39 should be understood against the backdrop of the imperial cult.[57] In Winn's estimation, "Son of God" here and elsewhere in the Gospel functions in direct response to the imperial title as part of Mark's larger purpose to pit "Jesus's impressive résumé against that of Vespasian."[58] Whatever one makes of these individual proposals, collectively, they call attention to an important

---

[51] See Bousset, *Kyrios Christos*, 93–7. Even Hengel quickly dismisses the emperor's designation as "son of god" as one more example within the Hellenistic world with no apparent relevance to the New Testament; see Hengel, *Son of God*, 30. One notable early exception, however, is Adolf Deissmann, who suggests that "there arises a polemical parallelism between the cult of the emperor and the cult of Christ, which makes itself felt where [Septuagint or Gospel terminology] happen to coincide [with imperial concepts] which sounded the same or similar"; see *Light from the Ancient East: The New Testament Illustrated by Recently Discovered Texts of the Graeco-Roman World*, trans. Lionel R. M. Strachan, New and completely revised. (London: Hodder and Stoughton, 1927), 342.

[52] Hengel, *Son of God*, 30; Collins, "Son of God among Greeks and Romans," 85–100; Peppard, *Son of God*, 138 n. 11; Gamel, *Mark 15:39*, 49.

[53] Peppard, *Son of God*, 4.

[54] See Bruce W. Winter, *Divine Honours for the Caesars: The First Christians' Responses* (Grand Rapids: Eerdmans, 2015), 67–71.

[55] Peppard, *Son of God*, 46–9.

[56] See Evans, *Mark 8:27–16:20*, 510; Winn, *Purpose, passim*. Peppard also proposes that Mark presents Jesus as a counter-emperor at Mark 15:39; see Peppard, *Son of God*, 132–33.

[57] Craig A. Evans "Mark's Incipit and the Priene Calendar Inscription: From Jewish Gospel to Greco-Roman Gospel," *JGRChJ* 1 (2000): 67–81; idem, *Mark 8:27–16:20*, 510; For a contrasting perspective, however, see Tae Hun Kim, "The Anarthrous Υἱός Θεοῦ in Mark 15,39 and the Roman Imperial Cult," *Bib* 79 (1998): 221–41, who argues that the appellation evokes Augustus in particular, who alone was honored as θεοῦ υἱός.

[58] Winn, *Purpose*, 201. See further idem, "Resisting Honor: The Markan Secrecy Motif and Roman Political Ideology," *JBL* 133 (2014): 583–601; idem, "Tyrant or Servant?: Political Ideology and Mark 10.42-45," *JSNT* 36 (2014): 325–52.

and previously overlooked facet of Mark's socio-linguistic world. (Winn's study is also significant for placing Jesus's identity as Son of God near to the heart of Mark's purpose.)

Finally, the most recent contribution to the study of Mark's "Son of God," Brian Gamel's dissertation, *Mark 15:39 as a Markan Theology of Revelation*, stands in a long line of interpreters who recognize the centurion's confession as the "punch line of the whole Gospel narrative."[59] Gamel's study is commendable for its attention to Mark's rhetoric and the range of associations Mark's son-of-God language would have had in the ancient world (from Jewish messianism via Ps 2:7 to the emperor's cult), as well as its argument that the centurion's confession is the result of the "direct, apocalyptic action of God," which represents the revelatory climax of Mark's Gospel.[60] Inasmuch as Gamel focuses on the meaning of Mark 15:39, however, he does not explore the dynamics of Son of God in Mark's Gospel as a whole.

Despite the enormous contributions that have been made to our understanding of Mark's Son of God, then, the fact remains that no study to date has examined the story Mark tells *through* Son of God from beginning to end. We are often left instead with vague statements about filial "obedience," Jesus's "nearness" to God, or "election."[61] Yet some positive conclusions have emerged. It can no longer be said that the language of divine sonship was unknown in Judaism; to the contrary, the language of divine sonship was demonstrably applied to the Messiah, often in dependence on Psalm 2. The majority of scholars thus recognize the messianic use of Ps 2:7 in Mark 1:11 and 9:7. At the same time, Mark's audience cannot have been ignorant of the broad resonances of such language in the Roman world—i.e., the emperor's designation. Finally, there are clear hints even on a structural level of a dynamic plot attending Mark's portrayal of Jesus as Son of God. The purpose of this study is to unfold that plot so central to Mark's Gospel.

1.2 Methodology and Presuppositions

It is perhaps obvious by now that grasping the meaning of Mark's Son of God requires equal attention to the Markan narrative *qua* narrative, its historical context, and Mark's use of Scripture at once. Indeed, one reason why previous studies in this area have fallen short is due to a methodological tunnel-vision that precludes seeing the whole

---

[59] Cf. M. Eugene Boring, *Truly Human/Truly Divine: Christological Language and the Gospel Form* (St. Louis: CBP, 1984), 78; and similarly Joachim Gnilka, *Das Evangelium nach Markus*, 2 vols, EKKNT 2 (Zürich: Neukirchen-Vluyn, 1978), 1:26; Philip G. Davis, "'Truly This Man Was The Son Of God': The Christological Focus of the Markan Redaction," (PhD diss, McMaster University, 1979), *passim*; idem, 'Mark's Christological Paradox', *JSNT* 35 (1989): 3–18; Kingsbury, *Christology*, 152; Harry L. Chronis, "To Reveal and to Conceal: A Literary-Critical Perspective on 'the Son of Man' in Mark," *NTS* 51 (2005): 459–81, here 461.

[60] Gamel, *Mark 15:39*, 176.

[61] So, e.g., Cullmann, *Christology*, 275; Malbon, *Mark's Jesus*, 76–7; Rudolf Schnackenburg, *Jesus in the Gospels: A Biblical Christology* (Louisville: Westminster John Knox, 1995), 50–1; and much of the commentary literature.

picture at once. What is needed is ultimately a three-dimensional approach that accounts for the Gospel's narrative shape, as well as its production within a particular time and place, and relationships to other texts—or what Stefan Alkier calls the *intratextual*, *extratextual*, and *intertextual* planes of the text.[62]

1.2.1 Intratextuality—or Reading Mark as a Story

The first of Alkier's planes, the intratextual, closely aligns with the principles of narrative criticism, which considers the "relative value of individual passages" in relation to the whole.[63] Said differently, "Any interpretation given of a portion of text can be accepted if it is confirmed by, and must be rejected if it is challenged by, another portion of the same text."[64] The initial impetus for reading Mark in this way emerges from the character of the Gospel itself, for Mark is first and foremost a *narrative*: a story with a definite beginning, middle, and end told in a sequential order.[65] To quote Kavin Rowe, then, "stories written as stories are probably meant to be read as such."[66] Numerous studies by now have reached the same conclusion about Mark, which served as an early testbed for narrative criticism of the Gospels.[67] These are, in turn, supported by studies

---

[62] Stefan Alkier, "Intertextuality and the Semiotics of Biblical Texts," in *Reading the Bible Intertextually*, eds. R. B. Hays, S. Alkier, and L. A. Huizenga (Waco: Baylor University Press, 2009), 8–9. No one has done as much as Alkier to bring Piercean semiotics, especially as mediated by Umberto Eco, into conversation with New Testament interpretation: see also Stefan Alkier, *Wunder und Wirklichkeit in den Briefen des Apostels Paulus: ein Beitrag zu einem Wunderverständnis jenseits von Entmythologisierung und Rehistorisierung*, WUNT 34 (Tübingen: Mohr Siebeck, 2001), 55–86; and esp. idem, "Intertextualität-Annäherungen an ein texttheoretisches Paradigma," in *Heiligkeit und Herrschaft: Intertextuelle Studien zu Heligkeitsvorstellungen und zu Psalm 110*, ed. Dieter Sänger (Neukirchen-Vluyn: Neukirchener, 2003), 1–26.

[63] See Mark Allan Powell, *What Is Narrative Criticism?* (Minneapolis: Fortress, 1990), 2. Alkier ("Intertextuality," 8) refers to the "universe of discourse" in dependence on Charles Sanders Pierce, by which he means "the text as a world for itself." In particular, the type of narrative criticism endorsed here falls between Powell's (11–2) "author-centered" and "text-centered" approaches.

[64] Umberto Eco, *Interpretation and Overinterpretation*, ed. Stefan Collini (Cambridge: Cambridge University Press, 1992), 65; cf. Stephen D. Moore, *Literary Criticism and the Gospels: The Theoretical Challenge* (New Haven: Yale University Press, 1989), 59: following the plot of a Gospel from beginning to end is "essential to its adequate interpretation."

[65] Papias's comment (as quoted by Eusebius, *Hist. eccl.* 3.39.15 [*PG* 20:296–97]) that Mark did not write a proper σύνταξις notwithstanding, it is obvious that his Gospel flows in a basic chronological sequence, even if his narrative is not of a very polished sort; cf. Loveday Alexander, "What Is a Gospel?" in *The Cambridge Companion to the Gospels*, ed. Stephen C. Barton (Cambridge/New York: Cambridge University Press, 2006), 13–33.

[66] C. Kavin Rowe, *Early Narrative Christology: The Lord in the Gospel of Luke* BZNW 139 (Berlin: de Gruyter, 2006), 15.

[67] See, e.g., Robert C. Tannehill, "The Disciples in Mark: The Function of a Narrative Role," *JR* 57 (1977): 386–405; idem, "The Gospel of Mark as Narrative Christology," *Semeia* 16 (1979): 57–95; Frank Kermode, *The Genesis of Secrecy: On the Interpretation of Narrative* (Cambridge: Harvard University Press, 1979); David M. Rhoads and Donald Michie, *Mark as Story: An Introduction to the Narrative of a Gospel* (Philadelphia: Fortress Press, 1982); Ernest Best, *Mark: The Gospel as Story* (Edinburgh: T&T Clark, 1983); Kingsbury, *Christology*; Mark Allan Powell, "Toward a Narrative-Critical Understanding of Mark," *Int* 47 (1993): 341–46; Stephen H. Smith, *A Lion with Wings: A Narrative-Critical Approach to Mark's Gospel* (Sheffield: Sheffield Academic, 1996); Bastiaan M. F. van Iersel, *Mark: A Reader-Response Commentary*, JSNTSup 164 (Sheffield: Sheffield Academic, 1998); Sharyn Echols Dowd, *Reading Mark: A Literary and Theological Commentary on the Second Gospel* (Macon, GA: Smyth &

of Mark's genre in recent decades, which invariably recognize Mark as some variety of broadly historical narrative.[68]

A second impetus for reading this way derives from both ancient and contemporary understandings of *identity*. Aristotle was perhaps the first to suggest a link between the concepts of identity and narrative by linking "character" (ἦθος) to "custom" or "habit" (ἔθος).[69] Building on Aristotle, Paul Ricoeur has argued that neither "identifying reference" (e.g., titular christology) nor "utterance" (e.g., sayings approaches to Jesus) constitute a person's identity; rather identity resides in the journey of the self through time, or what Ricoeur himself calls "the temporal dimension of human existence."[70] In other words, identity is comprised of one's whole history, or story, wherein individual episodes, actions, utterances, and so forth become meaningful and intelligible.[71] Hence,

---

Helwys, 2000); Francis J. Moloney, *Mark: Storyteller, Interpreter, Evangelist* (Peabody: Hendrickson, 2004); Malbon, *Mark's Jesus*; Kelly R. Iverson and Christopher W. Skinner, eds., *Mark as Story: Retrospect and Prospect*, RBS 65 (Atlanta: SBL, 2011); Elizabeth E. Shively, *Apocalyptic Imagination in the Gospel of Mark: The Literary and Theological Role of Mark 3:22-30*, BNZW 189 (Berlin/New York: De Gruyter, 2012); David M. Rhoads, Joanna Dewey, and Donald Michie, *Mark as Story: An Introduction to the Narrative of a Gospel*, 3rd ed. (Minneapolis: Fortress, 2013).

[68] Whether a "historical monograph" (so Adela Yarbro Collins, "Narrative, History, and Gospel," *Semeia* 43 [1988]: 145-53; idem, "Is Mark's Gospel a Life of Jesus? The Question of Genre," in *The Beginning of the Gospel: Probings of Mark in Context* [Minneapolis: Fortress, 1992], 1–38; idem, *Mark: A Commentary*, Hermeneia [Minneapolis: Fortress, 2007], 15–43), or "Greco-Roman biography" (so, esp., Richard A. Burridge, *What Are the Gospels? A Comparison with Graeco-Roman Biography*, 2nd ed. [Grand Rapids: Eerdmans, 2004], *passim*; as well as Charles H. Talbert, *What Is a Gospel? The Genre of the Canonical Gospels*, [Philadelphia: Fortress, 1977], *passim*; David Edward Aune, *The New Testament in Its Literary Environment* [Philadelphia: Westminster, 1987], 64; Christopher Bryan, *A Preface to Mark: Notes on the Gospel in Its Literary and Cultural Settings* [New York: Oxford University Press, 1993]; Detlev Dormeyer, "Mk 1,1-15 als Prolog des ersten idealbiographischen Evangeliums von Jesus Christus," *BibInt* 5 [1997]: 181–211; Helen K. Bond, *The First Biography of Jesus: Genre and Meaning in Mark's Gospel* [Grand Rapids: Eerdmans, 2020], 15–37), or at least a "broadly biographical" narrative (so Alexander, "What Is a Gospel?," 15). Recently, Matthew D. C. Larsen (*Gospels before the Book* [New York: Oxford University Press, 2018], 121–46) has argued that Mark is a ὑπομνήματα in the literal sense: a narrative of an unpolished and even unfinished sort; yet Larsen does not deny Mark's basic narrative quality. According to Larsen (144), "making *hypomnēmata* is an act of unifying the disparate."

[69] Aristotle, *E.N.* 3.2.1112a13ff.; 6.2.1139a23-24; 6.13.1144b27. In this way Aristotle recognized that a person's identity is the result, or sum, of a process of repeated actions.

[70] Paul Ricoeur, "Personal Identity and Narrative Identity," in *Oneself as Another* (Chicago: University of Chicago Press, 1992), 114–16. Ricoeur (141) further describes the outworking of personal identity as a dialectic between sameness and selfhood: that is, a person's recognition of being the *same* entity, though changing through time. There is, then, a constancy as well as a temporality to a person's identity, which exist in tension with one another. In Ricoeur's language, the dialectic between sameness and selfhood involves "competition between a demand for concordance and the admission of discordances." Identity is the synthesis of "discordant concordance" into a narrative. Cf. Hans W. Frei (*The Identity of Jesus Christ: The Hermeneutical Bases of Dogmatic Theology* [Eugene, OR: Wipf & Stock, 2000], 96): "Identity has, in addition, a temporal reference, indicated by a term much in vogue in contemporary thought—'identity crisis'"; and Jürgen Straub ("Temporale Orientierung und narrative Kompetenz," in *Geschichtsbewusstsein: psychologische Grundlagen, Entwicklungskonzepte, empirische Befunde*, ed. Jörn Rüsen [Köln: Böhlau, 2001], 39).

[71] See Ricoeur, *Oneself*, 141. Alasdair MacIntyre articulates a similar understanding: the self "resides in the unity of a narrative which links birth to life to death as a narrative beginning to middle to end"; see Alasdair MacIntyre, *After Virtue*, 3rd ed. (Notre Dame: University of Notre Dame Press, 2007), 205. The apprehension of the self in historical terms is analogous to the relationship between the present perception of oneself and memory. Hence Augustine (*Confessions* X.8.14 in *Basic Writings of Saint Augustine*, ed. Whitney Jennings Oates, trans. J. G. Pilkington, vol. 1 [Grand Rapids: Baker, 1980]): 'There [in memory] . . . do I meet with myself, and recall myself–what, when, or where I did

"it is in narrating that Mark interprets the identity of Jesus"—or, as Hans Frei states, Jesus's identity "is grasped only by means of the story told about him."[72]

According to literary critic Mieke Bal, it is precisely the principle of *order* that shapes a mere series of events into a story.[73] Earlier scenes in the narrative become "frames of reference" guiding our interpretation of subsequent scenes.[74] This is particularly true concerning the formation of a character's identity in a story since it is "on the basis of [successive] bits of information" that a character gradually becomes "more or less predictable."[75] Bal's use of frames is similar to Umberto Eco's discussion of frames and presuppositions within a text: "our presuppositions," when reading a given portion of a text, "are governed by pre-existing frames," which are in turn "activated" by prior uses of the same words or concepts.[76] Every use of a word or concept thus activates some "frame of reference," which imposes a "positional power" on the narrative henceforth.[77] Within a text, it is not only the context that defines the word, but "the word which sets and defines the context moving forward."[78] The result is that earlier frames exert a kind of "contextual pressure" on what comes after.[79] In plain terms, what comes before sets the perameters for the interpretation of what follows.

In Mark's case, scholars have long noted the evangelist's use of concentric structures, repetitions, and other framing devices: intratextual relationships that demonstrate the author's purposeful arrangement of material and suggest time and time againthat what comes before is to be understood in the light of what comes after, and vice versa.[80] Malbon aptly characterizes Mark's rhetoric as:

> one of juxtaposition—placing scene over against scene in order to elicit comparison, contrast, and insight. This juxtaposition includes repetition, not only of scenes, but

---

a thing, and how I was affected when I did it.'" So too Udo Schnelle (*Theology of the New Testament*, trans. M. Eugene Boring [Grand Rapids: Baker Academic, 2009], 39): "The New Testament narratives about Jesus Christ express a memory process, and they form a consciousness of history."

[72] Paul Ricoeur, "Interpretative Narrative," in *The Book and the Text: The Bible and Literary Theory*, ed. Regina M. Schwartz (Cambridge/Oxford: Blackwell, 1990), 241; Frei, *Identity*, 133.

[73] Mieke Bal, *Narratology: Introduction to the Theory of Narrative*, trans. Christine van Boheemen, 3rd ed. (University of Toronto Press, 2009), 8. Cf. Seymour Chatman, *Story and Discourse: Narrative Structure in Fiction and Film* (Ithaca, NY: Cornell University Press, 1980), 45–8, 63–67; Powell, *Narrative Criticism*, 36–42.

[74] Bal, *Narratology*, 120–26, here 120.

[75] Ibid., 120.

[76] Umberto Eco, *Semiotics and the Philosophy of Language* (Bloomington: Indiana University Press, 1986), 72–4, 117–18, here 72.

[77] Eco, *The Limits of Interpretation* (Bloomington; Indianapolis: Indiana University Press, 1990), 233.

[78] Ibid., 232.

[79] Eco, *Semiotics*, 117–18.

[80] See, e.g., Ernst von Dobschütz, "Zur Erzählerkunst des Markus," *ZNW* 27 (1928): 193–98; James R. Edwards, "Markan Sandwiches: The Significance of Interpolations in Markan Narratives," *NovT* 31 (1989): 193–216; Joanna Dewey, "Mark as Interwoven Tapestry: Forecasts and Echoes for a Listening Audience," *CBQ* 53 (1991): 221–36; Tom Shepherd, "The Narrative Function of Markan Intercalation," *NTS* 41 (1995): 522–40; B. M. F. Van Iersel, "Concentric Structures in Mark: 1:14-3:35 (4:1) With Some Observations on Method," *BibInt* 3 (1995): 75–98; Marcin Moj, "Sandwich Technique in the Gospel of Mark," *BibAn* 8 (2018): 363–77. For an overview of Mark's various literary devices with numerous examples of each, see Deppe, *Literary Devices*.

also of words and phrases: duality is widespread ... In addition, juxtaposition includes foreshadowing and echoing of words, phrases, and whole events.[81]

"Juxtaposition ... forshadowing and echoing of words, phrases, and whole events" precisely describes the types of intratextual relationships we find between 1:11; 9:7; and 15:39 (which many regard as either a chiastic structure or an *inclusio*), to say nothing of the additional linguistic parallels we will see with 3:11; 5:7; 12:6; and 14:61 in coming chapters.[82]

As one considers this structure, it matters immensely that Jesus is first introduced as God's Son in a frame utilizing Ps 2:7 (Mark 1:11)—and that υἱὸς θεοῦ first appears in combination with Χριστός (1:1), if one deems those words original—for this sets the perameters for our understanding of "Son of God" moving forward. And it is significant that this information is repeated several chapters later at the climax of one of the Gospel's most vivid scenes (9:7).[83] Literary critics such as Bal and Eco bear witness to the fact that such rhetorical relationships within the narrative are not simply interesting material for footnotes on Mark's literary style, but clues to the meaning of the Gospel as a whole, thereby significant for exegesis. To echo Frei once more, "meaning and narrative shape bear significantly on each other."[84]

1.2.2 Extratextuality—A Story within a Place in Time

In the preface to a collection of addresses given during the Second World War, C. S. Lewis comments that he had intented to remove from the printed essays certain remarks resembling sentences of his that had already appeared in print elsewhere; yet he could not, for "there comes a time ... when a composition belongs so definitely to the past that the author himself cannot alter it much without the feeling that he is producing a kind of forgery."[85] If Lewis's remark rings true of essays, it is even more true of stories. So while it is possible to conduct narrative criticism in a manner that is more or less ahistorical, to do so is to forfeit insight into the world of the text itself. Instead, with Robert Alter, I take for granted that historical research is "a necessary first

---

[81] Elizabeth Struthers Malbon, "Narrative Criticism: How Does the Story Mean?," in *Mark and Method: New Approaches in Biblical Studies*, ed. Janice Capel Anderson and Stephen D. Moore (Philadelphia: Fortress, 1992), 27–45. In addition to Malbon, Joanna Dewey, "Oral Methods of Structuring Narrative in Mark," *Int* 43 (1989): 32–44 claims that oral narrative, "'operates on the acoustic principle of the echo.' Ring composition (*inclusio*) is endemic in oral narrative, marking the boundaries of individual episodes and of much longer sections. Individual episodes and clusters of episodes are narrated in balanced patterns in either parallel or chiastic order." See also Robert L. Humphrey, *Narrative Structure and Message in Mark: A Rhetorical Analysis*, SBEC 60 (Lewiston, NY: E. Mellen, 2003), 12, 22 on Mark's regular use of "framing episodes" or "inclusions."

[82] Favoring a chiastic structure, see, e.g., Ched Myers, *Binding the Strong Man: A Political Reading of Mark's Story of Jesus* (Maryknoll, NY: Orbis, 1988), 390–91; favoring *inclusio*, see, e.g., David Ulansey, "The Heavenly Veil Torn: Mark's Cosmic Inclusio," *JBL* 110 (1991): 123–25.

[83] Bal (*Narratology*, 126–28) notes that repeated frames of reference are among the most important principles (or methods) of character construction.

[84] Hans W. Frei, *The Eclipse of Biblical Narrative: A Study in Eighteenth and Nineteenth Century Hermeneutics* (New Haven: Yale University Press, 1974), 11.

[85] C. S. Lewis, *The Weight of Glory and Other Addresses* (San Francisco: HarperOne, 2001), 24.

step to understanding" any biblical narrative.[86] The reason for this, as illustrated in Lewis's comment, is summarized in what Alasdair MacIntyre describes as "historically situated rationality": in short, the truth that all ideas belong to a particular place and time in history within which they make the sense they make.[87] Even the terms of our discourse are finally conditioned by our context.

In order to realize the goal of historically sensitive narrative reading, I draw upon Eco's concept of the *encyclopedia*: i.e., "the cultural framework in which the text is situated and from which its gaps are filled," or, in Eco's own words, "the common core of factual beliefs [the author and intended readers] share about the referents of a word."[88] So in our case, we ought to begin by asking what associations Mark and his intended readers (i.e., first-century Mediterraneans) would have had with [ὁ] υἱὸς [τοῦ] θεοῦ.[89] When we do so, historical studies at least as far back as Deissmann's *Licht vom Osten* alert us to basic tensions in the narrative that Mark weaves that are invisible to the reader who neglects historical research.[90]

Not all "entries" in the reader's encyclopedia are of equal relevance, however. Similar to Bal's model of narrative interpretation, Eco's concept of encyclopedic competence relies on the idea of frames. Circumstances within a narrative evoke certain "frames" or "scripts" that effectively act as a set of instructions guiding the reader's selections from the encyclopedia, which is to say the reader's understanding of a given term.[91] For instance, Eco gives the example of a wife exclaiming to her husband, "Honey, there is a man on the lawn!" The sentence requires the husband to make some judgment about the meaning of "man" based on "the *ad hoc* dictionary that both speakers, in that situation, take for granted."[92] Presumably, "the wife was not interested in the fact that men are mortal or hot-blooded animals"; but only once he has "evaluated the situation of the utterance" can the husband conjecture that his wife means to evoke something along the lines of "burglars in the night."[93]

---

[86] Robert Alter, *The Art of Biblical Narrative*, Rev. & updated ed. (New York: Basic Books, 2011), 14. Cf. Adela Yarbro Collins: "whatever tension there may appear to be between literary- and historical-critical methods, the two approaches are complementary"; see "Narrative, History, and Gospel," *Semeia* 43 (1988): 145–53, here 153.

[87] MacIntyre, *After Virtue*, 207; idem, *Whose Justice? Which Rationality?* (Notre Dame: University of Notre Dame Press, 1988), 349–69.

[88] Alkier, "Intertextuality," 8; Eco, *Theory*, 99. Descriptions of the encyclopedia abound; see also Kavin Rowe's helpful description: "the wider cultural knowledge (tacit and explicit) assumed by the author and embedded in the text by virtue of its origin in a particular time and place in history"; *World Upside Down: Reading Acts in the Graeco-Roman Age* (Oxford/New York: Oxford University Press, 2009), 8–9. In recent years, a number of scholars have applied Eco's encyclopedia to the study of the New Testament. In addition to Alkier and Rowe, see, e.g., Leroy Andrew Huizenga, *The New Isaac: Tradition and Intertextuality in the Gospel of Matthew*, NovTSup 131 (Leiden/Boston: Brill, 2009), 21–41; Joshua E. Leim, *Matthew's Theological Grammar: The Father and the Son*, WUNT 2/402 (Tübingen: Mohr Siebeck, 2015), 24; Botner, *Son of David*, 27–8.

[89] This very approach is exemplified, in fact, by Collins's pair of articles, "Mark and His Readers: Son of God among Jews/Greeks and Romans," mentioned above.

[90] See Gustav Adolf Deissmann, *Licht Vom Osten: Das Neue Testament Und Die Neuentdeckten Texte Der Hellenistisch-Römischen Welt* (Tübingen: J. C. B. Mohr, 1908), 243–76.

[91] Eco, *Semiotics*, 68–9.

[92] Ibid., 79.

[93] Ibid.

16   *The Gospel of the Son of God*

In other words, certain portions of the encyclopedia are activated by particular "frames" or "scripts" that "blow up" (or *actualize*) some possibilities and "narcotize" others.[94] As a result, we must ask what associations the use of the Jewish Scriptures in 1:11 and 9:7 actualizes (and narcotizes), just as we must ask what associations the identity of the speaker, a Roman centurion, in 15:39 might actualize (and narcotize). (As Bousset implicitly recognized, to do so may of course lead us to a seeming discontinuity between the meaning of Son of God in the first two instances versus the last [which the structure of the narrative seemingly denies], or, if not, to a radical continuity.)[95]

Before moving on, I should add that the aims of this study are ultimately historical: to recover a central component of the earliest Gospel's proclamation about Jesus Christ. Yet this is a goal that cannot be realized without attention to narrative and history alike.

1.2.3 Intertextuality—How One Story Takes its Cue from Another

Finally, the present work stands in the long line of studies that recognize that Mark's identification of Jesus as the Son of God refers at least in part to the Jewish Scriptures (in particular, Psalm 2). As such, it necessarily concerns Mark's use of Scripture. To speak of Mark's use of Scripture, however, is to refer to the broader phenomenon of intertextuality—or "the relationships texts can have with other texts."[96] Julia Kristeva's original definition of the term is apt here. According to Kristeva, "every text is the absorption and transformation of another text."[97] So also, every story takes its cue from some other(s). In Mark's case, Kristeva's point is plainly demonstrated from the fact that the Gospel begins by situating itself in the past story of Israel's Scriptures, as Origen and others recognized long ago.[98] In total, Mark contains an estimated seventy-three citations and allusions to the Jewish Scriptures, including the widely acknowledged allusions to Ps 2:7 in 1:11 and 9:7.[99]

Precisely because intertextuality involves not only citations but, frequently, more subtle allusions to other texts, we require some criteria to detect and interpret them. Toward this end, I assume the now well-established criteria originally developed by Richard Hays (namely, [1] *availability*, [2] *volume*, [3] *recurrence*, [4] *thematic coherence*, [5] *historical plausibility*, [6] *history of interpretation*, and [7] *satisfaction*), as well as

---

[94] Ibid. See also Eco, *Semiotics*, 117–18. For additional discussions of the encyclopedia, see idem, *Theory*, 98–114; idem, *Limits*, 266–82.

[95] When Bousset (*Kyrios Christos*, 95) argues that "when the Gospel of Mark places in the mouth of the Gentile captain the confession of the Son of God, still the υἱὸς τοῦ θεοῦ here cannot be understood in the sense of a confession to the Jewish Messiah," he is, in effect, recognizing that the centurion's identity at once actualizes certain frames and narcotizes others (namely, "the Jewish Messiah").

[96] Alkier, "Intertextuality," 3. Implicit in Alkier's definition is an awareness that texts can have more than one type of relationship with one another.

[97] The term was originally coined in the 1960s by the French philosopher Julia Kristeva to refer to the infinite matrix of relationships between texts. Implicit in the term is an awareness that texts are capable of more than one type of relationship with one another; see Julia Kristeva, *[Sēmeiōtikē] Recherches pour une sémanalyse* (Paris: Points, 1969). The present quotation, however, is from idem, *Revolution in Poetic Language* (New York: Columbia University Press, 1984), 59–60.

[98] According to Origen (*Cels.* 2.4 [*PG* 11:801]), Mark's opening in 1:1-3 shows "that the beginning of the Gospel is connected to the Jewish writings." Theophylact *Enarrat. Marc.* 1:1 (*PG* 123:493) is even more direct: "the end (τέλος) of the Old is the beginning of the New Testament."

[99] Watts, "Mark," in *CNTUOT*, 111.

more recent emendations of these guidelines to account for the way intertextuality functions in narrative.[100] In particular, I note the work of Holly Carey, who factors the importance of *genre* into studies of intertextual allusion. Carey observes that the narrative genre allows for "a wider possibility for the inclusion of allusions" owing to the potential for shared elements of "plot, setting, and character development."[101] The possibility exists, in other words, of a story portrayed as repeating itself for a second time, or perhaps even the actualization of an earlier story within the present narrative. In narratives, as opposed to epistles, moreover, an allusion "may or may not include shared vocabulary, since the author has more room to place his/her protagonist in shared or similar circumstances with that of the person [or text] to whom he alludes."[102]

In order to better account for the way in which allusions present themselves in narratives, Carey suggests the following modification of Hays's criteria, which will be assumed here as well: (1) *shared circumstances*; (2) *shared vocabulary*; (3) *recurrence in the narrative*; (4) *interruption of the immediate syntax*; (5) *illumination of the passage*; (6) *availability*; (7) *historical likelihood*; (8) *historical parallels* (i.e., do other texts exhibit an awareness of this intertext?).[103] I employ these criteria in the manner that Hays originally intended of his own criteria: as "rules of thumb" rather than strict demands that must be satisfied.[104] In theory, the fulfilment of any of these may signal an allusion to an earlier text, though the more, the better.

Of specific importance to this study is the concept of *metalepsis*, or an allusion to "a brief part of another text" in order to evoke "the entire context, message, or story of that other text."[105] In her recent studies of metalepsis, Jeannine K. Brown emphasizes that *metalepsis* in general has "a basic storied quality" to it since it involves the association of two texts on the level of story, including such characteristics as setting, plot, and characters.[106] Metalepsis

---

[100] See Hays, *Letters of Paul*, 29–31. For a discussion of the similar lists and revisions proposed by other scholars, see David Allen, "The Use of Criteria: The State of the Question," in *Methodology in the Use of the Old Testament in the New: Context and Criteria*, ed. David Allen and Steve Smith, LNTS 597 (London/New York: T&T Clark, 2020), 129–41.

[101] See Carey, *Jesus' Cry*, 41–2.

[102] Ibid., 42.

[103] Ibid., 43–4.

[104] Hays, *Letters of Paul*, 29.

[105] Jeannine K. Brown, *Scripture as Communication: Introducing Biblical Hermeneutics* (Grand Rapids: Baker Academic, 2007), 110. Cf. Richard Hays's often cited definition: "a rhetorical and poetic device in which one text alludes to an earlier text in a way that evokes resonances of the earlier text *beyond those explicitly cited*"; Richard B. Hays, *Echoes of Scripture in the Letters of Paul* (New Haven: Yale University Press, 1989), 15. The term was coined by John Hollander; see *The Figure of Echo: A Mode of Allusion in Milton and After* (Berkeley: University of California Press, 1981), 133–49. There is longstanding debate in the field of New Testament studies, of course, as to whether or not biblical allusions regularly recall their larger contexts. This debate lies beyond the scope of this study and, thus, is not one I aim to solve here. My general observation, however, is that some allusions rather obviously evoke larger contexts, while others may not. The present study will provide ample reasons to conclude that Mark's use of Psalm 2 is a case of the former.

[106] See Jeannine K. Brown, "Metalepsis," in *Exploring Intertextuality: Diverse Strategies for New Testament Interpretation of Texts*, ed. B. J. Oropeza and Steve Moyise (Eugene, OR: Cascade, 2016), 29–42 (29). In a related thought, Steve Smith ("The Use of Criteria: A Proposal from Relevance Theory," in *Methodology in the Use of the Old Testament in the New*, 145]) applies "relevance theory" to the subject of intertextuality, suggesting that readers or hearers stumbling across an initial shared word or theme will then follow the mental process known as relevance process to search for texts that have the something in common with the present text, "stopping when expectations of relevance are achieved."

within a narrative, then, regularly suggests the repetition or the actualization of an earlier story by the present one. This is what I suggest happens in the case of Psalm 2 in Mark. Mark's use of son-of-God language, so I will argue, consistently entails the transumption of the entire second psalm, beckoning the reader to see its actualization in the life of Jesus.

1.3 Clarifications

Given my commitment to reading Mark within its historical context, it is important to summarize some matters pertaining to the Gospel's actual location in history. Tradition claims that Mark, the interpreter of Peter, wrote from Rome in the mid to late 60s CE.[107] Nearly as many today would argue for a Syrian provenance around 70–71 CE, possibly reflecting the *Sitz im Leben* of the Jewish War.[108] A few have also argued for a Galilean provenance.[109]

For transparency's sake, I tentatively maintain the traditional view that Mark was written from Rome in the late 60s, though the possibility of a Syrian provenance cannot be ruled out. It is important to state, however, that the present argument does not depend on this position. To read Mark in light of the text's cultural encyclopedia is not to presume any precise *Sitz im Leben*. Rather, I assume only what can be known with reasonable certainty. For instance, I assume that Mark lived in a world whose contours were shaped by the daily realities of Roman imperial rule.[110] I take for granted the

---

[107] So Papias as quoted by Eusebius, *Hist. eccl.* 3.39.15 (*PG* 20:296–97); Justin, *Dial.* 106 (*PG* 6:721–24); Irenaeus, *Haer.* 3.1.2 (*PG* 7a:845); Clement of Alexandria and Origen, both quoted by Eusebius, 2.15.1-2, 6.14.6-7, 6.25.5 (*PG* 20:172, 349, 580); Jerome, *Vir. ill.* 8 (*PL* 23:621–23). Modern scholars who maintain this view include C. E. B. Cranfield, *The Gospel According to Saint Mark: An Introd. and Commentary* (Cambridge: University Press, 1959), 8; Walter Grundmann, *Das Evangelium nach Markus* (3rd ed.; THKNT 2; Berlin: Evangelische, 1965), 18–20; Vincent Taylor, *The Gospel According to St. Mark* (New York: St. Martin's Press, 1966), 31–2; Rudolf Pesch, *Das Markusevangelium* (2 vols; THKNT 2; Freiburg: Herder, 1976), 1:12-14; Raymond E. Brown and J. P. Meier, *Antioch and Rome: New Testament Cradles of Catholic Christianity* (New York: Paulist, 1983), 191–97; Martin Hengel, *Studies in the Gospel of Mark* (Philadelphia: Fortress, 1985), 23–9; 64–84; Robert H. Gundry, *Mark: A Commentary on His Apology for the Cross* (Grand Rapids: Eerdmans, 1993), 1029–034; Craig A. Evans, *Mark 8:27-16:20*, Word Biblical Commentary 34b (Nashville: Thomas Nelson Publishers, 2001), lxxxi–xcii; John R. Donahue and Daniel J. Harrington, *The Gospel of Mark*, SP 2 (Collegeville, MN: Liturgical, 2002), 42; Brian J. Incigneri, *The Gospel to the Romans: The Setting and Rhetoric of Mark's Gospel*, BIS 65 (Leiden ; Boston: Brill, 2003); Thomas C. Oden, *The African Memory of Mark: Reassessing Early Church Tradition* (Downers Grove: IVP Academic, 2011).

[108] See especially Joel Marcus, "The Jewish War and the *Sitz im Leben* of Mark," *JBL* 111 (1992): 441–62; and Gerd Theissen, *The Gospels in Context: Social and Political History in the Synoptic Tradition* (Minneapolis: Fortress, 1991), 236–51; and also S. Schulz, *Die Stunde der Botschaf: Einführung in die Theologie der vier Evangelisten* (Hamburg: Furche, 1967), 9; W. G. Kümmel, *Introduction to the New Testament* (Nashville: Abingdon, 1975), 97–8; H. C. Kee, *Community of the New Age: Studies in Mark's Gospel* (Philadelphia: Fortress, 1977), 100–05; Helmut Koester, *Introduction to the New Testament* (Philadelphia: Fortress, 1982), 2:166–67; Boring, *Mark*, 20.

[109] E.g., Hendrika Nicoline Roskam, ed., *The Purpose of the Gospel of Mark in Its Historical and Social Context*, NovTSup 114 (Leiden/Boston: Brill, 2004).

[110] See, e.g., E. Mary Smallwood, *The Jews under Roman Rule: From Pompey to Diocletian: A Study in Political Relations*, SJLA 20 (Leiden: Brill, 1981); Fergus Millar, *The Emperor in the Roman World, 31 BC–AD 337* (Ithaca, NY: Cornell University Press, 1977); idem., *The Roman Near East, 31 B.C.–A.D. 337* (Cambridge: Harvard University Press, 1993); Christopher Bryan, *A Preface to Mark: Notes on the Gospel in Its Literary and Cultural Settings* (New York: Oxford University Press, 1993); Incigneri, *Gospel*.

author's and audience's familiarity with Roman religious and political realities, such as the emperor's cult. Likewise, whoever the evangelist was, he was obviously well versed in Israel's Scriptures (as well as later Jewish tradition), and expected his readers to be as well.[111]

Some may object that the approach here treats the evangelist too much like a literary genius. Is this not the Mark whom Papias criticized for not having written his account "in order," and whom Bultmann claimed was "not sufficiently master of his material"?[112] In response, I echo Hays's response to a similar concern in *Echoes of Scripture in the Gospels*: "I do not want to be understood as suggesting that the Evangelists were engaged in fanciful Promethean poetic creativity."[113] But I do contend that Mark displays thoughtfulness in his rhetorical arrangement of his materials, and that the structure he gives to the story of Jesus is not entirely haphazard but concomitant with the message of the story itself.[114]

There is at least one obvious piece of historical evidence to support this claim: the evangelist could write. Though we now exceedingly little about the author of the Second Gospel, we do know that he could read and write, which to say that he possessed some education. Education itself, in turn, suggests a basic knowledge of rhetoric.[115] The same, of course, would be true of Mark's original readers (ἀναγνῶσται).[116] So to assume that Mark was capable of constructing a narrative with some rhetorical structure is not, after all, to assume that he was a literary genius, but rather to take seriously what we know for certain: that he was an ancient person who had an education.

1.4 The Argument

Broadly speaking, Herman Melville's 1851 novel *Moby-Dick* has little in common with the Gospel of Mark. Yet the two works share at least one characteristic: both are replete with allusions to Scripture, some more obvious than others. Among the most

---

[111] Marcus (*Way*) demonstrates throughout that Mark was acquainted not only with Scripture but also Scripture as interpreted in post-biblical Jewish tradition.

[112] Bultmann, *History*, 350.

[113] Hays, *Gospels*, 8.

[114] In any case, scholarship has traveled a long way from Bultmann's estimation of Mark as an author. So, e.g., Ben Witherington, *The Gospel of Mark: A Socio-Rhetorical Commentary* (Grand Rapids: Eerdmans, 2001), 11: Mark is "rhetorically sensitive and has rhetorical purposes"; cf. Marcus, *Mark 1–8*, 60; Moloney, *Mark: Storyteller*, 31–59; also Kermode, *Secrecy, passim*; and Ricoeur, "Interpretative Narrative," 241, who contests the notion that Mark is "maladroit."

[115] See David E. Aune, *The New Testament in Its Literary Environment* (Philadelphia: Westminster, 1987), 158: "rhetoric occupied a central place in education." Rhetoric also governed the writing of both history and biography (30–1); cf. Burridge, *Gospels, passim*; Alexander, "Gospel," 22. Moreover, as Martin Hengel, *Judaism and Hellenism: Studies in Their Encounter in Palestine during the Early Hellenistic Period*, trans. John Bowden (London: SCM, 1974), 65–83 demonstrated, the influence of Greco-Roman παιδεία was pervasive even in Palestine well before the beginning of the first century CE; even the counter-formation of Jewish schools in response to the Hellenistic movement did not escape the influence of παιδεία, insofar as it appropriated the educational model of those schools.

[116] Again, Aune, *Literary*, 13: "All levels of the population of the Roman world were exposed to the variety of structures and styles found in the rhetoric, literature, and art that were on public display throughout the Empire."

conspicuous in Melville's novel are the names of characters such as Captain Ahab and Elijah (the prophetic stranger who warns against joining Ahab's crew), Father Mapple's sermon on Jonah, and the quotation of Job that introduces the Epilogue. But the attuned reader will also notice more subtle allusions in the details such as the names of the captains, Peleg and Bildad, in the early chapters of the book. Carl F. Hovde illuminates an extended and complex interplay with the biblical story of Ishmael:

> The biblical Ishmael is the illegitimate son of Abraham by Rebecca's servant Hagar, and even though the Lord is good to Ishmael later in Genesis, his half-brother, Isaac, inherits the Lord's covenant through their father (Genesis 16, 17, 21, and 25). Melville's narrator promptly describes dark thoughts approaching self-destruction: He pauses before coffin warehouses and follows every funeral he meets. But in the novel things don't remain so grim for long. Just as the Lord in Genesis is good to Ishmael despite his illegitimacy, so Melville's Ishmael floats to rescue with his best friend's burial box.[117]

So what initially appears to be an incidental allusion in the opening line "Call me Ishmael" gains a fullness of meaning through continued, subtle interplay with the Genesis narrative. The argument of this book is that something similar happens in Mark's Gospel.

I contend that Mark portrays Jesus's earthly life from baptism to crucifixion as the actualization of Psalm 2: a coronation hymn that looks to God's enthronement of the Davidic king as the essential turning point of history, the means by which he overcomes the forces of chaos and establishes his kingdom on earth. To say so is not merely to say that Psalm 2 is the primary background behind Mark's Son of God, but rather that, *for Mark, to call Jesus the "Son of God" is to locate the entire progression of the psalm unfolding in the person and work of Jesus*. One might, as such, speak of the story of Psalm 2 *encoded* in the narrative's refrain that Jesus is God's son.[118] Like Melville's novel, Mark provides enough overt allusions to the psalm to allow us to pick up the trail and compel us to follow it further. And follow it we must, if we are to perceive the whole story of the Son of God.

Accordingly, the chapters of this book will follow Mark's story of Jesus Christ, the Son of God from his first introduction as such in the prologue to his crucifixion near the end of the Gospel, demonstrating at each turn how Mark's description of Jesus as God's Son evokes the themes of Psalm 2. The unexpected *peripeteia* occurs, however, with the centurion's confession, "Truly, this man was the Son of God," from the foot of

---

[117] Carl F. Hovde, "Introduction," in Herman Melville, *Moby-Dick: Introduction and Notes by Carl F. Hovde* (New York: Barnes & Noble Classics, 2003), xxii.

[118] In an important sense, the proposed scenario is not unique. A wealth of studies has highlighted the existence of large-scale narrative analogies or figural readings in each of the Synoptic Gospels: e.g., Ulrich Mauser, *Christ in the Wilderness: The Wilderness Theme in the Second Gospel and Its Basis in the Biblical Tradition*, SBT 39 (Naperville, IL: Allenson, 1963), Watts, *New Exodus*; Dale C. Allison, Jr., *The New Moses: A Matthean Typology* (Minneapolis: Fortress, 1993); Joel Kennedy, *The Recapitulation of Israel: Use of Israel's History in Matthew 1:1-4:11*, WUNT 2/257 (Tübingen: Mohr Siebeck, 2008); and Rowe, *Early Narrative Christology*; see also Hays, *Gospels*. I am simply proposing one more, with significant implications for our understanding of Mark.

the cross (15:39). In a shocking narrative twist, Mark suggests through the centurion's words that the triumphant conclusion of Psalm 2 has, ironically, begun to be realized through Jesus's death on the cross: the Son inherits the nations (cf. Ps 2:7-8).

In retrospect, it becomes possible to see how the entire life of Jesus, the Son of God, as narrated by Mark has been the actualization of Psalm 2, culminating with the victory of God's Messiah over every power and his inheritance of the whole earth. What is shocking about Mark's narrative, however, is *how* the Messiah's victory, per Psalm 2, is accomplished—i.e., through his death on the cross. Paradoxically, Jesus's death becomes the beacon of eschatological hopes in realization.

Before turning directly to Mark, however, it is imperative that we retrace the story of Psalm 2 in ancient Jewish and Christian interpretation alike, for, if I am correct, the story of Markan Son of God begins there. Moreover, much of the import to which Mark evokes the psalm becomes apparent only when one is aware of the various uses made of the psalm by ancient Jews and Christians alike. To that end, we turn now to the story recalled by Mark's own story of the Son of God: Psalm 2.

2

The Son of God and the Story of Psalm 2

When God declares Jesus to be his Son in both Mark 1:11 and 9:7, he does so in words borrowed from Ps 2:7: "You are my Son." In fact, Psalm 2 is the only source to which Mark expressly draws our attention when describing Jesus as God's Son.[1] In the chapters that follow, I will argue that Psalm 2 is indeed determinative for Mark's entire conception of Jesus as the Son of God. In order to appreciate this point, however, we must first understand the story of Psalm 2 itself.

In short, Psalm 2 was (a) a foundational text for the identification of the Davidic king as God's son; (b) almost universally read in an eschatological, messianic sense in early Jewish literature; and (c) inseparable from both the idea of Jesus's kingship and the events of his passion in early Christian literature. Together these facts provide the necessary context within which to understand Mark's own use of the psalm (and concept of Jesus's sonship). Additionally, the widespread influence of the psalm in early Jewish and Christian literature alike amounts to a preliminary reason to consider its potential influence in Mark: what Hays calls "historical plausibility."[2]

2.1 The Story within Psalm 2

To speak of the "story" of Psalm 2 may seem odd since a psalm is not, strictly speaking, a narrative. Yet numerous interpreters have discerned a distinct plot, or "drama," in this particular psalm.[3] At the outset, the nations and kings rebel against YHWH and his

---

[1] While the actual argumentation to this end will comprise the rest of this book, it is worth noting one basic reason for considering the significance of Psalm 2 upfront: namely, that Ps 2:7 is the only specific background Mark ever alludes to, in 1:11 and 9:7—see similarly Collins, "The Son of God among Jews," 393–408. Thus, while both Collins ("The Son of God among Greeks and Romans," 85–100) and Peppard (*Son of God*, 87, 95–124) rightly call attention to other associations readers in the Roman world might have made with son-of-God language, Mark's narrative inherently privileges Psalm 2 above these other possibilities. Marcus (*Mark 1–8*, 70) is instructive here: "the only writing that is extensively quoted in the NT is the OT. The OT—not Homer, Plato, or Cicero." During an SBL panel in 2015, Larry Hurtado made a related observation that intertextual allusions are, among other things, a way of paying a compliment to one's intended audience. If Mark intended for his audience to think primarily along Roman rather than Jewish lines in 1:11 and 9:7, then he has made counterintuitive choices.
[2] See Hays, *Letters of Paul*, 30.
[3] See Hermann Gunkel, *Einleitung in Die Psalmen*, Göttinger Handkommentar Zum Alten Testament [Göttingen: Vandenhoeck & Ruprecht, 1933], 145): Psalm 2 "erfindet ein ganzes Drama."

anointed (מְשִׁיחוֹ). In response, YHWH establishes his king on Mount Zion, who, in turn, recounts YHWH's decree of sonship and promise of dominion over the whole earth. At last, the psalm envisions the kings and nations submitting to YHWH though his "son," the anointed king. This drama in four acts is, in fact, embodied in the very structure of the psalm, which is arranged chiastically:

A. The kings of the earth rebel against YHWH and his Anointed (vv. 1-3)
    B. YHWH responds by setting his king on Zion (vv. 4-6)
    B.' The king responds by recounting YHWH's decree (vv. 7-9)
A.' The kings submit to YHWH and his anointed son (vv. 10-12).[4]

Despite this four-part structure, however, the result is something like a triptych in which the first and third panels depict the rebellion of the kings and nations and their eventual submission, respectively, while the center panel highlights God's enthronement of the king as the hinge on which the drama turns.[5]

The thoroughgoing focus on the king and his enthronement by YHWH combined with the language of ancient Near Eastern enthronement rituals (including the pivotal metaphors of begetting and sonship in v. 7) have sensibly led most interpreters to the conviction that the second psalm was, from the beginning, a coronation liturgy for the Davidic king, probably used at successive enthronements.[6] In any case, the psalm is deeply rooted in the ideology of the Davidic monarchy, looking to the king as the one who will instantiate God's rule and justice on earth (cf. 2 Sam 7:4-29).

---

[4] So Peter C. Craigie, *Psalms 1-50*, WBC 19 (Waco: Word, 1983), 65; James Luther Mays, *Psalms*, Interpretation (Louisville: Westminster John Knox, 1994), 45; Frank-Lothar Hossfeld and Erich Zenger, *Die Psalmen*, 3 vols, Neue Echter Bibel, Kommentar zum Alten Testament mit der Einheitsübersetzung 29 (Würzburg: Echter, 1993), 1:49; J. Clinton McCann, Jr., *The Book of Psalms: Introduction, Commentary, and Reflections*, NIB 4 (Nashville: Abingdon, 1996), 689; Robert L. Cole, *Psalms 1-2: Gateway to the Psalter*, HBM 37 (Sheffield: Sheffield Phoenix, 2012), 80. The relationship between the stanzas is confirmed by antithetical word pairs wherein every feature in the first half of the psalm is answered in the second half. For example, the nations (גוים) that rage against God and his anointed in 2:1 are the nations (גוים) that the son inherits in 2:8; the "kings of the earth" (קְרָא־יכלם) rebel in 2:2, yet the the "kings" (מלכים) and "rulers of the earth" (יפטש ארא) are rebuked in 2:10; and in contrast to these plural uses of מלכים, the singular מלך appears only once when God enthrones his king in v. 6. As Cole (79–80) observes, "God's king "is identified as the anointed one [וחישמ] at the outset, as the son of God [בני] in the middle, and son [בר] again at the conclusion"; and just as the kings' rebellion has been against YHWH and his anointed (v. 2) ... their submission is appropriately to both YHWH and his son (vv. 11-12a)."

[5] I.e., what John Eaton (*Kingship and the Psalms*, 2nd ed. [Sheffield: JSOT, 1986], 111) describes as a "schematized" pattern of revolt, response, and resolution. Cf. Hans-Joachim Kraus, *Psalms 1-59: A Commentary* (Minneapolis: Augsburg, 1988), 125; Mitchell J. Dahood, *Psalms I: 1-50: Introduction, Translation, and Notes*, AB 16 (Garden City, NY: Doubleday, 1966), 7; John Goldingay, *Psalms*, 3 vols (Grand Rapids: Baker Academic, 2006), 1:96.

[6] So, *inter alia*, Charles A. Briggs and Emilie G. Briggs, *A Critical and Exegetical Commentary on the Book of Psalms*, ICC 19 (New York: Scribner's, 1906), 1:12, 16; Gunkel, *Psalmen*, 5; Samuel L. Terrien, *The Psalms: Strophic Structure and Theological Commentary* (Grand Rapids: Eerdmans, 2003), 80–81; Collins and Collins, *Son of God*, 11; Allen P. Ross, *A Commentary on the Psalms* (Grand Rapids: Kregel Academic & Professional, 2011), 199. Alternatively, Sigmund Mowinckel (*Psalmenstudien*, 2 vols [Amsterdam: P. Schippers, 1961], 2:114, 177, 310) hypothesized an annual festival celebrating the king's enthronement and YHWH's kingship alike as the *Sitz im Leben* of the psalm; see also Kraus, *Psalms 1-59*, 126; Eaton, *Kingship*, 111–13; J. J. M. Roberts, "Mowinckel's Enthronement Festival: A Review," in

As various commentators have noted, the opening image of the kings and rulers of the earth gathered together (נוֹסְדוּ־יָחַד/συνήχθησαν) against YHWH and his anointed in 2:1-2 exemplifies the *Völkersturm* motif (cf. Psalms 46; 48; 76; 84): what Richard J. Clifford describes as a "narrative of a prototypical attack on the Lord's agent and place."[7] At the same time, vv. 1-3 also display parallels with Egyptian texts in which the king, as divine vice-regent, is the guarantor of peace against the cosmic forces of chaos.[8] At stake, then, is not only Israel's fate, but the entire created order.

The language of enthronement appears immediately in YHWH's response. As Mitchell Dahood observes, יוֹשֵׁב in v. 4 ("*he who sits* in the heavens laughs") "pregnantly connotes 'throne-sitter, king'" (cf. 1 Kgs 8:25; 22:19; Ps 123:1; Isa 6:1; Amos 1:5, 8).[9] Thus, the image of YHWH on his throne forms a parallel with 2:6 where we read, "I have set my king on Zion, my holy mountain."[10]

At the heart of the psalm stands the enthronement of the king itself. As Gerhard von Rad demonstrated, the "decree" (חֹק) in 2:7 probably refers to a physical document given to the king at his coronation.[11] In any case, the words of the decree, בְּנִי אַתָּה אֲנִי הַיּוֹם יְלִדְתִּיךָ/υἱός μου εἶ σύ ἐγὼ σήμερον γεγέννηκά σε ("You are my son, today I have begotten you"), seemingly recall the founding promise of the Davidic dynasty in 2 Sam 7:14: "I will be to him a father and he will be to me a son."[12] When

---

[7] *The Book of Psalms: Composition and Reception*, ed. Peter W. Flint et al., VTSup 99 (Leiden/Boston: Brill, 2005), 104. J. Clinton McCann, Jr. (*The Book of Psalms: Introduction, Commentary, and Reflections*, NIB 4 [Nashville: Abingdon, 1996], 689) entertains both possibilities. In view of the shared language and motifs with ANE enthronement rituals, it seems best to maintain a pre-exilic date for the psalm: so Gerald B. Cooke, "Israelite King as Son of God," *ZAW* 73 (1961): 202-25, esp. 217; Tryggve N. D. Mettinger, *King and Messiah: The Civil and Sacral Legitimation of the Israelite Kings*, ConBOT 8 (Lund: LiberLäromedel/Gleerup, 1976), 265–66; Eckart Otto, "Psalm 2 in neuassyrischer Zeit. Assyrische Motive in der judäischen Königsideologie," in *Textarbeit. Studien zu Texten und ihrer Rezeption aus dem Alten Testament und der Umwelt Israels. Festschrift für Peter Weimar*, ed. Klaus Kiesow and Thomas Meurer, AOAT 294 (Münster: Ugarit, 2003), 335–49; *contra* Zenger (*Psalmen*, 1:49–54), who suggests a post-exilic *Sitz im Leben* in light of the psalm's seemingly eschatological interests.

[7] Richard J. Clifford, *Psalms 1-72*, AOTC (Nashville: Abingdon, 2002), 46. Cf. Ps 48:5: "For behold, the kings gathered, they advanced together." The key phrase נוֹסְדוּ־יָחַד (συνήχθησαν in the LXX) is not common, but typically indicates a hostile alliance or conspiracy wherever it occurs (cf. Ps 31:14); see 'Amos Ḥakham, *Sefer Tehilim* סֵפֶר תְּהִלִּים, Torah, Nevi'im, Ketuvim 'im perush "Da'at Miḳra" (Jerusalem: Mossad Harav Kook, 1979), 6 n. 1; Cole, *Psalms 1-2*, 92.

[8] See Hossfeld and Zenger, *Psalmen*, 1:50, 52; Eric M. Orlin, "Politics and Religion: Politics and Ancient Mediterranean Religions," in *ER* 11:7276; Ronald S. Hendel, "Israelite Religion," in *ER* 7:4243; Henri Frankfort, *Kingship and the Gods: A Study of Ancient Near Eastern Religion as the Integration of Society & Nature*, Phoenix ed., An Oriental Institute Essay (Chicago: University of Chicago Press, 1978), 159; Craigie, *Psalms 1-50*, 66; and Collins and Collins, *Son of God*, 22.

[9] Dahood, *Psalms I*, 8-9; cf. Clifford, *Psalms 1-72*, 44; Markus Saur, *Die Königspsalmen: Studien zur Entstehung und Theologie*, BZAW 340 (Berlin/New York: de Gruyter, 2004), 30.

[10] On the metaphorical use of נסך for the installation of a ruler see BDB, s.v. נסך III. Though נסך more typically means to "pour out," the term is also a cognate of נָסִיךְ ("prince"). Thus, *HALOT*, s.v. נסך I suggests "to be consecrated" or "made leader" in Ps 2:6. Cf. Cole, *Psalms 1-2*, 107.

[11] Gerhard von Rad, "Das judäische Königsritual," *TLZ* 72 (1947): 211-16. See also Albrecht Alt ("Jesaja 8,23-9,6. Befreiungsnacht und Krönungstag," in *Festschrift Alfred Bertholet zum 80. Geburtstag gewidmet*, ed. Walter Baumgartner [Tübingen: Mohr Siebeck, 1950], 29–49]; Eaton, *Kingship*, 111–12; Collins and Collins, *Son of God*, 14. According to Hossfeld and Zenger (*Psalmen*, 1:50), the bestowal of a royal protocol to the king was also a part of Egyptian enthronement rituals.

[12] See, e.g., Berlin and Brettler, "Psalms," 1286; also Hossfeld and Zenger, *Psalmen*, 1:51. The promise of 2 Sam 7:14 is also recalled in Pss 72:1; 89:27-28; 132:11.

viewed against the backdrop of enthronement rituals throughout the ancient Near East, the substance of such language is clear: for God to declare the king his "son" is to install him as his personal vice-regent on earth who will enact his will.[13] God and the king work in one accord as father and son.[14] Accordingly, 2:8-9 anticipates the king's dominion over all the earth as his "inheritance" (נחל/κληρονομία).[15] Together, vv. 7-9 articulate the overarching hope expressed through the psalm: that of God's rule on earth instantiated through his son, the king.[16]

As a result, the psalm's final stanza (vv. 10-12) entreates the rebellious rulers who once opposed God and his anointed to be sensible (שכל/συνίημι). In place of their hostility, they are to "serve YHWH with fear and rejoice with trembling" and likewise "kiss the son" (vv. 10-12).[17] Despite the militant imagery of v. 9 and dire warnings of vv. 10-11, however, mercy is extened to the kings insofar as they are enjoined to gain wisdom and rejoice in YHWH's rule. Indeed, the psalm does not end on the note of wrath (אפו), but with the promise of blessing (אשרי) constituted by God's universal rule.[18]

---

[13] There is no firm agreement as to whether the Israelite motif reflected in 2 Sam 7:14 and Ps 2:7 should be conceived as adoption or some other legal metaphor, but either way it clearly resembles the practices of other ANE cultures in which the king could be known as a deity's son, most notably Egypt, but also Mesopotamia. What is extremely rare in ancient sources, however, is the notion that the king is the ontological offspring of the deity; see Ivan Engnell, *Studies in Divine Kingship in the Ancient Near East* (Oxford: Blackwell, 1967); John Baines, "Ancient Egyptian Kingship: Official Forms, Rhetoric, Context," in *King and Messiah in Israel and the Ancient Near East*, JSOTSup 270 (ed. John Day; Sheffield: Sheffield Academic, 1998), 19-20; Collins and Collins, *Son of God*, 5-7, 12-13; Cole, *Psalms 1-2*, 115. Cole helpfully observes similar metaphorical uses of birth language in Pss 87:3-6 and 110:2-3. The function of ילדתי in Ps 2:7, in any case, appears to parallel the function of יהיה in 2 Sam 7:14 (David's offspring will *be* a son to God) and of אתן in Ps 89:28 ("I will *appoint* him my firstborn . . .").

[14] As Cole (*Psalms 1-2*, 92) observes, "[t]he anointed monarch is the divine representative in every sense of the word." Both are mentioned precisely three times at the beginning, middle, and end of the psalm; rebellion against the one is tantamount to rebellion against the other; and the imperatives to "serve YHWH" and "kiss the son" (vv. 11-12) are synonymous. Cf. Luis Alonso Schökel and Cecilia Carniti, *Salmos: traducción introducciones y comentario*, Nueva Biblia Española (Estella: Editorial Verbo Divino, 1992), 156; Adele Berlin and Marc Zvi Brettler, "Psalms," in *The Jewish Study Bible: Jewish Publication Society Tanakh Translation*, ed. Adele Berlin, Marc Zvi Brettler, and Michael Fishbane (New York/Oxford: Oxford University Press, 2004), 1285

[15] Although there are disagreements concerning some of the details, the imagery of v. 9 apparently recalls coronation rituals throughout the ANE, in which the king would strike an earthen pot with the royal scepter or staff, destroying it. See the helpful summary in Sam Janse, *You Are My Son: The Reception History of Psalm 2 in Early Judaism and the Early Church* (Leuven: Peeters, 2009), 21; and the claims of Assyrian and/or Egyptian parallels by Gunkel, *Psalmen*, 5; Kraus, *Psalms 1-59*, 132; Hossfeld and Zenger, *Psalmen*, 1:54; and Bob Becking, "'Wie Töpfe sollst du sie zerschmeissen': mesopotamische Parallelen zu Psalm 2:9b," *ZAW* 102 (1990): 59–79, all cited by Janse; *contra* Othmar Keel, *Die Welt der altorientalischen Bildsymbolik und das Alte Testament: am Beispiel der Psalmen*, 5th ed. (Göttingen: Vandenhoeck & Ruprecht, 1996), 272-74, who maintains that the violent imagery of v. 9 constitutes a literal threat rather than an allusion to a coronation ritual.

[16] Cf. Hossfeld and Zenger, *Psalmen*, 1:50.

[17] The latter term most likely alludes to the kiss of fealty, wherein a vassal would kiss the sovereign's feet. See Gunkel, *Psalmen*, 8 citing parallels in texts from Babylonia and Assyria; and Artur Weiser (*The Psalms: A Commentary*, OTL [Philadelphia: Westminster, 1962], 70) citing parallels in texts from Babylonia and Egypt; see also Kraus, *Psalms 1-59*, 133; Janse, *Son*, 21. The LXX differs at v. 12, substituting δράξασθε παιδείας in place of נשקו-בר. The imperative to "accept correction" agrees with the entreaty to wisdom in v. 10, though it disrupts the series of parallels between YHWH and his son.

[18] Cf. Kraus, *Psalms 1-59*, 133; Hossfeld and Zenger, *Psalmen*, 1:54.

In summary, the second psalm looks to God's enthronement of his anointed king, his "son," as the hinge on which the fate of Israel and the world depends. In its progression it moves from the distinct images of widespread rebellion to YHWH's installation of his king and son, to the son's dominion over the whole world. Finally, Ps 2:7 is one of a small family of texts that identify David's heir as God's son in the Jewish Scriptures (2 Sam 7:14; 1 Chr 17:13; 22:10; 28:6; Pss 2:7; 89:27-28).[19] It is important to note, however, is that Psalm 2 is the only text to pair the terms משיח (v. 2), מלך (v. 6), and בן (v. 7)—a three-way linkage that proves significant in subsequent interpretation.

2.2 Psalm 2 in Early Judaism

In the absence of any king on David's throne following the exile, eschatological and messianic interpretation of Psalm 2 became the norm.[20] It was not hard, after all, to find the realization of oppression and tumult described in Ps 2:1-3 in the unhappy circumstances of the Hasmonean and Roman periods, but what many Jews longed for all the more so was the final hope of God's reign through his Messiah promised in the second half of the psalm.[21]

Accordingly, a number of texts find in Ps 2:1-2 the paradigmatic image of the nations and rulers gathered against Israel and/or the Messiah. Others highlight God's enthronement of the Messiah by alluding to Ps 2:6-7. Still others look forward to the Messiah's triumph over the nations, alluding to Ps 2:8-9. All of these patterns are catalogued in Table 2.1.

Notably, the early Jewish interest in the psalm corresponds closely to the threefold plot of rebellion, divine response, and resolution. Such even interest in virtually every portion of the psalm suggests that it was typically read with a view toward the total drama it envisions.[22] This suggestion is confirmed as we take a closer look at the individual texts.

2.2.1 Psalm of Solomon 17

As Rikk Watts observes, *Psalm of Solomon* 17 "is virtually a commentary on Ps. 2."[23] These eighteen psalms comprise the response of a group of devout Jews to the capture

---

[19] All of these can be traced back to the common ancestor of 2 Sam 7:14. As with Ps 2:7, Ps 89:27-28 is a seeming paraphrase of 2 Sam 7:14; see Georg Fohrer, "υἱός," *TDNT* 8:350. Effectively, then, Pss 2:7 and 89:27-28 are sibling texts in the tradition of the divine sonship of the Davidic king.

[20] Thus, as Janse (*Son*, 24–7, 34) discusses, interpreters ranging from John Calvin to von Rad have insisted that the psalm must be understood eschatologically.

[21] See the discussions in James H. Charlesworth, "From Messianology to Christology: Problems and Prospects," in *The Messiah: Developments in Earliest Judaism and Christianity*, ed. James H. Charlesworth (Minneapolis: Fortress, 1992), 3–4; John J. Collins, "A Messiah Before Jesus?" in *Christian Beginnings and the Dead Sea Scrolls*, ed. John J. Collins and Craig A. Evans (Grand Rapids: Baker Academic, 2006), 15.

[22] See Hays's description of metalepsis: "Allusive echo functions to suggest to the reader that text B should be understood in light of a broad interplay with text A, encompassing aspects of A beyond those explicitly echoed"; Hays, *Letters of Paul*, 20.

[23] Watts, "Mark," 123; cf. Janse, *Son*, 64–6.

Table 2.1 Quotations and Allusions to Ps 2 in Early Judaism[24]

	Ps 2:1-2 The kings of the earth oppose the Lord and his Messiah.	Ps 2:6-7 God sends /enthrones the Messiah.	Ps 2:8-9 The Messiah/Son inherits & reproves the nations.
Ps. Sol. 17	17:12, 22		17:23-24
1 En. 48	48:8		48:8-10
1Q28ª		II, 11-12	
4Q174	I, 18-19		
4Q246		I, 9-2, 1	
Sib. Or. 3	3:663-664	3:652-656	3:652-656
4 Ezra 13	13:31	13:32, 35, 37	13:37
Midr. Ps. 2	ad loc.	ad loc.	ad loc.
b. Sukkah 52a		52a	52a

of Jerusalem by a foreign invader, most likely Pompey's incursion in 63 BCE.[25] Against this backdrop, the seventeenth psalm opens and closes by declaring "the Lord himself is our king forever and ever" (17:1, 46), and further anticipates the triumph of ἡ βασιλεία τοῦ θεοῦ ἡμῶν ("the kingdom of our God") over the nations forever (17:3).[26] In vv. 23-24, the influence of Ps 2:9 is unmistakable; "the Son of David," will "destroy the sinner's arrogance *like a potter's jar; with a rod of iron* he will *shatter* all their substance."[27] See below:

Ps 2:9 LXX
ποιμανεῖς αὐτοὺς <u>ἐν ῥάβδῳ</u>
<u>σιδηρᾷ ὡς σκεῦος κεραμέως</u>
<u>συντρίψεις</u> αὐτούς

***Ps. Sol.* 17:23-24**
ἐκτρῖψαι ὑπερηφανίαν ἁμαρτωλοῦ
<u>ὡς σκεύη κεραμέως· ἐν ῥάβδῳ σιδηρᾷ</u>
<u>συντρῖψαι</u> πᾶσαν ὑπόστασιν αὐτῶν

Meanwhile, the "wicked rulers" (ἄρχοντας ἀδίκους) in v. 22 and "gentile peoples" (λαοὺς ἐθνῶν) in v. 30 recall the language of Ps 2:1-2 (cf. ἄρχοντες, ἔθνη, λαοί). The psalmist goes on to depict the nations coming "from the ends of the earth to see [the Messiah's] glory, bearing as gifts [Jerusalem's] scattered children" (17:31; cf. Ps 2:8, 10).[28]

---

[24] This inventory is not quite exhaustive. Absent from it are some rather subtle echoes to Ps 2:5, 10-12 in *Sib. Or.* 3:670; *Ps. Sol.* 17:31; and *1 En.* 50:4, all of which will be discussed below.

[25] See 2:2; 8:1-3, 15; 17:11-18; cf. Robert B. Wright, "Psalms of Solomon," *The Old Testament Pseudepigrapha*, 2 vols (Peabody, MA: Hendrickson, 2013), 2:639–41; idem, *The Psalms of Solomon: A Critical Edition of the Greek Text*, JCTCRSS 1 (New York: T&T Clark, 2007), 1; Kenneth Atkinson, *I Cried to the Lord: A Study of the Psalms of Solomon's Historical Background and Social Setting*, JSJSup 84 (Leiden/Boston: Brill, 2004), 21–2.

[26] Cf. *Ps. Sol.* 17:1 (κύριε σὺ αὐτὸς βασιλεὺς ἡμῶν εἰς τὸν αἰῶνα καὶ ἔτι) and 17:46 (κύριος αὐτὸς βασιλεὺς ἡμῶν εἰς τὸν αἰῶνα καὶ ἔτι). The repetition forms an *inclusio* highlighting the main theme of the psalm.

[27] Cf. Wright, "Psalms of Solomon," OTP 2:666; Kenneth Atkinson, *An Intertextual Study of the Psalms of Solomon: Pseudepigrapha*, SBEC 49 (Lewiston, NY: E. Mellen, 2001), 347–49. The translation above is my own.

[28] Trans. Wright, *Psalms of Solomon*, 193.

Although *Psalm of Solomon* 17 never alludes to Ps 2:6-7 directly, it anticipates the coming of the "Lord Messiah" (χριστὸς κυρίου; v. 32), who is also the "Son of David" (v. 21) and the "righteous king" (v. 32). All told, the overarching theme of *Psalm of Solomon* 17 is, like that of Psalm 2, God's establishment his kingdom through his Messiah, wherein justice will be done for God's people.[29] As in Psalm 2, the Lord's reign meshes with that of his Anointed, since the latter amounts to the realization of the former. Although this text directly cites only one verse from Psalm 2, it plainly reflects the broader plot and themes of Psalm 2 throughout.

2.2.2 4 Ezra

One finds a similar interpretation of Psalm 2 in *4 Ezra*: a text responding to Roman oppression following the destruction of the temple in 70 CE.[30] Several times in *4 Ezra*, God refers to the Messiah as "my son" (7:28-29; 13:32; 37, 52; 14:9; cf. Ps 2:7). The most significant discussion of this figure occurs in 13:31-37. Here, v. 31 describes a situation of widespread warfare ("kingdom against kingdom") reminiscent of Ps 2:2. Then, in v. 32, God's "son," the Messiah, appears, and in vv. 33-34 the nations gather against him (cf. Ps 2:1-2).[31] Yet the son finally "stand[s] atop Mount Zion" (vv. 35; cf. Ps 2:6-7) and reproves the nations (v. 37; cf. Ps 2:8-9). Fourth Ezra thus retraces the total plot of the psalm, interpreting it as a prophecy of the Messiah's exaltation and dominion over the hostile nations opposed to God's rule.[32]

---

[29] According to Kenneth Atkinson ("On the Use of Scripture in the Development of Militant Davidic Messianism at Qumran: New Light from Psalm of Solomon 17," in *The Interpretation of Scripture in Early Judaism and Christianity: Studies in Language and Tradition*, ed. C. A. Evans [Sheffield: Sheffield Academic, 2000], 108-09), Ps. Sol. 17, from v. 21 onward, depicts the Messiah as "a righteous counterpart to the 'man that is foreign to our race' (v. 7)." The Messiah's arrival answers the plight described in the first half of the psalm. Cf. Kenneth Pomykala, *The Davidic Dynasty Tradition in Early Judaism: Its History and Significance for Messianism*, EJL 7 (Atlanta, GA: Scholars, 1995), 161.

[30] See the discussions in Metzger, "Fourth Ezra," OTP 1:520-21; Michael E. Stone, *Fourth Ezra: A Commentary on the Books of Fourth Ezra* (Fortress, 1990), 10; George W. E. Nickelsburg, *Jewish Literature between the Bible and the Mishnah: A Historical and Literary Introduction*, 2nd ed. (Minneapolis: Fortress, 2005), 275. Knibb (R. J. Coggins and Michael A. Knibb, *The First and Second Books of Esdras*, CBC [Cambridge/New York: Cambridge University Press, 1979], 168), comments on 7:28-29: "[f]rom these other passages [12:31-34; 13:25-52] it emerges that one important function of the Messiah in 2 Esdras 3-14 was to judge and destroy the Romans and other nations (cp. Ps. 2:8-9)."

[31] Stone (*Fourth Ezra*, 207-13) believes that the Latin *filius* in the examples above is more likely a translation of παῖς rather than υἱός. Numerous others, however, believe "son" to reflect the original reading of the text: see Coggins and Knibb, *1-2 Esdras*, 168-69; Stephen Gero, "'My Son the Messiah': A Note on 4 Esr 7:28-29," *ZNW* 66 (1975): 264-67; John J. Collins, "The Background of the 'Son of God' Text," *BBR* 7 (1997): 51-61; Collins and Collins, *Son of God*, 96. James H. Charlesworth (*Jesus within Judaism: New Light from Exciting Archaeological Discoveries* [New York: Doubleday, 1988], 151) observes that "the Syriac version, which is independent of and just as important as the Latin, has *bar*: 'son.'"

[32] See similarly Coggins and Knibb, *1-2 Esdras*, 169, 266; John J. Collins, *The Scepter and the Star: Messianism in Light of the Dead Sea Scrolls*, 2nd ed. (Grand Rapids: Eerdmans, 2010), 186; Janse, *Son*, 68-9. Even Stone (*Fourth Ezra*, 403), though he discounts the potential influence of Ps 2:7 behind *filius* throughout *4 Ezra*, admits in 13:35 that "[a] most interesting parallel is to be seen in Ps 2:6, a text often given a messianic interpretation in the Second Temple period. There in the context of the attack made upon the king by the nations it states, 'I have set my king on Zion, my holy hill.'"

2.2.3 The Similitudes of Enoch

The *Similitudes of Enoch* 48-50 likewise display a broad interplay with Psalm 2. Where chapters 48-49 describe the coming of the "Son of Man" (48:2), who is variously designated God's "Chosen One" (48:9) and his "Anointed" (48:10), they do so in language dependent on the Isaiah's Servant Songs (e.g., Isaiah 42; 49) and Davidic oracles such as Psalm 2 and Isaiah 11.[33] *First Enoch* 48:8-10, for example, warns of the judgment coming against "the kings of the earth, and the strong who possess the land" before the vindication of the righteous.[34] The mention of "the kings of the earth" in v. 8, who are charged with having "denied the Lord of Spirits and his Anointed" in v. 10, frames this small unit as a riff on Ps 2:2.[35] Moreover, as Nickelsburg and Vanderkam note, the condemnation of these kings executed by the Lord's Anointed One "is consonant with the decree that is issued in vv. 7-9" of Psalm 2.[36] Again, in 50:4, the Anointed One is given dominion over the earth "reminiscent of the sovereignty of 'his Anointed One' over 'the ends of the earth' and the 'rulers of the earth' in Ps 2:8, 10."[37] If Nickelsburg and Vanderkam are correct, then Psalm 2 in its entirety appears to have helped shape the *Similitudes*' vision of the coming Messiah.

2.2.4 Sibylline Oracles 3

Sibylline Oracles 3:652-654 announces the coming of a deliverer-king sent by God, who will end war throughout the earth. Although not explicitly identified as the eschatological Messiah, both Collins and Janse observe that "the close connection of this ruler to God reminds us of the Messianic Ruler of texts like Ps.2."[38] Shortly thereafter, the text relates a familiar scene of warfare between "the kings of the nations" (βασιλῆες ἐθνῶν; cf. Ps 2:1-2), who "want to destroy the Temple of the great God" (ll. 663-665).[39] Yet ll. 669-670 declare that "God will speak with a great voice" (cf. Ps 2:5) in judgment against "the ignorant, empty-minded people" (λαὸν ἀπαίδευτον κενεόφρονα), which is reminiscent of the language found in Ps 2:10, 12 LXX (παιδεύθητε/δράξασθε παιδείας) and Ps 2:1 LXX (κενά).[40] Although the allusions found in Sibylline Oracles 3

---

[33] Nickelsburg and Vanderkam, *1 Enoch*, 2:167.
[34] Trans. Ibid., 2:166.
[35] So also J. C. Vanderkam, "Righteous One, Messiah, Chosen One, and Son of Man in 1 Enoch 37-71," in *The Messiah*, 171, 187; Nickelsburg and Vanderkam, *1 Enoch*, 2:174; and Grant Macaskill, "Matthew and the Parables of Enoch," in *Parables of Enoch: A Paradigm Shift*, ed. James H. Charlesworth and Darrell L. Bock, JCTCRSS 11 (London: T&T Clark, 2013), 218-29, here 229.
[36] Nickelsburg and Vanderkam, *1 Enoch*, 2:176.
[37] Nickelsburg and Vanderkam, *1 Enoch*, 2:189. Vanderkam, "Righteous One," 171 further suggests that "a biblical allusion [to Psalm 2] conditions the use of 'anointed one'" throughout this section of 1 Enoch.
[38] Janse, *Son*, 70; cf. Collins, "Sibylline Oracles," *OTP* 1:376-377; *contra* Rieuwerd Buitenwerf (*Book III of the Sibylline Oracles and Its Social Setting*, SVTP 17 [Leiden/Boston: Brill, 2003], 277), who is more hesitant to describe this figure as the Messiah. According to Collins (1:356), "[t]he main historical interest of Sibylline Oracles 3 lies in its attestation of a Jewish community that could hail a Ptoelmaic king as a savior figure or Messiah."
[39] So also Collins, "Sibylline Oracles," *OTP* 1:376-377; Buitenwerf, *Sibylline Oracles*, 277; Janse, *Son*, 69-70.
[40] Cf. Janse, *Son*, 70.

2.2.5 Psalm 2 in the Qumran Scrolls

One finds several references to Psalm 2 in the sectarian literature from Qumran. One of the most famous is found in 4QFlorilegium. As Jacob Milgrom observes, "*Florilegium* (4Q174) is more appropriately entitled '*A Midrash on 2 Samuel and Psalms 1-2*.'"[41] The initial midrash on 2 Sam 7:10b-16 in the first thirteen lines of column I identifies the "son" of 2 Sam 7:14 as "the Branch of David" (I, 11), who is elsewhere identified as the Messiah (4Q252 V, 1-4).[42] Immediately following this interpretation, Florilegium launches into another midrash on Psalms 1-2 (I, 14-II, 6), here read as a single text. Psalm 2:1-2 is quoted in I, 18-19 and applied to the uprising of the nations against "Israel in the last days." Significantly, the lines that follow interpret the rebellious kings and nations of Ps 2:1-2 as representatives of Belial, thus adding a cosmic dimension to Ps 2:1-2 (4Q174 1, 3 II, 2).[43] Lines 3-5 of frag. 4 expand on this reference: "This is the time when Belial will unleash severe things against the house of Judah to hate them [...] and shall seek with all his strength to scatter them."[44] According to 4Q174, then, the battle in Ps 2:1-2 transcends the earthly sphere.

Much is sometimes made of the fact that Florilegium does not explicitly mention the Messiah in its interpretation of Psalm 2.[45] Yet Florilegium offers an eschatological reading of Psalm 2 in conjunction with a reading of 2 Samuel 7 that identifies God's son as the Messiah. To suppose that the community did not identify the royal "son" in Ps 2:7 as the Messiah while identifying the "son" in 2 Sam 7:14 as such is to privilege silence over the obvious. On the contrary, the fact that 4Q174 cites Psalm 2 alongside 2 Sam 7:14 suggests that *Florilegium*, like other Second Temple literature, bears in mind the psalm's broader plot, beginning with the tumult of the nations and kings in 2:1-2, but ending with the Messiah's exaltation per Ps 2:6-7 and following.

Indeed, 1QRule of the Congregation (1Q28ª) II, 11-12 contains a probable allusion to Ps 2:7. The relevant portion reads: "At [a ses]sion of the men of renown, [those

---

[41] Jacob Milgrom, "Florilegium: A Midrash on 2 Samuel and Psalms 1-2," in *The Dead Sea Scrolls: Hebrew, Aramaic, and Greek Texts with the English Translations*, ed. James H. Charlesworth, PTSDSSP 6b (Tübingen: Mohr Siebeck; Louisville: Westminster John Knox, 1994), 248; cf. Dale Goldsmith, "Acts 13:33-37: A Pesher on II Samuel 7," *JBL* 87 (1968): 321-24; George J. Brooke, *Exegesis at Qumran: 4Q Florilegium in Its Jewish Context*, JSOTSup 29 (Sheffield: JSOT, 1985), 217-19; John J. Collins, "Jesus, Messianism, and the Dead Sea Scrolls," in *Qumran-Messianism: Studies on the Messianic Expectations in the Dead Sea Scrolls*, ed. James H. Charlesworth, Hermann Lichtenberger, and Gerbern S. Oegema (Tübingen: Mohr Siebeck, 1998), 111.

[42] In the lines that follow, the son is further identified as "the booth of David that is fallen" (Amos 9:11), whom God will raise up to save Israel: "He is the booth of David that is falle[n w]ho will arise to save Israel" (I, 12-13). Trans. Milgrom, *Florilegium*, 253.

[43] Cf. Marcus, *Way*, 62–3.

[44] Personal translation, following the restorations by Milgrom, *Florilegium*, 254.

[45] So Janse (*Son*, 51), who argues that "Ps.2 is interpreted non-Messianically" here since the battle is said to be against the elect of Israel rather than the Messiah. In view of the overall messianic context within which the citation of Ps 2:1-2 occurs, however, the implied alternative between a battle against the elect of Israel and Israel's Messiah is both unnecessary and unwarranted.

summoned to] the gathering of the community council, when [God] begets [יוליד] the Messiah with them: [the] chief [priest] of all the congregation of Israel shall enter ..."⁴⁶ The use of יוליד likely recalls ילדתיך in Ps 2:7, given that Psalm 2 is the only Scriptural text to speaks of God "begetting" the Messiah. In this case, we have yet another messianic interpretation of the psalm.⁴⁷

Though controversial, it is likely that 4QAramaic Apocalypse (4Q246), commonly known as the "Son of God text," also reflects the influence of Ps 2:7. In column II, line 1, the text refers to a figure who is called both "son of God" (ברה די אל) and "son of the Most-High" (בר עליון). Although the identity of the son of God figure in this text is notoriously debated, the view that the term refers to a Davidic Messiah has gained increasing support over the years.⁴⁸ Not only is "the individual most often designated as 'the son of God' in the Hebrew Bible ... the Davidic king," as Collins observes, but the vision of the son's unending rule and judging of the earth recalls other scriptural passages associated with either God's eternal kingdom or the Root of Jesse (i.e., the Davidic Messiah):

Dan 4:3	His kingdom is an everlasting kingdom, and his dominion endures from generation to generation (cf. Ps 145:13; Dan 4:34; 7:14, 27).
4Q246 II, 5	His kingdom will be an eternal kingdom ...
4Q246 II, 9	His rule will be an eternal rule ...
Isa 11:4	... he will judge the poor, and decide with equity for the meek of the earth ...⁴⁹
4Q246 II, 6	He will jud[ge] the earth in truth and all will make peace. The sword will cease from the earth.

---

⁴⁶ Trans. Florentino García Martinez and Eibert J. C. Tigchelaar (eds.), *The Dead Sea Scrolls Study Edition*, 2 vols; 2nd ed. (Grand Rapids: Eerdmans, 2000).

⁴⁷ So also Craig A. Evans, "Are the 'Son' Texts at Qumran 'Messianic'? Reflections on 4Q369 and Related Scrolls," in *Qumran-Messianism*, 138-39; Aquila H. I. Lee, *From Messiah to Preexistent Son: Jesus' Self-Consciousness and Early Christian Exegesis of Messianic Psalms*, WUNT 192 (Tübingen: Mohr Siebeck, 2005), 248; Janse, *Son*, 53.

⁴⁸ Some have suggested that the "son of God" refers to a negative ruler, described in the preceding column, who claimed divine titles for himself: either a Seleucid ruler (so J. T. Milik, "Du Livre d'Esther Dans La Grotte 4 De Qumrân," *RevQ* 15 [1992]: 321-406) or a pre-Christian version of the "anti-christ" (so David Flusser, "The Hubris of the Antichrist in a Fragment from Qumran," in *Judaism and the Origins of Christianity* [Jerusalem: Magnes Press, 1988], 207-13). Joseph A. Fitzmyer ("4Q246: The 'Son of God' Document from Qumran," *Bib* 74 (1993): 153-74) views the figure as a positive Jewish ruler, but not a messianic one. Florentino García Martínez ("The Eschatological Figure of 4Q246," in *Qumran and Apocalyptic: Studies on the Aramaic Texts from Qumran*, STDJ 9 [New York: Brill, 1992], 162-79; idem, "Messianic Hope in the Qumran Writings," in *The People of the Dead Sea Scrolls: Their Writings, Beliefs and Practices*, ed. Florentino García Martínez and Julio Trebolle Barrera, STDJ 30 [Leiden: Brill, 1995], 159-89) argues that the "son of God" is a heavenly eschatological figure. Supporting the present view (Davidic messianism), see, *inter alia:* John J. Collins, "The Son of God Text from Qumran," in *From Jesus to John: Essays on Jesus and New Testament Christology in Honour of Marinus de Jonge*, ed. Martinus C. De Boer, JSNTSup 84 (Sheffield: JSOT, 1993), 76-82; idem, *Scepter*, 155-64; Johannes Zimmerman, "Observations on 4Q246—The 'Son of God,'" in *Qumran-Messianism*, 188; Frank Moore Cross, "The Structure of the Apocalypse of 'Son of God' (4Q246)," in *Emanuel: Studies in Hebrew Bible, Septuagint, and Dead Sea Scrolls in Honor of Emanuel Tov*, ed. Shalom M. Paul, VTSup 94 (Leiden: Brill, 2003), 151-58; Karl A. Kuhn, "The 'One like a Son of Man' Becomes the 'Son of God,'" *CBQ* 69 (2007): 22-42; Tucker S. Ferda, "Naming the Messiah: A Contribution to the 4Q246 'Son of God' Debate," *DSD* 21 (2014): 150-75; Michael Segal, "Who Is the 'Son of God' in 4Q246?: An Overlooked Example of Early Biblical Interpretation," *DSD* 21 (2014): 289-312.

⁴⁹ Collins (*Scepter*, 178) notes that in 4QpIsaᵃ col. 3, frag. 7.26, "his sword will judge [al]l the peoples."

The close similarities between 4Q246 and Luke 1:32-35 also speak in favor of a messianic reading:

4Q246 I, 9–II, 1	Luke 1:32-35
He will be called great	He will be great
He will be called the son of God	He will be called the son of God
and they will call him son of the Most-High	he will be called the son of the Most-High[50]

In Luke's text, there can be no doubt that this combination of terms springs from the well of Davidic messianism. Luke 1:32 reads:

καὶ δώσει αὐτῷ κύριος ὁ θεὸς τὸν θρόνον Δαυὶδ τοῦ πατρὸς αὐτοῦ.

And the Lord God will give him the throne of David, his ancestor.

Indeed, most commentators assert that Luke 1:32-35 almost certainly alludes to 2 Sam 7:11-16 and possibly Ps 2:7.[51] Given, then, the messianic interpretations of 2 Sam 7:11-16 and Psalm 2 in both 4Q174 and 1Q28ᵃ, there is more than enough evidence to conclude, as Janse and others do, that texts such as Ps 2:7 and 2 Sam 7:14 must stand in the background of the title "Son of God" for the messianic figure in 4Q246.[52] Moreover, as we will see in the following chapter, Jewish literature pairs Isaiah 11 (especially Isa 11:4) alongside Psalm 2 more than any other text.[53]

Finally, the theme of eschatological battle leading to the establishment of an eternal kingdom in 4Q246 presents a striking parallel with Psalm 2. If this text does allude to Ps 2:7, then it seemingly does so while evoking the larger plot of the psalm. Indeed, the anticipation of an eternal kingdom in 4Q246 matches the interpretation of Psalm 2 in *4 Ezra*, Sibylline Oracles 3, and especially Psalm of Solomon 17.

One should also mention 4QPrayer of Enosh (4Q369). The text speaks of a "firstborn son" (בן בכור; II, 1, 6), which reminds one of Exod 4:22 where Israel is called God's "firstborn son" (בן רוכב).[54] In the surrounding context, however, 4Q369 also describes an "inheritance" (נחלתו; II, 1) given by God to the firstborn son and to "his seed (לזרעו) according to their generations, an eternal possession (אחזת)" (II, 4). The son is also "a prince and ruler" (שר ומושל; II, 7) crowned (עטרת; II, 8) by God himself and commanded to obey God's "righteous statutes" (חוקים צדיקים; II, 10), precisely in the context of their father-son relationship. The same terms apply to David in 2 Sam 7:12-16, Psalms 2 and

---

[50] An identical chart to this one appears in Johnson, "Romans 1:3-4," 474.

[51] See e.g., Joseph A. Fitzmyer, *The Gospel According to Luke (I-IX): Introduction, Translation, and Notes*, AB 28a–28b (Garden City, NY: Doubleday, 1981), 1:206–07; 347–52; Joel B. Green, *The Gospel of Luke*, NICNT (Grand Rapids: Eerdmans, 1997), 88–90; François Bovon, *Luke*: A Commentary on the Gospel of Luke 1:1-9:50. Hermeneia (Minneapolis: Fortress, 2002), 51.

[52] Janse, *Son*, 53; see also Collins, *Scepter*, 208; idem, "Jesus, Messianism, and the Dead Sea Scrolls," 111; Zimmerman, "Observations," 180.

[53] Isa 11:4 is referenced alongside portions of Ps 2 in *Ps. Sol.* 17:24, 35-36; *4 Ezra* 13:10, 38; *Midr. Ps.* 2:3; Rev 2:16; 19:11, 15; as well as Isa 11:2 in *Ps. Sol.* 17:32; *1 En.* 49:1, 3; Isa 11:6-9 in *Sib. Or.* 3:788-795; and Isa 11:12 in *Ps. Sol.* 17:26. There is also a high likelihood that Isa 11:2, 6 is alluded to alongside Ps 2:7 in Mark 1:10-13, which we will be explore in the following chapter.

[54] James Kugel, "4Q369 'Prayer of Enosh' and Ancient Biblical Interpretation," *DSD* 5 (1998): 119–48.

89, wherein the Davidic king is also called God's "firstborn" (בכור; cf. Ps 89:28) and "son" (בן; cf. 2 Sam 7:14; Ps 2:7).[55] Thus, it is more likely that the "firstborn son" in this text is again a royal Davidic figure.[56] Although Psalm 2 is surely not the sole background of 4Q369 1 II, 1-8 (indeed, the most plentiful echoes are of Ps 89), the verbal links between "inheritance" (נחלה) and "possession" (אחזה) with Ps 2:8 do suggest that we have here further evidence of the messianic reading of the psalm at Qumran, alongside the closely related texts of 2 Sam 7:11-16 and Ps 89.[57]

2.2.6 Psalm 2 in Rabbinic Literature

The messianic intrepretation of Psalm 2 continues in rabbinic literature. While the reticence of rabbinic literature to refer to the Messiah as God's "son" (probably in reaction to the Christian use of "Son of God") is well-known,[58] it is striking that some of the most explicit messianic interpretations of Ps 2:7 nevertheless come from rabbinic sources.

For example, *Midr. Ps.* 2.3 states that the entire psalm is about "the lord Messiah in the time to come."[59] The decree and promise of vv. 7-8 are spoken directly to the Messiah (2.9, 10). Intriguingly, *Midr. Ps.* 2.9 interprets the words "You are my son" in relation to each of the three divisions of Scripture. From the Torah, *Midr. Ps.* 2.9 cites Exod 4:22; from the Nevi'im, Isa 42:1; 52:13; and from the Kethuvim, Ps 110:1 and Dan 7:14. In this way, the text likens the Messiah's sonship to Israel's own, on the one hand, and fuses the "son" in Ps 2:7 with Isaiah's "servant" and Daniel's "son of man," on the other.

According to *b. Sukkah* 52a:6, Ps 2:7-8 is addressed to the Davidic Messiah (cf. *Midr. Ps.* 2.9, 10):

> To Messiah ben David, who is destined to be revealed swiftly in our time, the Holy One, Blessed be He, says: Ask of Me anything and I will give you whatever you wish, as it is stated: "I will tell of the decree; the Lord said unto me: You are My son, this day have I begotten you, ask of Me, and I will give the nations for your inheritance, and the ends of the earth for your possession"[60]

In contrast to some modern interpretations of Mark that draw a contrast between "Son of God" and "Son of David," *b. Sukkah* identifies the two: the Son of God in Ps 2:7 *is* the

---

[55] Cf. Johnson, "Romans 1:3-4," 472.
[56] Craig A. Evans, "A Note on the 'First-Born Son' of 4Q369," *DSD* 2 (1995): 185–201; Johnson, "Romans 1:3-4," 472.
[57] Though one could conceivably stop at labeling the reading in 4Q369 "Davidic" rather than "messianic," the text was likely composed at Qumran between 30 BCE and 68 CE (see Emanuel Tov and Martin G. Abegg, *Indices and an Introduction to the "Discoveries in the Judean Desert" Series*, DJD 39 [Oxford: Clarendon, 2002], 424); thus, the clear messianic readings of the same texts elsewhere at Qumran can and should be taken into consideration here too.
[58] See, e.g., Steichele, *Sohn Gottes*, 139–47; and Marcus, *Way*, 77–8.
[59] All translations of *Midr. Ps.* 2 are from William Gordon Braude, *The Midrash on Psalms*, 2 vols, YJS 13 (New Haven; London: Yale University Press, 1976).
[60] All quotations from the Babylonian Talmud herein are from I. Epstein, *The Babylonian Talmud* (London: Soncino, 1938).

Son of David, just as it is David's offspring to whom God issues the promise of sonship in 2 Sam 7:14.[61]

In general, the rabbinic interpretation of Psalm 2 is distinctly eschatological. As Lövestam observes, the rebellious nations of Ps 2:1-2 are so frequently interpreted as the eschatological anti-god forces of Gog and Magog in rabbinic literature[62] that "Ps. 2 is sometimes called 'the chapter of Gog and Magog' (פרשת גוג ומגוג)" (e.g., *Midr. Ps.* 3.2; *b. Ber.* 10a).[63] Lövestam concludes that "Ps. 2:1f is thus, in its messianic-eschatological usage within Judaism, associated with the idea of [demonic] opposition, rebellion, and the hostile attack upon God, the Messiah, and Israel."[64] This association will be of some relevance when we examine Mark's exorcism passages later. We may add to Lövestam's assessment that the psalm just as often evokes the Messiah's enthronement, triumph, and dominion over the whole earth in response to hostile attack. In other words, the rabbinic interpretation of Psalm 2, like earlier Jewish interpretations, conforms to the threefold drama contained within the psalm.

2.2.7 Summary

In summary, the interpretation of Psalm 2 in early Jewish literature is everywhere messianic and eschatological.[65] The central figure known as God's "son" is not just any Davidic king, but David's great heir, the Messiah. The hostility against him is universal, sometimes even cosmic, in scale, and his triumph over them is likewise total and final. Moreover, the universal tendency appears to have been to allude to Psalm 2 with a view toward the total drama it envisions. There are no clear exceptions on this point.

Before moving forward, we should note that Psalm 2 appears to have been the *locus classicus* for the concept of the Messiah as the Son of God.[66] Not only does the psalm accounts for the only linkage of the terms משיח and בן in the Jewish Scriptures, but, in fact, *all* of the early Jewish texts that identify the Messiah as God's "son," or vice versa, do so via the probable influence of Psalm 2.[67] All of this, we shall see, has important implications for the exegesis of Mark.

---

[61] E.g., Kingsbury, *Christology*, 112–13. Botner ("What Has Mark's Christ to Do with David's Son?" 50–70) cites further examples of this dichotomous thinking.

[62] E.g., in *Midr. Ps.* 2.2, 4; *Midr. Ps.* 3.2; *Midr. Ps.* 92.10; *Midr. Ps.* 118.12; *Tanḥ. B, Gen.* 2.24, *Tanḥ. B, Lev.* 8.18, *b.* Ber 7b; *b. Ber.* 10a; *Lev. Rab.* 27:11; *Esth. Rab.* 7:23; *Mek. Shir.* 7.

[63] Evald Lövestam, *Son and Saviour: A Study of Acts 13, 32-37, with an Appendix, "Son of God" in the Synoptic Gospels*, ConBNT 18 (Lund: Gleerup, 1961), 17. See also Isadore Epstein, ed., *The Babylonian Talmud*, vol. 1: Seder Zera'im (London: Soncino, 1978), 52 n. 4: Ps 2; K. G. Kuhn, "Γὼγ καὶ Μαγώγ," *TDNT*, 1:789–91; Marcus, *Way*, 63.

[64] Lövestam, *Son and Saviour*, 22–3.

[65] The only possible exception to this rule may be Wisdom of Solomon. Van Iersel (*Der Sohn und den synoptischen Jesusworten: Christusbezeichnung der Gemeinde oder Selbstbezeichnung Jesu?* [Leiden: Brill, 1961], 75), followed by Janse (*Son*, 71), finds a series of possible verbal parallels with Psalm 2 in Wis 1:1; 2:18; 4:18; 5:5; and 6:1, but without any interest in the prominent themes of the psalm. Yet it may be that these parallels amount to no more than a case of borrowed language rather than real interaction with the psalm (so Janse, *Son*, 71).

[66] Cf. Collins and Collins (*Son of God*, 12–15), who regard Ps 2 as an essential background for this identification.

[67] Namely, 1Q28ᵃ II, 11-12; 4Q246 I, 9–II, 1; *4 Ezra* 7:28-29; 13:32, 37, 53; 14:9; cf. *Midr. Ps.* 2.9; *b. Sukkah* 52a; and perhaps 4Q369 II, 6. This is not to discount the accompanying influence of 2 Sam 7:14 and Ps 89:27-28, in some texts, yet Psalm 2 is the one text that *consistently* informs those cited above.

2.3 Psalm 2 in the New Testament and Early Christianity

If the rule among early Jewish sources is to read Psalm 2 with a view toward the coming Messiah, the *rule* among early Christian sources is to identify the psalm's plot with the life of Jesus, especially the events of his passion. As Gerard Rouwhorst and Marcel Poorthuis state, early Christian uses of the psalm "are based on the conviction that Jesus, who was proclaimed as the Messiah at his baptism and during the transfiguration, and who was sentenced to death, suffered, died and resurrected, is the anointed one of v. 7 and the entire psalm is understood from that perspective."[68] Rouwhorst and Poorthuis, however, view this understanding as a departure from the eschatological interpretation found in Jewish sources, which is instead replaced by "a prophetic-christological" reading of the text.[69] Yet this assessment seems to miss the point: to locate the fulfillment of the psalm in the life of Jesus is not necessarily to de-eschatologize the psalm so much as it is to find its eschatological hopes realized in the person and work of Jesus.[70] In any case, scholars have long recognized that the conviction that Jesus is the Messiah is starting point for the NT's interest in Psalm 2.[71] This interpretation found there will, in turn, provide the basis for the interpretations of the psalm found throughout the patristic period.[72]

2.3.1 Psalm 2 in the New Testament

Although the fact is seldom observed, Psalm 2 is perhaps the most referenced Scripture in the NT.[73] Even by a minimalist assessment, the psalm is recalled more than thirty times between the Gospels, Acts, Hebrews, and Revelation. These references are summarized in Table 2.2.

---

[68] Gerard Rouwhorst and Marcel Poorthuis, "'Why Do the Nations Conspire': Psalm 2 in Post-Biblical Jewish and Christian Traditions," in *Empsychoi Logoi—Religious Innovations in Antiquity*, ed. Alberdina Houtman, Albert de Jong, and Magda Misset-Van de Weg, AJEC 73 (Leiden: Brill, 2008), 435.

[69] Ibid.

[70] As James W. Watts ("Psalm 2 In the Context of Biblical Theology," *HBT* 12 [1990]: 73–91 [here, 80]) recognizes, "the tension between prophetic and royal ideologies is dissolved in the eschatological hope for the coming of God and his Messiah." Likewise, the tension between the eschatological and prophetic dissolves in the identification of Jesus as the Messiah.

[71] E.g., Martin Hengel ("Christological Titles in Early Christianity," in *Studies in Early Christology* [Edinburgh: T&T Clark, 1995], 375) states that Ps 2 "is one of the most important Old Testament messianic proof texts in the entire New Testament." See also Barnabas Lindars (*New Testament Apologetic: The Doctrinal Significance of the Old Testament Quotations* [London: SCM Press, 1961], 138–44), who suggests that the interest in the psalm is an apologetic one aimed at establishing Jesus's messiahship. Again, W. G. Kümmel ("Das Gleichnis von den Bösen Weingärtnern (Mark 12, 1-9)," in *Aux sources de la tradition chrétienne: mélanges offerts à M. Maurice Goguel à l'occasion de son soixante-dixième anniversaire*, ed. J. J. von Allmen et al. [Neuchâtel: Delachaux & Niestlé, 1950], 131) suggests that "[i]n the early church ... the title 'Son of God' was used early on in the messianic sense for the risen Jesus, and probably emerged in connection with the relationship of Ps 2:7 to Jesus." Yet while B. M. F. Van Iersel (*Der Sohn und den synoptischen Jesusworten: Christusbezeichnung der Gemeinde oder Selbstbezeichnung Jesu?* [Leiden: Brill, 1961], 66–76) substantiates Kümmel's claim, he notes that, in Acts at least, Psalm 2 is associated with Jesus's *death* as well as his resurrection.

[72] See similarly Watts, "Pslam 2," 83.

[73] But see Hossfeld and Zenger, *Psalmen*, 49. Clifford (*Psalms 1–72*, 46) mistakenly claims that "[t]he New Testament cites this psalm more than any other." That prize goes to Ps 110; however, Clifford's statement would be correct if one added the words "or alludes to."

Table 2.2 *Quotations* and Allusions to Ps 2 in the NT[74]

Psalm 2	NT Reference	Connection to the Person of Jesus
Ps 2:1-2 (Hostility)	Matt 26:3-4, 57; 27:1, 7, 17, 27; 28:12; Luke 22:63-23:43	Jesus's Passion (Trial)
	Acts 4:25-26; cf. 4:5; 13:27	
	Rev 11:15, 18; 17:18; 19:19	The kings of the earth gather for eschatological war against Christ
	John 1:41, 49	Jesus is "Messiah," "Son of God," "King of Israel"
	Matt 3:17; Mark 1:11; Luke 3:22	Baptism (declared God's "Son")
	Matt 4:1-11, Luke 4:1-13	Temptation (called "Son of God," offered authority over the nations)
	Matt 17:5, Mark 9:7; Luke 9:35; 2 Pet 1:17	Transfiguration (delcared God's "Son")
	Luke 1:32-35	Annunciation (called "Son of God," inherits "throne of David")
Ps 2:6-7 (Coronation)		
	John 1:34	
	John 1:49	Possible allusion to Ps 2:7 (see below) See above ("Son of God" and "King of Israel")
	Matt 27:37-54	Crucifixion (the "King of the Jews" set on Zion)
	Acts 13:33	Resurrection/enthronement (quotes Ps 2:7)
	Rom 1:3-4	Resurrection (Seed of David & Son of God)
	Heb 1:5	Exaltation & Enthronement (quotes Ps 2:7)
	Heb 5:5	Exaltation & Enthronement (quotes Ps 2:7)
Ps 2:8-9 (Reign)	Rev 2:26, 28	Authority over the nations (as Son of God)
	Rev 2:27; 19:15	Authority over the nations (quotes Ps 2:9)
	Rev 12:5	Authority over the nations (quotes Ps 2:9)

At a glance, one can see that the NT, broadly speaking, applies the entire psalm to the entire story of Jesus. Notably, these uses of the psalm, like the early Jewish readings above, also correspond closely to the threefold plot intrinsic to the psalm itself. Though much could be said about the psalm's use in the NT, I content myself here with three observations pertinent to the interpretation of Mark's Gospel: (1) the interpretation of Psalm 2 is everywhere Davidic and messianic; (2) true to its origins as a coronation hymn, it principally evokes Jesus's enthronement; and (3) perhaps surprisingly, it is associated with Jesus's passion more than any other event or occasion.

---

[74] I have excluded possible allusions to Ps 2:11 in 1 Cor 2:3; 2 Cor 7:15; Eph 6:5; and Phil 2:12 (see Janse, *Son*, 80), which I deem too vague and uncertain to warrant further consideration.

2.3.1.1 Foretelling Jesus, the Messiah: Psalm 2 in the Acts of the Apostles

The book of Acts is not the earliest document in the NT to take up Psalm 2, but it offers a convenient entry point due to the breadth and clarity of its references. In Acts 4:5, Peter and John stand before "the rulers and elders and scribes ... gathered together in Jerusalem" (συναχθῆναι αὐτῶν τοὺς ἄρχοντας καὶ τοὺς πρεσβυτέρους καὶ τοὺς γραμματεῖς ἐν Ἰερουσαλήμ) in a scene reminiscent of Jesus's own trial (cf. Luke 23:13; Matt 26:3; Mark 15:1). The use of συναχθῆναι in combination with τοὺς ἄρχοντας, in particular, recalls the language of Ps 2:2 LXX.[75] Shortly thereafter, the believers quote Ps 2:1-2 LXX verbatim in a prayer offered upon Peter and John's release:

> [24]And when they heard it, with one accord they took up a cry to God and said, "Master, you are the one who made heaven and earth and the sea and all that is in them, [25]who said through the Holy Spirit by the mouth of our ancestor David, your servant, 'Why do the nations rage and the peoples plot in vain? [26]The kings of the earth take their stand and the rulers take counsel against the Lord and his Messiah" (ἵνα τί ἐφρύαξαν ἔθνη καὶ λαοὶ ἐμελέτησαν κενά; παρέστησαν οἱ βασιλεῖς τῆς γῆς καὶ οἱ ἄρχοντες συνήχθησαν ἐπὶ τὸ αὐτὸ κατὰ τοῦ κυρίου καὶ κατὰ τοῦ χριστοῦ αὐτοῦ); [27]for truly they were gathered together in this very city against your holy servant, Jesus, whom you anointed (ἔχρισας), both Herod and Pontius Pilate, together with the Gentiles and peoples of Israel,[28] to do whatever your hand and counsel predestined to happen.[29] And now, Lord, look upon their threats and grant your servants all boldness to speak your word."
>
> Acts 4:24-29

Scholars have long suspected that these verses preserve earlier tradition.[76] But the interpretation in vv. 27-28 is also so precise that some have likened these verses to a

---

[75] See Peter Doble, "The Psalms in Luke-Acts," in *The Psalms in the New Testament*, 83–117, here 101; Janse, *Son*, 92.

[76] This is largely due to the apparent use of liturgical formulae and awkward transitions in vv. 25 and 29: see, e.g., Dibelius, "Herodes und Pilatus," 124–25; Van Iersel, *Sohn*, 69; Gustav Stählin, *Die Apostelgeschichte* (Göttingen: Vandenhoeck & Ruprecht, 1968), 78; Ernst Haenchen, *The Acts of the Apostles: A Commentary* (Philadelphia: Westminster, 1971), 228; I. Howard Marshall, *The Acts of the Apostles: An Introduction and Commentary*, TNTC (Grand Rapids: Eerdmans, 1980), 104; Marion L. Soards, "Tradition, Composition, and Theology in Luke's Account of Jesus before Herod Antipas," *Bib* 66 (1985): 344–64; Rudolf Pesch, *Die Apostelgeschichte*, 2 vols, EKKNT 5 (Zürich: Benziger; Neukirchen-Vluyn: Neukirchener, 1986), 1:176–79; Darrell L. Bock, *Proclamation from Prophecy and Pattern: Lucan Old Testament Christology*, JSOTSup 12 (Sheffield: JSOT Press, 1987), 203–05; Hans Conzelmann, *Acts of the Apostles*, trans. James Limburg, A. Thomas Kraabel, and Donald H. Juel, Hermeneia (Philadelphia: Fortress, 1987), 35; C. K. Barrett, *A Critical and Exegetical Commentary on the Acts of the Apostles*, ICC 44 (Edinburgh: T&T Clark, 1994), 242; Joseph A. Fitzmyer, *The Acts of the Apostles: A New Translation with Introduction and Commentary*, AB 31a (New York: Doubleday, 1998), 307; Jervell, *Apostelgeschichte*, 189; contra Lindars, *Apologetic*, 143; Gerd Lüdemann, *The Acts of the Apostles: What Really Happened in the Earliest Days of the Church* (Amherst, NY: Prometheus, 2005), 73. In an earlier version of this work, however, Lüdemann (*Early Christianity According to the Traditions in Acts: A Commentary*, trans. John Bowden [Minneapolis: Fortress, 1989], 59) argues that it "seems necessary in one case [to say that elements of the prayer were derived from tradition], since the interpretation of Ps.2.1f. in terms of Herod and Pilate probably underlies the prayer—cf. similarly Luke 23.6."

pesher on Ps 2:1-2.[77] Herod and Pilate are identified as the βασιλεῖς and ἄρχοντες, while the ἔθνη and the λαοί are similarly identified as the Gentiles and Israel, all engaged in a conspiracy against Jesus, the Lord's χριστός (cf. Ps 2:2). Acts thus attests a tradition that sees the hostility toward the Lord's Anointed realized in the circumstances of Jesus's passion. The interpretation offered here is not without reference to the figure of David, either. Not only is the psalm attributed to David (v. 25), but the description τὸν ἅγιον παῖδά σου Ἰησοῦν ("your holy servant, Jesus") in v. 27 parallels Δαυὶδ παιδός σου ("David, your servant") in v. 25.[78] According to Acts, then, Jesus is the Messiah in whom God's ancient promises to David find their fulfillment, and this is (ironically) signified in part by the events of his passion.

The same interpretation appears to underlie Acts 13:27, where the ἄρχοντες are implicated for condemning Jesus to death just before another reference to Pilate in v. 28.[79] Here, however, the allusion is closely followed by a quotation of Ps 2:7 LXX:

> We bring you good tidings that what God promised to our ancestors, he has fulfilled for us, their children, by raising Jesus, as also it is written in the second psalm: '*You are my son, today I have begotten you*' (υἱὸς μου εἶ σύ, ἐγὼ σήμερον γεγέννηκά σε).
>
> Acts 13:32-33

Notably, the quotation occurs within a segment of Paul's speech at Pisidian Antioch concerned with God's choice of David as king and his promise to raise up a savior "from this man's seed" (σπέρματος) (v. 23; cf. 2 Sam 7:12). It is precisely this promise that Acts finds realized in Jesus's resurrection in 13:33. Just as God once "raised up (ἤγειρεν) David to be their king" (v. 22), he raised (ἤγειρεν) Jesus from the dead (v. 30; cf. v. 33).[80] As Jacob Jervell states, "[t]hrough the resurrection Jesus becomes the King of Israel. So it is not the resurrection as such, but the eternal kingdom of salvation that is decisive. And so the resurrection equals enthronement."[81] In other words, Ps 2:7 does not refer to Jesus's resurrection *per se* but to his *enthronement*, of which the resurrection is proof.[82]

Peter Doble connects the overarching interpretation of Psalm 2 in Acts 4 and 13 nicely: "[w]hen read as part of Luke's substructure, this surfacing of Ps. 2:7 [in chapter 13] can be seen as part of a development that began in Acts 4:25-27.... David's throne is now occupied by Jesus. This fulfillment was possible only because God raised from

---

[77] E.g., Pesch (*Apostelgeschichte*, 1:176–77); and Janse (*Son*, 94), who compares these verses to the *pesher* on Ps 2:1-2 in 4Q174.

[78] Cf. Pesch (*Apostelgeschichte*, 1:176); Doble, "Luke-Acts," 104.

[79] So also Van Iersel, *Sohn*, 77; Janse, *Son*, 93.

[80] Cf. Pesch, *Apostelgeschichte*, 2:38, who summarizes the implications of Ps 2:7 here: "Jesus wird als der von Gott gezeugte messianische Davidssohn und 'Retter für Israel' (vgl. 4Qflor I, 13) ausgewiesen."

[81] Jacob Jervell, *Die Apostelgeschichte*, KEK 3 (Göttingen: Vandenhoeck & Ruprecht, 1998), 359: "Durch die Auferstehung wird Jesus ziun König Israels. Also ist nicht die Auferstehung als solche, sondern das ewige Heils-Königreich entscheidend. Und so ist die Auferstehung Inthronisation." Cf. Werner R. Kramer, *Christ, Lord, Son of God*, SBT 50 (London: SCM, 1966), 109; Janse, *Son*, 102.

[82] Indeed, Ps 2 contains no resurrection language in the first place, and v. 34 points instead to Isa 55:13 as a prooftext for the resurrection.

the dead this Jesus whom the rulers crucified."[83] We can summarize the use of Psalm 2 in Acts as follows:

	Acts		Psalm 2
4:5	The rulers (ἄρχοντας) gather together (συναχθῆναι) with the elders and scribes to try Peter and John in Jerusalem.	2:2	οἱ ἄρχοντες συνήχθησαν
4:25-28	Herod and Pilate are the βασιλεῖς and ἄρχοντες who put Jesus, the Lord's χρίστος, to death; the Gentiles and people of Israel are ἔθνη and λαοί.	2:1-2	ἵνα τί ἐφρύαξαν ἔθνη καὶ λαοὶ ἐμελέτησαν κενά; παρέστησαν οἱ βασιλεῖς τῆς γῆς καὶ οἱ ἄρχοντες συνήχθησαν ἐπὶ τὸ αὐτὸ κατὰ τοῦ κυρίου καὶ κατὰ τοῦ χριστοῦ αὐτοῦ.
4:27	"In this city, i.e., Jerusalem, God's holy (ἅγιον) servant, Jesus, whom he anointed (ἔχρισας), was killed.	2:2, 6-7	τοῦ χριστοῦ ... Σιων ὄρος τὸ ἅγιον αὐτοῦ[84]
13:27	The rulers (ἄρχοντες) condemned Jesus in Jerusalem; Pilate named again (v. 28)	2:2	οἱ ἄρχοντες
13:33	The Son's enthronement) is fulfilled by Jesus's resurrection.	2:7	υἱός μου εἶ σύ, ἐγὼ σήμερον γεγέννηκά σε.

Ultimately, Acts attests an early application of Psalm 2 to the person of Jesus founded on the conviction that he is David's eschatological heir, the Messiah. Accordingly, the hostility against the Lord's Anointed (Ps 2:1-2) is realized in events of Jesus's passion and his enthronement (Ps 2:7) is evidenced, in turn, by his resurrection. From this perspective, one can see how Jesus's passion and kingship are intimately related: Jesus's passion, like the opposition against the Lord's Anointed in Psalm 2, is the context of his enthronement.[85]

2.3.1.2 Jesus's Passion and Enthronement of God's Son Elsewhere

The same patterns of interpretation are visible elsewhere in the NT. For instance, the tradition linking Psalm 2 to Jesus's passion also informs the Gospel passion narratives. As Wim Weren has shown, Luke 22:67–23:39 contains a number of verbal correspondences with Psalm 2, including ἄρχοντες (23:13, 35/Ps 2:2), which is twice paired with λαός/λαοί (23:5, 13, 14, 35/Ps 2:1), χρίστος (22:67; 23:2, 35, 39/Ps 2:2), βασιλεύς (23:2, 3, 37, 38/Ps 2:6), υἱός (22:70/Ps 2:7), ἐκμυρτηρίζω (23:35/Ps 2:4), and παιδεύω (23:16, 22/Ps 2:10).[86] Weren is not novel in linking Psalm 2 to this passage;

---

[83] Doble, "Luke-Acts," 110.
[84] Doble argues from an analysis of Ps 2's use in the substructure of Luke-Acts as a whole, within which, he argues, "whom you anointed" (ὃν ἔχρισας) refers to Jesus's baptism in Luke 3:22 where Ps 2:7 is quoted, that Acts 4:27 may also allude to Ps 2:6-7; see "Luke-Acts," 103–04.
[85] According to Van Iersel (*Sohn*, 70), the psalm in Acts points back to an early stage of tradition, in which the psalm was already associated with Jesus's suffering, death, and resurrection. For the apostles, the psalm embodied the whole narrative of the passion and resurrection, which were never separated from each other.
[86] Wim J. C. Weren, "Psalm 2 in Luke-Acts: An Intertextual Study," in *Intertextuality in Biblical Writings: Essays in Honour of Bas van Iersel*, ed. J. Draisma (Leuven: Peeters, 1989), 189–204, esp. 200–01; More recently, Luke Timothy Johnson, Joel B. Green, John T. Carroll have all observed some of the parallels with Psalm 2 noted by Weren; see Luke Timothy Johnson, *The Gospel of Luke*, SP 3 (Collegeville, MN: Liturgical, 1991), 368; Joel B. Green, *The Gospel of Luke*, NICNT (Grand Rapids: Eerdmans,

ancient interpreter commonly associated Psalm 2 with Jesus's trial, whether in Luke, Matthew, or Mark.[87] Yet some of these verbal correspondences, such as the addition of τοὺς ἄρχοντας καὶ τὸν λαὸν in 23:13, are the result of Lukan redaction. Especially intriguing is Luke's use of the rare verb ἐκμυκτηρίζω to describe Jesus's mockery by the ἄρχοντες in 23:35. The same verb is used in Ps 2:4 LXX to refer to *God's* mockery of the *rulers*.[88] Overall, the concentration of language from Psalm 2 in Lukan redactional material suggests that the evangelist consciously associates Psalm 2 with Jesus's passion.[89]

Matthew also alludes to Ps 2:1-2 several times in his passion narrative. Unlike Luke, however, Matthew's clearest allusions involve his redactional use of the verb συνάγω.[90] For instance, Matt 26:3-4 replaces Mark's ἐζήτουν (14:1) with συνήχθησαν (cf. Ps 2:2) so as to portray the chief priests (cf. οἱ ἀρχιερεῖς, ἄρχοντες) and elders of the people (τοῦ λαοῦ) "gathered together" and conspiring (συνεβουλεύσαντο) against Jesus to put him to death (cf. 26:57; 27:17, 27; 28:12).[91] It is also likely that, in Matthew, "taking counsel" (συμβούλιον ἔλαβον) against Jesus is a gloss on σύναγω from Ps 2:2, which amounts to several more allusions (27:1-2, 7; 28:12).[92] So both Matthew and Luke connect Ps 2:1-2 to Jesus's trial, but in ways independent of Mark and each other. This state of affairs deepens the sense that Psalm 2 was already associated with Jesus's passion in an earlier stratum of tradition.

1997), 796, 798; Janse, *Son*, 88; John T. Carroll, *Luke: A Commentary*, NTL (Louisville: Westminster John Knox, 2012), 453, 458. John Nolland (*Luke*, WBC 35c [Dallas: Word, 1989], 1122) even argues against the "older view" that Luke's account of Jesus before Herod "has been spun out of an exegesis of Ps 2:1-2," arguing that there are no good reasons to doubt the episode's historicity. There is also, however, no reason why Luke could not have woven allusions to Psalm 2 into an historical account.

[87] Francois Bovon (*Luke: A Commentary on the Gospel of Luke 19:28–24:53*, trans. James E. Couch [Minneapolis: Fortress, 2012], 3:257–58) correctly notes that Tertullian (*Marc.* 4.42; *PL* 2.464a) interpreted Jesus's trial before Pilate as the fulfillment of Ps 2:1-2, but, in n. 73, mistakenly claims that "Tertullian seems to be the only one who relates this biblical passage to the passion of Jesus." On the contrary, the association is commonplace among the church fathers, as we will see below.

[88] This verb occurs elsewhere in biblical literature only in Ps 21:8; 34:16; 1 Esd 1:49; and Luke 16:14. The reversal of the situation from Ps 2 in Luke's PN is, according to Weren, "Psalm 2," 201, part of Luke's theological aim.

[89] Hence, C. H. Dodd (*Historical Tradition in the Fourth Gospel* [Cambridge: Cambridge University Press, 1989], 118) suggests that the features of the Lukan trial narrative could, "not improbably, be traced back to a form of the tradition shaped largely under the influence of the *testimonium* from Ps 2." In this case, however, it is notable that Luke does not draw the explicit connections between the psalm and Herod and Pilate found in Acts, which suggests all the more that the latter is traditional material rather than Luke's own.

[90] For a detailed discussion of these allusions, see Tucker S. Ferda, "Matthew's Titulus and Psalm 2's King on Mount Zion," *JBL* 133 (2014): 561–81, esp. 569–70.

[91] Others who have observed this series of allusions include Brian M. Nolan, *The Royal Son of God: The Christology of Matthew 1-2 in the Setting of the Gospel*, OBO 23 (Göttingen: Vandenhoeck & Ruprecht, 1979), 88; Robert H. Gundry, *Matthew: A Commentary on His Literary and Theological Art* (Grand Rapids: Eerdmans, 1982), 518; W. D. Davies and Dale C. Allison, Jr., *A Critical and Exegetical Commentary on the Gospel according to Saint Matthew* ICC 40, 3 vols (New York: T&T Clark, 1988–97), 3:438; Eugene Boring, "Matthew," in *NIB* (Nashville: Abingdon, 1995), 8:464 n. 550.

[92] Origen, *Hom. Ps. ad loc.* (*PG* 12:1102b); Theodoret, *Comm. Ps. ad loc.* (*PG* 80:874d); Ferda, "Psalm 2," 569–570.

In addition to Ps 2:2, Tucker Ferda argues that Matthew's *titulus* in 27:37 may contain an allusion to Ps 2:6, as Origen, Augustine, Aquinas, and others supposed.[93] Whereas the psalm envisions the king's coronation on Zion's hill, Jesus is crucified on a hilltop outside Jerusalem as ὁ βασιλεὺς τῶν Ἰουδαίων ("the King of the Jews"), mocked, and derided (27:39, 41, 44) for claiming to be the "Son of God" (27:40, 43).

Psalm 2 is linked with Jesus's passion, as well as his exaltation and enthronement, outside the Gospels as well. For instance, two verbatim quotations of Ps 2:7 LXX appear in Heb 1:5; 5:5, both bearing reference to Jesus's death and exaltation, while also recalling the psalm's Davidic character. The first pairs Ps 2:7 LXX with 2 Sam 7:14 LXX, thereby bringing the Davidic covenant to the forefront.[94] But these two quotations also follow the image of Jesus seated "at the right hand of the Majesty on high (cf. Ps 110:1), "having made the purification for sins" (Heb 1:3), calling to mind Christ's exaltation and enthronement, on the one hand, and his death, on the other hand.[95] Again, Heb 5:5 declares that "Christ did not exalt himself (ἑαυτὸν ἐδόξασεν) to become high priest, but [was exalted by] he who said to him, '*You are my son, today I have begotten you.*'"[96] This quotation is then followed by a reference to Jesus's suffering in 5:7-8: "who in the days of his flesh cried out to God, offered up both prayers and supplications to the one who was able to save him from death with loud cries and tears, and he was heard because of his reverence. Although he was a son, he learned obedience through what he suffered."[97] So in Hebrews, as elsewhere, Psalm 2 functions as a key text for the enthronement of the Davidic Messiah realized in his death and resurreciton alike.

A similar reading of Ps 2:7 may underlie Rom 1:3-4 (a couplet almost universally accepted as pre-Pauline tradition) in which God's "Son born of the seed of David" (τοῦ γενομένου ἐκ σπέρματος Δαυὶδ) is "designated Son of God by resurrection from the dead" (τοῦ ὁρισθέντος υἱοῦ θεοῦ).[98] The linkage of Davidic descent with the designation Son of God calls to mind such texts as 2 Sam 7:12-14 and Ps 2:7.[99] While some of the

---

[93] Ferda, "Psalm 2," 568–88.
[94] As we have seen, Psalm 2 and 2 Sam 7:14 are also cited together in 4Q174, and may also underlie Luke 1:32-35 and 4Q246. All three texts bear connotations of Davidic messianism.
[95] See similarly Harold W. Attridge, "The Psalms in Hebrews," in *The Psalms in the New Testament*, 198–200.
[96] On the connotations of enthronement in Heb 5:5 see also Koester, *Hebrews*, 298–9; Gareth Lee Cockerill, *The Epistle to the Hebrews*, NICNT (Grand Rapids: Eerdmans, 2012), 246–48. As in Heb 1:3-5, Ps 2:7 again appears in conjunction with Ps 110, v. 4 of which Heb 5:6 cites.
[97] Craig R. Koester (*Hebrews: A New Translation with Introduction and Commentary*, AB 36 [New York: Doubleday, 2001], 188) argues that "[t]he death of Jesus is presupposed by the statement that God's Son 'made purification for sins' (1:3)." Moreover, several scholars have demonstrated that Heb 5:7-8 likely recalls Jesus in Gethsemane: e.g., Dodd, *Tradition*, 71; Raymond E. Brown, *The Death of the Messiah: From Gethsemane to the Grave: A Commentary on the Passion Narratives in the Four Gospels*, 2 vols (New York: Doubleday, 1994), 1:227–33; Dale C. Allison, Jr., *Constructing Jesus: Memory, Imagination, and History* (Grand Rapids: Baker, 2010), 417.
[98] See, e.g., J. D. G. Dunn, *Romans*, WBC 38a-b (Dallas: Word, 1988), 5; Matthew W. Bates, "A Christology of Incarnation and Enthronement: Romans 1:3-4 as Unified, Nonadoptionist, and Nonconciliatory," *CBQ* 77 (2015): 107–27.
[99] Indeed, these verses have reminded many interpreters of these scriptural verses and others: see the history of interpretation in Johnson, "Romans 1:3-4," 467–90; Joshua W. Jipp, "Ancient, Modern, and Future Interpretations of Romans I:3-4: Reception History and Biblical Interpretation," *JTI* 3 (2009): 241–59. Linkage is indeed the right word to describe the relationship between Rom 1:3 and

specific terminology (e.g., σπέρματος Δαυὶδ) more closely resembles 2 Samuel 7, the notion of *designating* reminds one of God's decree in Ps 2:7. In any case, Rom 1:3-4 appears to recall God's promise that one of David's descendants would occupy his throne forever, which places it in the tradition of Psalm 2 and 2 Samuel 7 alike (cf. Ps 89:26-27; 4Q174).[100] Hengel recognizes this when he states that "the title 'Son of God'" is here an "interpretation of the title '*Christos*,' the Messiah from the house of David."[101] So what is sometimes construed as the Son of David's adoption as God's Son is actually his coronation, signified by the resurrection. As Joshua Jipp argues, "Jesus' resurrection and his Davidic sonship are integrally linked, as it is the resurrection that marks out (one might say 'coronates' or 'enthrones') Jesus as Israel's royal Messiah."[102] This, of course, corresponds to the interpretation of Ps 2:7 that we have now seen in both Acts and Hebrews.

2.3.1.3 Psalm 2 Elsewhere in the New Testament

Allusions to Psalm 2 appear elsewhere in the NT without direct reference to Jesus's death or resurrection. Yet these instances, too, are united by an emphasis on Jesus's enthronement as the Davidic Messiah, either as prospect or in retrospect.

We have already seen that Ps 2:7 may have influenced Luke 1:32-35, in which Jesus is called υἱὸς ὑψίστου and υἱὸς θεοῦ. In addition, John's Gospel contains a series of likely allusions to Psalm 2:6-7 in 1:29-49. First, in 1:34, John the Baptist's testimony, οὗτός ἐστιν ὁ υἱὸς τοῦ θεοῦ, bears a striking resemblance to God's pronouncement at Jesus's baptism in the Synoptics, which recall Ps 2:7.[103] Consider the comparison below:

Ps 2:7	υἱός μου εἶ σύ
Mark 1:11	σὺ εἶ ὁ υἱός μου
Luke 3:22	σὺ εἶ ὁ υἱός μου
Matt 3:17	οὗτός ἐστιν ὁ υἱός μου
John 1:34	οὗτός ἐστιν ὁ υἱὸς τοῦ θεοῦ.

1:4. As Johnson argues, the parallelism between son of David and Son of God in these verses should be understood synonymously rather than antithetically; "[h]istorically, the relationship is not antithetical but complementary"; see "Romans 1:3-4," 476. Likewise, Janse (*Son*, 105) observes that "the text moves along the line of 2Sam. 7 and Ps. 2:7: the son of David is acknowledged as the Son of God"; *contra* Bates, "Christology of Incarnation," 107-27.

[100] So Dennis Duling, "The Promises to David and Their Entrance into Christianity: Nailing Down a Likely Hypothesis," *NTS* 20 (1973-74): 55-77.
[101] Hengel, "Christological Titles," 375-76.
[102] Jipp, "Romans I:3-4," 258.
[103] On the likely allusion to Ps 2:7 in John 1:34 see F. F. Bruce, *The Gospel of John* (Grand Rapids: Eerdmans, 1983), 55; and Craig S. Keener, *The Gospel of John: A Commentary*, 2 vols (Peabody, MA: Hendrickson, 2010), 1:464; cf. Robert Mercier, *L'Évangile Pour Que Vous Croyiez: Le Quatrième Évangile*, Collection Gratianus (Montréal: Wilson & Lafleur, 2010), 126; D. Moody Smith, *John*, ANTC (Nashville: Abingdon, 1999), 70. Alternatively, some, such as Rudolf Schnackenburg (*Gospel According to St. John* [London: Burns & Oates, 1982], 1:305), favor the variant ἐκλεκτός in place of υἱός; but in defense of υἱός, see Rudolf Bultmann, *The Gospel of John: A Commentary* (Philadelphia: Westminster, 1971), 93; Ernst Haenchen, *John: A Commentary on the Gospel of John* (Philadelphia: Fortress, 1984), 154; and Herman N. Ridderbos, *The Gospel According to John: A Theological Commentary* (Grand Rapids: Eerdmans, 1997), 77 n. 43.

Although John conspicuously omits the actual event of Jesus's baptism, the fact that he agrees with the Synoptics in placing a version of these words near the scene of John's baptism (cf. 1:29-34) raises suspicion that Ps 2:7 belonged to the baptism account in early tradition.[104] Shortly thereafter, Jesus is called τὸν Μεσσίαν (1:41; cf. Ps 2:2) just before Nathaniel declares, σὺ εἶ ὁ υἱὸς τοῦ θεοῦ, σὺ βασιλεὺς εἶ τοῦ Ἰσραήλ (v. 49; cf. Ps 2:6-7). Given that the words σὺ εἶ ὁ υἱὸς τοῦ θεοῦ closely resemble Ps 2:7 LXX (υἱὸς μου εἶ σύ) and that the triad of Messiah, king, and son [of God] appears in Psalm 2 alone, an allusion to the psalm is probable.[105] Appropriately, when John proclaims Jesus's messianic kingship, he does so by echoing the very decree of enthronement from Psalm 2. In the chapters to come, I will argue that the uses of Ps 2:7 at Jesus's baptism (Matt 3:17; Mark 1:11; Luke 3:22) and transfiguration (Matt 17:5; Mark 9:7; Luke 9:35) serve a similar purpose.

Finally, Revelation makes extensive use of Psalm 2 in order to emphasize the authority and dominion granted to the Son as a consequence of his enthronement (Ps 2:8-9). Portions of Ps 2:9 LXX appear three times in book, along with at least one allusion to Ps 2:8. In Rev 2:26-27 Christ declares that "the one who conquers and the one who keeps my works until the end, to him I will give authority over the nations [Ps 2:8]. *And he will rule them with a rod of iron*, as pottery pieces are shattered [Ps 2:9]." Though the promises of Psalm 2 are applied to Christ's followers, they are rooted in the conviction that Christ himself has already received such authority. Hence, Rev 3:21 portrays Jesus having already conquered and seated on the throne, and promising to bestow the same authority on those follow in his wake. Revelation 12:5 likewise applies Ps 2:9 directly to Christ, along with a likely allusion to Ps 2:7: "she gave birth to a male child (υἱὸν ἄρσεν), who is to shepherd all the nations with a rod of iron (ἐν ῥάβδῳ σιδηρᾷ)."[106] Revelation 19:15 repeats the previous reference to Ps 2:9 and combines it with an allusion to Isa 11:4 ("And out of his mouth will come a sharp sword that, with it, he may strike the nations").

Elsewhere, Revelation recalls the psalm's inherent threefold drama. The statement in 11:15, ἡ βασιλεία τοῦ κόσμου τοῦ κυρίου ἡμῶν καὶ τοῦ χριστοῦ αὐτου, followed by "the nations raged, but your wrath came" in v. 18, plainly recalls Ps 2:1-2, 5, as do τῶν βασιλέων τῆς γῆς in 17:18 and 19:19, where they "make war against him was sitting on the horse [i.e., Christ]."[107] The imagery of Ps 2:1-2 thus refers to the rebellion of the

---

[104] Dodd (*Tradition*, 259–60) observes certain agreements between John 1:32–34 and each of the Synoptics, though he considers John to be independent. Among the agreements, Dodd considers 1:34 to recall "the Matthean form of the *bath qol* at the Baptism." Haenchen (*John*, 154) refers to "intrusive traces of the synoptic tradition" in 1:29-34. Others, including C. K. Barrett (*The Gospel According to St. John: An Introduction with Commentary and Notes on the Greek Text*, 2nd ed. [Philadelphia: Westminster, 1978], 178) and J. Ramsey Michaels (*The Gospel of John*, NICNT [Grand Rapids: Eerdmans, 2010], 115), observe the close similarities between 1:34 and Mark 1:11, Matt 3:17.

[105] Barrett, *John*, 182; Raymond E. Brown, *The Gospel According to John: Introduction, Translation, and Notes*, 2nd ed., AB 29 (Garden City, NY: Doubleday, 1979), 1:88; Bruce, *John*, 61; Ridderbos, *John*, 91; Smith, *John*, 77; Michaels, *John*, 132; Hays, *Gospels*, 324; cf. Bultmann (*John*, 93 n. 1, 104 n. 7), who also recognizes Son of God as a title for the King of Israel with origins in the OT.

[106] Υἱὸν ἄρσεν is noticeably redundant in 12:5; one might rather expect τέκνον ἄρσεν. Since 12:5 already cites Ps 2:9, it is plausible that the choice of υἱὸν defers to Ps 2:7.

[107] Cf. Moyise, "Revelation," in *Psalms*, 232.

kings and kingdoms of the world against Jesus, the Lord's Anointed, in the last days. In summary, Revelation takes up the entire drama of Psalm 2 and interprets it christologically from beginning to end.

Revelation's use of Psalm 2 is unique in the NT in that it applies the psalm directly to Christ's future triumph rather than the past events of his death and resurrection. Yet it would be a mistake to suppose that Psalm 2 bears no connection to those prior events in Revelation. In fact, the *leitmotiv* of "conquering," with which Revelation's use of Psalm 2 begins, is inseparable from Jesus's death and resurrection, as 5:6 makes plain: "the Lion of the tribe of Judah, the Root of David, [who] has conquered" is the Lamb on the throne, "standing as though having been slain" (Rev 5:5-6).[108] All is predicated on the statement in 1:18: "I was dead, and behold I am living forever and ever." So the authority and dominion which Revelation seizes upon from Ps 2:8-9 are but the consequence of Jesus's prior death and resurrection. Finally, Revelation offers an ecclesiocentric reading of Psalm 2 by applying the violence of the nations and kingdoms of the earth to Christ's followers under persecution, and, likewise, transferring Christ's (the Son's) victory to his church (e.g., 2:26-27; 11:18).[109] The ecclesiocentric reading, however, derives from the christological one.

2.3.1.4 Summary: Psalm 2 in the New Testament

In summary, the NT authors variously find the drama of Psalm 2, understood messianically, realized in the person of Jesus, who is David's eschatological heir. True to its origins as a coronation hymn, the psalm is associated with Jesus's enthronement as God's Davidic Messiah-Son. Yet the NT authors also consistently relate the psalm to the events of Jesus's death and resurrection as the events in which his enthronement and inheritance of the nations come to fruition. Finally, all of these ideas appear to have their roots in prior tradition since the same interpretations are attested in various ways, shapes, and forms across the NT writings.

2.3.2 Psalm 2 in Patristic Literature

Like the NT authors, the church fathers universally read Psalm 2 as "a prophecy of Christ," to quote Diodore of Tarsus.[110] In particular, the fathers continue to read Psalm 2 as a foretelling of the events of Jesus's passion. According to John Chrysostom, Ps 2:1-2 describes the very "judgment hall" of Christ.[111] So also, they continue to associate

---

[108] For the connection of conquering with Rev 5:5-6, see also David E. Aune, *Revelation*, WBC 52a–b (Dallas: Word, 1997), 353. On the interpretation of the lion and the lamb generally, cf. G. B. Caird, *A Commentary on the Revelation of St. John the Divine*, BNTC (London: Black, 1966), 74–5; Craig R. Koester, *Revelation: A New Translation with Introduction and Commentary*, AB 38a (New Haven: Yale University Press, 2014), 385–90.

[109] Cf. Koester, *Revelation*, 302.

[110] *Comm. Ps.* 2 (CChr 6), 11; cf. Justin, *1 Apol.* 40 (PG 6:388–89).

[111] Chrysostom, *Hom. Matt.* 36 ad loc. (PG 57:415c).

the psalm chiefly with Christ's kingship. Hence, Theodoret asserts that Psalm 2 "foretells both the human sufferings and the kingship of Christ the Lord."[112] As Theodoret implies, the Christ's passion and kingship are inseparable in patristic exegesis of the psalm.

At the same time, the church fathers sometimes extend their readings of Psalm 2 beyond what is explicitly found in the NT, thereby offering further insight into the early Christian interpretation of the psalm. For instance, patristic readings of Psalm 2 display a widespread emphasis on the extension of Christ's rule over the nations (the Gentiles), realized by way of the Gentiles' worship of Christ. So Augustine, commenting on Ps 2:7-8, speaks of the "kings of the earth now happily subdued by Christ, and all nations serving him."[113] Eusebius favorably compares Christ's reign over the nations (Ps 2:8) to Vespasian's, who ruled only the Romans.[114] Elsewhere, Augustine sees the fact that even the emperors bow the knee to Christ as a fulfillment of Ps 2:11 ("Serve the Lord with fear and rejoice in him with trembling").[115] These and other uses are summarized in Table 2.3, which is only a representative sample of the numerous patristic citations of Psalm 2.

Table 2.3 Quotations of Psalm 2 in Patristic Literature[116]

Psalm 2	Patristic Reference	Interpretation
Entire Psalm	Justin, *1 Apol.* 40	
	Eusebius, *Hist. eccl.* 1.3.6	
	Diodore, *Comm. Ps.* 2	Psalm 2 is a "prophecy of Christ"
	Augustine, *Enarrat. Ps.* 2	
	Theodoret, *Comm. Ps.* 2	Foretells Jesus's passion and kingship
Ps 2:1-2	Hippolytus, *On Gen.* 49.5	
	Tertullian, *Marc.* 3.22; 4.39; 5.3, 4, 17	
	Origen, *Princ.* 3.3; *Comm. Matt.* 12:1, 13:9	
	Eusebius, *Comm. Ps.* 2.2	
	Athanasius, *Ep. fest.* 11	Foretells Jesus's trial and death, especially the conspiracy of the nations and rulers against him.
	Apos. Con. 5.3	
	Chrysostom, *Hom. Matt.* 26:19; *Hom. Matt.* 36	
	Augustine, *Ep.* 93.3.9; *Faust.* 13.7; *Don.* 5.19	
	Theodoret, *Ep.* 146	
	Tertullian, *Marc.* 4.42; *Res.* 20	
	Irenaeus, *Epid.* 74	
	Athanasius, *Hom. Matt.* 21:2 8.3-4	Refers to Herod & Pilate in conspiracy against Jesus

---

[112] *Comm. Ps.* 2, ad loc. (PG 80:871); trans. Robert C. Hill, *Theodoret of Cyrus: Commentary on the Psalms, 1–72*, FC 101 (Washington, DC: Catholic University of America Press, 2000), 52.
[113] Augustine, *Faust.* 13.7 (PL 42:285).
[114] Eusebius, *Hist. eccl.* 3.8.11 (PG 20:240b).
[115] Augustine, *Ep.* 93.3.9, 185.5.19 (PL 33:325, 891).
[116] The usual practice of the patristic writers was to cite Ps 2 rather than allude to it. All of the references listed here indicate verbatim quotations.

Verse	Source	Interpretation
	Diodore, *Comm. Ps.* 2	
	Augustine, *Serm. Dom.* 21.72; *Cons.* 3.16.53	
	Theodoret, *Comm. Ps.* 2	
	Theodoret, *Ep.* 146	Ps 2:1-2, 6-8: Christ's reign with God
Ps 2:3	Tertullian, *Marc.* 5.3-4	Refers to new age ushered in by Christ's passion
	Origen, *Comm. Matt.* 13:9	God laughs at those who crucified Jesus by raising him from the dead
Ps 2:4	Athanasius, *Ep. fest.* 11	
Ps 2:5	Hippolytus, *Against the Jews*	Christ speaks to his persecutors in wrath
	1 Clem. 36	Ps 2:7-8/9 refers to Christ's reign over
	Justin, *Dial.* 122	the nations (esp. the Gentiles)
	Tertullian, *Marc.* 3.20; 4.25, 39; 5.17, 27	
	Irenaeus, *Haer.* 4.21	
	Chrysostom, *Catech. Illum.* 1.4	
Ps 2:6-9	Augustine, *Tract. Ev. Jo.*, 115, 117; *Cons.* 2.4	
	Theodoret, *Ep.* 146	
	Cyprian, *Test.* 2.29	Ps 2:6: Christ will reign forever
	Athanasius, *Apol. sec.*, 2.20	Ps 2:6: the Son in the body upon Zion
	Gregory of Nyssa, *Eun.* 9.4, 11.3	Ps 2:6: Christ's kingship absorbs his
	Augustine, *Enarrat. Ps.* 47:5	humiliation
		Ps 2:6: Christ dies as a king
	Origen, *Comm. Matt.* 130, *Comm. Jo.* 6.23	The *titulus* on the cross fulfills Ps 2:6
	Augustine, *Tract. Ev. Jo.*, 115, 117,	
	Serm. 218.5-6	
	Bede, *Exp. Marc.* 15.26	
	Apos. Con., 5.3	Ps 2:7-8 fulfilled by Christ's death &
	Augustine, *Fid.* 7; *Faust.* 12.43	resurrection
	Eusebius, *Hist. eccl.* 3.8.11	Ps 2:8: Christ superior to Vespasian
	Cyril of Jerusalem, *Cat.* 12	Ps 2:7, 9, Christ's reign superior to the Romans
	Theodore, *Comm. Ps.* 2.9	Nations are crushed to be reformed
	Leo the Great, *Serm.* 29.3	Ps 2:8 means the salvation of the nations
	Polycarp, *Phil.* 2.1, 6.3	Ps 2:11: Christ's enthronement
	Cyril of Jerusalem, *Cat.* 14.13	Ps 2:11: refers to Jesus's passion
Ps 2:10-12	Augustine, *Ep.* 93.3.9; 185.5.19	Ps 2:11 foretells emperors worshiping Christ
	Augustine, *Enarrat. Ps.* 47:5	Ps 2:10-11: Christ supplants earthly kings

2.3.2.1 Psalm 2 and Jesus's Passion

To begin with, the fathers widely echo the interpretation of Ps 2:1-2 found in Acts 4:24-29. Diodore is representative in this regard: "By *nations and peoples* he means either the Israelites themselves or those of Herod's company in being Gentiles, and by *peoples* the Jews."[117] Diodore, like several others explicitly cites Acts 4:25-28 for support.[118]

---

[117] Diodore, *Comm. Ps.* 2 in *Diodore of Tarsus: Commentary on Psalms 1–51*, trans. Robert C. Hill, WGRW 9 (Atlanta: SBL Press, 2005), 7.
[118] Cf. Augustine, *Cons.*, 3.16.53 (*PL* 34:1191); and Theodoret, *Comm. Ps.* 2 (*PG* 80:873).

Yet many of the fathers go beyond Acts in their application of the psalm to Jesus's passion. For instance, Tertullian extends his interpretation of Ps 2:1-2 to include v. 3 ("Let us break their bonds asunder, and cast off their yoke from us").[119] According to Tertullian, this verse refers to the freedom of Christ's followers, who are justified "by the liberty of faith, not by servitude to the law," which they have as a consequence of Jesus's death and resurrection.[120] Tertullian then exhorts his readers to "'break their bonds asunder and cast away their cords from us,' [precisely] because 'the rulers have gathered themselves together against the Lord and against his Christ,'" who triumphed over them.[121]

Both Origen and Athanasius expand their application of Ps 2:1-2 to Jesus's trial to v. 4 of the psalm, which they see fulfilled in his resurrection.[122] According to Origen, the kings and rulers handed Jesus over to death only to be "*laughed at by Him who dwells in the heavens* and *mocked by the Lord* [since], contrary to their expectation, it was to the destruction of their own kingdom and rule, that they received from the Father the Son, who was raised on the third day, by having abolished His enemy death."[123] So Psalm 2 encompasses Jesus's death and resurrection alike, which together comprise the occasion of his enthronement.

Elsewhere, Origen also sees Ps 2:6 realized by Jesus's crucifixion. "And for a crown," he writes, "'over his head' is written 'this is Jesus King of the Jews.' And there is no other cause for his death (nor indeed was there) than that he was the King of the Jews. And concerning this it was spoken, 'But I have been made King by him on Zion, his holy mountain [Ps 2:6].'"[124] For Origen, then, while Jesus's enthronement is demonstrated by his resurrection, his crucifixion can be thought of as the coronation itself.

Augustine attests the same interpretation of Ps 2:6: "a title was placed over his cross, on which was written *The king of the Jews* (Jn 19:19), which showed that not even by killing him could they manage not to have him as king.... This is why we sing in the Psalm, *I, however, have been established by him as king on Zion his holy mountain*."[125] What makes Augustine's comment especially intriguing, however, is his reference to the ancient hymnody of the church. Apparently, the association of Ps 2:6 with Jesus's crucifixion had already become a traditional part of the church's liturgy. His comment may even remind one of Dibelius's contention that Acts 4:24-28 preserves an early

---

[119] *Marc.* 5.3-4 (*PL* 2:474c, 478b).
[120] *Marc.* 5.3 (*PL* 2:474c).
[121] *Marc.* 5.4 (*PL* 2:478b).
[122] Origen, *Comm. Matt.* 13.9 (*PG* 13:1117c); Athanasius, *Ep. fest.* 11 (*PG* 26:1411); cf. Augustine, *Enarrat. Ps.* 2.3 (*PL* 36:70). Augustine does not associate Ps 2:4 with the resurrection directly but nevertheless interprets God's laughter in the light of the fact "that the name of Christ and his lordship will spread to future generations and be acknowledged among the nations."
[123] *Comm. Matt.* 13.9 (*PG* 13:1117c). Italics mine.
[124] *Comm. Matt.* 130, in *Origenes Werke*, vol. 11, *Origenes Matthäuserklärung*, part 2, ed. Erich Klostermann, Ernst Betz, and Ursula Treu, 2nd ed. (Berlin: Akademie, 1976), 267. I am indebted to Tucker Ferda ("Psalm 2," 565) for bringing this passage to my attention. The translation above is his. For the same interpretation of Ps 2:6 elsewhere in Origen's works, see *Comn. Jo.* 6.23 (*PG* 14:265d).
[125] Augustine, *Serm.* 218.5 in *The Works of Saint Augustine: A Translation for the 21st Century*, ed. John E. Rotelle, trans. Edmund Hill (New York: New City, 2001), III/11: 239. Italics Hill's; *PL* 38:1085; cf. *Cons.*, 2.4.8 (*PL* 34:1075); *Enarrat. Ps.* 47:5 (*PL* 36:536); *Tract. Ev. Jo.*, 115, 117 (*PL* 35:1939, 1946).

liturgical use of Psalm 2.[126] In any case, the interpretation of the *titulus* on the cross as the fulfillment of Ps 2:6 also appears in Pseudo-Cyprian, Bede, and a number of later interpreters.[127]

2.3.2.2 Psalm 2 and the Crucified King

Elsewhere, too, the fathers plainly view Christ's passion as the context of his enthronement. Justin is instructive in this regard. Just before citing Psalm 2, Justin indicates that while the psalm relates Jesus's passion on the one hand, it foretells Christ's reign as the Son of God, on the other. In Justin's words, David foretold that:

> the conspiracy which was formed against Christ by Herod the king of the Jews, and the Jews themselves, and Pilate, who was your governor among them, with his soldiers; and how He should be believed on by men of every race; and how God calls Him His Son, and has declared that He will subdue all His enemies under Him; and how the devils, as much as they can, strive to escape the power of God the Father and Lord of all, and the power of Christ Himself; and how God calls all to repentance before the day of judgment comes.[128]

Justin then quotes Psalms 1–2 in their entirety. So for Justin, the whole of Psalm 2 is about Christ's passion *and* kingship, which are not easily separable from one another.

Cyril of Jerusalem is even more suggestive. In his instructions to catechumens, Cyril offers the following intertwined interpretation of Jesus's passion and Psalm 2:

> *And the Angel says to them again, Fear not; I do not say to the soldiers, fear not, but to you. As for them, let them be afraid, so that, having learned by trial, they may bear witness and say, Truly this was the Son of God. . . . Go, tell His disciples that He is risen*; and the rest. And they depart with joy, yet fearfully. Is this also written? Yes, so says the second psalm, which narrates the passion of Christ, *Serve the Lord with fear, and rejoice in Him with trembling. Rejoice* on account of the risen Lord; but *with trembling*, because of the earthquake, and the angel who appeared as lightning.[129]

Cyril, like others before him, is of the opinion that Psalm 2 *in toto* "narrates [διαγορεύων] the passion Christ."[130] That Cyril really does mean that the psalm as a whole relates to

---

[126] Dibelius, "Herodes," 124; cf. Weren, "Psalm 2," 200.
[127] See Pseudo-Cyprian, *De duobus montibus Sina et Sion* 9.1-2, in Anni Maria Laato, *Jews and Christians in De duobus montibus Sina et Sion: An Approach to Early Latin Adversus Iudaeos Literature* (Åbo: Åbo Akademi University Press, 1998), 177; Cassiodorus, *Expl. Ps.* 2 (ACW 51:61); Bede, *Exp. Marc.* (ed. D. Hurst; CChr 120; Turnhout: Brepols, 1960), 632; *Gloss. ord.* on Mark 15:26 (*PL* 114:239c); Albert the Great, *Enarrat. Jo.*, in *Opera Omnia*, vol. 24 (ed. Auguste Borgnet; Paris: Ludovicum Vives, 1899), 657; Thomas Aquinas, *Super Evangelium S. Matthaei: Lectura* (ed. P. Raphaelis Cai; Turin: Marietti, 1951), 363.
[128] *1 Apol.* 40 (*PG* 6:389).
[129] Cyril of Jerusalem, *Cat.* 14.13 (*PG* 33:841a).
[130] See also LSJ, s.v. "διαγορεύω": not merely to mention, but to "relate in detail." Cyril does not state that Ps 2 mentions the passion but more nearly that it *narrates* the passion.

Jesus's passion is evident from the particular verse he actually cites in application to the centurion's confession: Ps 2:11, which reads, "Serve the Lord with fear, and rejoice in him with trembling." What makes Cyril's interpretation particularly intriguing is that he applies a less cited verse from the psalm to a seemingly atypical segment of the passion narrative. Cyril thus demonstrates that *all* of Psalm 2 could be applied to Jesus's passion and death. As with other patristic interpretations, Cyril's application makes no sense unless he operates under the *prima facie* assumption that Psalm 2 is entirely about Jesus's passion and kingship. Indeed, Cyril does not argue his case; he simply assumes it as a matter of common knowledge.

2.3.2.3 The Son's Inheritance and the Worship of the Gentiles

Even apart from the examples above, many of the fathers cite Ps 2:6 in reference to Jesus's enthronement.[131] In addition, many cite Ps 2:7-9 as a prophecy of Christ's universal reign over the nations in a manner resembling the use of these verses in Revelation.[132] Notably, the largest number of patristic citations of Ps 2:7 belong to this category, which further suggests that early Christians associated Ps 2:7 primarily with the idea of Christ's *enthronement*, rather than any specific event, such as the resurrection.[133]

As with Ps 2:1, the "nations" in 2:8 are commonly understood as the Gentiles.[134] Patristic exegesis thus displays a prominent concern for the extension of Christ's rule

---

[131] So Cyprian, *Test.* 2.29 (*PL* 4:720b); Athanasius, *C. Ar.* 2.20.52 (*PG* 26:257); Gregory of Nyssa, *Eun.* 11.3 (*PG* 45:872); Jerome, *Comm. Ps.* 2; Theodoret, *Ep.* 146 (*PG* 83:1395); *Comm. Ps.* 2.7 (*PG* 80:873); Theodore of Mopsuestia, *Comm. Ps.* 2.6; see *Commentary on Psalms 1–81*, trans. Robert C. Hill, WGRW 5 (Atlanta: SBL Press, 2006), 22–5.

[132] Within the NT, only Revelation cites Ps 2:9. Yet it is more likely that the patristic citations of Ps 2:9 display evidence of an earlier tradition than that they are dependent on Revelation. In the first place, *1 Clem.* 36.4 is almost certainly not dependent on Revelation since Clement displays no acquaintance with the work. Instead, Clement cites Ps 2:7-8 following Heb 1:7 and preceding Ps 110:1 (cf. Heb 1:13), clearly recalling the use of Ps 2:7 in Heb 1:5. So although Clement interprets Ps 2:8 in a manner consistent with Revelation, the latter work is not Clement's source. Other patristic sources tend to follow the pattern witnessed in Clement, *contra* Revelation, by offering their interpretations of Ps 2:8-9 as an extension of their interpretations of Ps 2:7 (see esp. Tertullian, *Marc.* 5.17 [*PL* 2:507b], who also pairs Ps 2:8 with Ps 110:1). Given that Revelation and several patristic sources attest the same interpretation of Ps 2:8-9 in apparent independence of one another, the evidence suggests that the association of Psalm 2 with Christ's triumphant reign, like its association with the passion, belongs to earlier tradition.

[133] So *1 Clem.* 36 (*PG* 1:281); Justin, *Dial.* 122 (*PG* 6:760); Tertullian, *Marc.* 3.20, 4.25, 39, 5.17 (*PL* 2:349b, 423a, 457c, 464a); Irenaeus, *Haer.* 4.21 (*PG* 7:1045), Cyril of Jerusalem, *Cat.* 12.18 (*PG* 33:748); Chrysostom, *Catech. Illum.* 1.4 (*PG* 49:227); Augustine, *Fid.* 7 (*PL* 40:176), *Faust.* 12.43 (*PL* 42:277), *Tract. Ev. Jo.* 115, 117 (*PL* 35:1939, 1946); Theodoret, *Ep.* 146 (*PG* 83:1395). This statistic holds true even when one accounts for the later use of Ps 2:7 to support the eternal generation of the Son after the Arian controversy: see Athanasius, *C. Ar.* 4.24 (*PG* 26:504); Cyril of Jerusalem, *Cat.* 10.1 (*PG* 33:665); Gregory of Nazianzus, *Or.* 30.9 (*PG* 36:113); Theodoret, *Hist. eccl.* 1.3 (*PG* 82:900). In any case, such use of Ps 2:7 is not mutually exclusive with its use in relation to Christ's kingship, as demonstrated by the fact that Cyril and Theodoret cite Ps 2:7 to both ends.

[134] So Eusebius, *Hist. eccl.* 3.8.11 (*PG* 20:240); Chrysostom, *Catech. Illum.* 1.4 (*PG* 49:27); Augustine, *Tract. Ev. Jo.*, 115, 117 (*PL* 35:1939, 1946).

to all the Gentiles (cf. Acts 4:25-28; Rev 11:15).[135] Yet patristic sources are more explicit than the NT in specifying that Christ's inheritance of the nations and rule over the Gentiles "with a rod of iron" (Ps 2:8-9) is realized precisely through their worship of him. Hence, in *De Consensu*, just after applying Ps 2:1-2 to Jesus's passion and Ps 2:6 to his crucifixion, Augustine applies Ps 2:9 ("you shall rule them with a rod of iron and shatter them like a potter's vessel") to Christ's subsequent reign over the nations.[136] Elsewhere, Augustine refers to the "kings of the earth now happily subdued by Christ, and all nations serving him."[137] In another comment on Ps 2:7-9, Christ's rule is equated with the nations' salvation: "the nations are to be joined to the name of Christ and so redeemed from death and become God's possession."[138] In the view of Leo the Great, Christ's inheritance of the nations means their merciful adoption by him.[139] According to Didymus of Alexandria, the words of Ps 2:8 are "spoken for our sake, not for the Son's."[140] Commenting on Ps 2:9, both Origen and Theodore of Mopsuestia maintain that Christ rules the nations with a rod of iron in order to reform them.[141]

Finally, although Cyril of Jerusalem stands alone in relating Ps 2:11 to Jesus's passion, others draw an indirect connection between the two. Polycarp, for instance, exhorts the Philippians to "serve God in fear" in view of Christ's death, resurrection, and eternal reign.[142] Augustine is even more interesting: in two separate texts he reads Ps 2:11 as a prophecy concerning the Roman emperors who would one day bow the knee to Christ and serve him.[143] Such an interpretation is consistent with the widespread view that vv. 8-9 relate Christ's universal and eternal authority over the nations, as well as Eusebius's comparison of Christ's reign over against Vespasian's. In one text Augustine links this same interpretation to the usual interpretation of Ps 2:1-2.[144] Plainly, then, his reading of 2:11 as the submission of the nations and rulers to Christ is predicated on the psalm's thoroughgoing association with the passion, inseparable from his kingship.

2.3.2.4 Summary

In summary, patristic exegesis attests the same tradition as the NT by reading Psalm 2 christologically. Jesus is the Davidic Messiah, whose death is ironically the occasion of

---

[135] Several others assert that Christ's reign is superior to that of the Roman emperor. E.g., Eusebius, *Hist. eccl.* 3.8.11 (*PG* 20:240) compares Christ's reign to Vespasian's, finding Christ's to be superior. Augustine, *Ep.* 93.3.9, *Ep.* 185.5.19 (*PL* 33:325, 891) envisages the emperors submitting to Christ by worshiping him.

[136] *Cons.*, 2.4.8 (*PL* 34:1075); cf. Augustine, *Enarrat. Ps.* 47:5 (*PL* 36:536); *Serm.* 218.5 (*PL* 38:1085); *Tract. Ev. Jo.*, 115, 117 (*PL* 35:1939, 1946).

[137] *Faust.* 13.7 (*PL* 42:285).

[138] Augustine, *Enarrat. Ps.* 2.7 (*PL* 36:71).

[139] Leo I, *Serm.* 29.3 (*PL* 54:229b).

[140] Didymus, *Frag. Ps.* 2.8 (*PG* 39:160b-d).

[141] Origen, *Exg. Ps.* 2.9 (*PG* 12:1108-09); Theodore of Mopsuestia, *Comm. Ps.* 2.9; see *Psalms 1-81*, 28-30; cf. Augustine, *Enarrat. Ps.* 2.8 (*PL* 36:71); *Serm.* 366.6 (*PL* 39:1649) where Augustine likens the rod of Christ's rule to the rod of discipline and correction.

[142] *Phil.* 2:1 (*PG* 5:1005).

[143] *Ep.* 93.3.9; 185.5.19 (*PL* 33:325, 891); cf. the similar interpretation of Ps 2:10-11 in *Enarrat. Ps.* 47:5 (*PL* 36:536).

[144] *Ep.* 93.3.9 (*PL* 33:325).

his enthronement and whose resurrection is the proof thereof. Yet patristic literature also demonstrates the extent to which the *entire* psalm was applied to Jesus's passion and kingship at once. Finally, patristic exegesis corresponds, in one sense to early Jewish interpretations of Psalm 2: whereas early Jewish readings anticipate the Messiah's reign over all nations, so the church fathers regularly emphasize *Christ's* reign over the Gentiles', realized through their worship.

2.4 Summary: The Story of Psalm 2

With remarkable consistency, the interpretation of Psalm 2 appears never to have departed from its origins as a coronation hymn for the Davidic king. God himself enthrones his anointed king as his vice-regent or "son," who will instantiate his reign on earth, bringing peace in place of hostility. In early Judaism, Ps 2:7 thus becomes the *locus classicus* for the concept of the Messiah as God's son (see, e.g., 1Q28ᵃ II, 11-12; 4Q246 I, 9–II, 1; *4 Ezra* 7:28-29; 13:32, 37, 53; 14:9; cf. *Midr. Ps.* 2.9; *b. Sukkah* 52a). There is evidence that the NT likewise understands Jesus as God's Son in conjunction with Davidic messianism (e.g., Acts 13:33; Rom 1:3-4; Heb 1:5; 5:5), as I will argue of Mark in the coming chapters. But in the NT and patristic literature alike, the psalm is seen to prefigure Jesus's passion and resurrection, as the occasion and realization of his enthronement, as well as his consequent reign over the nations.

Finally, it is remarkable that the interpretation of Psalm 2 in early Jewish and Christian sources alike never departs from the threefold plot inherent in the psalm: the hostility of the nations, the enthronement of God's anointed son, and God's enduring reign on earth through his king. That is to say, Psalm 2 appears to have been read as a plot—an implicit narrative of sorts—with many ancient readers displaying extended interaction with the psalm as a whole (e.g., *Ps. Sol.* 17; *1 En.* 48–50; Acts 4; 13; Revelation; and nearly all of the church fathers). The idea that Mark might do the same is not out of the ordinary; rather, it is the ordinary. What is hard to imagine is that Mark, in contrast to virtually every other example we possess, would allude to part of Psalm 2 without a view toward its total plot. With this in mind, we turn to Mark's Gospel itself.

3

The Beginning of the Gospel

The preamble is the beginning of a speech, as the prologue in poetry and the prelude in flute playing; for all these are beginnings, and as it were a paving the way for what follows.

Aristotle, Rhetoric

[Mark's] prologue . . . puts into the readers' hands at the outset the key which is designed to unlock the meaning of the contents of the book.

R. H. Lightfoot, History and Interpretation in the Gospels

The story of the Son of God in Mark begins, quite literally, with the beginning of the Gospel itself. Even if one discounts the debated occurrence of υἱοῦ θεοῦ in 1:1, Jesus is first introduced into the narrative as God's "Son" in 1:11 in words drawn primarily from Ps 2:7: "*You are my Son*, the beloved; in you I am well-pleased."

In order to appreciate the significance of this point, we may begin by considering the significance of the prologue itself. Ancient writers, like modern literary critics, universally agreed that the purpose of any introduction is to pave the way for what follows by providing a "swift sketch of the plot," as it were.[1] Mark's Gospel is no exception to this rule.[2] Although Markan interpreters have not always agreed on the extent of the prologue, all agree that 1:1-13/15 sets the stage for the narrative that follows by announcing many of the core themes of the Gospel as well as the identity of Jesus himself.[3] In the following chapter, I will argue that Mark's use of Ps 2:7 in conjunction with Jesus's introduction into the narrative and at the very climax of the

---

[1] See Quintilian, *Inst.* 10.1.48; Aristotle, *Rhetoric* 3.1414b (quoted above); Lucian, *Hist.* 53; Polybius, *Hist.* 11.1a; and the discussion in Michael Winterbottom and D. A. Russell, eds., *Ancient Literary Criticism: The Principal Texts in New Translations* (Oxford: Clarendon Press, 1972), 158–59, 387, and 545. Cf. Francis J. Moloney (*Mark: Storyteller, Interpreter, Evangelist* [Peabody: Hendrickson, 2004], 59): "A prologue will generally inform the reader about *who* the hero is and *what* the hero does, but the reader must enter the story that follows to discover *how* the hero manifests what has been said in the prologue"; and (cited by Moloney) D. E. Smith, "Narrative Beginnings in Ancient Literature and Theory," *Sem* 52 (1991): 1–9.

[2] So already the earliest extant commentary on Mark: see *Exp. Marc.* 1:1 in Michael Cahill, ed., *Expositio Evangelii secundum Markum*, CChr 82 (Turnhout: Brepols, 1997), 5; idem, *The First Commentary on Mark: An Annotated Translation* (New York: Oxford University Press, 1998), 5, 19–20.

[3] Following R. H. Lightfoot (*The Gospel Message of St. Mark* [London: Oxford University Press, 1962], 15–20), some contend that the prologue ends at v. 13; cf. Frank J. Matera, "The Prologue as the

prologue (1:9-11) indeed sets the parameters for the meaning of Son of God in the rest of the narrative. Likewise, we will see that Psalm 2 is not incidental for Mark's prologue, but rather consonant with the themes of the prologue as a whole. We begin, then, with "the beginning of the gospel" (ἀρχή τοῦ εὐαγγελίου) itself.

3.1 Mark's Incipit: The Son of God in the Beginning

The Gospel of Mark opens with the words ἀρχὴ τοῦ εὐαγγελίου Ἰησοῦ Χριστοῦ [υἱοῦ θεοῦ] ("the beginning of the good news of Jesus Christ Son of God"). Yet we are immediately confronted by the question of whether the final words, υἱοῦ θεοῦ, are original in 1:1.[4] Although the majority of ancient witnesses support their inclusion, some significant ones do not.[5] Since it is *prima facie* unlikely that a scribe would omit the *nomina sacra* ($\overline{YY\Theta Y}$) in the first line of the text, either due to *homoioteleuton* or theological motivations, the criterion of transcriptional probability would appear to favor the shorter reading (lacking υἱοῦ θεοῦ).[6] In actuality, however, omissions occurred

---

Interpretive Key to Mark's Gospel," *JSNT* 34 (1988): 3–20. Others (perhaps most) follow Leander Keck's ("The Introduction to Mark's Gospel," *NTS* 12 [1966]: 352–70) argument for v. 15; cf. M. Eugene Boring, "Mark 1:1-15 and the Beginning of the Gospel," *Semeia* 52 (1990): 43–81. I follow Marcus's (*Mark 1–8*, 138) position that vv. 14-15 serve a transitional function at the close of the prologue; cf. Joanna Dewey, *The Oral Ethos of the Early Church: Speaking, Writing, and the Gospel of Mark* (Eugene, OR: Wipf & Stock, 2013), 68.

On the importance of Mark's prologue as a preview of the Gospel, see, e.g., R. H. Lightfoot, *History and Interpretation in the Gospels: The Bampton Lectures 1934* (London: Hodder and Stoughton, 1935), 61; Gnilka, *Markus*, 1:39; Matera, "Prologue," 3–20; Watts, *New Exodus*, 53–4. Many have noted that 1:11 in particular anticipates later moments in the Gospel, especially 9:7 and 15:39: see Lane, *Mark*, 45, Morna Hooker, *The Message of Mark* (London: Epworth, 1983), 5; Pesch, *Markusevangelium*, 1:97; Kingsbury, *Christology*, 60; Marcus, *Mark 1–8*, 163, 168.

4   Arguing for the shorter reading, see Jan Slomp, "Are the Words 'Son of God' in Mark 1.1 Original?," *BT* 28 (1977): 143–50; Peter Head, "A Text-Critical Study of Mark 1.1: The Beginning of the Gospel of Jesus Christ," *NTS* 37 (1991): 621–29; Bart D. Ehrman, "The Text of Mark in the Hands of the Orthodox," *LQ* (1991): 143–56; idem, *The Orthodox Corruption of Scripture: The Effect of Early Christological Controversies on the Text of the New Testament*, updated ed. (New York: Oxford University Press, 2011 (1993), 85–8; Adela Yarbro Collins, "Establishing the Text: Mark 1:1," in *Texts and Contexts: Biblical Texts in Their Textual and Situational Contexts*, ed. Tord Fornberg and David Hellholm (Olso; Copenhagen; Stockholm; Boston: Scandinavian University Press, 1995), 111–25. Arguing for the longer reading, however, see Alexander Globe, "The Caesarean Omission of the Phrase 'Son of God' in Mark 1:1," *HTR* 75 (1982): 209; Tommy Wasserman, "The 'Son of God' Was in the Beginning (Mark 1:1)," *JTS* 62 (2011): 20–50; Max Botner, "The Role of Transcriptional Probability in the Text-Critical Debate on Mark 1:1," *CBQ* 77 (2015): 467–80. Finally, J. K. Elliott ("Mark 1.1-3—A Later Addition to the Gospel?," *NTS* 46 [2000]: 584–88) and N. Clayton Croy ("Where the Gospel Text Begins: A Non-Theological Interpretation of Mark 1:1," *NovT* 43 [2001]: 105–27) argue that v. 1 is a later addition.

5   Those witnesses that include the words υἱοῦ θεοῦ are ℵ¹ A B D E F G^{suppl} H K L M S U V W Y Γ Δ Π Σ Φ Ω $f^{1.13}$ 22 579 582^c 820^c 1555^c 𝔐 a aur b c d f ff² l q r¹ VL₉A vq sy$^{p.ph.h}$ got sa^{mss} bo geo² aeth arab^{mss} slav Ir^{lat} Sever Cyr Ps-Ath Vic Ambr Chrom Hier^{pt} Aug. Lacking υἱοῦ θεοῦ, see ℵ* Θ 28^c 530 582* 820* 1021 1436 1555* 1692 2430 2533 *l*211 sy^{pal} sa^{ms} arm geo¹ arab^{ms} Or$^{gr.lat}$ Serap Bas CyrJ AstI Hes.

6   So, e.g., Head, "Mark 1.1," 621–29; and Ehrman, "Text," 143–56; idem, *Orthodox*, 85–8. Bruce Metzger (*A Textual Commentary on the Greek New Testament* [London: UBS, 1971], 73) had previously suggested that the use of *nomina sacra* combined with the occurrence of six genitives in a row could account for the possible omission of υἱοῦ θεοῦ due to *homoioteleuton*, but this argument is dismissed by Head (628).

frequently in the first lines of manuscripts, including the omission of the *nomen sacrum* Χριστοῦ ($\overline{XY}$) in 28* and even the very first word of the text, ἀρχή, in syr^pal.[7] Likewise, C. H. Turner long ago demonstrated the tendency of patristic sources to omit from the Gospel beginnings, and Mark 1:1 in particular, whatever was not relevant to their immediate purposes.[8] Far from theologically problematic, Turner shows that the shorter reading could at times be theologically *favorable* in some instances.[9] The typical arguments against the longer reading are not so strong as they first appear, then.

Finally, it should be noted that the argument against the longer reading has historically been motivated to a large degree by the absence of υἱοῦ θεοῦ in Sinaiticus (*א).[10] Yet Sinaiticus has become notorious for its high number of errors and subsequent corrections—a number surpassing that of any other NT manuscript.[11] The first wave of corrections (which already contains υἱοῦ θεοῦ in Mark 1:1) is thought to have occurred quickly, possibly even before the codex left the scriptorium.[12] If א* is the primary witness for the shorter reading, then, it must be admitted that it rests on shaky ground in terms of external evidence. The external evidence, in any case, strongly favors the longer reading.[13]

---

[7] For examples elsewhere in the NT, see Barbara Aland et al., eds., *Novum Testamentum Graecum: editio critica maior III: Die Apostelgeschichte*, 2nd ed. (Stuttgart: Deutsche Bibelgesellschaft, 1997), 1:2; idem, *Novum Testamentum Graecum: editio critica maior IV: Die Katholischen Briefe*, 2nd ed. (Stuttgart: Deutsche Bibelgesellschaft, 1997), 1:2, 104, 204, 264, 370, 388, 404. As Globe ("Mark 1:1," 215) observes 28* was later corrected (28^c) to include the missing *nomen sacrum* ($\overline{XY}$, indicating that the omission was indeed a mistake. For further examples of copying errors in Mark 1:1 see Wasserman, "Mark 1:1," 47.

[8] C. H. Turner, "Text of Mark 1," *JTS* 28 (1927): 150–58. Turner specifically cites Irenaeus and Victorinus, both of whom omit not only υἱοῦ θεοῦ from Mark 1:1-3, but other material as well, according to their immediate theological purposes, despite demonstrating an awareness of the omitted material elsewhere. Cf. Globe ("Mark 1:1," 210), who offers several more examples of church fathers (including Irenaeus, Severian, and Jerome) who vary between the longer reading and an abridged reading per their immediate purposes.

[9] As Botner ("Transcriptional," 477) writes, the fathers do indeed view Mark 1:1 "as a text freighted with theological significance—however, not the sort of significance that modern interpreters might expect."

[10] As Globe ("Mark 1:1," 209) recounts, the first doubts concerning the longer reading appeared shortly after the discovery of Sinaiticus. Neither Tischendorf nor Westcott & Hort included it in their texts of Mark. By far, the two most credible witnesses for the shorter reading are א* and Origen. Yet Turner ("Text," 150) suggests that, in view of the "close relation" between א* and Origen, we have "really not two witnesses to deal with but one."

[11] According to D. C. Parker (*Codex Sinaiticus: The Story of the World's Oldest Bible* [London: British Library, 2010], 3, 79–80), the total number of corrections between the six groups of editors comes to over 23,000, including frequent spelling corrections and insertions of accidentally omitted text. Curiously, each successive wave of corrections brings Sinaiticus into closer alignment with Vaticanus, which is, by comparison, a pristine manuscript, and may be slightly older than Sinaiticus. Thus, according to Parker (18), "where they differ in the New Testament, most editors believe that the text of Codex Vaticanus is generally more reliable than that of Codex Sinaiticus"; cf. T. C. Skeat, "Four Years' Work on the Codex Sinaiticus: Significant Discoveries in Reconditioned MS," in *The Collected Biblical Writings of T. C. Skeat*, ed. J. K. Elliott (Leiden: Brill, 2004), 115; and Frederic G. Kenyon and A. W. Adams, *The Text of the Greek Bible*, 3rd ed. (London: Duckworth, 1975), 82.

[12] Parker (*Sinaiticus*, 80) suggests within the first fifty years; however, Bruce Metzger and Bart D. Ehrman (*The Text of the New Testament: Its Transmission, Corruption, and Restoration*, 4th ed. [New York/Oxford: Oxford University Press, 2005], 66) suggest "before the manuscript left the scriptorium." See similarly, Wasserman, "Mark 1:1," 46; and Skeat ("Four Years," 116), who believes the first corrections took place "almost as soon as the Codex was written."

[13] The most complete analysis of the external evidence to date is that of Wasserman, "Mark 1:1," 22–41. As Wasserman demonstrates, manuscript evidence, patristic evidence, and versional evidence all favor the longer reading.

So while the argument that follows does not depend on the originality of υἱοῦ θεοῦ in 1:1, it would seem an interpretive error to ignore them in light of the total evidence.

Proceeding on the likelihood that the longer reading is original, then, Mark begins by declaring that the εὐαγγέλιον he narrates is the proclamation of one who is both Χριστός, "Christ/Messiah," and υἱὸς θεοῦ, "son of God," implying that the narrative cannot be understood apart from these two titles.[14] Yet, as Elizabeth Struthers Malbon states, Mark's Son of God "resists easy comprehension and full definition at this beginning point";[15] such definition is instead left to the ensuing narrative. That is not to say that Mark leaves us without any clues, however.[16]

On the contrary, the language of Mark 1:1 bears multiple analogies in the ancient world.[17] On the one hand, "perhaps the best analogue we have in antiquity" for the collocation Ἰησοῦ Χριστοῦ υἱοῦ θεοῦ, as Botner observes, is *Caesar Augustus Divi filius*/Καῖσαρ Σέβαστος θεοῦ υἱός, whose birth was also described in imperial inscriptions as "the beginning of good news for the world ..." (ἦρξεν δὲ τῶι κόσμωι τῶν δι' αὐτὸν εὐαγγελίων).[18] For those who heard the imperial proclamation echoed or mimicked by Mark's incipit, the message would be clear: Jesus is a royal figure whose significance in some way rivals the claims made by Caesar.[19]

---

[14] According to some (e.g., M. Eugene Boring, "Mark 1:1-15 and the Beginning of the Gospel," *Semeia* 52 [1990]: 43–82; John G. Cook, *The Structure and Persuasive Power of Mark: A Linguistic Approach* [Atlanta: Scholars Press, 1995], 138–40, 173; Collins, *Mark*, 130), 1:1 probably functions in as a title for the entire work. As Collins comments, "It would seem, then, that the introductory sentence summarizes the content of the work."
There is also debate as to whether Ἰησοῦ Χριστοῦ should be understood as an objective genitive ("about Jesus Christ") or subjective genitive ("proclaimed by Jesus Christ"); see Black, *Mark*, 46–7. Given that the entire narrative is, in fact, *about* Jesus Christ and since Jesus is the object of εὐαγγέλιον elsewhere in Mark (8:35; 10:29; 13:10; 14:9), the objective nuance is more likely (so Guelich, *Mark 1–8:26*, 9).

[15] Malbon, *Mark's Jesus*, 66; cf. Boring, *Mark*, 32.

[16] As Malbon (*Mark's Jesus*, 66) recognizes: "[Mark 1:1] alludes to previous uses of 'Christ' and 'Son of God' in Jewish Scripture."

[17] This point is nicely captured in a pair of articles by Adela Yarbro Collins: "Mark and His Readers: The Son of God among Jews," 393–408; followed by "Mark and His Readers: The Son of God among Greeks and Romans," 85–100. The ambiguity in Mark 1:1 is not, as such, the result of the evangelist's terseness alone but, firstly, the polysemy inherent within his terms in antiquity.

[18] Botner, *Son of David*, 77. For a comparison of the two collocations, see furhter Matthew V. Novenson, *Christ among the Messiahs: Christ Language in Paul and Messiah Language in Ancient Judaism* (New York: Oxford University Press, 2012), 93–6. The inscription quoted above is the famous Priene Calendar Inscription (OGIS 458; *c.* 9 BCE). For discussion of this inscription in relation to Mark's incipit, see, *inter alia*, Craig A. Evans, "Mark's Incipit and the Priene Calendar Inscription: From Jewish Gospel to Greco-Roman Gospel," *JGRChJ* 1 (2000): 67–81; Boring, *Mark*, 30; Peppard, *Son of God*, 92; Karl Galinsky, *Augustus: Introduction to the Life of an Emperor* (Princeton: Princeton University Press, 2012), 162–63. Far from unique, this inscription is but a single example of the rhetoric that permeated Mark's theatre of discourse (see, e.g., IGR 1.901; 4.309, 315; ILS107,113; P.Ryl.601; P.Oslo26; *IG* II 1077; IvP II 384).

[19] Cf. Boring, *Mark*, 30; and already Deissmann, *Light from the Ancient East*, 341–42. Some, such as Evans ("Incipt," 70, 77, 81) and Winn (*Purpose*, 98–9; 102), go so far as to suggest that Mark deliberately mimics the rhetoric of the imperial cult so as to assert assert that Jesus, rather than Augustus, is the true Son of God whose reign brings salvation (σωτηρία) and good tidings (εὐαγγέλιον) for the world. Whether or not this is so, anyone who heard the similarity to the imperial claims at all must have sensed the implicit rivalry.

On the other hand, nearly every word of Mark's opening verse—including ἀρχή, εὐαγγελίον, χριστός, and υἱοῦ θεοῦ—also recalls the language of the Septuagint.[20] And while both χριστός and υἱὸς θεοῦ alone could recall any number of passages, their combination calls to mind Ps 2:2, 7 LXX in particular.[21] As the very next lines of the Gospel indicate, it is this scriptural backstory that is determinative for Mark.

According to Mark 1:2, the gospel unfolds "*as it is written* in Isaiah the prophet":[22]

Καθὼς γέγραπται ἐν τῷ Ἡσαΐᾳ τῷ προφήτῃ·
ἰδοὺ ἀποστέλλω τὸν ἄγγελόν μου πρὸ προσώπου σου,
 ὃς κατασκευάσει τὴν ὁδόν σου·
φωνὴ βοῶντος ἐν τῇ ἐρήμῳ·
ἑτοιμάσατε τὴν ὁδὸν κυρίου,
εὐθείας ποιεῖτε τὰς τρίβους αὐτοῦ ...

Mark 1:2-3[23]

Although Mark's prologue cites Scripture directly only this once, the effect of this single citation is to frame the narrative that follows as "part of a much larger story, which we see stretching back as far as the prophets."[24] Indeed, it is probably no coincidence that Mark quotes Isaiah 40 in close connection with εὐαγγέλιον (1:1); as Peter Stuhlmacher has demonstrated, Isa 40:9 appears to be the primary background of the εὐαγγέλιον concept throughout the NT.[25] The gospel Mark announces is not a generic one, then, but rather the fulfillment of that which was foretold by Isaiah.[26] To quote Richard Hays, "Mark signals to his readers that the εὐαγγέλιον of Jesus Christ is

---

[20] Cf., for instance, ἀρχή in Gen 1:1; Hos 1:1; εὐαγγελία in 2 Sam 4:10; 2 Kgs 7:9; as well as εὐαγγελίζομαι in 1 Sam 31:9; 2 Sam 1:20, 4:20, 18:19-31; 1 Kgs 1:42; 1 Chr 10:9; Pss 39:10, 67:12, 95:2; Isa 41:27; 52:7; 60:6; 61:1; Jer 20:15; Joel 2:32; Nah 1:15; and esp. Isa 40:9; χριστός in Lev 4:5; 1 Sam 2:10; 12:3; 24:6; 2 Sam 1:14; 22:51; Pss 17:51; 88:39, 51; 131:10; and God's υἱός in Exod 4:22; Hos 11:1; 2 Sam 7:14; Jer 31:20.

[21] In addition to Ps 2:7, David's seed is also called God's υἱός in 2 Sam 7:14, but χριστός does not occur in that passage. Likewise, God's king is called χριστός in numerous instances (see above), but only in Psalm 2 is this χριστός also his υἱός.

[22] According to Robert A. Guelich ("'The Beginning of the Gospel': Mark 1:1-15," *BR* 27 [1982], 6) καθὼς γέγραπται in the NT always forms "a bridge between what has preceded and the quotation that follows." Although I am not necessarily persuaded by his contention that 1:2 cannot, therefore, begin a new sentence, we should nevertheless understand 1:2-3 as an elaboration on 1:1.

[23] As is well known, Mark's citation is actually a conflation of Exod 23:20; Mal 3:1; and Isa 40:3 (see, e.g., Marcus, *Way*, 12-7; Watts, *New Exodus*, 61-3; idem, "Mark," in *CNTUOT*, 113-20). Yet Isaiah seems to be of primary significance for Mark—hence, Mark refers to Isaiah alone by name (see Watts, *New Exodus*, 90).

[24] Christopher Bryan, *A Preface to Mark: Notes on the Gospel in Its Literary and Cultural Settings* (New York: Oxford University Press, 1993), 85; cf. Kermode, *Genesis*, 133-34. This is, in fact, the only formula citation in Mark's Gospel.

[25] Peter Stuhlmacher, *Das paulinische Evangelium*, FRLANT 95 (Göttingen: Vandenhoeck & Ruprecht, 1968), 109-79, 218-25.

[26] As various scholars have noted, Isaiah 40 appears to have become the *locus classicus* for YHWH's eschatological restoration of Israel, often viewed as a new exodus, in early Judaism (see, e.g., Klyne R. Snodgrass, "Streams of Tradition Emerging from Isaiah 40:1-5 and Their Adaptation in the New Testament," *JSNT* 2 [1980]: 24-45; Marcus, *Way*, 18-36; Watts, *New Exodus*, 84). Examples of such interpretation occur in in 1QS 8:13-14; 4Q213a; 4Q176; Bar. 5:5-7; Sir. 48:24; *T. Moses* 10:1-5; *Ps. Sol.* 11:1-2, 4-6; *Pesiq. R.* 29/30a, 29 30b, 30, 33.

to be read within the matrix of Isaiah's prophetic vision: God will return to Zion [i.e., "the way of the Lord"] and restore Israel."[27] It is this story to which Mark's proclamation of Jesus Christ, the Son of God belongs.

3.2 Preparing the Way (Mark 1:4-8)

This impression is confirmed by the allusive nature of the prologue leading up to Jesus's first appearance in 1:9. When John appears "*baptizing* in the wilderness and *preaching* a *baptism* of repentance for the forgiveness of sins" (βαπτίζων ἐν τῇ ἐρήμῳ καὶ κηρύσσων βάπτισμα μετανοίας εἰς ἄφεσιν ἁμαρτιῶν) in v. 4, we are meant to understand that he is Isaiah's prophesied messenger *preparing* (κατασκευάσει) the way and "*crying* in the wilderness [βοῶντος ἐν τῇ ἐρήμῳ], '*prepare* [ἑτοιμάσατε] the way of the Lord'" (1:2-3).[28] And when Mark portrays "*all* Judea and *all* the Jerusalemites" (πᾶσα ἡ Ἰουδαία χώρα καὶ οἱ Ἱεροσολυμῖται πάντες) coming to receive John's baptism, we are meant to see the entire nation symbolically being prepared for the coming restoration.[29] Mark then presents John in the garb of Elijah (1:6; cf. 2 Kgs 1:8) and offers only a brief account of his preaching, centered entirely on the coming of "the stronger one" (ὁ ἰσχυρότερός).[30]

But Mark's succinct presentation of John and his preaching has another purpose as well, which relates to both 1:1 and (as we shall see) 1:9-11: to prepare the way for the coming Messiah. What, after all, might be the significance of portraying John as a new Elijah or Elijah returned (cf. Mal 3:22 LXX)?[31] More than likely, the significance resides in the fact that Elijah was expected to return in the last days ahead of the Messiah himself (cf. Mark 9:11; Matt 11:14; 17:10; Luke 1:17).[32] Additionally, while ὁ

---

[27] Hays, *Gospels*, 21.
[28] So Origen, *Comm. Jo.* 1.14 (*PG* 14:48); Basil, *Ad. Eunom.* 2.15 (*PG* 29b:601); *Exp. Marc.* 1:4 (*CChr* 82); Bede, *Exp. Marc.* 440; *Hom. 1.1*; and, in the modern era, C. H. Turner, "Marcan Usage: Notes, Critical and Exegetical, on the Second Gospel IV: Parenthetical Clauses in Mark," *JTS* 26 (1925): 145–56; Thomas R. Hatina, *In Search of a Context: The Function of Scripture in Mark's Narrative*, SSEJC 8 (London/New York: Sheffield Academic Press, 2002), 141–42; Joel Marcus, *John the Baptist in History and Theology* (Columbia: University of South Carolina Press, 2018), 143.
[29] Though an obvious exaggeration (Boring, *Mark*, 41; Black, *Mark*, 54), it would seem to be hyperbole with a theological purpose (so Lohmeyer, *Markus*, 15; Mauser, *Wilderness*, 92; Kingsbury, *Christology*, 59–60; Marcus, *Way*, 24).
[30] Cf. the much longer summaries in Matt 3:1-12; and Luke 3:1-20. On the likelihood that Mark 1:6 alludes to Elijah's appearance in 2 Kgs 1:8, see Grundmann, *Markus*, 28; Gnilka, *Markus*, 1:46; Marcus, *Mark 1–8*, 156; Collins, *Mark*, 145; Benoît Standaert, *Évangile selon Marc: commentaire*, 3rd ed., 3 vols, EBib 61 (Pendé: J. Gabalda, 2010), 53.
[31] As Dormeyer ("Mk 1,1-15," 186) observes, Mark 1:6 is one of only five occasions on which Mark mentions anyone's clothing (cf. 9:3; 14:51-52; 15:17-20; 16:5). In each instance other than the infamous young man in 14:51-52, the symbolic significance of the clothing is obvious.
[32] Outside the NT, this expectation appears in *Tg. Ps.-J. Deut* 30:4; *b. ʿErub.* 43a–b; *m. Sotah* 9:15; *Pesiq R.* 35:3; and *Pirqe R. El.* 43. On the probable existence of this tradition in the time of the NT, see Dale C. Allison, Jr., "Elijah Must Come First," *JBL* 103 (1984): 256–58; and Anthony Ferguson, "The Elijah Forerunner Concept as an Authentic Jewish Expectation," *JBL* 137 (2018): 127–145; *contra* Joseph A. Fitzmyer, "The Aramaic 'Elect of God' Text from Qumran Cave IV," *CBQ* 27 (1965): 348–72; idem, "More about Elijah Coming First," *JBL* 104 (1985): 295–96; and Morris M. Faierstein, "Why Do the Scribes Say That Elijah Must Come First?," *JBL* 100 (1981): 75–86. As Allison, in particular, argues:

ἰσχυρός/τερός is not a messianic title *per se*, it takes little effort to recognize that, in the narrative flow of Mark 1:1-15, "the stronger one" who "is coming after" John (ἔρχεται ὁ ἰσχυρότερός μου ὀπίσω μου) is Jesus, who comes after John in 1:9 and who is χριστός (1:1).³³ Luke, in fact, makes this connection explicit in his adaptation of Mark 1:7, which interprets ὁ χριστός as ὁ ἰσχυρότερός (Luke 3:15-16).³⁴ Moreover, as Botner observes, the pairing of a verb of coming (ἔρχεται) and a temporal marker (ὀπίσω) is "one of the most common ways to introduce a Messiah" in Jewish literature (cf. 1QS 9:11; CD 19:10-11; 4Q252 5:3; *4 Ezra* 12:32).³⁵ So John's allusion to "the stronger one" who is coming after him immediately following his own depiction as Elijah returned readily serves to paint him as the forerunner of the Messiah.³⁶

Likewise, while a number of texts look forward to the outpouring of God's Spirit in the last days, sometimes in connection with the coming of the Messiah, the pairing of *water* and the *Spirit* in 1:8 (ἐγὼ ἐβάπτισα ὑμᾶς ὕδατι, αὐτὸς δὲ βαπτίσει ὑμᾶς ἐν πνεύματι ἁγίῳ) reminds many of Ezek 36:25-27 in particular ("I will sprinkle clean water on you, and you will be clean from all your uncleanness, and from all your idols I will cleanse you ... I will put my Spirit within you, and cause you to walk in my statutes").³⁷ In its broader context, this passage anticipates the gift of God's Spirit in connection with the coming of a figure who is called "my servant David" (עבדי דויד) and "prince" (נשיא) among God's people (34:23-24; 37:24-25).³⁸ In summary, every detail of

---

(1) Elijah's return was expected in earlier texts (Mal 3:22 LXX/3:23 MT; Sir. 48:9-10; 1 Macc. 4:46; 14:41; 4Q558 II.4-5); (2) it is difficult to explain why early Christians would have attributed their eschatological beliefs to the scribes; and (3) later Jewish sources presumably did not adopt their views from Christian sources. The logical conclusion, therefore, is that the expectation of Elijah as a messianic forerunner existed by the time of the NT.

³³ The Davidic Messiah is characterized by divinely bestowed "strength" in Isa 11:2 LXX; *1 En.* 49:3; and *Ps. Sol.* 17:37. In Isaiah, ἰσχυρός/ἰσχύς frequently characterizes YHWH himself (40:10, 26; 29, 31; 45:24; 50:2; 63:1, 15), so the possibility also exists of a direct reference to God in 1:7. Yet, as Collins (*Mark*, 64) suggests, evoking the language of Isaiah's Divine Warrior "could well have had connotations of the Davidic messiah as God's agent in the eschatological battle."

³⁴ Cf. Darrell L. Bock, *Mark*, NCBC (New York: Cambridge University Press, 2015), 113.

³⁵ Botner, *Son of David*, 78. Botner also notes and affirms Simon Gathercole's (*The Preexistent Son: Recovering the Christologies of Matthew, Mark, and Luke* [Grand Rapids: Eerdmans, 2006], 111–12) objection that verbs of "coming" are not messianic *termini technici*. But to observe a linguistic pattern is not to postulate *termini technici*. In addition to the evidence Botner cites, it worth noting that the articular participle ὁ ἐρχόμενος connotes a messianic figure in *all* of its occurrences in the canonical Gospels: Matt 11:3; 21:9; 23:39; Mark 11:9; Luke 7:19-20; 13:35; 19:38; John 6:14, 35; 12:13; cf. Heb 10:37.

³⁶ See similarly Marcus, *Mark 1–8*, 157–58; cf. Collins, *Mark*, 64.

³⁷ So Guelich, *Mark 1–8*:26, 25; Marcus, *Mark 1–8*, 152; Collins, *Mark*, 138. As Marcus notes, this passage is also followed by a "classic expression" of the wilderness theme (Ezek 36:33-36), which is also a feature of Mark's prologue (1:3-4, 12-13). The eschatological outpouring of God's Spirit appears elsewhere in Isa 32:15; 44:3; 63:10-14; Ezek 36:25-27; 39:29; Joel 2:28-29; 1QS 4:20-22; *m. Yoma* 8:9; and with the Messiah in *T. Levi* 18:11; *T. Jud.* 24:2; 4Q521 2:6; *m. Sotah* 9:15. In other texts, God's anointed/the Messiah himself is specially endowed with God's Spirit: see 2 Sam 23:1-2; Isa 11:1-2; 61:1; *Ps. Sol.* 17:37; *1 En.* 49:3; 62:2; *Tg. Isa.* 42:1-4; cf. Mark 1:10.

³⁸ Ezek 34:23-24 is interpreted messianically in CD 7:20; 1QS^b 5:20; 1 QM 5:1; and 4Q161. See further J. D. G. Dunn, "Messianic Ideas and Their Influence on the Jesus of History," in *The Messiah*, 367; J. J. M. Roberts, "The Old Testament's Contribution to Messianic Expectations," in *The Messiah*, 46.

Mark's terse account of John and his preaching serves a single purpose: to create an atmosphere of messianic expectation—that is, to "prepare the way."[39]

3.3 Introducing God's Son (Mark 1:9-11)

And so Jesus himself appears for the first time in the narrative:

Καὶ ἐγένετο ἐν ἐκείναις ταῖς ἡμέραις ἦλθεν Ἰησοῦς ἀπὸ Ναζαρὲτ τῆς Γαλιλαίας καὶ ἐβαπτίσθη εἰς τὸν Ἰορδάνην ὑπὸ Ἰωάννου.

Mark 1:9

That the scene of Jesus's baptism (1:9-11) marks the climax of the prologue is indicated on a linguistic level by the introductory expression καὶ ἐγένετο ἐν ἐκείναις ταῖς ἡμέραις ("and it happened in those days"). Not only is this phrase obviously septuagintal in diction,[40] but it is also a means of slowing down the narrative in order to focus attention on the specific event that follows.[41] The dramatic intensity in the scene itself builds swiftly as Jesus rises up out of the Jordan to see the heavens rent and the Spirit descending to him like a dove (αἱ εὐθὺς ἀναβαίνων ἐκ τοῦ ὕδατος εἶδεν σχιζομένους τοὺς οὐρανοὺς καὶ τὸ πνεῦμα ὡς περιστερὰν καταβαῖνον εἰς αὐτόν) until, at last, a voice from heaven (i.e., God) declares:[42]

σὺ εἶ ὁ υἱός μου ὁ ἀγαπητός, ἐν σοὶ εὐδόκησα.

Mark 1:11

With these words the definition for which υἱὸς θεοῦ begs in 1:1 begins to materialize via God's own speech about his Son. To say so, however, is to say [MEPR1]that Mark's Son of God is, from the beginning, defined with reference to Israel's Scriptures, specifically Ps 2:7, to which the heavenly voice here alludes.[43] As Malbon appropriately

---

[39] So also Taylor (*Mark*, 156): "Mark's account of the Baptist's preaching is very brief.... Everything is concentrated on the prophecy of the coming of the Mightier One and the baptism which, in contrast to his own baptism by water, the Messiah will dispense." Similar observations have been made by others, such as Lohmeyer, *Markus*, 9; N. B. Stonehouse, *The Witness of Matthew and Mark to Christ*, 2nd ed. (Grand Rapids: Eerdmans, 1958), 16; Cranfield, *Mark*, 33; Gnilka, *Markus*, 1:39; Kingsbury, *Christology*, 60; Simon Légasse, *L'Evangile de Marc*, 2 vols, LD 5 (Paris: Cerf, 1997), 1:53; Marcus, *Mark 1–8*, 166; Standaert, *Marc*, 1:72; and Black, *Mark*, 55.

[40] Cf. Marcus (*Mark 1–8*, 158): "these words ... are an OT idiom that is not found in nonbiblical Greek."

[41] Stephen H. Levinsohn, *Discourse Features of New Testament Greek: A Coursebook on the Information Structure of New Testament Greek*, 2nd ed. (Dallas: SIL International, 2000), 177. Likewise, the shift from the imperfect, which dominates 1:5-8, to the aorist in 1:9 indicates a return from the narrative "background" to the "foreground"; see Levinsohn, *Discourse*, 173–75; cf. Constantine R. Campbell, *Verbal Aspect, the Indicative Mood, and Narrative: Soundings in the Greek of the New Testament*, SBG 13 (New York: Peter Lang, 2007), 241. The aorist ἐβάπτισα in v. 8 is already "backgrounded" since it occurs in direct discourse.

[42] The voice from heaven is often (rightly in my view) likened to the rabbinic *bat-qôl*: a voice from heaven expressing the will of God, sometimes with a quotation from Scripture: see Taylor, *Mark*, 161; Marcus, *Mark 1–8*, 160–61; Black, *Mark*, 59.

[43] For a useful summary of the positions maintained by modern interpreters, see Watts, "Mark," in *CNTUOT*, 122. The main contenders have been (in the following order) Ps 2:7; Isa 42:1; and Gen

remarks, "Not too surprisingly, (God) seems to be quite familiar with Scripture, but not constrained to quote it exactly."[44] In order to fully appreciate the weight that these words bear in the prologue (and Mark's Gospel as a whole), it is important to note several points before we examine their meaning in detail.

1. As Kavin Rowe writes, "Literarily speaking, it would be hard to overstress the importance of a character's first introduction into what [W. J.] Harvey called the 'web of human relationships.'"[45] Whereas we first *see* Jesus in 1:9, God's pronouncement in 1:11 constitutes the first word *about* Jesus in Mark's narrative. Quite simply, God's "Son" is how he is introduced into the "web of human [and divine] relationships" that is Mark's Gospel. Bal further explains the manner in which initial introductions bear on our future understanding of a character: the initial "bits of information" we receive about a character effetively "determine him or her so inconspicuously that the reader processes the information without giving it a second thought."[46] This insight is not modern, however; Cicero makes the same observation about the importance of first impressions in general.[47] In short, whatever we learn about Jesus in the subsequent narrative necessarily builds on this foundation.

2. The strength of this entire point is bolstered by the fact that God himself is the speaker in 1:11. The concept of "point of view" is a familiar one among narrative critics.[48] Plainly stated, some characters possess a more credible voice than others. But as Kingsbury rightly suggests, the normative, or "evaluative," point of view within the Gospels is consistently aligned with God's own, which is to say that what God says

---

22:1, with the majority of scholars today supporting some combination of these three. Alternatively, Paul G. Bretscher ("Exodus 4:22-23 and the Voice from Heaven," *JBL* 87 [1968]: 301–11) suggests Exod 4:22-23; John Paul Heil ("Jesus with the Wild Animals in Mark 1:13," *CBQ* 68 [2006]: 63–78) suggests Jer 38:20 LXX in passing; and Hooker (*Mark*, 47) rightly notes that Mark 1:11 is also reminiscent of a number of passages that describe Israel as God's "son," including Exod 4:22; Deut 1:31; Jer 2:2; 31:9; and Hos 11:1.

[44] Malbon, *Mark's Jesus*, 76.

[45] Rowe (*Early Narrative Christology*, 43), citing not only W. J. Harvey, *Character and the Novel* (Ithaca, New York: Cornell University Press, 1965), 52; but also Hannah Arendt, *The Human Condition* (Chicago: University of Chicago Press, 1958), 184; and Viktor Pöschl's study of the Aeneid: *The Art of Vergil: Image and Symbol in the Aeneid* (trans. Gerda Seligson; Ann Arbor: Unversity of Michigan Press, 1962), 91.

[46] Bal, *Narratology*, 120. This is not, of course, to assume that Mark's original audience has no preconceived notions of Jesus. Bal herself continues: "To begin with, there is information that is 'always-already' involved, that relates to the extratextual situation, in so far as the reader is acquainted with it." In terms of the story, however, it still matters immensely which facet of the character's identity the author chooses to actualize from the start since this choice will guide the reader's (or listener's) apprehension of the character moving forward. On a further note, Bal (121) stresses that the narrative logic of character construction applies no less to historical characters than to fictional ones.

[47] Cicero, *De Or.*, 2.78.315: "the opening passage contains the first impression and the introduction of the speech, and this ought to charm and attract the hearer straightaway" (trans. E. W. Sutton and H. Rackham, LCL 348:439). Cicero's comment refers to the beginning of a speech; however, the same logic can easily be applied to the introduction of the main character in a narrative.

[48] See, e.g., Boris Upensky, *A Poetics of Composition: The Structure of the Artistic Text and Typology of a Compositional Form* (Berkeley: University of California, 1973), 8–16; Chatman, *Story and Discourse*, 151–58; N. R. Petersen, "'Point of View' in Mark's Narrative," *Semeia* 12 (1978): 97–121; James L. Resseguie, "Point of View," in *How John Works: Storytelling in the Fourth Gospel*, ed. Douglas Estes and Ruth Sheridan, RBS 86 (Atlanta: SBL Press, 2016), 79–96.

counts the most in the Gospel narratives.⁴⁹ In Mark's case, moreover, God's speech in 1:11 is all the more notable when contrasted with the author's overall reserve in speaking directly about God.⁵⁰ In a rare instance, Mark lifts the veil and unequivocally discloses God's own point of view.

3. Furthermore, in their immediate context, the words "You are my Son..." comprise the content of a divine revelation. The opening or parting of the heavens is a common motif indicating a divine revelation or theophany.⁵¹ Specifically, Mark's phrase σχιζομένους τοὺς οὐρανούς in 1:10 echoes the ancient prayer found in Isa 63:19b that God would "rend the heavens and come down" (ἐὰν ἀνοίξῃς τὸν οὐρανόν/ירדת לוא־קרעת שמים).⁵² Mark, that is to say, presents the events of Jesus's baptism as God's answer to Isaiah's prayer for God to restore Israel in a manner recalling the original exodus.⁵³

So also, the Spirit's descent (τὸ πνεῦμα ... καταβαῖνον εἰς αὐτόν) recalls a motif found throughout Isaiah (notably, in 11:2; 42:1: 61:1; and 63:14) signifying God's anointing to a special task or office—e.g., "the root of Jesse" in 11:2 or the "Servant of YHWH" in 42:1 and 61:1.⁵⁴ Altogether, the imagery leading up to the voice in 1:11 suggests that Israel's eschatological turning point is at hand. As Boring writes, "the time of waiting and longing is over, the ultimate act of God's revelation is already beginning," and Jesus's anointing is its epicenter.⁵⁵

---

⁴⁹ See Kingsbury, *Christology*, 47–50; cf. Powell (*Narrative Criticism*, 24): "All four New Testament Gospels depict a world that includes supernatural beings and events.... The right way of thinking, furthermore, is aligned with God's point of view.... What God thinks is, by definition, true and right."

⁵⁰ See John R. Donahue, "A Neglected Factor in the Theology of Mark," *JBL* 101 (1982): 563–94.

⁵¹ See, e.g., Gen 7:11; Ps 77:23; Isa 24:18; Ezek 1:1; John 1:51; Acts 7:56; 10:11; Rev 4:1; 11:19; 19:11; *2 Bar.* 22:1; *Apoc. Abr.* 19:4; *T. Levi* 2:6; 5:1; 18:6; *T. Jud.* 24:2; Herm. Vis. 1:4. See also Lohmeyer, *Markus*, 21; Taylor, *Mark*, 160; Pesch, *Markusevangelium*, 1:90; Steichele, *Sohn Gottes*, 113, 119; Marcus, *Way*, 56–7; idem, *Mark 1–8*, 165–66; and Black, *Mark*, 58.

⁵² See, *inter alia*, Ivor Buse, "The Markan Account of the Baptism of Jesus and Isaiah LXIII," *JTS* 7 (1956): 74–5; cf. Marcus, *Way*, 49–50; idem, *Mark 1–8*, 159; Schenck, *Isaiah*, 44–7; Watts, *New Exodus*, 102–08; Donald Juel, *Mark* (Minneapolis: Augsburg, 1990), 34; James R. Edwards, "The Baptism of Jesus According to the Gospel of Mark," *JETS* 34 (1991): 44–5; *contra* Pesch, *Markusevangelium*, 1:90–1, who observes that "*Joseph and Aseneth* 14:2 uses ἐσχίσθη ὁ οὐρανός in a description of a vision that bears no relation to Isa 63:19." But as Buse and Marcus both point out, the heavenly rending is not the only point of contact between Mark 1:10 and Isaiah 63. In Isa 63:11, Yahweh brings his people up out of the sea, just as Jesus here rises up from the water; and in 63:14 the Spirit descends. Note: although Mark's σχίζω differs from Isaiah's ἀνοίγω, σχίζω is actually the closer equivalent of the Hebrew קרע, and ἀνοίγω in Isa 63:19 is actually a unique rendering of this Hebrew verb in the LXX; cf. Watts, *New Exodus*, 103.

⁵³ See Isa 63:11, 12, 13, 15, 16, 19; cf. Joseph Blenkinsopp, *Isaiah 40–55: A New Translation with Introduction and Commentary*, AB 19a (New York: Doubleday, 2002), 263–64.

⁵⁴ Each of these verses has been plausibly suggested behind Mark 1:10, but Guelich (*Mark 1–8:26*, 32) may ultimately be correct that Mark ultimately alludes to the entire leitmotif rather than any one of these texts over the others; cf. Pesch, *Markusevangelium*, 1:91; Gundry, *Mark*, 35. Notably, Collins (*Mark*, 149) observes that the Spirit's descent in Isa 61:1 (πνεῦμα κυρίου ἐπ᾽ ἐμέ) coincides with Yahweh's anointing (ἔχρισεν), which parallels Jesus's description as χριστός in 1:1. Yet the verbal agreements in Mark 1:10 are stronger with Isa 11:2 and 63:14. Mark also alludes to both Isaiah 11 and 42:1 in the immediately following context, as we will see shortly.

⁵⁵ Boring, *Mark*, 45.

From any number of angles, then, we may conclude with Watts that Mark 1:11 is the very "pinnacle of the prologue."[56] And so, as Taylor comments, "The importance of i. 11 cannot be exaggerated."[57]

3.3.1 Defining God's Son: Ps 2:7 in Mark 1:11

It matters all the more, then, that Mark draws the words of 1:11 from Scripture. It is widely agreed that the words σὺ εἶ ὁ υἱός μου ὁ ἀγαπητός, ἐν σοὶ εὐδόκησα are primarily a conflation of Ps 2:7 and Isa 42:1.[58] Aside from a slight variation in word order, the principal clause, σὺ εἶ ὁ υἱός μου, is a near citation of Ps 2:7b LXX: υἱός μου εἶ σύ.[59] The allusion was recognized early on by ancient interpreters including including Justin, Clement of Alexandria, and one NT manuscript.[60] Many, in fact, quote the pronouncement as Ps 2:7 verbatim (υἱός μου εἶ σύ ἐγὼ σήμερον γεγέννηκά σε).[61] According to these interpreters, the pronouncement at Jesus's baptism *is* the pronouncement in Ps 2:7.

As we observed in the previous chapter, Psalm 2 was originally a coronation liturgy for the Davidic king, understood messianically in subsequent Jewish literature. Verse 7, in particular, recounts the psalm's pivotal moment: the decree by which the Lord's "anointed" (משיח/χριστός) is enthroned as "[le] véritable lieutenant de Yahvé sur terre."[62] To allude to the decree in Ps 2:7, then, is to recall the very words with which God enthrones the Messiah as his vice-regent. Even the rhetoric of the pronouncement,

---

[56] Watts, *New Exodus*, 109.
[57] Taylor, *Mark*, 162.
[58] See, *inter alia*, Taylor, *Mark*, 162; Schweizer, *Mark*, 36–8; Lane, *Mark*, 57; Gundry, *Mark*, 49; Donald Juel, *A Master of Surprise: Mark Interpreted* (Minneapolis: Fortress, 1994), 36–7; idem, *Messianic*, 79; Marcus, *Way*, 48–56; idem, *Mark 1–8*, 162, 165–66; Légasse, *Marc*, 91–2; Watts, *New Exodus*, 108–18; Focant, *Marc*, 69; Collins, *Mark*, 150; Black, *Mark*, 59; Hays, *Gospels*, 48, 92, 96. Other scholars over the years have argued for either Ps 2:7 alone (e.g., Lindars, *Apologetic*, 140 n. 2; Vielhauer, "Erwägungen," 205–06; Gnilka, *Markus*, 1:53; Steichele, *Sohn Gottes*, 131–35); or Isa 42:1 alone (e.g., Cullmann, *Christology*, 66; Joachim Jeremias, "παῖς θεοῦ," *TDNT* 5:700–02; Pesch, *Markusevangelium*, 1:92–3).
[59] The difference in word order can be explained as a shift to a more natural word order once the words were removed from the chiasm to which they belong in the psalm, as well as a more emphatic form of personal address, typical of Mark's style elsewhere; cf. Marcus, *Way*, 50; idem, *Mark 1–8*, 162; Watts, *New Exodus*, 111. For the same pattern of address (σύ εἶ...) see 3:11; 8:29; 14:61; and 15:2. Additionally, John S. Kloppenborg ("Variation in the Reproduction of the Double Tradition and an Oral Q?," *ETL* 83 [2007]: 53–80) has demonstrated that ancient writers did not always aim to reproduce source texts verbatim. Among other phenomena that might account for re-phrasings, Kloppenborg calls attention to the common rhetorical practice of *aemulatio*: "the emulation of predecessor texts, a practice that could involve modest verbal transformation, or complete paraphrase, expansion, contraction, or elaboration" (61); cf. Raymond F. Person, "The Ancient Israelite Scribe as Performer," *JBL* 117 (1998): 601–09. To place too much emphasis on the difference in word order is therefore misleading.
[60] Justin, *Dial.* 88.8, 103.6 (*PG* 6:688, 717); Clement of Alexandria, *Paed.* 1.6.25 (*PG* 8:280); and Luke 3:22 in Codex D.
[61] In addition to Justin and Luke 3:22 D above, *Apos. Con.* 2.32; *Gos. Eb.*, frg. 4 (*NTApoc* 1:170); Origen, *Comm. Jo.* 1.32 (*PG* 14:77); Methodius, *Symp.*, 8.9 (*PG* 18:152); Lactantius, *Inst. Div.*, 4.15 (*PL* 6:491a); and Hilary, *Trin.*, 11.18 (*PL* 10:412b) all quote the baptismal voice as Ps 2:7. For these interpreters, the words at Jesus's baptism were apparently interchangeable with those of the psalm.
[62] Jean-Bernard Dumortier, "Un Rituel D'Intronisation: Le Ps. Lxxxix 2-38," *VT* 22 (1972): 176–96, here 187.

σὺ εἶ ὁ υἱός μου, mimics the rhetoric of God's decree in the psalm as a performative utterance meant to establish the authority of his Messiah over the nations.[63] The effect is to transfer the climax of the psalm to the climax of the prologue, so as to say, "this is that and then is now."

3.3.2 "My Servant in Whom My Soul Delights" (Isaiah 42:1)

The allusion to Isa 42:1 that follows is initially less obivous, but ultimately stands on firm evidence.[64] Although Mark's phrase, ἐν σοὶ εὐδόκησα, shares no words in common with Isa 42:1 LXX, it bears a strong resemblance to several other versions of Isa 42:1. Both Theodotion and Symmachus render the Hebrew רצתה εὐδόκησεν rather than προσεδέξατο, as does Matt 12:18 (ὁ ἀγαπητός μου ὃν εὐδόκησεν ἡ ψυχή μου).[65] The equivalent of "in whom I have been well pleased" also appears throughout *Targum Isaiah*, not only in *Tg. Isa.* 42:1, but also 41:8-9, 43:1, 10, and 44:1-2.[66] When one also takes into account the motif of the Spirit's descent in Mark 1:10 (cf. Isa 42:1: ἔδωκα τὸ πνεῦμά μου ἐπ' αὐτόν), the allusion is readily apparent.[67]

As Marcus comments, the allusion to Isa 42:1 "points in a similar eschatological direction [to Ps 2:7], since in that passage the Lord's righteous servant has been chosen for an eschatological task (cf. the messianic interpretation in *Tg. Isa.* 42:1)."[68] Yet many Markan interpreters continue to assume that Mark here holds in tension two distinct Christologies: a "servant" Christology, represented by Isa 42:1, in addition to the royal, messianic Christology, represented by Ps 2:7.[69] This notion seemingly has its roots in an earlier stratum of scholarship once championed by Bousset and Jeremias, which

---

[63] So also Botner, *Son of David*, 87. On performative utterances, see J. L. Austin, *How to Do Things with Words*, 2nd ed., The William James Lectures (Oxford: Clarendon, 1975), 53–66. As Austin explains, a performative utterance differs from merely descriptive language; rather it comprises a kind of action in which something is made to be so precisely by pronouncing it so: e.g., "I now pronounce you husband and wife," or "Out!" in a baseball game.

[64] It is unclear to me when this connection was first made since it is seemingly absent from the writings of the church fathers, medieval interpreters, and Reformers. However, it is already known to Reimarus (*Fragments*, 83); and appears in John Owen (*The Works of John Owen*, 16 vols, ed. W. H. Goold [London: Banner of Truth Trust, 1965], 1:88); C. H. Spurgeon (see *Sermon 1727* in C. H. Spurgeon, *The Metropolitan Tabernacle Pulpit: Containing Sermons Preached and Revised*, 56 vols [Pasadena, Texas: Pilgrim Publications, 1973], 29:351); Matthew Henry (*Matthew Henry's Commentary on the Whole Bible*, 6 vols [Peabody: Hendrickson, 2009], 5:24); and John Gill (*Gill's Commentary*, 6 vols [Grand Rapids: Baker, 1980], 5:23).

[65] Additionally, Watts ("Mark," in *CNTUOT*, 122) observes that εὐδοκέω is the most common rendering of התרצ elsewhere in the LXX.

[66] So also Bruce D. Chilton, *A Galilean Rabbi and His Bible: Jesus' Use of the Interpreted Scripture of His Time* (London: SPCK, 1984), 128–30; Marcus, Way, 53; Watts, "Mark," in *CNTUOT*, 122–23.

[67] Cf. Jeremias, "παῖς θεοῦ," *TDNT* 5:701-02.

[68] Marcus, *Mark 1-8*, 166. Additionally, Marcus, building on the earlier scholarship of B. W. Bacon, argues persuasively that the aorist εὐδόκησα signifies "God's past election of Christ ... *for an eschatological work*" (emphasis original); see Marcus, Way, 73–4; B. W. Bacon, "Notes on New Testament Passages," *JBL* 16 (1897): 136-39; idem, "Supplementary Note on the Aorist εὐδόκησα, Mark i. 11," *JBL* 20 (1901): 28–30; cf. Lohmeyer, *Markus*, 24; Gundry, *Use*, 31–2.

[69] See e.g, Boring (*Mark*, 46), who finds a "tension between royal power as God's anointed Son and human weakness as the Suffering Servant"; or Collins (*Mark*, 150): "Mark interprets Jesus as both the messiah and the Servant of the Lord."

postulated the existence of a servant Christology represented by παῖς μου beneath υἱὸς μου in Mark 1:11.[70] But while the identity of Isaiah's servant varies among ancient sources, in some corners of Jewish tradition, the servant is explicitly the Messiah Son of David (e.g., *Tg. Isa.* 43:10; 52:13; cf. Acts 4:25, 27, 30; *Did.* 9:2).[71]

Indeed, Botner has recently shown that some features of Isaiah 42 help facilitate a Davidic interpretation.[72] First, the language used to describe this figure is decidely royal; the terms עבדי, "my servant," and בחירי, "my chosen one," "show strong affinity within Davidic traditions."[73] Second, in the overarching scheme of the Isaianic corpus, the servant takes up "the same vocation" as the root of Jesse from Isa 11:1-10.[74] Indeed, many Jewish and Christian Messiah texts view the servant of YHWH (Isa 42:1-7) and the root of Jesse (Isa 11:1-10) as "the *same* figure."[75]

For our purposes, however, there is an even more important fact at hand. In some Jewish texts, the servant of Isa 42:1 and the royal Messiah of Psalm 2 are also the *same* figure. References to Psalm 2 and Isa 42:1 appear alongside one another not only in the Gospels, but in *Ps. Sol.* 17:21, *1 Enoch* 48–49, and *Midr. Ps.* 2.9. Midrash Psalm 2:9 is especially noetworthy since it cites Isa 42:1 (as well as 52:13) as a gloss on Ps 2:7, identifying Psalm 2's "son" and Isaiah's "servant" alike as the Davidic Messiah.[76] More likely than not, these two texts appear together in Mark 1:11 for the same reason that they appeared together elsewhere: both were understood to refer to the Davidic Messiah.

In view of such evidence, it is worth reiterating two of Juel's conclusions from over forty years ago: (1) "There is no basis for speaking of a 'paidology,' as if there existed in early Christian circles a distinct constellation of images revolving aroud Isaiah's servant"; and (2) "There is no cause to separate Psalm 2 and Isaiah 42 into distinct

---

[70] See the excursus below.

[71] Acts 4:25-30 clearly links Jesus's designation as παῖς to David's designation as παῖς; cf. *Did.* 9:2. As Juel (*Messianic*, 131) recognizes, this is "royal language, appropriate ... to the Messiah-King." Alternatively, Isa 42:1 LXX intrepets the Servant as Jacob/Israel; while Isa 48:9-10; 49:6 speak of the Servant as one who will restore the tribes of Jacob/Israel. Sirach 11:12-13 also appears to understand the Servant as an individual. Targum Isaiah 52:13 explicitly refers to "My servant, the Messiah"; cf. Juel, *Messianic*, 121–24. Juel (127) concludes that "there is no evidence of an overall interpretation of the servant passages in Isaiah." With respect to Targum Isaiah, however, it should be noted that *Tg. Isa.* 41:8-9 also identifies the servant as "Israel" and "Jacob." For the targumist, then, it is also possible that "Israel" and "Messiah" are not mutually exclusive options.

[72] Botner, *Son of David*, 91–2.

[73] See דוד עבדי or עבדי דוד 1 Chr 17:4; Ps 89:4, 21-22; Isa 37:35; Jer 33:21, 22, 26; Ezek 34:23, 24; 27:24; Hag 2:23; Zech 3:8; as well as יריחבל in Ps 89:4. Botner (*Son of David*, 91) claims that such language is "unequivocally royal." But as Juel (*Messianic*, 125) observes, servant-of-God language can apply to a number of figures in Scripture, including Abraham (Gen 26:24); Moses (Num 12:7; Josh 1:2, 7, 13; Dan 9:11); Elijah (1 Kings 18:36); Jacob/Israel (Isa 41:8; 48:20); the righteous (Proverbs and Psalms, *passim*; cf. Wis. 2:13); or the prophets (2 Chr 36:5 LXX; Jer 35:15). Nevertheless, Botner's basic point stands insofar as "servant" and "chosen" language refers to David far more often than to any other figure.

[74] Both (1) receive YHWH's Spirit (11:2/42:1); (2) to establish justice (11:3-5/42:1-4); (3) bring about Israel's "new exodus" (11:10-16/42:6-7); and (4) draw the gentiles to worship YHWH (11:9-10/42:4, 10-13).

[75] Botner, *Son of David*, 92.

[76] Cf. *Midr. Ps.* 2.4, which also applies Isa 42:13 to the Messiah. A close relationship between Psalm 2 and Isaiah's Servant Songs permeates the entire midrash.

branches of interpretive tradition."[77] On the contrary, we have cause to do just the opposite. Properly understood, Mark's allusion to Isa 42:1 reinforces the use of Ps 2:7 suggested above: Mark points to Jesus as the Spirit-anointed royal Messiah who will accomplish God's purposes at the turn of the ages, and this takes place precisely where Mark first introduces Jesus into the narrative. As Hays writes, Jesus's baptism is thus a "disguised royal anointing"—but for those with ears to hear, the disguise is a thin one.[78]

3.4 Excursus: Mark 1:11 in Twentieth-Century Interpretation

Despite the strength of the evidence above, some scholars have occasionally doubted Mark's use of Ps 2:7 in 1:11. In recent years, a few scholars have challenged the majority view, arguing that the connection between the heavenly voice and the psalm is precise at only two words (υἱός μου) since Mark's word order differs from that of Ps 2:7 LXX (υἱός μου εἶ σύ).[79] More substantially, such scholars commonly argue that υἱός has replaced παῖς (from Isa 42:1) in the original text of Mark.

In point of fact, the entire lineage of objections against Ps 2:7 can be traced back to a single comment by Gustaf Dalman near the turn of the twentieth century, even though Dalman himself did not doubt the presence of Ps 2:7 in the baptismal voice.[80] Given the importance of this allusion for Markan interpretation, it is worth retracing this history in detail. In actuality, there have never been many objections to the proposed allusion to Ps 2:7, but essentially one objection, raised on faulty premises, which has been repeated too often.

3.4.1 From Dalman to Bousset and Bousset to Jeremias and Onward

In his influential work, *Die Worte Jesu*, Gustaf Dalman argued the conclusion shared by most interpreters today that the voice at Jesus's baptism represents a conflation of Ps 2:7 and Isa 42:1. Sensibly, Dalman also asked what might account for the conflation of these two verses in the first place. To this end, Daman observed that παῖς, which translates עבד in Isa 42:1 LXX, can also mean "child" or "son."[81] So Dalman proposed that, owing to this semantic overlap, the παῖς of Isa 42:1 was later connected with the υἱός of Ps 2:7.[82] Although Dalman himself did not doubt the presence of Ps 2:7 in addition to Isa 42:1, his suggestion provided the basis for others who did.

---

[77] Juel, *Messianic*, 132.
[78] Hays, *Gospels*, 48.
[79] See, e.g., Bretscher, "Exodus 4:22-23," 301–11; Jeffrey A. Gibbs, "Israel Standing with Israel: The Baptism of Jesus in Matthew's Gospel (Matt 3:13-17)," *CBQ* 64 (2002): 511–26; Heil, "Wild Animals," 70–1; Huizenga, *New Isaac*, 156–58.
[80] Gustaf Hermann Dalman, *Die Worte Jesu: mit Berücksichtigung des Nachkanonischen Jüdischen Schrifttums und der Armäischen Sprache* (Leipzig: J. C. Hinrichs'sche, 1898); ET: *The Words of Jesus: Considered in the Light of Post-Biblical Jewish Writings and the Aramaic Language*, trans. D. M. Kay (Edinburgh: T&T Clark, 1902).
[81] Dalman, *Words*, 276–80.
[82] Ibid.

Dalman's claim that the terms παῖς and υἱός were interchangeable was assumed, yet taken in a different direction by Bousset, who proposed that Isa 42:1 comprised the original background of the heavenly voice to the exclusion of any reference to Ps 2:7. As noted earlier, Bousset believed "Son of God" had "a much too mythical ring" to have arisen from the early Palestinian (i.e., Jewish) Christian community.[83] Instead, he proposed that the designation παῖς μου ("my servant"), which he claimed was a product of the "primitive Christian messianology of Deutero-Isaiah," lay beneath the designation υἱός μου ("my son").[84] The designation was later changed to υἱός μου only after the primitive Palestinian tradition came under the influence of Hellenism. On this reconstruction, Ps 2:7 originally played no part in the voice at Jesus's baptism or transfiguration (Mark 1:11; 9:7).[85] So originated the "paidology," or servant Christology, hypothesis, as well as its supposed contrast with an exalted, royal Christology.

Bousset's hypothesis proved influential to both Cullmann and Jeremias, the latter of whom explicitly acknowledged his dependence on Bousset.[86] It was Jeremias who then gave the argument its lasting shape. Jeremias began by noting that Isa 42:1 not only contains several terms thought to have influenced Mark 1:11, but also mentions the descent of the Spirit found in Mark 1:10. Since, Jeremias reasoned, 1:11 serves as a confirmation that the promise of the Spirit has just been fulfilled, Isa 42:1 fits the context better than Ps 2:7. Jeremias also observed that one variation of the heavenly pronouncement (Luke 9:35) contains ἐκλελεγμένος instead of ἀγαπητός, which forms a parallel with ὁ ἐκλεκτός μου in Isa 42:1.[87] These two factors, combined with the basic premise inherited from Bousset that υἱός μου could easily have replaced the more primitive designation παῖς μου, led Jeremias to the conclusion that Isa 42:1 accounts for the wording of the baptismal voice in its entirety, without any influence from Ps 2:7.

What is crucial to note at this point is that seemingly every interpreter who has doubted the allusion to Ps 2:7 at Jesus's baptism since Jeremias has done so in explicit dependence on him.[88] Indeed Juel, when countering this view, cites Jeremias.[89] To reiterate, however, Jeremias himself cites Bousset, who cites Dalman.

Under scrutiny, the entire chain of arguments above proves problematic.

1. To begin with, many of Jeremias's arguments are in fact good arguments for the presence of Isa 42:1; yet Jeremias's positive argument *for* the presence of an allusion to Isa 42:1 in no way diminishes the possibility that Mark may have alluded to other texts as well, such as Ps 2:7.[90] The impetus for thinking so derives purely from the *a priori*

---

[83] Bousset, *Kyrios*, 93.
[84] Ibid., 96–7.
[85] Ibid., 95–6.
[86] See Jeremias, "παῖς θεοῦ," *TDNT* 5:701–02; Oscar Cullmann, *Die Tauflehre des Neuen Testaments Erwachsenen- und Kindertaufe*, ATANT 12 (Zürich: Zwingli, 1948), 11–13. Jeremias explicitly mentions Bousset and, secondarily, Ernst Lohmeyer (*Gottesknecht und Davidsohn*, SymBU 5 [Västervik: C.O. Ekblad, 1945], 9).
[87] Jeremias, "παῖς θεοῦ," *TDNT* 5:701–02.
[88] So, e.g., Reginald H. Fuller, *The Mission and Achievement of Jesus: An Examination of the Presuppositions of New Testament Theology* (Chicago: Alec R. Allenson, 1956), 55; Cranfield, *Mark*, 54–5; Cullmann, *Christology*, 66; Jeremias, "παῖς θεοῦ," *TDNT* 5:700–02; Pesch, *Markusevangelium*, 1:92–3; Gibbs, "Israel," 511–12; Heil, "Wild Animals," 70–1; Huizenga, *New Isaac*, 156–58.
[89] Juel, *Messianic*, 79.
[90] See similarly Marshall, "Son of God," 328.

assumption that the presentation of Jesus as the Isaianic *servant* stands in conflict with his portrayal as the *Son* of God. As we have already seen, however, this assumption runs counter to the actual evidence. In reality, Psalm 2 and Isa 42:1 are cited together in at least three other Jewish texts, including two that certainly predate Mark (see above). The reason for this textual association—and the more likely answer to Dalman's original question—is that both the psalm's "son" and Isaiah's "servant" could be (and were) interpreted as the Davidic Messiah. Hence, the two designations are anything but incompatible.

2. Even if the variant of ἀγαπητός (ἐκλελεγμένος) in Luke 9:35 does point toward Isa 42:1, it is a variant of ἀγαπητός, *not* υἱός or any other feature from Ps 2:7.[91] This, too, is only an argument *for* Isa 42:1, not an argument *against* Ps 2:7.

3. Even more critical, the base assumption that παῖς and υἱός were interchangeable is highly questionable. Despite some semantic overlap between the two words, Steichele demonstrates that, in fact, the LXX distinguishes between the two terms with remarkable consistency, and the NT appears to follow suit. When used of Christ, παῖς is never interchanged with υἱός.[92]

4. As Juel points out, "in the NT, *pais* is not even a title" at all.[93] Likeiwse, "'Servant of God,' whether in Greek or Hebrew, is never treated as a title like Christ."[94]

5. Bousset and Jeremias each postulate that the designation παῖς θεοῦ was "avoided" very early on in Hellenistic circles because of its perceived incompatibility with the confession of Jesus as υἱὸς θεοῦ. But in that case, it is an unexplained mystery that παῖς (θεοῦ) continues to appear, not only in Acts (3:13, 26; 4:27, 30), but also in the writings of apostolic Christianity (*1 Clem.* 59:2, 3, 4; *Mart. Pol.* 14:1, 3; 20:2; *Diog.* 8:9, 11; 9:1; *Did.* 9:2-3; 10:2-3). Why should this supposed "pre-Marcan" stratum of early tradition be preserved in these later texts, yet not in so much as a single textual variant of the baptism pericopae in any one of the Gospels?[95]

6. Finally, there is simply no actual evidence for the conjecture that a substitution from παῖς (θεοῦ) to υἱός (θεοῦ) ever took place in the Gospels or in any text whatsoever.

What should be recognized in retrospect is that Bousset's original conjecture was driven less by firm evidence than by three critical assumptions that: (a) υἱός θεοῦ is mythological in character and so could not have arisen on Palestinian soil;[96] (b) "Servant of God" and "Son of God" are contradictory and incompatible designations;[97] and

---

[91] See again Marshall, "Son of God," 328. Yet it is not entirely certain that Luke 9:35 does allude to the ἐκλεκτός of Isa 42:1. Ἐκλεκτός also appears in Ps 88:20 LXX, as an epithet of David, and in Ps 105:23, where it refers to Moses. None of these would be out of place in the context of Jesus's transfiguration in Luke 9:28-36.

[92] Steichele, *Der leidende Sohn*, 126–7. As Steichele observes, υἱός is never a translation for the 807 occurrences of the Hebrew עבד in the LXX and, apart from Prov 4:1, παῖς is never a translation for the 207 occurrences of בן. In a several instances in the NT in which παῖς bears the sense of "boy" or "child" (e.g., Matt 2:16; 17:18; 21:15; Luke 2:43; 8:51, 54; 9:42), and one in which παῖς and υἱός are used interchangeably (John 4:46-53); but παῖς clearly bears the sense of "Servant," as in "Servant of God," in all of its uses as a designation of Jesus, most of which are in Acts (Matt 12:18; Acts 3:13, 26; 4:27, 30).

[93] Juel, *Messianic*, 79.

[94] Ibid., 124.

[95] Quotation from Jeremias, "παῖς θεοῦ," *TDNT* 5:702; Bousset (*Kyrios*, 95–6) implies the same.

[96] Bousset, *Kyrios*, 93.

[97] Ibid., 96.

(c) the Messiah was never thought of as Son of God in early Judaism (in his own words, "Son of God" has "nothing ... to do with Jewish-primitive Christian messianology").[98] Each of these assumptions has proven false in light of subsequent research.

3.4.2 Reassessing the Assumptions

Already in 1898, Dalman was able to write that "The second Psalm is generally reckoned the principal biblical source of the designations, 'Son of God' and 'Anointed' (Messiah), as applied to the King of the Messianic age."[99] As we have observed, Ps 2:6-7 probably recalls the promise of divine sonship to David's heirs in 2 Sam 7:14, which is echoed in other texts as well. But it is Psalm 2 that accounts for the fundamental linkage of the terms משיח/χριστός and בני/υἱός μου.

At the time, however, Dalman was able to account for only a few messianic readings of Psalm 2 in later literature (*Ps. Sol.* 17:23-24; *Midr. Ps.* 2:7; *b. Sukkah* 52a).[100] These few examples notwithstanding, he concluded from the paucity of evidence that "Ps. 2 was not of decisive importance in the Jewish conception of the Messiah, and that 'Son of God' was not a common Messianic title."[101] Yet, as we witnessed in the previous chapter, more recent discoveries have led many scholars to conclude otherwise on the basis of nine examples rather than three.[102]

But even if Dalman were entirely correct, Bousset and many others after him unfortunately disregarded his important qualifier "common" in the sentence quoted above. In actuality, Dalman did not say that Son of God was *never* used as a messianic title.[103] To the contrary, Dalman affirmed that, insofar as the Messiah was thought of as the Son of God, Psalm 2 is the principal source of that association. In any case, Psalm 2 now appears to have been more influential for Jewish messianism than Dalman or those soon after him realized, and the Davidic Messiah was likewise thought of as God's "son" more commonly than earlier generations of scholars supposed.[104] The clear precedents for son-of-God language in Jewish literature in and outside of the Bible are enough to discredit Bousset's first assumption that "Son of God" could not have arisen out of early Jewish Christianity.[105] Given such precedents, neither can one assume that the designation is "mythical" (i.e., metaphysical) in origin (Bousset's third assumption).[106]

---

[98] Ibid., 93, 97.
[99] Dalman, *Words*, 268. Dalman's comment remains in force today; see e.g., Collins and Collins, *King and Messiah, passim.*
[100] Dalman, *Words*, 268–73.
[101] Ibid., 272.
[102] Again, see 1Q28a II, 11-12; 4Q174 I, 18-19; 4Q246 I, 9–II, 1; *Ps. Sol.* 17:23-24; *1 En.* 48:8-10; *Sib. Or.* 3:652-664; *4 Ezra* 13:31-37; *Midr. Ps.* 2; *b. Sukkah* 52a:6.
[103] Yet, the claim that Son of God was *never* a messianic title is precisely the point in support of which Bousset (*Kyrios*, 93) cites Dalman.
[104] See Collins and Collins, *Son of God, passim* on this very point.
[105] For that matter, one could also note the frequent description of Israel as God's Son: e.g., Exod 4:22; Jer 31:9; 31:20; Hos 11:1; *Jub.* 2:20; 19:29; 4Q504 III.5-6; *Pss. Sol.* 13:9; 18:4; and in the plural: Deut 1:31; 14:1; Hos 1:10; 11:10; Isa 63:8; Sir 36:11; Wis 18:13; cf. 5:5, *T. Levi* 18:8; *T. Jud.* 24:3; *Jub.* 1:24-25, 28; *Sib. Or.* 3:702.
[106] Or even if the designation *is* found to imply metaphysical content, it is a misstep in logic to assume that it could not then have roots in Israel's Scriptures.

As it happens, Reimarus was much closer to the mark when he reasoned (more than a century before Dalman) that "to be called 'Son of God' and 'Christ the Messiah' mean one and the same thing."[107] Though Reimarus's compression of these titles into one is ultimately reductionistic, he had the foresight to see what subsequent research has indicated: that Son of David, Messiah, and Son of God (and, in some cases, even "Servant of Yahweh") alike served as messianic epithets derived from the Jewish Scriptures. Wherever Son of God (or "my son," per Ps 2:7) is found to be messianic, it can hardly be said to contradict Son of David or any other messianic epithets. As we have seen, *b. Sukkah* 52a identifies the "son" of Psalm 2 as the "Messiah, *Son of David*." Similarly, it is a mistake, in view of the messianic and Davidic uses of παῖς in *Targum Isaiah* and in Acts to suggest that υἱός (θεοῦ) and παῖς (θεοῦ) stand in conflict with one another. Properly understood, the two designations are complementary rather than contradictory. So crumbles the last of Bousset's (and Jeremias's) assumptions.

The upshot of the foregoing rehearsal is that the perennial case against the presence of Ps 2:7 in Mark 1:11, which has been repeated on occasion with little variation for more than a century now, was conceived on entirely erroneous premises in the first place. The best evidence has always supported the original contention, unquestioned prior to the twentieth century, that the words σὺ εἶ ὁ υἱός μου are a distinct allusion to Ps 2:7. The arguments to the contrary should be laid to rest.

3.5 A Storied Metalepsis: Psalm 2 in Mark's Prologue

So far, we have seen that Mark alludes to Ps 2:7 (the climax of Psalm 2) at the climax of his own prologue and that there are good reasons to expect this initial definition of what it means to be υἱὸς θεοῦ to exert a shaping influence over the narrative moving forward.[108] As it happens, the first hints that it actually does so occur immediately in Mark's brief temptation narrative (1:12-13) and the transition that follows (1:14-15). The thematic connections to Psalm 2 in these verses are not immediately obvious, yet they become apparent when one glances back at 1:9-15 as a whole, and even more so in light of Mark's broader use of Scripture in these verses.

3.5.1 The Wilderness Battle: Jesus's Temptation in Mark 1:12-13

Scholars regularly acknowledge the continuity between Jesus's baptism and temptation in all three of the Synoptic Gospels.[109] In Mark, both the quick transition (καὶ εὐθὺς)

---

[107] Reimarus, *Fragments*, 83.

[108] As we saw in the previous chapter, the norm among Jewish and Christian sources alike was, in fact, to allude to Psalm 2 with the enitre plot of the psalm in mind, with many texts making extended allusions to the psalm throughout (e.g., *Ps. Sol.* 17; *1 En.* 48–50; Acts 4; 13; Revelation; and nearly all of the church fathers). Both the broader and the more specific tendency again exemplify what Jeannine Brown ("Metalepsis," 29) calls "storied metalepsis": the recollection of an entire story, or plot, by another.

[109] So Alan Richardson, *An Introduction to the Theology of the New Testament* (New York: Harper, 1959), 150; Birger Gerhardsson, *The Testing of God's Son. (Matt. 4: 1-11 & Par.): An Analysis of an Early Christian Midrash*, ConBNT 2 (Lund: Gleerup, 1966), 20; William Richard Stegner, *Narrative*

and the ongoing action of the Spirit in 1:12 (cf. 1:10) suggest that what transpires in the wilderness somehow follows as a consequence of the Spirit-anointing that took place with Jesus's baptism. Yet precisely *how* 1:12-13 coheres with 1:9-11 is a matter of some debate.

On the one hand, the setting in the wilderness, the specific duration of forty days, and the theme of testing remind many of Israel's forty years of testing in the wilderness.[110] So, as Alan Richardson suggests, Jesus recapitulates Israel's experience in his baptism and temptation alike: "[a]s Israel of old, the 'son' whom God called out of Egypt, was baptized in the Red Sea and tempted in the Wilderness, so also Jesus is baptized in the Jordan and tempted in the wilderness."[111] In support of such an interpretation, J. P. Heil observes a number of thematic and linguistic parallels with Deut 8:1-16 in particular (see Table 3.1).[112]

Others focus on Ps 91 (90 LXX):10-13 as the key to understanding Mark 1:13, since the psalm is unique for its depiction of an individual standing between beasts, on the one hand, and ministering angels, on the other.[113] The relevant portion of the psalm reads:

> No evil shall come before you, and no scourge shall come near your tent, for he will command his angels concerning you to guard you in all your ways (ὅτι τοῖς ἀγγέλοις αὐτοῦ ἐντελεῖται περὶ σοῦ τοῦ διαφυλάξαι σε ἐν πάσαις ταῖς ὁδοῖς σου); on their hands they will bear you up, lest you strike your foot against a stone. On the asp and the basilisk you will tread, and you will trample the lion and the dragon under foot.
>
> Ps 90:10-13 LXX

Table 3.1 Comparison of Mark 1:12-13 and Deut 8:1-16

Mark 1:12-13	Deut 8:1-16
God's Spirit "drives out" (ἐκβάλλει) Jesus into the wilderness (ἔρημον) (1:12)	God "led out" (ἐξαγαγόντος) Israel through the wilderness (ἐρήμου) (8:14-15)
"forty days" (1:13)	"forty years" (8:2, 4)
tested/tempted (πειραζόμενος) (1:13)	"to test/tempt" (ἐκπειράσῃ) them (8:2, 16)
As God's Son (1:11)	... and so train/teach Israel as God's son (8:5)

Theology in Early Jewish Christianity (Louisville: Westminster John Knox, 1989), 49; Jeffrey B. Gibson, "Jesus' Wilderness Temptation According to Mark," *JSNT* 53 (1994): 3-34, here 8. As Gerhardsson also notes, every account of Jesus's temptation is linked to a preceding account of his baptism (cf. Matt 3:13-4:13; Luke 3:21-4:13).

[110] See, e.g., Robert W. Funk, "The Wilderness," *JBL* 78 (1959): 205-14; Mauser, *Wilderness*, 77-102; Stegner, *Narrative*, 49; idem, "Wilderness and Testing in the Scrolls and in Matthew 4:1-11," *BR* 12 (1967): 18-27; Gibson, "Wilderness Temptation," 3-34.
[111] Richardson, *Introduction*, 150; also quoted in Stegner, *Narrative*, 49.
[112] Heil, "Wild Animals," 73-4.
[113] So Gibson, "Wilderness Temptation," 21-2; Hooker, *Mark*, 51; Ardel B Caneday, "Mark's Provocative Use of Scripture in Narration: 'He Was with the Wild Animals and Angels Ministered to Him,'" *BBR* 9 (1999): 19-36; Boring, *Mark*, 48; Collins, *Mark*, 151-53; Botner, *Son of David*, 97-8.

Mark's phrase, καὶ οἱ ἄγγελοι διηκόνουν αὐτῷ, is particularly evocative of the psalm (cf. Matt 4:11). At Qumran (11Q11) and in other early Jewish texts (e.g., *LAB* 59:4; *b. Šebu.* 15b), Psalm 91 is also closely associated with exorcism and protection against the demonic.[114]

For our purposes, it is important to note that the psalm may have been associated with the king from the start and is, in any case, associated with David both in the LXX and at Qumran.[115] Intriguingly, *Tg. Ps.* 91:2-8 not only makes David the speaker, but imagines his son, Solomon, as the recipient of David's words in these verses.[116] In response, Solomon turns to God and expresses his total confidence in him (v. 9), whereupon God speaks vv. 10-13 to Solomon directly. Though the targum dates to a later century (c. fourth–sixth CE), Psalm 91 is already associated with Solomon's triumph over demonic forces in 11Q11.[117] There is substantial evidence, then, that many readers in Mark's time assumed that the speaker/addressee was not only a royal figure, but in fact a Davidide, thus offering another point of continuity between Mark 1:12-13 and 1:9-11, and with Psalm 2.[118]

The two scriptural backgrounds noted above are not mutually exclusive; both Matthew and Luke quote Deut 8:3 and Ps 91:11-12 alike in their expansions of Mark 1:12-13, and there is a unifying thread between these intertexts themselves since Psalm 91 also appears to recall Israel's time in the wilderness—particularly in the image of YHWH spreading his "pinions" (אברתו) and "wings" (כנפיו) to protect Israel through the wilderness (cf. Ps 91:4; Deut 32:10-11).[119] As John Goldingay comments, the psalm implies that "the king will continue to have Israel's experience."[120] Throughout Jesus's baptism and temptation together (1:9-13), then, we may say (in modification of Richardson's words above) that, just as God's royal son, the king, was expected to recapitulate God's son, Israel's, experience, so Jesus realizes the king's and Israel's destinies at once as God's anointed Son, the royal Messiah (cf. Psalm 2).

---

[114] Cf. Susan R. Garrett, *The Temptations of Jesus in Mark's Gospel* (Grand Rapids: Eerdmans, 1998), 58; Collins, *Mark*, 151-52; Botner, *Son of David*, 99-101 (especially concerning *LAB* 59.4).

[115] Though Though the (see, e.g., Zenger, *Psalms 2*, 432), many interpreters also consider the speaker in the psalm to be most probably the king (so Eaton, *Kingship*, 17; Mitchell J. Dahood, *Psalms 2: 51–100: Introduction, Translation, and Notes*, AB 16b (Garden City, NY: Doubleday, 1966), 329; Goldingay, *Psalms*, 3:39). Ps 90 LXX contains the ascription Αἶνος ᾠδῆς τῷ Δαυείδ; 11Q11 5.4 similarly reads לדויד.

[116] In particular, *Tg. Ps.* 91:4-8 reads: "You [Solomon] will not be afraid of the terror of the *dermons that go about in* the night, nor of the arrow *of the angel of death that he shoots* in the daytime ... You [Solomon] will only look with your eyes, and you will see *how the wicked are being destroyed*" (trans. David M. Stec, *The Targum of Psalms: Translated with a Critical Introduction, Apparatus, and Notes*, ArBib 16 [London: T&T Clark, 2004], 174–75, his italics.).

[117] See 11Q11 2.2-3; 5:4-13. The recension of Psalm 91 in column 5 follows fragments of several apocryphal psalms intended for use in exorcism, in which Solomon is mentioned explicitly; cf. Collins, *Mark*, 152.

[118] See similarly Botner, *Son of David*, 99.

[119] Cf. Matt 4:4, 6; Luke 4:4, 10-11; and see, e.g., David C. Mitchell, *The Message of the Psalter: An Eschatological Programme in the Book of Psalms*, JSOTSup 252 (Sheffield: Sheffield Academic, 1997), 277–78; cf. Goldingay, *Psalms 3*, 40–7. Deuteronomy 32, in turn, is closely tied to Deuteronomy 8. Moreover, Psalm 91 is generally thought to have been attached to (and possibly composed with) Psalm 90, "the Song of Moses"; see Zenger, *Psalms 2*, 432; Marvin E. Tate, *Psalms 51-100*, WBC 20 (Dallas: Word, 1990), 452–53.

[120] Goldingay, *Psalms*, 2:47; cf. 3:41.

Finally, Richard Bauckham has presented a compelling case that Mark's reference to Jesus "with the wild animals" (καὶ ἦν μετὰ τῶν θηρίων) may be an allusion to the messianic peace envisioned by Isa 11:1-9. Contrary to the general assumption that the wild animals are hostile to Jesus in 1:13, Bauckham observes that μετ generally expresses a sense of "close, friendly association elsewhere" in Mark (3:14; 5:18; 14:67; cf. 4:36).[121] Rather than hostility, then, Bauckham argues that Mark's phrase naturally implies Jesus's peaceful coexistence with the animals—an image that readily recalls the peace between animals and humans alike enacted by the root of Jesse in Isa 11:6-9. Isaiah 11:6-9 was, in fact, the *locus classicus* for the concept of eschatological peace all members of creation, as recalled by *Sib. Or.* 3:788-95; *2 Bar.* 73:6; Philo, *Praem.* 87-90; and Irenaeus, *Ad. Haer.* 5.33.3. In this case, the image of Jesus with the wild animals continues the image of his anointing in 1:10-11 so that Mark 1:9-13 combined mirror the progression of Isa 11:1-9: following his receipt of God's Spirit, the Davidic Messiah begins to enact the messianic peace in the wilderness.

Although interpreters often feel the need to adjudicate between this interpretation and one or more of the others noted above, I do not believe it is necessary to do so. Instead, we should consider what these several probable intertexts share in common. We have already observed one common thread between Deuteronomy 8 and Psalm 91. Psalm 91 and Isa 11:1-9, in turn, are united by their mutual assocation with David's lineage, not unlike Ps 2:7 and Isaiah 42:1 in Mark 1:11. We will see still further connections between these intertexts below, but in the meantime, I wish to suggest the following interpretation of Mark 1:12-13: Jesus is portrayed as (a) the Davidic Messiah who (b) recapitulates Israel's experience of testing in the wilderness as he (c) battles Satan and d.) triumphs, so as to prefigure the messianic peace envisioned by Isaiah 11. In this way, Mark 1:12-13 advances virtually all of the themes in 1:9-11, including the recapitulation of Israel, the "new exodus," and, interwoven between them all, Jesus's identity as the royal Messiah-Son of God. Likewise, 1:12-13 carries over prominent themes found in Psalm 2.

3.5.2 Wrapping up the Prologue: Psalm 2 and Mark 1:12-15

Whereas in the psalm, the anointed king, God's "son," triumphs over the forces hostile to God's reign (often understood in cosmic terms by subsequent interpreters), so Jesus, the anointed Son of God overcomes Satan.[122] As we saw in the previous chapter, Psalm 2 was commonly associated with the Messiah's eschatological battle against the forces opposed to God's reign; indeed, it was recalled so often for the motif of eschatological, cosmic battle[123] that Lövestam suggests that Ps 2:1-2 is perhaps the classic text

---

[121] Bauckham, "Wild Animals," 5; cf. Marcus, *Mark 1–8*, 168. In addition to Bauckham's brief list of more obvious examples, one may add numerous others that indicate "friendly association" or, at the least, allegiance for the time being: 1:20, 29, 36; 2:16, 19, 25; 3:6, 7; 5:24, 40; 8:10, 38; 9:8; 11:11; 14:14, 17; 15:1, 7, 31. In no instance does Mark use μετά to indicate an adverse relationship between two parties.

[122] See especially 4Q174 1:18-19 where the hostile kings and nations in Ps 2:1-2 are understood to be the forces of "Belial" (לעילב); cf. Midrash Psalm 2; Rev 11:15, 18; 19:19.

[123] Recall, e.g., *Ps. Sol.* 17:12, 22; *1 En.* 48:8-10; 4Q174 1:18-19; *Sib. Or.* 3:663-664; *4 Ezra* 13:31; *Midr. Ps.* 2 *ad loc.*; Rev 11:15, 18; 17:18; 19:19; cf. Acts 4:25-29.

"associated with the idea of [demonic] opposition, rebellion, and the hostile attack upon God, the Messiah, and Israel."[124] In Ps 2:8-12, then, it is the son's charter to establish God's reign on earth over against the hostile powers. Similarly, Mark's prologue ends, in the aftermath of the battle with Satan, with Jesus's pronouncement that "the kingdom of God is at hand" (ἤγγικεν ἡ βασιλεία τοῦ θεοῦ; 1:14-15). "The time is fulfilled" (πεπλήρωται ὁ καιρὸς); and so the introduction of the "gospel" (τὸ εὐαγγέλιον) of the Son of God (1:1, 15) comes to a close.[125]

Marcus is one of few to recognize how strongly Psalm 2 resonates with the ending of Mark's prologue. According to Marcus, "Mark's use of Psalm 2, then, is not limited to the direct citation of it in 1:11. Rather, the whole series of short pericopes in 1:9-11, 12-13, and 14-15 reflects the basic 'plot' of the psalm, and its influence may extend even further into Mark's story."[126] Such is my contention here. In fact, it is not only Mark 1:9-15 that coheres with the themes and plot of Psalm 2, but the entire prologue from 1:1-15, which insists from first to last that the story of Jesus is that of Israel's eschatological renewal through God's coming Messiah.

3.5.3 Mark's Use of Psalm 2 in Intertextual Context: A Final Clue

The shared themes of Psalm 2 and Mark's prologue may be the first clue that the allusion to Ps 2:7 in 1:11 is a case of "storied metalepsis," but they are not the last. Even more telling is Mark's use of Ps 2:7 alongside certain passages from Isaiah, namely Isa 11:2 (and 6-9) and 42:1. Although seldom noted by Markan interpreters, Psalm 2 and Isaiah 11 appear alongside one another in six other texts outside the Gospels (*Ps. Sol.* 17; *1 En.* 48–50; *Sib. Or.* 3:652-795; *4 Ezra* 13:10-28; Rev 2:16, 26-27; 19:11, 15, 19; *Midr. Ps.* 2), three of which also allude to Isaiah 42 (*Ps. Sol.* 17; *1 En.* 48–50; *Midr. Ps.* 2). Moreover, two of these texts, both earlier than Mark, pair portions of Psalm 2 with precisely the same allusions to Isaiah 11 and 42 found in Mark 1:10-11: Isa 11:2 and 42:1. This basic data is summarized in Table 3.2.

As the chart above displays, no particular verse from Psalm 2 is associated with any particular verse from Isaiah 11 or 42; rather, the psalm *as a whole* appears to have been associated with these two chapters as well as Isaiah 49. Such patterns merit closer inspection.

We have already observed that *Psalm of Solomon* 17 displays an extended interplay with Psalm 2, including a virtual citation of Ps 2:9 in *Ps. Sol.* 17:23-24. In context, however, this near citation is bracketed by allusions to Isa 42:1 and Isa 11:4:[128]

---

[124] Lövestam, *Son and Saviour*, 22–3. To Lövestam's point, we should recall, again, that by the rabbinic period, Psalm 2 had become known as "the chapter of Gog and Magog" (*Midr. Ps.* 3.2; *b. Ber.* 10a).

[125] As Keck ("Introduction," 358–60) observed, the prologue begins and ends with εὐαγγέλιον, which is for Mark the announcement of Christ's appearance on earth (357). It should be noted that from the perspective articulated throughout this chapter, there is no contradiction in terms between τὸ εὐαγγέλιον Ἰησοῦ Χριστοῦ [υἱοῦ θεοῦ] (1:1) and τὸ εὐαγγέλιον τοῦ θεοῦ (1:14) inasmuch as the "gospel of God" as envisioned by Mark concerns the fulfillment of God's promises *about* the Christ-Son of God *through* Jesus. Too much has been made of an implicit contrast that likely never existed for Mark if indeed his "gospel" is the one forecast in Isaiah 40.

[126] Marcus, *Way*, 66–9.

[127] Cf. *Tanḥ. B, Lev.* 8.18, which cites Isa 42:13 in connection with Ps 2:2.

[128] Cf. Wright, "Psalms of Solomon," *OTP* 2:639; Janse, *Son*, 83.

Table 3.2 The Collocation of Psalm 2 and Isaiah in Mark and Other Literature

	Psalm 2	Isaiah 11	Isaiah 42	Isaiah 49
Mark 1:10-13	2:7	11:2, 6-9	42:1	
Ps. Sol. 17:21		11:4	42:1	49:3, 6
17:22-23	2:2	11:12		49:6
17:23-24	2:8-9	11:4		
17:24		11:2		
17:26				
17:28				
17:32	2:2			
17:35-36				
17:37				
1 En. 48:4	2:2, 7-9	11:2	42:6	49:6-8
48:4-7	2:8, 10		42:1	
48:8-10				
49:1, 3				
49:2, 4				
50:4-5				
Sib. Or. 3:652	2:6-7	11:6-9		
3:660-665	2:1-2			
3:663	2:2			
3:669-671	2:4-5			
3:670	2:1, 10, 12			
3:788-795				
4 Ezra 13:10	2:1-2	11:4		
13:31	2:7	11:4		
13:32	2:2			
13:33-34	2:6			
13:35	2:7-9			
13:37				
13:38				
Midr. Ps. 2:1-17	1-12	11:4	42:13[127]	49:23
2:3			42:1	
2:4				
2:9				
Rev 2:16	2:8-9	11:4		
2:26-27	2:9	11:4		
19:11	2:2	11:4		
19:15				
19:19				

Behold, O Lord, and raise up to them their king, the son of David, at the time, in the which you choose, O God, that he may reign over *Israel your servant* (ἐπὶ Ισραηλ παῖδά σου; Isa 42:1). *And gird him with strength, that he may shatter unrighteous rulers. And that he may purge Jerusalem from nations that trample (her) down to destruction. In the wisdom of righteousness he will thrust out sinners from (the) inheritance, he will destroy the pride of the sinner as a potter's vessel. With a rod of iron he will break in pieces all their substance* (Ps 2:9). *He will destroy the godless nations with the word of his mouth* (ὀλεθρεῦσαι ἔθνη παράνομα ἐν λόγῳ στόματος αὐτοῦ; Isa 11:4). At his rebuke nations will flee before him. And he will reprove sinners for the thoughts of their heart.

Ps. Sol. 17:21-25

Like Isa 42:1 LXX, Psalm of Solomon 17 understands the servant to be Israel. Nevertheless, it is significant that this allusion to Isa 42:1 occurs in the context of a prophecy about the Davidic Messiah, implying that the Isaiah passage was understood to be part and parcel with the messianic vision set forth by Psalm 2. Isaiah 11:4, meanwhile, functions as a kind of gloss on Ps 2:9. In the present psalmist's view, Ps 2:9 and Isa 11:4 describe one and the same future. *Psalm of Solomon* 17:26 then alludes to Isaiah 11 once more in order to describe those whom the Messiah will lead in righteousness. Thereafter, the allusion to Isa 11:4 is repeated in 17:35-36, this time following an allusion to Ps 2:2 (17:32). Lastly, 17:37 invokes Isa 11:2, declaring that God has "made him [the Messiah] powerful in the Holy Spirit and wise in the counsel of understanding, with strength and righteousness."[129] All told, *Psalm of Solomon* 17 contains an extensive interplay between Psalm 2 and Isaiah 11 with touches of Isa 42:1 as well. In this way, it serves as an important analogue for Mark 1:10-13.

A similar situation occurs in the *Similitudes of Enoch* 48–50, which intertwines allusions to Psalm 2 with Isaiah 11; 42; and 49. As Nickelsburg and Vanderkam observe, the *Similitudes* draw on *both* Isaiah's Servant Song's *and* the Davidic oracles of Psalm 2 and Isaiah 11 (*1 En.* 48:8, 10, 49:3) in their description of the Enochic "Son of Man."[130] Immediately prior to the allusions to Ps 2:2, 7-9 in *1 En.* 48:8-10 that we observed in the previous chapter, vv. 4-7 contain a kind of riff on Isa 49:6-8, presented below:[131]

1 Enoch 48	**Isaiah 49**
staff, lean, not fall (v. 4ab)	raise up the tribes (v. 6b)
light of the nations (v. 4c)	light to the nations (v. 6d; cf. Isa 42:6)
fall down and worship (5a)	prostrate themselves (v. 7f)
chosen, hidden (v. 6a)	hid, chose (vv. 2bd, 7h)
preserved the portion/lot (v. 7b)	restore the preserved (v. 6c); apportion the heritages (v. 8f)
they are saved (v. 7e)	a day of salvation (v. 8b).

Interspersed with these allusions to Isaiah 49 are possible nods toward Isa 42:1, 6 with the phrases "chosen" (*1 En.* 48:6) and "light of the Gentiles" (48:4).[132] These are followed by an almost certain allusion to Isa 42:1 in *1 En.* 49:2-4, which declares that the "Chosen One" is chosen "according to [the Lord's] good pleasure."[133] Intermixed with these

---

[129] On the correspondences between *Psalm of Solomon* 17 and Isaiah 11, see further the research of Max-Alain Chevallier, *L'Esprit et le Messie dans le bas-judaïsme et le Nouveau Testament*, Études d'histoire et de philosophie religieuses 49 (Paris: Presses Universitaires de France, 1958), 5–7, 12–25; Atkinson, *Intertextual*, 330; Janse, *Son*, 63.

[130] Nickelsburg and Vanderkam, *1 Enoch*, 2:167.

[131] The chart below has been reproduced from Nickelsburg and Vanderkam, *1 Enoch*, 2:168.

[132] The same phrase appears in both Isa 42:6 and 49:6.

[133] The pairing of Ps 2 and Isa 42:1 is noted again by Loren T. Stuckenbruck, "The Building Blocks for Enoch as the Son of Man in the Early Enoch Tradition," in *Parables of Enoch*, 315–28, here 329, who argues that both of these texts, among others, helped form the vision of the Son of Man found in the *Parables of Enoch*.

descriptions of God's Chosen One are further references to Isa 11:2 in both *1 En.* 49:2 ("wisdom is poured out like water") and especially 49:3 ("in him dwells the spirit of wisdom, and the spirit of insight, and the spirit of understanding and might..."). As this section of the *Similitudes*, we encounter a further reference to Ps 2: 8, 10 in 50:4-5. As with *Psalm of Solomon* 17, the *Similitudes* take up different sections of Psalm 2 than Mark, yet they pair Psalm 2 with the same texts from Isaiah. Like Mark, moreover, the *Similitudes* apparently regard Isaiah's "servant" and the messianic "son" in Psalm 2 as one and the same figure.

An extended allusion to Isa 11:6-9 also occurs in *Sib. Or.* 3:788-795:

Wolves and lambs will eat grass together in the mountains.
Leopards will feed together with kids.
Roving bears will spend the night with calves.
The flesh-eating lion will eat husks at the manger
like an ox, and mere infant children will lead them in bonds,
for he will make the beasts on earth harmless.
Serpents and asps will sleep with babies,
and not not harm them: for the hand of God will be upon them.[134]

As noted above, these lines recall Isaiah 11's classic expression of the messianic peace. But these lines also follow several messianic uses of Psalm 2 in lines 652-670. Janse understandably doubts whether this is a true connection since the allusions occur more than 100 lines apart.[135] But the two allusions nevertheless operate within the same overarching context to precisely the same effect, and both are extensive.[136] Moreover, in the grand, 829-line scheme of Sibylline Oracles 3, the distance between the allusions is not necessarily as significant as Janse suggests.

Isaiah 11 and Psalm 2 appear together again in *4 Ezra* 13, where the image of the Messiah slaying the wicked with the breath of his lips (Isa 11:4) appears on either side of the allusions to Psalm 2 found in vv. 31-37.[137] First, in 13:10, the Messiah (God's "Son") sends forth "from his mouth something like a stream of fire, and from his lips a flaming breath." Then, in 13:38, the image of fire stands for the law: "he will destroy them without effort by means of the law, which was symbolized by the fire." As in *Psalm of Solomon* 17, *4 Ezra*'s interpretation of Psalm 2 is bracketed by allusions to Isaiah 11.

In the NT, Revelation 2 and 19 evidence a similar relationship between Isaiah 11 and Psalm 2. In 2:16, the "sword of my mouth" (cf. Isa 11:4) is at least loosely connected with Christ's "authority over the nations" and the "rod of iron" (Ps 2:9), which he has received from his Father (2:26-27). The connection between the two texts is much more obvious in 19:11-19. Already in v. 11, Christ both judges and makes war in

---

[134] See Collins, "Sibylline Oracles," *OTP* 1:379.
[135] Chevallier, *L'Esprit*, 6; Janse, *Son*, 70.
[136] Furthermore, see Collins, "Sibylline Oracles," *OTP* 1:357, who observes that "[t]he eschatology of *Sibylline Oracles* 3 finds its closest parallels in pre-exilic Jewish literature such as Isaiah and the Psalms. The assault of the gentiles on Jerusalem is especially reminiscent of Psalms 2 and 48, while the transformation of the earth in verses 785–95 is obviously dependent on Isaiah 11."
[137] Cf. Janse, *Son*, 69.

righteousness, recalling the context of Isa 11:4. Shortly thereafter, v. 15 combines the imagery of Isa 11:4 and Ps 2:9 in a single sentence: καὶ ἐκ τοῦ στόματος αὐτοῦ ἐκπορεύεται ῥομφαία ὀξεῖα, ἵνα ἐν αὐτῇ πατάξῃ τὰ ἔθνη, καὶ αὐτὸς ποιμανεῖ αὐτοὺς ἐν ῥάβδῳ σιδηρᾷ. Again, the two texts interpret one another just as they do in *Ps. Sol.* 17:23-24 and *4 Ezra* 13:37-38. These references are followed by a pair of allusions to Ps 2:2 in Rev 19:19, which precedes a final reference to Isa 11:4 (cf. *Ps. Sol.* 17:35-36).

Finally, *Midr. Ps.* 2.3 also cites Isa 11:4 when elaborating on Ps 2:2, noting that if a rebellion should come against the Messiah in the time-to-come, he "shall smite the land with the rod of his mouth" and "with the breath of his lips shall he slay the wicked." Then, when the wicked kings realize their error, "they shall bow down to thee with their face to the earth, and lick up the dust of thy feet" (Isa 49:23). Soon after these references to Isaiah 11 and 49, *Midr. Ps.* 2.4 applies Isa 42:13 ("He will behave Himself mightily against his enemies") to the same section of Psalm 2. Most importantly, however, *Midr. Ps.* 2.9 cites Isa 42:1 as a comment on Ps 2:7, identifying YHWH's "son" with YHWH's "servant," linking the two verses to one another just as we find in Mark 1:11.

In summary, the examples above demonstrate that (1) Mark's use of Ps 2:7 alongside Isaiah 11 and 42 is not novel, but has its roots in Jewish tradition; and (2) this tradition associates the total plot of Psalm 2 with the Isaiah texts precisely because these texts were were understood to describe one and the same eschatological drama centered around the expectation of God's Messiah who would establish his reign on earth. In all probability, then, Mark also alludes to Ps 2:7 with the entire script of the psalm in mind, just as our analysis of the prologue has otherwise suggested.

3.6 Looking Ahead: Mark 1:11 and the Rest of the Story

The foregoing chapter has argued that the use of Ps 2:7 in Mark 1:11 is foundational for Mark's definition of Son of God moving forward, just as the prologue itself is foundational to the Gospel. Our exegesis of Mark 1:11 would be incomplete, as such, if we did not note the ways in which it does, in fact, point to future moments in the narrative. As noted in the introduction, Jesus is called God's Son at the relative beginning, middle, and end of the Gospel—that is, his baptism (1:11), transfiguration (9:7), and crucifixion (15:39). Both of these latter moments, in fact, recall God's pronouncement at Jesus's baptism in distinct ways.[138]

---

[138] Already, Ambrose (*Spir.*, 2.6.57 [*PL* 16.755b]) had noted the threefold rhetorical connection between these moments: "And that you might know that he spoke of the descent of Jesus, [Mark] added that he declared his Christ to men, for in his baptism he declared him, saying: 'You are my beloved Son, in whom I am well pleased.' He declared him on the mount, saying: 'This is my beloved Son, listen to him.' He declared him in his passion, when the sun hid itself and the sea and earth trembled. He declared him in the centurion, who said: 'Truly this was the Son of God.'" Others besides Ambrose must have noticed the connection too, but, sadly, ancient exegetes paid little attention to Mark's distinct account (as opposed to Matthew's). Yet the threefold connection is most distinct in Mark, where it comprises the beginning, middle, and end of Jesus's story with no human confessions of Jesus's sonship in between.

First, the "voice from the cloud" in 9:7 repeats the essential declaration from 1:11:

1:11   καὶ φωνὴ ἐγένετο ἐκ τῶν οὐρανῶν· σὺ εἶ ὁ υἱός μου ὁ ἀγαπητός,
ἐν σοὶ εὐδόκησα
9:7   καὶ ἐγένετο φωνὴ ἐκ τῆς νεφέλης· οὗτός ἐστιν ὁ υἱός μου ὁ ἀγαπητός,
ἀκούετε αὐτοῦ.

While not identical, the divine voice in 9:7 plainly echoes the allusion to Ps 2:7 in 1:11 with only a change from a second to third person address in order to suit the specific narrative context.[139] So in the grand scheme of Mark's Gospel, we are presented with not one but *two* instances in which God declares Jesus to be his Son by echoing the royal decree from Ps 2:7. *Prima facie*, such repetition suggests that the echo of Psalm 2 at Jesus's baptism is indeed foundational—not only to Jesus's identity as God's Son in Mark, but to the fabric of the story itself.

Second, and even more intriguing, Mark 1:10-11 appears to form an *inclusio* with 15:38-39 at the opposite end of the narrative.[140] At Jesus's baptism, the heavens are rent and a voice from heaven declares, "You are my Son"; at the moment of his death on the cross, the temple veil is rent and a Roman centurion declares, "Truly, this man was Son of God":[141]

1:10-11   Καὶ εὐθὺς ἀναβαίνων ἐκ τοῦ ὕδατος εἶδεν *σχιζομένους* τοὺς οὐρανοὺς καὶ τὸ πνεῦμα ὡς περιστερὰν καταβαῖνον εἰς αὐτόν· καὶ φωνὴ ἐγένετο ἐκ τῶν οὐρανῶν· *σὺ εἶ ὁ υἱός μου ὁ ἀγαπητός, ἐν σοὶ εὐδόκησα.*
15:38-39   Καὶ τὸ καταπέτασμα τοῦ ναοῦ *ἐσχίσθη* εἰς δύο ἀπ' ἄνωθεν ἕως κάτω. Ἰδὼν δὲ ὁ κεντυρίων ὁ παρεστηκὼς ἐξ ἐναντίας αὐτοῦ ὅτι οὕτως ἐξέπνευσεν εἶπεν· *ἀληθῶς οὗτος ὁ ἄνθρωπος υἱὸς θεοῦ ἦν.*

---

[139] See, e.g., Schweizer, *Mark*, 182; Black, *Mark*, 206.
[140] Among the numerous scholars who have observed this inclusio, see Elizabeth Struthers Malbon, *Narrative Space and Mythic Meaning in Mark* (New York: Harper & Row, 1986), 187 n. 93; Howard M. Jackson "The Death of Jesus in Mark and the Miracle from the Cross," *NTS* 33 (1987): 16–37; Stephen Motyer, "The Rending of the Veil: A Markan Pentecost?," *NTS* 33 (1987): 155–57; David Ulansey, "The Heavenly Veil Torn: Mark's Cosmic Inclusio," *JBL* 110 (1991): 123–25; Juel, *Mark*, 225; idem, *Master*, 34; A. B. Caneday "Christ's Baptism and Crucifixion: The Anointing and Enthronement of God's Son," *SBJT* 83 (2004): 70–85; Collins, *Mark*, 762; Focant, *Mark*, 41; Dean B. Deppe, *Theological Intentions of Mark's Literary Devices: Markan Intercalations, Frames, Allusionary Repetitions, Narrative Surprises, and Three Types of Mirroring* (Eugene, OR: Wipf & Stock, 2015), 218. Whether employing the term "inclusio" or not, others who have noted the distinct parallels between these two passages include Schweizer, *Mark*, 358; Lane, *Mark*, 576; Best, *Story*, 132–33; Hooker, *Mark*, 45; Gundry, *Mark*, 48; Johannes Heidler, "Die Verwendung von Psalm 22 im Kreuzigungsbericht des Markus. Ein Beitrag zur Frage nach der Christologie des Markus," in *Christi Leidenspsalm: Arbeiten zum 22. Psalm; Gestchrift zum 50. Jahr des Bestehens des Theologischen Seminars "Paulinum" Berlin*, ed. H. Genest (Neukirchen-Vluyn: Neukirchen, 1996), 26–34; Matera, *Christology*, 8; Marcus, *Mark 1–8*, 163–64; Evans, *Mark*, 509; Edwards, *Mark*, 36; France, *Mark*, 49, 77; Boring, *Mark*, 45, 432, 434; Black, *Mark*, 330–33. The connection is seldom doubted, but see Fritzleo Lentzen-Deis, *Die Taufe Jesu nach den Synoptikern: Literarkritische und gattungsgeschichtliche Untersuchungen* (Frankfurt: Knecht, 1970), 280–81; and Stein, *Mark*, 56, 719, who admits a number of parallels but counters that the circumstances are not "identical."
[141] See similarly Juel, *Master*, 34.

Significantly, these two episodes are linked by the only two uses of the verb σχίζω in Mark's Gospel, and there are reasons to think this parallel is intentional.[142] While all three Synoptists employ ἐσχίσθη to describe the rending of the temple veil (cf. Matt 27:51; Luke 23:45), only Mark employs the same verb to describe the rending of the heavens at Jesus's baptism. Mark's choice of σχιζομένους likewise represents a change from his source text, Isa 63:19 LXX, which reads: ἐὰν ἀνοίξῃς τὸν οὐρανόν.[143] By contrast, Matthew and Luke retain Isaiah's ἀνοίγω, which is more typical where the motif of the heavens opening occurs elsewhere in Jewish literature.[144] Mark's choice of σχίζω in 1:10 would appear to be his own, then—likely a deliberate rhetorical move intended to connect Jesus's baptism and crucifixion to one another.[145] Besides the principal parallels above, scholars have also observed several other parallels between these two scenes: (1) in each instance, "something is said to *descend*," whether the Spirit (1:10), or the tear in the veil (15:38), which Mark describes as a downward motion (ἀπ' ἄνωθεν ἕως κάτω); (2) "Elijah is symbolically present" on both occasions (cf. 1:9; 15:36); and (3) the verb used to describe Jesus's last breath in 15:37, 39, ἐκπνέω, is a cognate of πνεῦμα, used in 1:10.[146]

According to Quintilian, the point of an *inclusio* is that *respondent primis et ultima*.[147] If we are to take Quintilian seriously, then Mark's *inclusio* suggests that the meanings of 1:11 and 15:39 each depend, in part, on the other.[148] Boring and Collins capture opposite sides of Quintilian's dictum by stating that Mark 1:10 points *forward* to 15:38 (Boring), while 15:38 refers *back* to 1:10 (Collins).[149] According to Quintilian, both are correct.

Yet, although many interpreters have acknowledged Mark's *inclusio*, virtually none have asked what this might mean for Mark's overarching portrayal of Jesus as the Son of God.[150] This is surprising given that the declarations of Jesus's identity are arguably the the climax of each scene: the content of each ἀποκάλυψις, so to speak.[151]

---

[142] Cf. Marcus, *Mark 1–8*, 163.
[143] Cf. Buse, "Baptism," 74–5; Marcus, *Way*, 49–50.
[144] Cf. Matt 3:16; Luke 3:22. In addition to Isa 63:19 LXX, ἀνοίγω describes the opening of the heavens in Gen 7:11; Ps 77:23; Ezek 1:1; John 1:51; Acts 7:56; 10:11; Rev 4:1; 11:19; 19:11; *T. Levi* 2:6; 5:1; 18:6; and *T. Jud.* 24:2. By contrast, σχίζω is used to describe such an event in only two other instances: *Jos. Asen.* 14:2; and *1 Apoc. John* 17.10. A TLG search shows that Mark 1:10 is, in fact, the earliest known use of σχίζω in connection with οὐρανός. Cf. Collins (*Mark*, 148): "The phrase 'the heavens split' is an unusual expression. It does not occur in the LXX. It occurs nowhere else in the New Testament or in the apostolic literature."
[145] So also Collins (*Mark*, 762): "it is likely that Mark formulated the tradition about Jesus' baptism in his own words and chose to use the verb ('to split')"; cf. Deppe, *Literary Devices*, 219.
[146] See Ulansey, "Inclusio," 123; cf. Motyer, "Rending," 155–57; Caneday, "Baptism and Crucifixion," 72.
[147] Quintilian, *Inst.* 9.3.34. Accordingly, an *inclusio* creates mutuality between two passages, as well as a parenthesis around the material encompassed between them.
[148] *Inclusio* is one of a number of devices that exemplify "repetition as parenthesis," along with the related devices of *redditio* (Gk. προσαπόδοσις); see Heinrich Lausberg, *Handbook of Literary Rhetoric: A Foundation for Literary Study*, ed. David E. Orton and R. Dean Anderson, trans. Matthew T. Bliss, Annemiek Jansen, and David E. Orton (Leiden/Boston: Brill, 1998), §625.
[149] Boring, *Mark*, 45; Collins, *Mark*, 762.
[150] For example, Jackson ("Death," 16–37); Motyer ("Rending," 155–57); Ulansey ("Inclusio," 123–25); Juel (*Mark*, 225); and Collins (*Mark*, 762) all focus on the intpretive significance of the parallel between the rent heavens and the temple veil rather than the declarations of Jesus's sonship at the beginning and end of Jesus's story.
[151] As Gurtner ("Rending," 293) recognizes, "the rending of the heavens led to God's proclamation of Jesus as his 'beloved son' (1:11)," whereas "the rending of the veil led to the proclamation by the centurion of Jesus as the 'son of God' (15:39)."

How exactly God's pronouncement and the centurion's confession can answer one another, especially in light of the former's echo of Ps 2:7, is a matter for another chapter. But whatever the answer to his question may be, Mark's *inclusio*, along with the repetition of 1:11 in 9:7, constitutes one more piece of evidence that the use of Ps 2:7 in 1:11 is foundational to Mark's Gospel. Yet it suggests that the story has only begun in Mark's prologue. So while Mark 1:11 must bear heavily on our understanding of these later moments in the Gospel, so also the meaning of 1:11 finally depends on the rest of the story. On the immediate horizon, then, we turn to the Son's war against the kingdom of Satan.

4

The Son of God in Conflict

For this purpose the Son of God was revealed: to destroy the works of the devil.
1 John 3:8

The previous chapter demonstrated that God's pronouncement, "You are my Son," in Mark 1:11 draws meaningfully on God's decree, "You are my Son," in Ps 2:7 so as to superimpose the psalm's eschatological hopes onto Jesus's ministry from the very start of the Gospel. These eschatological expectations begin their realization early in Mark's narrative with Jesus's exorcisms of unclean spirits, which collectively demonstrate the anointed Son's overthrow of God's cosmic enemies as he instantiates God's reign on earth. As such, and as we shall see, Mark's use of son-of-God language in 3:11 and 5:7 has its bearings within the larger, programmatic actualization of Psalm 2 in Mark's Gospel.

4.1 An Unlikely Chorus: God's Word and the Demons' Words about Jesus

Following the prologue, Jesus is identified as God's Son by unclean spirits in Mark 3:11 and 5:7. These instances, in turn, account for Mark's only uses of son-of-God language before 9:7, which repeats the heavenly allusion to Ps 2:7 from 1:11. At a glance, there is an obvious (if ironic) intra-narrative resonance between what the demons' have to say about Jesus and God's own pronouncement about Jesus in 1:11 and 9:7:

Mark 1:11	σὺ εἶ ὁ υἱός μου
Mark 1:24	ὁ ἅγιος τοῦ θεοῦ
Mark 3:11	σὺ εἶ ὁ υἱὸς τοῦ θεοῦ
Mark 5:7	υἱὲ τοῦ θεοῦ τοῦ ὑψίστου
Mark 9:7	οὗτος ἐστιν ὁ υἱός μου

Parallels of diction and syntax unite all five of the pronouncements above. As Malbon observes, the "unclean spirits and demons are on the side of Satan in the cosmic struggle ... but oddly enough, what the unclean spirits and demons say to and about

Jesus is most like what God says in 1:11 and 9:7."[1] Malbon's point is enhanced by the fact that the demons, in fact, *characteristically* address Jesus as God's "Son" as opposed to any other epithet, not only in Mark but also in Matthew and Luke.[2]

On a narrative level, then, God's words in 1:11 provide the obvious interpretive frame within which to hear the demons' statements about Jesus, which are, likewise, framed on the opposite side by the repetition of God's own pronouncement in 9:7.[3] Yet this means that the demons' outbursts in 1:24; 3:11; and 5:7 somehow take their cue not only from what God says in 1:11 and 9:7 but from Ps 2:7. Taken at face value, the plain suggestion of Mark' intra-narrative parallels is that Ps 2:7 informs the meaning of Jesus's sonship in these in-between episodes as well as in 1:11 and 9:7. Likewise, both 3:11 and 5:7 (and, to a lesser degree, even 1:24) sound echoes of an echo of Ps 2:7.

4.2 Plundering Satan's Kingdom: Jesus's Exorcisms in the Gospel of Mark

In actuality, one does not have to look hard to see the thematic connection between Jesus's exorcisms and Psalm 2—at least not if one reads Psalm 2 in the way that many ancient readers appear to have done. We have seen in previous chapters that the Messiah's battle against God's (and Israel's) enemies in Ps 2:1-2 was sometimes interpreted in cosmic terms—so often so that *Midr. Ps.* 3.2 refers to Psalm 2 as "the chapter of Gog and Magog."[4] Notably, 4QFlor 2:1-2 interprets the kings of the earth and rulers who rise up against YHWH and his Messiah as Belial and his servants. According to Zenger and others, this cosmic dimension may have been a part of the psalm's original vision when it was composed.[5] In early Christian interpretation, Justin

---

[1] Malbon, *Mark's Jesus*, 80, 82, respectively. Malbon (82) adds "and what the narrator says in 1:1." Yet, while there is also an obvious parallel with 1:1 (υἱοῦ θεοῦ), the parallels with 1:11 and 9:7 are distinctly greater.

[2] Cf. Matt 8:29; Luke 4:41; 8:28. Matera (*Kingship*, 105) likewise observes that each of the two instances in which Jesus grants authority to his disciples to cast out demons (3:14-15; 6:7) follows a declaration of his sonship (3:11; 5:7); thus, power over the demons appears closely linked to Jesus's identity as the Son of God. The singular expception to this general rule occurs in Mark 1:24 (cf. Luke 4:34), which will be addressed below.

[3] See similarly Cranfield, *Mark*, 126; Pesch, *Markusevangelium*, 1:201; Légasse, *Marc*, 224; Trocmé, *Marc*, 93; France, *Mark*, 155; Collins, "The Son of God among Jews," 400; idem, *Mark*, 213. As Standaert (*Marc*, 256) writes: "Mais dans la structure dramatique de l'évangile, ces confessions des démoniaques sont au service de la tension entre ce que savent les destinataires, grâce au prologue, et ce que savent les gens dans le récit."

[4] E.g., in 4Q174 1:18–2:2; *Midr. Ps.* 2.2; cf. 2.4; *Midr. Ps.* 92.10; *Midr. Ps.* 118.12; *Tanḥ. B, Gen.* 2.24; *Tanḥ. B, Lev.* 8.18; *b. Ber* 7b; *b. Ber.* 10a; *Lev. Rab.* 27:11; *Esth. Rab.* 7:23; *Mek. Shir.* 7; as well as *Midr. Ps.* 3.2 (above). On Gog and Magog as supernatural, demonic forces see Johann Lust, "Gog," *DDD*, 373–375; idem, "Magog," *DDD*, 535–37.

[5] See again Hossfeld and Zenger, *Psalmen*, 1:50, 52; cf. Victor Sasson ("The Language of Rebellion in Psalm 2 and in the Plaster Texts from Deir 'Alla," *AUSS* 24 [1986]: 147–54, who observes the close similarity between the language of "universal rebellion" in Ps 2:1-2 and the language of "cosmic rebellion" in an inscription from Deir 'Alla in the Transjordan.

Martyr likewise understands the conflict described in Ps 2:1-2 on two planes at once: as a reference to "Herod and Pilate," on the one hand, and "devils," on the other.[6]

Such traditions are intriguing in light of the widespread agreement among scholars that Mark depicts Jesus's exorcisms as "enactment[s] of a dualistic cosmic battle in which the Spirit-empowered Jesus wages war against Satan to rescue those held captive in Satan's household."[7] The overarching motif is one of battle between rival kingdoms.[8] This is evident not only from the combative, sometimes militaristic language of the individual exorcism accounts themselves (1:23-27; 3:11-12; 5:1-20), but also from the framing provided by Jesus's wilderness temptation (1:12-13) and the Beelzebul controversy (3:22-30).[9]

On the one hand, in 1:12-13, the Spirit casts Jesus, the Spirit-anointed Son of God, into his initial conflict with Satan in the wilderness, after which we are to understand that Jesus emerges as victor, bringing forth the kingdom of God on earth over against the kingdom of Satan.[10] That this initial conflict, which forms a bridge between Jesus's anointing (1:10-11) and the formal beginning of his ministry (1:14-15), sets the stage for the various encounters with the demonic that follow is already hinted at by the intra-narrative parallels observed above; but we will see further links between 1:10-15 and Jesus's first exorcism in 1:23-27 below.

On the other hand, the most revealing glimpse into the purpose of Jesus's exorcisms arguably occurs with the Beelzebul controversy in 3:22-30.[11] In an effort to discredit Jesus, the Jerusalem scribes claim that it is "by the ruler of demons [that] he casts out demons" (ἐν τῷ ἄρχοντι τῶν δαιμονίων ἐκβάλλει τὰ δαιμόνια). Jesus, in turn, responds with two parables. First, he asks how Satan can cast out Satan (πῶς δύναται σατανᾶς σατανᾶν ἐκβάλλειν), and further explains that:

> If a kingdom is divided against itself, that kingdom cannot stand; and if a house is divided against itself, that house will not be able to stand. And if Satan has risen up against himself and become divided, he cannot stand but is at his end.
>
> Mark 3:24-26

---

[6] *1 Apol.* 40 (*PG* 6:389). Accordingly, Justin also understands Christ's victory with reference to his earthly and supernatural enemies alike.

[7] Elizabeth E. Shively, *Apocalyptic Imagination in the Gospel of Mark: The Literary and Theological Role of Mark 3:22-30*, BNZW 189 (Berlin/New York: De Gruyter, 2012), 106. Gerd Theissen (*The Miracle Stories of the Early Christian Tradition*, trans. John Riches [Philadelphia: Fortress, 1983], 90–1) similarly concludes that "[e]xorcisms are seen in the context of the universal struggle between the rule of God and the rule of Satan." See also James M. Robinson, *The Problem of History in Mark and Other Marcan Studies* (Philadelphia: Fortress, 1982), 35–8; Eric Sorensen, *Possession and Exorcism in the New Testament and Early Christianity*, WUNT 2/157 (Tübingen: Mohr Siebeck, 2002), 141; Graham H. Twelftree, *Jesus the Exorcist: A Contribution to the Study of the Historical Jesus*, WUNT 2/54 (Tübingen: Mohr Siebeck, 1993), 217–18; ibid, *In the Name of Jesus: Exorcism among Early Christians* (Grand Rapids: Baker Academic, 2007), 101–15; Marcus, *Mark 1–8*, 282–83; Malbon, *Mark's Jesus*, 80.

[8] See Theissen, *Miracle Stories*, 88–9.

[9] Twelftree, *Name*, 106–07; cf. Collins, *Mark*, 232.

[10] Van Iersel (*Reader Response*, 102–03) observes that Mark 1:12-13 introduces the fundamental conflict between the narrative's hero and its central antagonist.

[11] According to Pesch (*Markusevangelium*, 209), 3:20ff "illustriert die Wirkung des exorzistischen Wirkens Jesu." Gnilka (*Markus*, 150) similarly contends that 3:27 "ist ursprünglich als umfassende Erläuterung von Jesu Exorcismus und Heilungswirksamkeit zu verstehen." See similarly Boring, *Mark*, 108.

In so doing, Jesus implicitly suggests that the people are, in reality, witnessing a struggle between two kingdoms.[12] Rather than commanding demons by their ruler, he implicitly wages war on Satan's kingdom by the power of the Holy Spirit (3:28-30; cf. 1:10-13).[13]

On an intratextual level, Jesus's second parable, the binding of the "strong man" (τοῦ ἰσχυροῦ) in 3:27, recalls his own characterization as "the stronger one" (ὁ ἰσχυρότερος) in 1:7, which we saw appears to have messianic connotations in Mark's prologue.[14] At the same time, on an intertextual level, Jesus's saying alludes directly to Isa 49:24-25, where God declares to those in doubt that "the captives of the mighty (ἰσχύοντος) shall be taken, and the prey of the tyrant be rescued" (49:25).[15] As Graham Twelftree argues, "So clearly does this parable echo Isa 49:24-25 ... that we can expect this Old Testament passage to have informed Mark's hearers' understanding of the parable": God is rescuing his people from their mighty enemy.[16] By way of analogy, Satan is the "strong man" and his "prey," which Jesus (the Messiah) now "plunders" (διαρπάσαι), are those illegitimately held captive by him. It follows that Jesus's exorcisms are examples of the kingdom of God in operation: with the arrival of the kingdom of God, the eschatological liberation of the captives and the disenfranchisement of evil have begun.[17]

Additionally, the binding of demonic powers in the messianic age occurs in a variety of Jewish literature, as does the release of Satan's captives.[18] By implication, the Messiah himself appears to overcome Satan by casting out his servants in at least some of these texts, just as Mark's narrative implies.[19] It is within this framework of cosmic and eschatological battle between God's Messiah and the forces of Satan that we are ultimately to understand Jesus's exorcisms in the Gospel of Mark. But what is vital to grasp at this point is that throughout the whole of ancient Jewish and

---

[12] Cf. Pesch, *Markusevangelium*, 214.
[13] Cf. Matt 12:22-30, which makes explicit Jesus's claim regarding the Spirit, which is implicit in Mark.
[14] Cf. Hooker, *Mark*, 116; Marcus, *Mark 1-8*, 282; Boring, *Mark*, 108.
[15] Pesch, *Markusevangelium*, 215; Gnilka, *Markus*, 1:150; Watts, *New Exodus*, 146-52; France, *Mark*, 173; Sorensen, *Possession*, 140-41; Twelftree, *Name*, 107; Shively, *Apocalyptic*, 84.
[16] Twelftree, *Name*, 107.
[17] Cf. Gnilka, *Markus*, 150; Twelftree, *Exorcist*, 217-18; Marcus, *Mark 1-8*, 283; Shively, *Apocalyptic*, 106.
[18] See, respectively, Isa 24:21-22; *1 En.* 54:3-5; 69:28; *T. Levi* 18:12; Rev 20:1-3; and *T. Dan* 5:11; *T. Zeb.* 9:8; 11QMelch 11-13, 24-25. Cf. Pesch, *Markusevangelium*, 215; France, *Mark*, 173; Boring, *Mark*, 108; Twelftree, *Exorcist*, 217-24; idem, *Name*, 114. God's expulsion of demonic powers in the age to come is already expected as early as Zech 13:2 ("On that day ... I will remove the unclean spirit [τὸ πνεῦμα τὸ ἀκάθαρτον in the LXX] from the land"), which is later associated with exorcisms in both *Num. Rab.* 19:8 and *Pesiq. Rab. Kah.* 4:7, and occurs in many of the texts considered by Twelftree below.
[19] E.g., in *T. Levi* 18:11-12; *T. Jud.* 25:3; *T. Dan* 5:10-11; *T. Zeb.* 9:8; *T. Reu.* 6:10-12; *Ass. Mos.* 10:1; *Sifra Lev.* 26:6; *Pesiq. Rab.* 36; *1 En.* 10:4; 55:4; cf. 4Q174 1:18–2:2. As Twelftree (*Exorcist*, 183-89) concludes, explicit evidence for a widespread expectation that the Messiah would be an exorcist is lacking; cf. Marcus, *Mark 1-8*, 261. Twelftree reaches this conclusion on the grounds that (a) many of the examples above come from the *Testaments of the Twelve Patriarchs*, which bear marks of possible Christian interpolation; (b) others, such as *Pesiqta Rabati*, are quite late; and (c) some, e.g., *1 En.* 10:4, though they anticipate the eschatological binding of demons, do not explicitly mention the Messiah or exorcism. Yet, as Twelftree (217-24) also notes, there is nevertheless a clear expectation that the demonic powers will be dealt with in the messianic age. Moreover, Twelftree does not consider those texts which link Psalm 2 with the defeat of demonic powers.

The Son of God in Conflict

Christian literature, only one text supplies a precedent for the unseating the demonic powers by God's anointed "Son" as we find in Mark 3:11-12 and 5:7: Psalm 2. With these preliminary considerations in mind, we are now in a position to examine Jesus's encounters with the unclean spirits in closer detail.

4.3 Mark 1:21-28: "I Know Who You Are"

For all intents and purposes, Jesus's exorcism of the unclean spirit in the Capernaum synagogue (1:21-28) comprises the first real episode in his ministry. Only a summary of Jesus's message (1:14-15) and the calling of the first disciples (1:16-20) precede it. Although "Son" of God does not actually occur in this pericope, the episode distinctly relates Jesus's exorcisms to his anointing and concomitant war against Satan (1:10-13), and so bears important implications for the exegesis of 3:7-12 and 5:1-20 as well.

Although we are not told *what* Jesus taught in the synagogue (1:21-23), Hooker is correct that Jesus's subsequent "overthrow of the demons must be seen as part of his proclamation of the kingdom of God."[20] The real focus of the scene, then, is on that very event: the confrontation between Jesus and the unclean spirit (v. 23),[21] who addresses Jesus by crying out, τί ἡμῖν καὶ σοί, Ἰησοῦ Ναζαρηνέ; ἦλθες ἀπολέσαι ἡμᾶς; οἶδά σε τίς εἶ, ὁ ἅγιος τοῦ θεοῦ (v. 24).

"*Holy One* of God" (ὁ ἅγιος τοῦ θεοῦ) is not "*Son* of God" (ὁ υἱὸς τοῦ θεοῦ); yet one is hard pressed, so soon after hearing the voice from heaven in 1:11, not to recall the declaration of Jesus's identity there, especially following the unclean spirit's outburst, οἶδά σε τίς εἶ. The unclean spirit's expression more readily bears the sense "I *recognize* you, who you are," rather than simply "I know who you are," as in most English translations.[22] The spirit's bold assertion thus instinctively prompts the reader/hearer (who also knows who Jesus is) to recall the one and only identity of Jesus voiced in the narrative so far, which, at any rate, occurred just thirteen verses earlier. Additionally, commentators have long observed that τὸ πνεῦμα τὸ ἀκάθαρτον (1:23, 26, 27) contrasts with the πνεῦμα ἅγιον of Jesus's anointing in 1:10 (cf. 1:8, 12).[23] And, as Jesus's first foray into ministry after 1:12-15, 1:21-28 inherently builds on the theme of Jesus, the anointed Son's, battle with Satan as he instantiates God's kingdom on earth.[24] The

---

[20] Hooker, *Mark*, 62; cf. Boring, *Mark*, 63. We are told only that Jesus teaches "as one with authority" (ὡς ἐξουσίαν ἔχων) in v. 22, which he thereafter demonstrates by his exorcism of the unclean spirit (see v. 27: διδαχὴ καινὴ κατ᾽ ἐξουσίαν).

[21] Literally "*in* an unclean spirit" (ἐν πνεύματι ἀκαθάρτῳ). Mark's expression seemingly indicates that it is not the man who has the unclean spirit so much as the unclean spirit who has the man under its control (see BDAG, "ἐν" 4.c.), perhaps even approximating a dative of possession (see BDF §220 on the use of ἐν for the dative proper). The same expression also occurs in 5:2.

[22] Οἶδα, being in reality the perfect of εἴδω, properly carries the sense of knowing by *seeing*: lit., "I have seen." See BDAG, "οἶδα" s.v.; LSJ, "εἴδω" s.v.

[23] E.g., Heinrich August Wilhelm Meyer, *Kritisch exegetisches Handbuch über die Evangelien des Markus und Lukas*, 2nd ed. (Göttingen: Vandenhoeck und Ruprecht, 1846), 21; Légasse, *Marc*, 127-28; Marcus, *Mark 1-8*, 188; Boring, *Mark*, 64; Black, *Mark*, 72.

[24] John R. Donahue and Daniel J. Harrington, *The Gospel of Mark*, SP 2 (Collegeville, MN: Liturgical, 2002), 82-3; Black, *Mark*, 72.

obvious implication of these various connections is that it is as the Spirit-anointed, royal Son of God (1:10-11) that Jesus now launches his exorcistic ministry.[25]

4.3.1 "The Holy One" and "the Son" of God

Such an implication naturally raises questions about the relationship between ὁ υἱὸς τοῦ θεοῦ (cf. 1:11; 3:11) and ὁ ἅγιος τοῦ θεοῦ in 1:24. Despite the obvious semantic difference between the two terms, the intra-narrative parallels with 1:11; 3:11; and 5:7 as well as the connections between the present episode and 1:10-15 suggest some sort of relationship. Unsurprisingly, some have viewed "Holy One" (ὁ ἅγιος) as a functional variation of or substitute for "Son" (ὁ υἱός) in 1:24.[26] Earlier scholars, such as Wrede, assumed that it essentially functioned as a messianic title, more or less synonymous with "Son" and "Son of God" in 1:11 and 3:11.[27] In 1960, Franz Mussner, linking Mark's phrase to a pun on "Nazarene" (see Ναζαρηνέ in v. 24), again concluded that the title ultimately has messianic connotations.[28] Yet, as Botner notes, in more recent scholarship, "[i]t has become almost obligatory to begin a discussion of ὁ ἅγιος τοῦ θεοῦ ('the Holy One of God') by conceding that it 'was not a messianic title in Judaism.'"[29] Botner, however, offers substantial evidence that the primary connotations of such language were indeed (a) Davidic and (b) specifically focused on the matter of royal anointing.

Specifically, Botner calls our attention to four texts that refer to David as "the holy one" in connection with his royal anointing (Ps 88:19 LXX; *LAB* 59:2; Pss 152:4; 153:3) and two others that refer to anointing Israel's king with "holy oil" (11QPsa 28:11; Josephus, *Ant.* 6.157, 165).[30] The association of the term "holy" with royal anointing first occurs in Psalm 89 (88 LXX), which is a sister-text of Psalm 2 in the tradition

---

[25] Cf. Pesch, *Markusevangelium*, 1:201; Matera, *Kingship*, 105; Twelftree, *Exorcist*, 106–07; Légasse, *Marc*, 127-28.

[26] E.g., France, *Mark*, 104.

[27] Wrede, *Messianic Secret*, 24–34; see similarly Meyer, *Markus*, 21.

[28] Franz Mussner, "Ein Wortspiel in Mk 1,24?," *BZ* 4 (1960): 285–86. Mussner plausibly suggests ἅγιος θεοῦ is the result of a wordplay (*Wortspiel*) on Ναζαρηνέ and ὁ ἅγιος τοῦ θεοῦ derived from the Samson story in Judg 13:5-7 LXX, which interchanges ναζεὶρ θεοῦ and ἅγιος θεοῦ, which both translate the Hebrew נזיר אלהים; cf. Eduard Schweizer, "'Er wird Nazoräer heissen' (zu Mc 1.24; Mt 2.23)," in *Judentum, Urchristentum, Kirche: Festschrift für Joachim Jeremias*, ed. Walter Eltester, BZAW 26 (Berlin: Töpelmann, 1960), 90–3; Pesch, *Markusevangelium*, 1:122 n. 20; Marcus, *Mark 1–8*, 188. This interpretation is not mutually exclusive with the interpretation presented below, however, since Mussner himself suggests that ὁ ἅγιος τοῦ θεοῦ has messianic connotations since Jesus is "*the* Holy One of God" par excellence.

[29] Max Botner, "The Messiah Is 'the Holy One': Ὁ Ἅγιος Τοῦ Θεοῦ as a Messianic Title in Mark 1:24," *JBL* 136 (2017): 417–33 (here, 417). To his point, Botner lists M.-J. Lagrange, *L'Évangile selon Saint Marc*, 6th ed. (Paris: Librairie Lecoffre, 1942), 22; Taylor, *Mark*, 174; Howard Clark Kee, *Community of the New Age: Studies in Mark's Gospel* (Philadelphia: Westminster, 1977; repr., Macon, GA: Mercer University Press, 1983), 120; Dieter Lührmann, *Das Markusevangelium*, HNT 3 (Tübingen: Mohr Siebeck, 1987), 51; Hooker, *Mark*, 64; and Gundry, *Mark*, 82. One may add to Botner's list Marcus, *Mark 1–8*, 188; and Trocmé, *Marc*, 52. This conclusion is typically drawn on the basis that ὁ ἅγιος τοῦ θεοῦ never occurs as a title for the Messiah in extant Jewish literature. But such an approach obscures more than it reveals by failing to account for the participation of words and phrases in a larger language game (see Wittgenstein, *P.I.* §7) or, in semiotic terms, the connotations of words within a given encyclopedia (Eco, *Theory*, 48–150). Simply put, that is not how language works. Cf. Novenson, *Christ among the Messiahs*, 41–63.

[30] Botner, "Holy One," 421–26.

identifying the Davidic king as God's Son (see vv. 27-28).³¹ After designating the king "the holy one of Israel" (ὁ ἅγιος Ἰσραήλ) in v. 18, Ps 88:21 LXX further links David's royal anointing with YHWH's holiness: "I have anointed [ἔχρισα] him with my holy oil [ἐλαίῳ ἁγίῳ]." A similar linkage of terms appears in the first-century CE text *LAB* 59:2: "Behold now is this the holy one, *the anointed of the Lord* [*sanctus christus domini*]?"³² As in Ps 88 LXX, "holy one" refers to the Lord's anointed. Finally, in Ps 152:4, David cries out, "Spare, O Lord, your *elect one*, and deliver your *holy one* from destruction," and Ps 153:3 declares, in turn, "he [the Lord] delivered the physical life of his *elect one* from the hands of death; and he redeemed his *holy one* from destruction."³³ Both psalms employ the designations "elect one" and "holy one" synonymously.

In addition to the texts Botner cites, the Davidic Messiah is called the "Holy Messiah" (משיח הקודש) in fragment 12 of 1Q30, and "the Holy One" in *B. Bat.* 75b. Moreover, Luke 4:34, 41 employs both ὁ ἅγιος τοῦ θεοῦ and ὁ υἱὸς τοῦ θεοῦ in parallel with one another and with χριστός.³⁴ Finally, one of the texts Botner cites (*LAB* 60:1-3) not only describes the Davidic Messiah as the "holy one," but also depicts the Messiah's dominion over unclean spirits.³⁵

What is important to note, then, is that insofar as ὁ ἅγιος τοῦ θεοῦ constitutes Davidic language and especially connotes the royal anointing of the Davidic Messiah, it is congruent with ὁ υἱὸς [τοῦ θεοῦ] in Ps 2:7, especially in the context of Mark 1:10-11: Jesus's royal anointing. Observing this connection likewise supports the overall connection between those earlier events in 1:10-15 and the present episode (1:21-28). Once again, it is precisely as the Spirit-anointed, royal Son of God spoken of in Ps 2:7 that Jesus now performs his exoristic ministry. One might say that the exorcism of the unclean spirit in 1:24-25 is the first outward manifestation of Jesus's identity declared in 1:11.

The rest of the pericope establishes a pattern that will repeat itself in 3:11-12 and 5:1-20. After the unclean spirit addresses Jesus and exclaims his identity aloud (1:24), Jesus responds by rebuking (ἐπιτίμησεν) and silencing (φιμώθητι) it before casting it out (1:25). The transcript is that of a battle between Jesus and the demonic.³⁶ The

---

³¹ Both Ps 2:7 ("I will recount the decree: YHWH said to me, 'You are my son . . .'") and Ps 89:26-27 ("He will call to me, 'You are my Father, my God and the Rock of my salvation!' And I also will make him the firstborn, the Most-High of the kings of the earth") bear the apparent influence of 2 Sam 7:14 ("I will be to him a father, and he will be to me a son"); cf. Georg Fohrer, "υἱός," *TDNT* 8:350.

³² Trans. D. J. Harrington, "Pseudo-Philo," in *OTP* 2:372.

³³ Trans. Charlesworth, *OTP* 2:617.

³⁴ So also Bock, *Mark*, 127; cf. Fitzmyer (*Luke*, 1:546) commenting on Luke 4:34: "In the Lucan context Jesus' 'holiness' would have to be explained by his 'sonship' (3:22) and 'anointing' with the Spirit (4:18)." Fitzmyer recognizes in Luke also an inherent connection between ὁ ἅγιος τοῦ θεοῦ, ὁ υἱὸς τοῦ θεοῦ, and God's anointing. See also the application of ἅγιος to υἱὸς θεοῦ in a Davidic context in Luke 1:35.

³⁵ In *LAB* 60:1-3, David wards off the unclean spirits from Saul and further declares, "one born from my loins will rule over you"; trans. Harrington, "Pseudo-Philo," in *OTP* 2:373. Marcus (*Mark 1-8*, 193) observes that the adjective "holy" also occurs numerous times in the War Scroll (1QM 1:16, 3:5, 6:6, etc.) in contexts describing the coming eschatological battle. In 1QM 13:2-6, God also curses "Belial (Satan) and all his spirits, to whom are attributed uncleanness and hostility to God." In Mark, as in the War Scroll, the holiness of God appears to confront the uncleanness (i.e., unholiness) of the demons— hence, the implicit opposition between God's πνεῦμα ἅγιον and the πνεύματα ἀκάθαρτα (see above).

³⁶ See also Hooker (*Mark*, 64), who considers 1:24-25 to be a picture of Jesus waging war against God's enemies.

plural pronouns ἡμῖν and ἡμᾶς in the unclean spirit's twofold question suggests that he recognizes in Jesus, the Holy One of God, the impending doom of the whole world of the demonic[37]—and Jesus's swift rebuke (ἐπιτίμησεν) suggests an affirmative answer in turn.[38] As Pesch writes, Jesus is the "*Vernichter*" of the demonic realm.[39]

4.4 Mark 3:6-11: "You Are the Son of God"

Following the initial episode in the Capernaum synagogue, Jesus continues to exorcise demons (1:32-34, 39), whom he does not allow to speak "because they [know] him" (v. 34: ὅτι ᾔδεισαν αὐτόν). Chapters 2–3 then describe a series of mounting conflicts between Jesus and (a) the scribes (2:6-7), (b) the scribes and Pharisees (2:16), (c) the Pharisees and the disciples of John (2:18), and (d) the Pharisees again in 2:23–3:6.

In Mark 3:11, then, we encounter the first use of son-of-God language since 1:11 at the close of what may be considered Mark's "opening act" (1:16–3:12).[40] Following Keck's treatment of the passage, most interpreters agree that 3:7-12 comprises a summary paragraph (*Sammelbericht*), which draws the opening section of the narrative to a meaningful close.[41] With yet another bold statement of Jesus's identity, 3:11 may

---

[37] The idiomatic question τί ἡμῖν καὶ σοί appears in both classical Greek and the LXX, where it translates the similar Hebrew idiom, מה־לי ולך (see Josh 22:24; Judg 11:12; 2 Sam 16:10; 19:23; 1 Kgs 17:18; 2 Kgs 3:13; 2 Chr 35:21; Hos 14:8). Though the question can carry the simple force of "What do we have in common?" (e.g., in 2 Kgs 3:13; 2 Chr 35:21), it often bears the more aggressive meaning "What do you have against me?" Guelich (*Mark*, 57) points out that the question "is almost always posed by an inferior to a superior"; thus, the unclean spirit recognizes Jesus's greater might from the beginning; cf. Otto Bächli, "Was habe ich mit Dir zu schaffen?: Eine formelhafte Frage im A.T. und N.T." *TZ* 33 (1977): 69–80; Koch, *Wundererzählungen*, 57–6. (The references in 2 Sam 16:10; 19:23, both spoken by David to the sons of Zeruiah, may be regarded as rare exceptions; however, even in these instances David poses the question while he is in a particularly despondent, even semi-defeated, state.) Given this apparent recognition, ἦλθες ἀπολέσαι ἡμᾶς, should be regarded as a sincere question expressing fear in the face of Jesus's identity and inherent mission: so Marcus, *Mark 1–8*, 188; *contra* Hooker, *Mark*, 64.

[38] So France, *Mark*, 103; see also Gnilka (*Markus*, 81), who observes that the question is almost a statement: Jesus's mission is to destroy the demonic forces. H. C. Kee ("The Terminology of Mark's Exorcism Stories," *NTS* 14 [1968]: 232–46, here 235) argued persuasively that Mark's use of ἐπιτιμάω in both 1:25 and 3:12 recalls its use in the LXX where it usually translates the Hebrew גער, a *terminus technicus* in both the OT and at Qumran for God's "subjugating word" by which "evil powers are brought into submission"; cf. Kazmierski, *Son of God*, 97–8; Guelich, *Mark*, 57; Gundry, *Mark*, 77; Marcus, *Mark 1–8*, 194; Boring, *Mark*, 65.

[39] Pesch, *Markusevangelium*, 122. Pesch also points out that the use of the plural ἡμῖν and ἡμᾶς implies that the unclean spirit speaks here as a representative of the entire collective group of demons; hence, the whole world of the demonic; cf. Hooker, *Mark*, 64; Malbon, *Mark's Jesus*, 80; Elizabeth E. Shively, "Purification of the Body and the Reign of God in the Gospel of Mark," *JTS* 71 (2020): 62–89 (here, 78).

[40] Mark's "structure" is notoriously difficult to identify. Yet in the view of almost all interpreters, 1:16–3:6/12 constitutes a broad unit and the first major section of the Gospel after the prologue; see, e.g., the literary outlines suggested by Guelich, *Mark 1–8:26*, xxxvi; Marcus, *Mark 1–8*, 64; Black, *Mark*, 8, 68.

[41] See Leander E. Keck, "Mark 3:7-12 and Mark's Christology," *JBL* 84 (1965): 341–58. Citing agreement with Keck, see Gnilka, *Markus*, 1:135; Kazmierski, *Son of God*, 84–5; Guelich, *Mark 1–8:26*, 142–44; Marcus, *Mark 1–8*, 259; Standaert, *Marc*, 249; Black, *Mark*, 103. Collins (*Mark*, 211) calls 3:7-12 an "editorial formulation" and agrees that the passage effectively recapitulates the preceding narrative

be deemed the climax of this summary and, by extension, 1:16–3:12 as a whole. Here we read that "the unclean spirits, whenever they beheld him, would customarily fall down before him and cry aloud saying, 'You are the Son of God!'" (καὶ τὰ πνεύματα τὰ ἀκάθαρτα, ὅταν αὐτὸν ἐθεώρουν, προσέπιπτον αὐτῷ καὶ ἔκραζον λέγοντες ὅτι σὺ εἶ ὁ υἱὸς τοῦ θεοῦ).[42]

Falling where they do, the words σὺ εἶ ὁ υἱὸς τοῦ θεοῦ work together with God's decree σύ εἶ ὁ υἱός μου in 1:11 to form an inclusion, or bracket, around the entire first section of Mark's narrative. Whoever Jesus is in Mark's narrative so far, he is the Son of God.[43] But this same Son of God has already been defined by Mark's narrative in terms of Ps 2:7—a definition we have reason to believe 3:11 recalls inasmuch as it appears to deliberately recall Mark 1:11 itself. It is possible, then, to lend sharper definition to the statement above: whoever Jesus is in Mark's early narrative, he is the anointed "Son" of Ps 2:7, whose charter is to overcome the powers opposed to God's rule and, conversely, instantiate God's reign on earth (see esp. Ps 2:1-2). In fact, just before we reach Mark's summary in 3:7-12, we encounter a seldom-noted, but probable, allusion to no other passage than Ps 2:1-2.

4.4.1 Taking Counsel against God's Son (Mark 3:6)

Although it falls outside the *Sammelbericht* itself, various interpreters have observed that Mark 3:6 serves a bridge-like function, linking 3:7-12 back to the very narrative of Jesus's ministry that it summarizes (1:16–3:5).[44] In any case, it would be a mistake to read 3:7-12 in isolation from 3:6 simply because they fall within different sections of an outline that is, to some degree, arbitrary in the first place.[45]

This single verse, then, concludes the whole series of conflicts in Chapters 2–3 by describing an unlikely alliance between the Pharisees and the Herodians against Jesus

---

(1:16–3:6). Earlier scholarship (see Taylor, *Mark*, 225; Cranfield, *Mark*, 124; Schweizer, *Mark*, 78; Egger, *Frohbotschaft*, 93; and Pesch, *Markusevangelium*, 1:201–02) maintained that the paragraph summarized what follows instead; and a few since Keck, such as T. A. Burkill ("Mark 3:7-12 and the Alleged Dualism in the Evangelist's Miracle Material," *JBL* 87 [1968]: 409–17) have argued that 3:7-12 summarizes *both* what precedes *and* what follows (see similarly Stein, *Mark*, 159). But Guelich (*Mark 1–8:26*, 144) rightly points out that the earlier view "gives too much prominence to the controversy unit [2:1–3:6] as an entity in itself, overlooks the thrust of 1:21-45, and fails to see how 3:7-12 functions to bring together Mark's portrait of Jesus's ministry from 1:16 to 3:6." It also need not surprise anyone to find some motifs and themes from Mark 1:16–3:12 repeated in the subsequent narrative.

[42] Note the customary (or iterative) use of the imperfect (see BDF §325) throughout 3:11-12 (ἐθεώρουν, προσέπιπτον, ἔκραζον, ἐπετίμα). Cf. Meyer, *Markus*, 41.

[43] Black (*Mark*, 103) describes Mark 3:7-12 as "bookending 1:14-15." So closely do 1:11 and 3:11 mirror one another that many interpreters suppose the latter intentionally recalls the former: e.g., Douglas R. A. Hare, *Mark* (Louisville: Westminster John Knox, 1996), 46; Collins, "Son of God among Jews," 394, 400; Marcus, *Mark 1–8*, 261; Donahue and Harrington, *Mark*, 121; Lars Hartman, *Markus evangeliet*, Kommentar till Nya testamentet 2a–2b (Stockholm: EFS-förlaget, 2004), 117; Standaert, *Marc*, 256; Fabio La Gioia, *Marco: analisi narrativa del Vangelo più antico*, Collana Logos (Todi: Tau editrice, 2019), 76.

[44] Marcus, *Mark 1–8*, 251; Donahue and Harrington, *Mark*, 121; Moloney, *Mark*, 71–2.

[45] So Hooker (*Mark*, 109), who considers the boundaries between 3:6 and 3:7 to be "largely arbitrary."

in the following words: καὶ ἐξελθόντες οἱ Φαρισαῖοι εὐθὺς μετὰ τῶν Ἡρῳδιανῶν συμβούλιον ἐδίδουν κατ' αὐτοῦ ὅπως αὐτὸν ἀπολέσωσιν. Among the peculiarities within this verse is Mark's unusual phrase συμβούλιον ἐδίδουν, which occurs nowhere else in extant ancient Greek literature.[46] Yet this phrase does bear a family resemblance to certain other expressions that occur in the Gospels, such as συμβούλιον ποιήσαντες in Mark 15:1 and Matthew's συμβούλιον ἔλαβον/λάβοντες (12:14; 22:15; 27:1-2, 7; and 28:12).[47] All three of these expressions, moreover, are limited to the Gospels and later Christian literature citing the Gospels and, more specifically, the plot to murder Jesus.[48] The present example is, in fact, the first foreshadowing of Jesus's death in Mark's Gospel, and the phrase συμβούλιον ἐδίδουν itself is often understood as an intra-narrative foreshadowing of the similar expression συμβούλιον ποιήσαντες in Mark 15:1 (Καὶ εὐθὺς πρωῒ συμβούλιον ποιήσαντες οἱ ἀρχιερεῖς μετὰ τῶν πρεσβυτέρων καὶ γραμματέων καὶ ὅλον τὸ συνέδριον, δήσαντες τὸν Ἰησοῦν ἀπήνεγκαν καὶ παρέδωκαν Πιλάτῳ).[49]

The plot thickens when one also recognizes the association of this whole family of expressions with Ps 2:2 (καὶ οἱ ἄρχοντες συνήχθησαν ἐπὶ τὸ αὐτὸ κατὰ τοῦ κυρίου καὶ κατὰ τοῦ χριστοῦ αὐτοῦ) throughout early Christian literature. Although the phrase συμβούλιον— does not occur in Ps 2:2 LXX, this verse was perhaps the *locus classicus* for the motif of conspiracy against the Lord's Anointed. As we have seen, Acts 4:24-28 cites Ps 2:1-2 with explicit reference to Jesus's passion. In Matthew, moreover, the phrase συμβούλιον ἔλαβον/λάβοντες regularly serves as a gloss for συναχθέντες, which alludes to Ps 2:2 throughout Matthew's passion narrative (Matt 26:3-4, 57; 27:17, 27).[50] Additionally, in Matt 26:3-4 the cognate verb συμβουλεύω immediately follows an allusion to Ps 2:2 (συνήχθησαν οἱ ἀρχιερεῖς καὶ οἱ πρεσβύτεροι τοῦ λαοῦ).

Origen and Theodoret seem to have picked up on the connection, for both view Matthew's συμβούλιον language in 27:1-2, 7 and 28:12 as allusions to Ps 2:2.[51] Similarly,

---

[46] Taylor (*Mark*, 224) thinks the phrase could be based on a Semitic idiom—a suggestion that coheres with the analysis below.

[47] Origen, *Comm. John* 28.12 (*PG* 14:709, 712); and Chrysostom, *Hom. Matt.* 86 (*PG* 58.760), in fact, use these expressions interchangeably.

[48] To be precise, a TLG search produces *one* occurrence of συμβούλιον λαμβάνω outside of the NT: in Aesop's Fables, which are notoriously difficult to date.

[49] So also Gundry, *Mark*, 152; Hooker, *Mark*, 108; Marcus, *Mark 1-8*, 250-54; Donahue and Harrington, *Mark*, 116; Moloney, *Mark*, 71; cf. Black, *Mark*, 100. Boring (*Mark*, 96) goes further by cataloging a whole series of parallels between 3:1-6 and later passion material in Mark, concluding that while 3:1-6 is "based on earlier tradition, Mark arranges the narrative so that the pattern ... of the passion permeates the story throughout." In my judgment, Gundry is probably correct to suggest that both verses (3:6; 15:1) belong to pre-Markan tradition. This is especially probable in view of a pre-Markan passion narrative (cf. Mark 15:1; Matt 27:1); see esp. Pesch, *Markusevangelium*, 2:364-77; Marion L. Soards, "Appendix IX: "The Question of a PreMarcan Passion Narrative," Brown, *The Death of the Messiah*, 2:1492-1524. Markan redaction in 3:6 is even more probable in this case, since the expression and motif here typically belong to the passion narratives. Mark has not invented 3:6 but interjected it from elsewhere in the tradition.

[50] On Matthew's use of συναχθέντες and other forms of συνάγω in the passion narrative as allusions to Ps 2 see e.g., Brian M. Nolan, *The Royal Son of God: The Christology of Matthew 1-2 in the Setting of the Gospel*, OBO 23 (Göttingen: Vandenhoeck & Ruprecht, 1979), 88; Robert H. Gundry, *Matthew: A Commentary on His Literary and Theological Art* (Grand Rapids: Eerdmans, 1982), 518; Davies and Allison, *Matthew*, 3:438; Eugene Boring, "Matthew," in *NIB* (Nashville: Abingdon, 1995). 8:464 n. 550; and esp. Ferda, "Psalm 2," 569-70.

[51] Origen, *Hom. Ps. ad loc.* (*PG* 12:1102b); Theodoret, *Comm. Ps. ad loc.* (*PG* 80:874d).

Athanasius later quotes Ps 2:2 in full as an exposition of the cognate expression συμβούλιον γενόμενον, and Leontius uses συμβούλιόν λαβόντες interchangeably with συναχθέντες when discussing Jesus's trial.[52] Both Origen and Chrysostom also use Mark's συμβούλιον ποιήσαντες interchangeably with συναχθέντες.[53] Once again, it is suggestive that none of these related expressions ever occurs in any context other than discussions of Jesus's passion or foreshadowings thereof.[54]

To summarize, the facts are these:

1. Συμβούλιον ἐδίδουν is unattested apart from Mark 3:6.
2. The clause belongs to a group of related expressions (συμβούλιον—).
3. Matthew, Origen, Chrysostom, Athanasius, and Leontius all employ or recognize expressions of this group as a gloss for συνήχθησαν from Ps 2:2.
4. None of these expressions ever occurs outside of a link to the plot against Jesus in his passion, which is also associated with Ps 2:1-2 in the tradition (e.g., Matt 26-27, Acts 4:25-26).

In his commentary on Mark 3:6, Pesch, recognizing the similar language and shared motifs between the two passages, wonders "whether the narrator thinks of Ps 2:1f in the face of the alliance against Jesus, as in Acts 4:24ff."[55] In view of the evidence presented above, I suggest that Pesch is more than justified in his curiosity. In all probability, Mark did indeed think of Ps 2:1-2, for wherever such language occurs in ancient literature, Ps 2:1-2 is near at hand.

4.4.2 Recapitulating the Son of God and His Mission (Mark 3:7-12)

If Mark 3:6 contrasts the murderous intent of the Pharisees and Herodians with Jesus's own "intention of giving life" (3:4), on the one hand, it likewise contrasts their conspiracy against him with the attraction of the crowds in 3:7-8, on the other.[56] With no further ado, Mark transitions to the summary of Jesus's early ministry in 3:7-12.

---

[52] Athanasius, *Ep. Fest.* 11 (*PG* 26:1411); Leontius, *Hom.* 6 (*CChr* 17).
[53] Origen *Comm. John*, 28.12 (*PG* 14:709, 712); Chrysostom *Hom. Matt.*, 86, 90 (*PG* 58:761, 787).
[54] In addition to Mark 3:6, on Matt 12:14 and 22:15 as foreshadowings of the passion, see Jack Dean Kingsbury, "The Developing Conflict between Jesus and the Jewish Leaders in Matthew's Gospel: A Literary-Critical Study," *CBQ* 49 (1987): 60; John Paul Heil, *The Death and Resurrection of Jesus: A Narrative-Critical Reading of Matthew 26-28* (Minneapolis: Fortress, 1991), 16-7; and esp. Dale C. Allison, Jr., "Foreshadowing the Passion," in *Studies in Matthew: Interpretation Past and Present* (Grand Rapids: Baker Academic, 2005), 217-35. Matt 12:14, parallel to Mark 3:6, is indeed an exact parallel with 26:4, where the verb συμβουλεύω is connected to an allusion to Ps 2:2 utilizing συνήχθησαν in the previous verse (26:3).
[55] See Pesch (*Markusevangelium*, 1:201): "Ob der Erzähler angesichts des Bündnisses gegen Jesus wie Apg 4,24ff an Ps 2,1f denkt, muß offenbleiben." Donahue and Harrington (*Mark*, 121–22) also hint at a connection between Mark 3:6 and Ps 2:1-2.
[56] So, respectively, Marcus (*Mark 1–8*, 251) and Kazmierski (*Son of God*, 85); Légasse (*Marc*, 223); Standaert (*Marc*, 250); and Gundry (*Mark*, 156–57). Gundry further observes that the atypical advancement of Jesus's name before the verb in 3:7 sets him in greater contrast to the Pharisees and Herodians in 3:6; thus, we may speak of a marked contrast in between 3:6 and 7, which implies an intentional linkage between the two verses.

This tightly constructed paragraph recapitulates the events of the narrative so far in three respects.⁵⁷ (1) The gathering of the crowds "following" (ἠκολούθησεν) Jesus from all around (3:7-8) recalls earlier moments in the narrative such as 1:45 (καὶ ἤρχοντο πρὸς αὐτὸν πάντοθεν) and 1:5, where "all Judea and all the Jerusalemites" come to receive John's baptism.⁵⁸ (2) The statement that Jesus "healed many" (3:10: πολλοὺς γὰρ ἐθεράπευσεν) summarizes Jesus's activity throughout 1:30-34, 40-45; 2:1-12; and 3:1-5. (3) We have seen Jesus cast out unclean spirits (3:11-12) in 1:23-27, 32-34, and 39. These observations are not new, but what is not usually stated is that this entire summary is designed to recapitulate Jesus's messianic identity and mission.

To begin with, Mark's list of geographic regions in 3:7b-8 has garnered a great deal of attention over the years.⁵⁹ According to Mark's depiction, "a great multitude followed [Jesus] from Galilee; and from Judea and from Jerusalem and from Idumea and beyond the Jordan and the regions around Tyre and Sidon, a great multitude, upon hearing what things he was doing came to him."⁶⁰ Mark's list has no exact parallel in Matthew or Luke;⁶¹ and, aside from the obvious fact that Mark depicts people coming to Jesus from all of the surrounding area, some of the idiosyncrasies of his list beg for further explanation.⁶² The most common explanation (rightly, in my view) is that Mark symbolically points toward the eschatological gathering of Israel around Jesus, just as he also appears to do with the commissioning of the "Twelve" in the next paragraph (3:13-19).⁶³ But even so, Marcus rightly points out that not all of the regions

---

⁵⁷ The construction of 3:7-12 has been the subject of much scholarly discussion, often attempting to decipher Mark's redaction of his material (see, e.g., Taylor, *Mark*, 225; Keck, "Mark 3:7-12," 346–47; Reploh, *Markus*, 37; Pesch, *Markusevangelium*, 1:198; Gnilka, *Markus*, 1:133; Schweizer, *Mark*, 79; Guelich, *Mark 1–8:26*, 144; Marcus, *Mark 1–8*, 259). But the evangelist's "tight focus" is also recognized by those who reject redaction criticism of Mark's Gospel—e.g., Black (*Mark*, 104): "Mark continues to keep a tight focus on Jesus' healing power and authoritative command."
⁵⁸ See also 1:28; 2:2, 4, 13. Cf. Hooker, *Mark*, 110; Collins, *Mark*, 211–13.
⁵⁹ For a helpful summary of past suggestions in addition to those given below, see Guelich, *Mark 1–8:26*, 146.
⁶⁰ Meyer (*Markus*, 41) insightfully observes that while the each of the principal regions of Israel is introduced independently by a repeated use of ἀπό, the additional regions are effectively grouped together and introduced by a single ἀπό (ἀπὸ τῆς Ἰδουμαίας καὶ πέραν τοῦ Ἰορδάνου καὶ περὶ Τύρον καὶ Σιδῶνα). Thus, the list effectively distinguishes between (a) the principal regions of Israel and (b) the extremities of its borders.
⁶¹ The closest approximations are in Matt 4:25 and Luke 6:17. See further below.
⁶² For instance, Mark 3:8 is the only mention of Idumea in the NT and the inclusion of Tyre and Sidon opposite the omission of the Decapolis and Samaria is striking. Taylor (*Mark*, 227); Karl L. Schmidt (*Der Rahmen der Geschichte Jesu: literarkritische Untersuchungen zur ältesten Jesusüberlieferung* [Darmstadt: Wissenschaftliche Buchgesellschaft, 1969], 106) and Lane (*Mark*, 129) speculate that Mark names the regions in which Jesus ministers throughout the Gospel, but this view fails since Jesus never ministers in Idumea and only passes through Tyre and Sidon. Others, such as Pesch (*Markusevangelium*, 1:200) and Ernst (*Markus*, 110) suggest that these are the locations of churches in the time of the evangelist, yet both Gnilka (*Markus*, 1:134) and Egger (*Frohbotschaft*, 102) note a lack of evidence for this view. Finally, Légasse (*Marc*, 223) suggests that Mark envisages the future expansion of Christianity beyond Israel's borders; yet, apart from Tyre and Sidon, most of the regions Mark names have to do precisely with Israel's regions and borders.
⁶³ So, e.g., Erich Klostermann, *Das Markusevangelium*, 4th ed., HNT 3 (Tübingen: Mohr Siebeck, 1950), 33; Karl-Georg Reploh, *Markus, Lehrer der Gemeinde: eine redaktionsgeschichtliche Studie zu den Jüngerperikopen des Markus-Evangeliums*, SBM 9 (Stuttgart: Katholisches Bibelwerk, 1969), 38; Grundmann, *Markus*, 76; Guelich, *Mark*, 146; Marcus, *Mark 1–8*, 254. Among those who consider

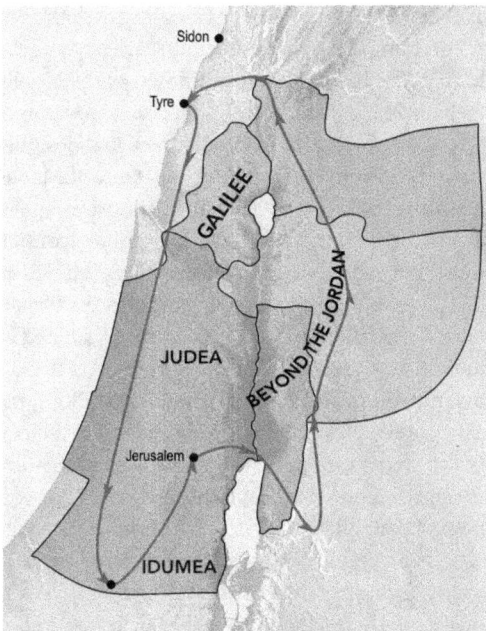

Figure 4.1 Mark's List with David's Census Route[64]

Mark names were part of Israel in the first century; indeed, Tyre and Sidon never belonged to Israel.[65] Marcus's observation suggests that there is room to sharpen the basic explanation offered by others.[66] To this end, I propose a variation of the typical explanation above: Mark may deliberately recall precisely the regions and boundaries of *David's* kingdom rather than those of Israel in his own day.

Mark's repeated emphasis on the number "twelve" (ἐποίησεν δώδεκα . . . ἐποίησεν τοὺς δώδεκα) in 3:13-19 a purposeful allusion to the twelve tribes of Israel pointing toward Israel's restoration, see Cranfield, *Mark*, 127; Pesch, *Markusevangelium*, 1:204; Schweizer, *Mark*, 81; Guelich, *Mark 1–8:26*, 165; Hooker, *Mark*, 111; Marcus, *Mark 1–8*, 266; Moloney, *Mark*, 78; Black, *Mark*, 106. As Bock (*Mark*, 164) writes, "within Israel, a picture of restoring Israel emerges." For comparison, Bock lists Matt 19:28; Luke 22:28-30; Isa 49:6; Ezek 45:8; Sir 36:10; 48:10; *Ps. Sol.* 17:26-32; *Sib. Or.* 2.170-176; *T. Jos.* 19:1-7; Josephus, *Ant.* 11.133. Matera (*Kingship*, 105) further observes that the authority given to them to exorcise demons (3:15), moreover, seems derivative of Jesus's own authority as the Son of God (3:11) and indicates an initial fulfillment of Israel's eschatological restoration.

[64] Map generated using Accordance 13 (OakTree Software, Inc., 2019).

[65] Marcus, *Mark 1–8*, 260. Idumea, for instance, could only be considered Jewish by virtue of having been forcibly converted under the Hasmoneans (see 1 Macc 4:36-59; 2 Macc 10:1-8; Josephus, *Ant.* 13.9; *War* 1.63); the Transjordan had been part of ancient Israel (Num 32:33-42), but Israelite control of the Transjordan (Perea) ended when the Assyrians conquered the area in 733 BCE (2 Kgs 15:29); see Diane I. Treacy-Cole, "Perea," *ABD* 5:224.

[66] Marcus's own suggestion (*Mark 1–8*, 260) is that Mark may wish to point toward the inclusion of Gentiles as well as the restoration of Israel; cf. Focant, *Marc*, 139; Black, *Mark*, 103–04. While plausible, however, this suggestion still does not explain why Mark mentions *Tyre and Sidon*, in particular, as opposed to a region like the Decapolis, in which Jesus actually ministers (5:20; 7:31; cf. Matt 4:25).

While the regions Mark lists do not line up perfectly with the boundaries of Israel in Mark's own day, they correspond nicely to the boundaries of Israel under David's reign. Idumea, for example, matches the region once known as the Negeb of Judah, bounded by the city of Beersheba in the south.[67] Mark's phrase πέραν τοῦ Ἰορδάνου, while less specific than "Perea" (cf. Josephus, *Ant.* 13.50), is the usual designation in the LXX for the Transjordan occupied Reuben, Gad, and the half-tribe of Manasseh: ancient Israel's eastern border.[68] And while the cities of Tyre and Sidon were never part of Israel, the regions around Tyre and Sidon (cf. Mark 3:8) are uniquely counted in David's census (2 Sam 24:5-7), which mentions that the census takers "circled round to Sidon and came to the fortress of Tyre" before proceeding south to the Negeb.[69] One can, in fact, superimpose the route of David's census onto the regions named by Mark as follows:

On the whole, Mark's list makes good sense if he means to portray not merely the gathering of all Israel, but the restoration of *David's* kingdom, in particular. On this reading, Mark not only presents Jesus bringing about Israel's eschatological restoration, as others have supposed, but more precisely as David's eschatological successor, the royal Messiah, who brings such restoration to bear via the Kingdom of God.

Within the framework established by the gathering multitude in 3:7-8, it is not difficult to imagine Jesus's healings (3:10) and exorcisms (3:11-12) as further evidence of his messianic identity. Though healings in and of themselves need not *necessarily* point to a messianic figure, there is evidence that healings *could* serve as messianic signs.[70] Most notoriously, 4Q*Messianic Apocalypse* (4Q521) declares that the Messiah's "spirit will hover over the poor"; "he will renew the faithful with his strength ... freeing the prisoners, giving sight to the blind, [and] straightening the twisted" (2:5-8).[71] A similar list appears in Matt 11:5 (cf. Luke 7:22 [Q 7:22]), dubbed τὰ ἔργα τοῦ Χριστοῦ (Matt 11:2).[72] What makes the comparison of these two texts particularly intriguing is that both appear to draw upon Isa 61:1-2—a text that figures prominently in the Synoptic tradition elsewhere (e.g., Luke 4:18-19).[73] It is possible, then, that, under

---

[67] Idumea is also mentioned in similar lists in Josephus, *War* 2:43; *Ant.* 17:254. For Beersheba as the southern boundary of Idumea, see Ulrich Hübner, "Idumea," *ABD* 3:382. Hübner also that the region of Idumea is geographically equivalent to that of the Negeb.

[68] See, e.g., Num 32:19, 32; 34:15; 35:14; Deut 3:20; 4:41, 46; Josh 1:15; 13:8; 18:7; 20:8; 21:36; 22:4, 7, 11; Judg 5:17; 10:8; 1 Sam 31:7; 1 Chr 6:63; 12:38.

[69] In addition to the fact that their environs are counted in David's census, Tyre and Sidon are closely associated with David elsewhere. Tyre, in particular, is perhaps David's (and Solomon's) closest ally, and it is Tyre's King Hiram who gives his aid in the construction of both kings' palaces and Solomon's temple. See 2 Sam 5:11, 7:13, 40-45, 9:11-14, 27, 10:11, 22. Cf. Scott P. Noegel, "Phoenicia, Phoenicians," *DOTHB*, 792-98, esp. 794-95.

[70] See Lidija Novakovic, *Messiah, the Healer of the Sick: A Study of Jesus as the Son of David in the Gospel of Matthew*, WUNT 2/170 (Tübingen: Mohr Siebeck, 2003), esp. 152-83. Novakovic demonstrates that Matthew portrays the Davidic Messiah (Jesus) as a healer through his creative interpretation of the Jewish Scriptures.

[71] Slightly adapted from García Martínez and Tigchelaar, *The Dead Sea Scrolls*.

[72] Matt 11:5 reads: "the blind receive sight, the lame walk, lepers are cleansed, the deaf hear, the dead are raised, and the poor receive good tidings."

[73] For a detailed comparison of 4Q521 2:5-8 and Q 7:22, see Dale C. Allison, Jr., *The Intertextual Jesus: Scripture in Q* (Harrisburg, PA: Trinity Press International, 2000), 110-12. As Allison (111) observes, the list in 4Q521 "is based upon Psalm 146[:6-8] with secondary influence from Isaiah, including Isa 61:1-2." Allison (112) concludes that "[t]he list in 4Q521 is far from identical with the recitation of

the influence of texts like Isa 61:1-2, healings were sometimes among those works expected of the Messiah.

In any case, Mark 3:7-12 presents Jesus's healings and exorcisms as the *de facto* reason for the gathering of the multitude around Jesus.[74] If 3:7-8 points to the eschatological restoration of David's kingdom, then Mark likewise presents Jesus's healings and exorcisms as the works affecting that restoration. Indeed, throughout the first three chapters of his narrative, Mark offers Jesus's healings and exorcisms as demonstrations of who Jesus is on some level; yet who Jesus is Mark has already told us: he is χριστός υἱὸς θεοῦ (1:1).

Yet when we come to 3:11, one commonly reads that "there seems to have been no general expectation in Judaism that the Messiah would be an exorcist."[75] True though this may generally be, we have nevertheless seen a number of texts that anticipate the binding or exile of demonic powers in the messianic age, including some in which the Messiah is directly involved in the overthrow of the demonic.[76] Nowhere is the Messiah's personal agency in the destruction of the demonic more evident than in the tradition emanating from Ps 2:1-2, in which the hostile rulers to be overcome by God's anointed "Son" were not infrequently associated with demonic forces.[77] Ὁ υἱὸς τοῦ θεοῦ, then, is precisely who Mark associates with the exorcisms of demons in 3:11-12.

The focus on Jesus's exorcisms in 3:11-12 repeats the general pattern and much of the language observed in the earlier Capernaum synagogue episode (1:23-27).[78] The demons routinely "fall before" (προσέπιπτον) Jesus and cry out (ἔκραζον) his identity, after which he rebukes (ἐπετίμα) and silences them. Such repetition, along with the renewed use of τὰ πνεύματα τὰ ἀκάθαρτα and the customary imperfect, helps give a certain paradigmatic character to the account: it is not simply once or occasionally, but indeed *customarily*, that the unclean spirits single Jesus out as ὁ υἱὸς τοῦ θεοῦ.[79] On a narrative level, this brief summary serves to reinforce the link between Jesus's identity as the Son of God and his role in vanquishing the supernatural powers opposed to God's rule.

All told, the unclean spirits' outcry ὁ υἱὸς τοῦ θεοῦ in Mark 3:11 forms the climax of a *Sammelbericht* that reinforces Jesus's messianic identity and mission from beginning to end. As Black aptly states, "3:7-12 summarizes what the shifting sovereignty from Satan (1:13) to God entails."[80] Its use, as such, at the end of the first broad section of Mark's narrative aligns closely with the use of ὁ υἱὸς μου in 1:11, which served to

---

Jesus' deeds in Q, and the parallels should not be exaggerated. Yet it does appear that phrases from Isa 61:1-2 were sometimes brought into connection with other scriptural sentences from Isaiah and elsewhere in order to paint a picture of the eschatological future." It should also be noted that Ps 146:6 is also used in Acts 4:24 (alongside Ps 2:1-2) and 14:15 to describe the new age ushered in by Jesus.

[74] As evidenced, first, by the causal phrase ἀκούοντες ὅσα ἐποίει in 3:8 and, again, by the inferential γάρ that introduces Jesus's healings and exorcisms at the beginning of 3:10.
[75] Marcus, *Mark 1–8*, 261.
[76] See n. 19 above.
[77] See n. 4 above.
[78] Cf. La Gioia, *Marci*, 76.
[79] See n. 41.
[80] Black, *Mark*, 105; cf. Theissen, *Miracle Stories*, 89–91.

distinguish Jesus as God's anointed Messiah (Ps 2:7): his royal vice regent commissioned to instantiate his rule on earth.

Glancing backward, it is highly suggestive that Mark places an allusion in 3:6 to Ps 2:1-2, alluding to the collusion of God's enemies against his anointed, just before this summary in 3:7-12, which concludes by hearkening back to his identity as God's anointed Son destined by him to overcome those same forces. So far as I am aware, only one commentator, Donahue, even hints at the implications of this connection. His words are thus worth quoting at length:

> The summary clearly culminates in the final words of 3:11, "You are the Son of God," which take the readers back to the first words of the gospel (1:1) and foreshadow the use of this same title in the trial and crucifixion episodes (14:62; 15:39). In the title "Son of God" there is an implicit hint of opposition. Christian adoption of the title reflects in part an apologetic use of Psalm 2, the psalm of royal adoption where the central point is the divine decree: "You are my son; today I have begotten you" (2:7; 2 Sam 7:14; Ps 89:26-27). The context of Psalm 2 is opposition to the king (vv. 1-3), followed by divine derision at this opposition and installation of the king (vv. 4-6). The adopted son is then assured of divine protection (vv. 7-12). *In this Markan summary, then, following immediately upon the plan to kill Jesus which will unfold in tragic inevitability, the readers are informed that, as in Psalm 2, such opposition is but a prelude to the victory of God's regent.*[81]

By now we have seen historical evidence and exegesis enough to support Donahue's comments on every level. Indeed, Ps 2:1-2, alluded to in Mark 3:6, is both the section of the psalm widely associated with opposition to God's anointed and, at times, demonic forces supposed to be behind that opposition. Psalm 2:7, recalled in roundabout way by 3:11, then evokes once more the assured enthronement and ensuing victory of God's anointed Son over against those powers. In the larger scheme of Mark 1:1–3:12, the evangelist presents Jesus as God's Messiah-Son (1:1) who, having been anointed by him to reign as his vice regent on earth (1:11), now enacts his identity by demolishing Satan's kingdom all around him (1:23-27; 3:11-12). As Donahue also hints, however, we have not yet reached the end of this burgeoning plot. Straightaway, we will see it continue in Mark's third and final account of Jesus's dialogue with the demons.

4.5 Mark 5:1-20: "You are the Son of the Most-High God"

On the other side of Mark's opening act, Jesus comes, in 5:1, to the country of the Gerasenes across the sea, where he is quickly met by a demoniac coming from the tombs, who addresses him as υἱὲ τοῦ θεοῦ ὑψίστου (5:7). In this and in other respects, Jesus's encounter with "Legion" (λεγιών) in 5:1-20 advances the same pattern we have seen above.[82] Upon seeing Jesus, the demoniac approaches and prostrates

---

[81] Donahue and Harrington, *Mark*, 121–22. Emphasis mine.

(προσεκύνησεν) himself before him (5:6; cf. 3:11), and cries aloud (κράξας φωνῇ μεγάλῃ) Jesus's identity as God's Son, which the unclean spirit associates with Jesus's intent to harm (βασανίσῃς) him (5:7, 10; cf. 1:24; 3:11). At once, Jesus commands the unclean spirit(s) to come out of the man and expels them (5:8-13; cf. 1:25; 3:11). The parallels in this episode are especially strong with the account in 1:23-27. For instance, the question, τί ἐμοὶ καὶ σοί, in 5:7 is a near verbatim repetition of τί ἡμῖν καὶ σοί in 1:24, and the plea that follows, ὁρκίζω σε τὸν θεόν, μή με βασανίςῃς, likewise reminds one of the question, ἦλθες ἀπολέσαι ἡμᾶς.[83]

In view of these intra-narrative parallels, the address υἱὲ τοῦ θεοῦ τοῦ ὑψίστου plainly belongs alongside the earlier cries ὁ ἅγιος τοῦ θεοῦ and ὁ υἱὸς τοῦ θεοῦ (1:24; 3:11). The expression itself is a kind of variation on ὁ υἱὸς τοῦ θεοῦ in the first place. Throughout the LXX, the base expression ὁ θεὸς ὁ ὑψίστος typically connotes YHWH's dominion over the nations and their gods at large (see, e.g., Pss 45:5; 70:19; 81:6; 90:1; 106:11; Sir 41:8), and likewise occurs often on the lips of Gentiles so as to distinguish the God of Israel over against all other gods (Gen 14:18-22; Num 24:16; Dan 3:93; 4:2, 17, 34; 5:18; 2 Macc 3:31; 1 Esd 2:3). Here, too, υἱὲ τοῦ θεοῦ τοῦ ὑψίστου occurs, fittingly, in a Gentile region.[84] By and large, it bears the same connotations as ὁ υἱὸς τοῦ θεοῦ in 3:11 and, for that matter, ὁ ἅγιος τοῦ θεοῦ—but with an added nuance that brings the notion of contest with other realms and powers (both natural and supernatural) to the fore. Though not an allusion to Ps 2:7 *per se*, within the overall scheme of Mark's narrative, it is only natural to read the demon's address in 5:7 in keeping with the previous expressions of Jesus's identity in 3:11; 1:24; and 1:11—in other words, as the royal Son of God named in Ps 2:7.

Significantly, the expression "Son of the Most-High" also occurs in Luke's annunciation narrative (1:32-35) and in 4Q246 2:1. As witnessed previously in Chapter 1, both of these texts use the term synonymously with "Son of God" in likely dependence on Ps 2:7.[85] The relevant passages read:

> *He will be great* and *he will be called the Son of the Most-High* (υἱὸς ὑψίστου). And the Lord God will give to him the throne of his ancestor David, and he will reign over the house of Jacob forever, and *of his kingdom there will be no end*.... The Holy Spirit will come upon you, and the power of the Most-High will overshadow you; and so the child to be born *will be called holy* (ἅγιος), *the Son of God* (υἱὸς θεοῦ).
> Luke 1:32-35

---

[82] Cf. Taylor, *Mark*, 280; Stein, *Mark*, 253.
[83] See similarly, France, *Mark*, 28; Standaert, *Marc*, 381.
[84] Marcus, *Mark 1-8*, 342-44; Bock, *Mark*, 189.
[85] See the previous discussion in Chapter 2. On the almost certain dependence of Luke 1:32-35 on 2 Sam 7:11-16 and possible dependence on Ps 2:7 as well, see also Fitzmyer, *Luke*, 1:206-07; 347-52; Green, *Luke*, 88-90; Bovon, *Luke*, 1:51. Meanwhile, just as as Fitzmyer suspects the influence of 2 Sam 7:14 and Ps 2:7 behind Luke 1:32-35, others suspect the same of 4Q246: so Collins, *Scepter*, 183-85; Gerbern S. Oegema, *The Anointed and his People: Messianic Expectations from the Maccabees to Bar Kochba* (Sheffield: Sheffield Academic Press, 1998), 122; Zimmermann, "Observations" in *Qumran-Messianism*, 180; Janse, *Son*, 53; and Ferda ("Naming the Messiah," 169), who notes that the naming convention in 4Q246 reminds one "in particular of the enthronement scenario envisaged in Ps 2."

He will be called [gr]eat and *he will be called son of God* (ברה די אל), and they *will call him son of the Most-High* (בר עליון).... *His kingdom will be an eternal kingdom* (מלכותה מלכות עלם) ... *his rule will be an eternal rule* (שלטנה שלטן עלם).

4Q246 1:9–2:9

Not only do both texts use similar biblical language to describe a ruler of an eternal kingdom who will be called both "Son of God" and "Son of the Most-High,"[86] but Luke, in particular, plainly assigns all of these terms to the realm of Davidic messianism with allusions to both 2 Sam 7:14 and (probably) Ps 2:7; the ruler spoken of will inherit the throne of his ancestor David and ruler over Israel forever. Intriguingly, Luke also interweaves the terms ὁ υἱὸς τοῦ θεοῦ, ὁ υἱὸς τοῦ θεοῦ τοῦ ὑψίστου, and ἅγιος all within the linguistic sphere of Davidic messianism, just as Mark appears to in 1:24; 3:11; and 5:7. The broader relationship between such terminology and Psalm 2 elsewhere only reinforces the natural implication of Mark's narrative otherwise: that it is the royal Son spoken of in Psalm 2 who now vanquishes the demonic powers.

Meanwhile, talk of rivalry with other gods and powers leads naturally to a discussion of the broader features of 5:1-20. Its fundamental similarities with prior episodes notwithstanding, the story of the Gerasene demoniac is by far the most detailed exorcism account in Mark (or any of the Gospels).[87] Among its more notable features are Mark's framing of the episode in terms of Isa 65:1-7 and his distinct use of military language—including the very name λεγιών (v. 9) and the accompanying emphasis on Legion's terrifying strength.

To begin with, the term λεγιών is a Latin loanword with its roots in the Roman army.[88] From the beginning of the episode (vv. 3-4), Mark lays special stress on the fact that no one has the strength to bind Legion, not even with a chain (καὶ οὐδὲ ἁλύσει οὐκέτι οὐδεὶς ἐδύνατο αὐτὸν δῆσαι), nor to subdue him (καὶ οὐδεὶς ἴσχυεν αὐτὸν δαμάσαι). Instead, Legion characteristically "shreds" (διεσπάσθαι) chains and "shatters" (συντετρῖφθαι) shackles. The use of ἴσχυεν in v. 4 reminds one of the earlier descriptions of Satan as ὁ ἰσχυρός in 3:27 and Jesus himself as ὁ ἰσχυρότερος in 1:7: whereas no one is strong enough to bind Legion, Jesus, "the stronger one," has already bound "the strong man," Satan.[89]

---

[86] As Collins ("Jesus, Messianism, and the Dead Sea Scrolls," in *Qumran-Messianism*, 109) states, "[t]he Greek titles 'Son of the Most High' and 'Son of God' [in Luke 1:32, 35] correspond exactly to the Aramaic fragment from Qumran."

[87] Mark's account in 5:1-20 is notably longer than the parallels in Matt 8:28-34 and Luke 8:26-39.

[88] See BDAG, "λεγιών," 587; D. Kennedy, "Roman Army," *ABD* 5:789; J. B. Campbell, "Legio," *BNP* 7:356-370. While it is possible that "legion" simply refers to the strength and number of the force Jesus faces (so Annen, *Heil*, 57–8; Witherington, *Mark*, 182; Standaert, *Marc*, 384–85; Bock, *Mark*, 190), the term's origin and strong association with the Roman army make it unlikely that a reader or hearer within in the Roman Empire would *not* think of the Roman army when encountering the word λεγιών (cf. Klaus Wengst, *Pax Romana: And the Peace of Jesus Christ*, trans. John Bowden [Philadelphia: Fortress, 1987], 66; and also Taylor, *Mark*, 281; Marcus, *Mark 1–8*, 344).

[89] Watts, *New Exodus*, 159; cf. Shively, *Apocalyptic*, 83.

Many of the terms that follow the unclean spirit(s) self-description as λεγιών are also common in military contexts, including ἀποστέλλω (v. 10), ἐπιτρέπω, and ὁρμάω (v. 13).⁹⁰ As Watts states, "[i]f we allow the clear military associations of λεγιών (v. 9) to establish the semantic parameters of the account," then ἀποστείλῃ connotes the dispatch of a military force; ἐπέτρεψεν, formal permission, or even a command, issued by a superior to a subordinate; and ὥρμησεν, the charge of troops into battle.⁹¹

For some exegetes, Mark's blatant use of military language points to nothing less than a polemic against Roman rule.⁹² On this reading, "Legion" is representative of the literal Roman legion occupying Judea, while Jesus's exorcism symbolizes future political liberation.⁹³ Others, however, doubt whether Mark has any such political aim.⁹⁴ Standaert, for instance, considers that, if Mark's purpose is to polemicize against Roman rule, he has blunted his own critique by portraying the true enemy as a spiritual one.⁹⁵ Twelftree, likewise, finds it hard for the story to evoke occupation since it takes place in Gentile, rather than Jewish, territory, and demonstrates broad use of the term λεγιών in non-political contexts.⁹⁶ As Shively concludes, then, "[i]n the context of Mark's unfolding narrative, λεγιών is best taken to refer to the army of demons under the control of Satan, their military king.⁹⁷ Whether or not Mark also intends some degree of double entendre implicating the Romans as earthly counterparts in league with the demonic powers (cf. the interpretation of Ps 2:1-2 in 4Q174 1:18–2:2) is unclear; but what is clear is that this episode fits within Mark's overall portrayal of

---

⁹⁰ J. Duncan M. Derrett, "Contributions to the Study of the Gerasene Demoniac," *JSNT* 2 (1979): 2–17 (here, 5); and more recently, Markus Lau, "Die Legio X Fretensis Und Der Besessene von Gerasa Anmerkungen Zur Zahlenangabe 'Ungefähr Zweitausend' (Mk 5,13)," *Bib* 88 (2007): 351–64, esp. 353.

⁹¹ Watts, *New Exodus*, 159. Watts also considers ἀγέλη (vv. 11, 13) to belong to this group of military terms, following Derrett ("Gerasene," 5–6), who maintains that the term is inappropriate for pigs, which are not herd animals, and are here acting more like an army. Yet Derrett's claim conflicts with the observations of animal behaviorists; see, e.g., J. P. Signoret, B. A. Baldwin, and D. Fraser, "The Behaviour of Swine," in *Behaviour of Domestic Animals*, ed. E. S. E. Hafez (London: Baillière Tindall, 1975), 295–29; as well as with the existence of a word for "swineherd" (συβώτης) already in Homer, *Od.*, 14.7; cf. LSJ, "συβώτης," s.v.

⁹² See, e.g., Theissen, *Miracle Stories*, 254–55; Klaus Wengst, *Pax Romana: Anspruch und Wirklichkeit: Erfahrungen und Wahrnehmungen des Friedens bei Jesus und im Urchristentum* (München: Kaiser, 1986), 111; Myers, *Binding*, 190–94; Richard Dormandy, "The Expulsion of Legion A Political Reading of Mark 5:1-20," *ExpTim* 111 (2000): 335–37; Christopher Burdon, "'To the Other Side': Construction of Evil and Fear of Liberation in Mark 5.1-20," *JSNT* 27 (2004): 149–67; Lau, "Legio X," 351–64; Warren Carter, "Cross-Gendered Romans and Mark's Jesus: Legion Enters the Pigs (Mark 5:1-20)," *JBL* 134 (2015): 139–55.

⁹³ Lau ("Legio X," 351–64) even sees the "pigs" (vv. 11-13) as a precise reference to the Legio X Fretensis, whose emblem was a boar. Yet it should be noted that the "boar" and the "pig" constituted very different symbols in the ancient world; the former was primarily associated with strength and ferocity, while the latter was primarily associated with sacrifice (see Annen, *Heil*, 163).

⁹⁴ E.g., Annen, *Heil*, 57–8; Twelftree, *Name*, 108–11; Standaert, *Marc*, 384–85; Shively, *Apocalyptic*, 83, 237; Hans M. Moscicke, "The Gerasene Exorcism and Jesus' Eschatological Expulsion of Cosmic Powers: Echoes of Second Temple Scapegoat Traditions in Mark 5.1-20," *JSNT* 41 (2019): 363–83. Marcus (*Mark 1-8*, 351–52) entertains the possibility of some anti-Roman polemic, but does not believe it to be the primary theme within the story; cf. Collins (*Mark*, 270): "The aim of the story is not—at least not primarily—to make a statement about the Romans."

⁹⁵ Standaert, *Marc*, 384–85.

⁹⁶ Twelftree, *Name*, 108–09.

⁹⁷ Shively, *Apocalyptic*, 237.

Jesus as the messianic Son of God who deposes the forces of Satan as he instantiates the kingdom of God.[98]

That is what Mark signifies, in turn, by framing "the actual deliverance with two uncharacteristic departures from his usual formal style in which he stresses the tomb dwelling [vv. 2-3, 5] and the presence of swine [vv. 11-16]."[99] Both features are allusions to Isa 65:1-7 LXX.[100]

The Isaiah text itself comprises a scathing critique against a group of apostate Israelites who have abandoned YHWH for the worship of idols (v. 1), behind which, according to Isa 65:3 LXX, stand demonic powers.[101] Whereas Mark depicts a man dwelling in the tombs and mountains and amid swine, Isaiah had previously spoken of those who "fall asleep in the tombs and in the caves for the sake of dreams, who eat swine-flesh and broth of sacrifices (all their vessels being defiled)" and "who burned incense on the mountains and reviled [YHWH] on the hills" (65:4, 7).[102] Isaiah 65:3 LXX, moreover, identifies the true recipients of this idolatrous behavior as δαιμόνια ("demons"). According to John Watts, v. 4 describes the "rituals of the cult of the dead, that is necromancy, in which one contacts the spirits of the dead by spending the night in the cemeteries."[103] Ancient interpreters also appear to have understood these verses to refer to an idolatrous cult. For example, where the LXX inserts δαιμόνια, Tg. Isa. 65:3 inserts טעות ("idols"), and Ibn Ezra comments on Isa 65:4 that the purpose of lying down in the tombs was "to inquire of the dead and to listen to the spirits."[104] Seemingly, eating swine-flesh and sleeping in tombs—both considered "unclean" in the Torah (see Lev 11:7; Deut 14:8; cf. Isa 66:17; m. 'Ohal. 17-18; b. Sanh. 65b; m. B. Qam. 7:7)—were

---

[98] See similarly Marcus, *Mark 1–8*, 352; Moscicke, "Gerasene," 378.

[99] Watts, *New Exodus*, 157 (I have modified the Scripture references from Watts's original quotation); cf. Guelich, *Mark* 277, 282; Kertelge, *Markusevangelium*, 104. In addition to Isa 65:1-7, Marcus (*Mark 1–8*, 348–49) observes possible allusions to several other scriptural passages, including Ps 68:8 LXX (cf. 5:2-3, 4, 19); Ps 65:7-8; and, chiefly, the crossing of the sea in Exodus 14–15; cf. Derrett, "Legend and Event," 64; idem, "Gerasene," 6–8; Gnilka, *Markus*, 1:199, following Harald Sahlin, "Die Perikope vom gerasenischen Besessenen und der Plan des Markusevangeliums," *ST* 18 (1964): 159–72; Stein, *Mark*, 247; Standaert, *Marc*, 394–96. The latter is possibility is intriguing and worth noting; as Marcus (348) writes, "[b]oth [Mark 5:1-20 and Exodus 14–15] are stories in which God displays his mercy on his people and his incomparable power over his enemies, and both climax in a scene in which a multitude is drowned; there are, besides, several verbal echoes of the Septuagint version of the Exodus tale." Thematically, an allusion to the exodus crossing would cohere with the Mark's presentation of Jesus delivering persons from bondage to Satan and into kingdom of God.

[100] Cf., *inter alia*, Taylor, *Mark*, 279; Gnilka, *Markus*, 1:199; Gundry, *Mark*, 258–59; Légasse, *Marc*, 321; Watts, *New Exodus*, 157–58; Marcus, *Mark 1–8*, 348; Stein, *Mark*, 247; Standaert, *Marc*, 377.

[101] Claus Westermann, *Isaiah 40–66: A Commentary*, trans. D. M. G. Stalker, OTL (Philadelphia: Westminster, 1969), 398–402; R. N. Whybray, *Isaiah 40-66*, NCB (Grand Rapids: Eerdmans, 1981), 266–71; John D. W. Watts, *Isaiah 34-66*, WBC 25 (Waco: Word, 1987), 912–13; John Goldingay, *A Critical and Exegetical Commentary on Isaiah 56-66*, ICC 24 (London: Bloomsbury, 2014), 440–53, esp. 440, 447. The notion that the powers standing behind the idols of foreign gods are actually demons reflects a widespread belief attested in Jewish literature; see Franz Annen, *Heil für die Heiden: zur Bedeutung u. Geschichte d. Tradition vom besessenen Gerasener (Mk 5, 1-20 parr.)*, FTS 20 (Frankfurt am Main: Knecht, 1976), 135–49.

[102] Translation adapted from NETS.

[103] Watts, *Isaiah 34-66*, 914; cf. Brooks Schramm, *The Opponents of Third Isaiah: Reconstructing the Cultic History of the Restoration*, JSOTSup 193 (Sheffield: Sheffield Academic, 1995), 156.

[104] Abraham ben Meïr Ibn Ezra, *The Commentary of Ibn Ezra on Isaiah*, 2 vols, trans. M. Friedländer, Society of Hebrew Literature (London: N. Trübner, 1873), 2:294.

practices of this cult. In its larger setting, however, Isa 65:1-7 ultimately looks toward an age when both idols and the demonic powers behind them will be no more. As Goldingay explains, within the larger scheme of Isaiah 56–66, judgment upon these acts comes as prelude to the restoration of Israel.[105] Insofar as they allude to Isaiah 65, then, tombs and pigs converge in Mark 5:1-10 to point not only toward idolatry and capitulation to the demonic, but also God's judgment upon the demonic and the concomitant deliverance of his people.

In further support of this reading, Franz Annen, in his detailed study of Mark 5:1-20, notes that swine were often associated with the worship of idols in the ancient world. In both Greece and Rome, pigs were choice animals for sacrifice.[106] Among Greeks, Annen contends, "[a]s a sacrificial animal, it is, above all, important in the cult of the chthonic deities [deities of the underworld], but was also sacrificed to almost all the gods," including Zeus (who was said to have been nursed by a pig as a child), Dionysius, Athena, Nemesis, Demeter, and Kore (Persephone).[107] The sacrificing of swine also played a role in various mystery cults.[108] Among Romans, swine were likewise sacrificed to almost all the gods, including Jupiter, Mars, Vulcan, Dis Pater, Hercules, Diana, Luna, Tellus, Maia, Ceres, and Dea Dia.[109] Pigs were, moreover, sacrificed in order to ratify contracts and alliances, at weddings, in private worship, and even for the purpose of atonement in at least two cases: (1) if one had shown neglect for the dead by failing to throw dirt on a corpse; (2) preventative atonement in advance of the harvest season.[110] Pigs were, however, particularly associated with the underworld and, thus, "[n]o Roman tomb was legally protected until a pig had been sacrificed."[111] Archaeological evidence noted by de Vaux and others demonstrates the existence of such cults in ancient Syria and Palestine.[112]

The same association of pigs and tombs under a broader umbrella of idolatry observed in Isaiah 65, then, was also a part of Mark's cultural foreground. Together, the background of Isaiah and the foreground of Mark's own world suggest that what we witness in Mark 5:1-20 is indeed a battle between rival powers: the unfolding conflict between God and the supernatural powers opposed to his rule.[113] As such, Mark 5:1-20 finally unveils to the fullest extent the battle between God's royal Son and the demonic powers that began as early as 1:10-13. In all of this, one can see the implications of Psalm 2 worked out, or actualized, across the narrative landscape of the Second Gospel.

---

[105] Goldingay, *Isaiah 56–66*, 453.
[106] Annen, *Heil*, 162–73; cf. J. Duncan M. Derrett, "Legend and Event: The Gerasene Demoniac: An Inquest into History and Liturgical Projection," in *Studia Biblica 1978*, ed. Elizabeth A. Livingstone, JSNTSup 2 (Sheffield: University of Sheffield Press, 1979), 63–73, here 68.
[107] Annen, *Heil*, 163. "Als Opfertier ist es vor allem im Kult der chthonischen Gottheiten wichtig wurde aber auch sonst fast allen Göttern geopfert."
[108] Ibid., 163.
[109] Ibid., 163–65.
[110] Ibid., 165.
[111] Derrett, "Legend and Event," 68; see also idem, J. Duncan M. Derrett, "Spirit-Possession and the Gerasene Demoniac," *Man* 14 (1979): 286–93, esp. 290; Cicero, *Leg.* 2.22.57 (cited by Derrett); and J. M. C. Toynbee, *Death and Burial in the Roman World*, AGRL (Ithaca, NY: Cornell University Press, 1971), 50.
[112] Roland de Vaux, *Les Sacrifices de l'Ancien Testament*, CahRB 1 (Paris: J. Gabalda, 1964), 250–53; see also Annen, *Heil*, 165–68.
[113] Cf. Theissen, *Miracle Stories*, 88–9.

4.6 Summary and Conclusions

In this chapter, we have seen that Mark presents Jesus's exorcisms as his plundering of Satan's kingdom (3:22-27) and, more specifically, the outworking of his identity decreed in 1:10-11 by way of Ps 2:7. The overall picture painted by the individual exorcism accounts is one of Jesus, God's royal vice-regent, demolishing the kingdom of Satan as he instantiates God's reign on earth (cf. Ps 2:1-2). Thus, in 1:21-28, Jesus begins to exorcise unclean spirits as God's royal "Son" (1:11), anointed by his Spirit (1:10). In 3:7-12 we read that the unclean spirits characteristically recognize Jesus as ὁ υἱὸς τοῦ θεοῦ, recalling God's decree (ὁ υἱὸς μου) in 1:11/Ps 2:7, just after a seeming allusion to Ps 2:1-2 (in which the powers opposed to God's rule convene against his anointed) in 3:6. Mark 5:1-20 then highlights the theme of eschatological battle with its use of military language. But the battle is yet only a prelude to the victory of the Son of the Most-High God (υἱὲ τοῦ θεοῦ τοῦ ὑψίστου) over the forces opposed to God's rule. Finally, each of the epithets with which the demons identify Jesus, whether ὁ ἅγιος τοῦ θεοῦ (1:24), ὁ υἱὸς τοῦ θεοῦ (3:11), or υἱὲ τοῦ θεοῦ τοῦ ὑψίστου (5:7), consistently connote Davidic messianism. The most obvious precedent for a plot in which God's messianic "Son" overthrows the demonic is, once again, Psalm 2.

All told, the recurrence of Davidic and son-of-God language in Mark's exorcism accounts advances the foundational use of Ps 2:7 in Mark 1:11 by displaying the actualization of the psalm's themes in the narrative of Jesus's earthly career. In these early chapters, Mark points to Jesus as the anointed Son of God dethroning and unseating the forces opposed to God's rule as he enacts God's reign on earth. Soon we will see Mark's "storied metalepsis" protracted still further through a second allusion to Ps 2:7 in his account of the transfiguration.

5

The Son on the Mountain

The transfiguration is at once the commentator's paradise and despair.

G. B. Caird[1]

Thus was shown to the apostles the glory of the body of Christ coming into his kingdom: for in the fashion of his glorious transfiguration, the Lord stood revealed in the splendor of his reigning body.

Hilary of Poitiers, *De trin.* 11.37

In Mark 9:7 we encounter the words of Ps 2:7 echoed for the second time in Mark's narrative atop the mount of the transfiguration—a revelatory highpoint in anyone's estimation.[2] On the one hand, the repetition of Ps 2:7 midway through the Gospel reinforces Mark's original identification of Jesus vis-à-vis Ps 2:7 at his baptism (1:11). On the other hand, its function within the transfiguration scene (9:2-8) bears its own implications for Mark's portrait of Jesus as God's Son.

Properly understood, Jesus's transfiguration in Mark functions something like an icon prefiguring his enthronement and alluding specifically to Dan 7:9-14's vision of the enthronement of the Son of Man (among other texts). Yet, as we shall see, the eschatological visions of Daniel 7 and Psalm 2 are conflated in a number of Jewish texts that anticipate the enthronement of God's Messiah in the last days. When we view Mark 9:2-8 against this backdrop, it becomes clear that the transfiguration, like previous passages we have seen, recalls Psalm 2 in order to presage the enthronement of God's Messiah (i.e., "Son").[3]

---

[1] G. B. Caird, "Expository Problems: The Transfiguration," *ExpTim* 67 (1956): 291–94 (here, 291).
[2] Hence, "die Offenbarungsszene" as it is styled in much of the German commentary literature (e.g., Pesch, *Markusevangelium*, 2:70). See also Hooker, *Mark*, 175–76; Marcus, *Mark 8–16*, 635; Black, *Mark*, 203.
[3] Whether or not many today would side with Meyer (*Markus*, 109)'s contention that Mark's is the original form of the transfiguration narrative, it is generally recognized that Mark has put considerable thought into the crafting and placement of 9:2-8 within the overall narrative; see Charles Masson, "La Transfiguration de Jésus (Marc 9:2-13)," *RTP* 14 (1964): 1–14; and (more recently) Marcus, *Mark 8–16*, 635.

5.1 Climbing the Mountain with Mark: Mark 9:7 in Narrative Perspective

If Mark's early chapters (1:16–3:12) offer a sweeping view of Jesus's ministry, emphasizing both the conflicts and manifestations of his identity along the way, the narrative from 3:13 and 9:1 presents an intensification of the earlier pattern, highlighting opposing reactions to Jesus (3:22-30; 6:1-6; 7:24-30; 8:11-13), even more dramatic signs of his authority (4:35-41; 5:1-43; 6:30-56; 8:1-10, 22-26), and ever the question of identity.[4] These culminate with Jesus's own question, "Who do you say I am?" (ὑμεῖς δὲ τίνα με λέγετε εἶναι) in 8:29, to which Peter responds, "You are the Christ" (σὺ εἶ ὁ χριστός).[5] Chapter 8 then concludes with Jesus's first prediction of his death and resurrection (8:31) and a cryptic statement about the coming of the Son of Man and the kingdom of God:

> "For whoever is ashamed of me and my words in this adulterous and sinful generation, so also the Son of Man will be ashamed of him when he comes in the glory of his Father with the holy angels." And he said to them, "Truly, I tell you: there are some standing here who will by no means taste death until they see the kingdom of God having come in power."
>
> Mark 8:38–9:1

Numerous commentators have observed that this saying and the foregoing episode alike set the stage for Jesus's transfiguration in 9:2-8. Jesus's transfiguration (and especially the voice from the cloud in 9:7) provides a dramatic confirmation of Peter's confession.[6] At the same time, Mark points to the transfiguration as an initial fulfillment of the promise made in 9:1 that some of those present will not die without having seen the arrival of God's future.[7] Finally, as if in answer to the previous questions of identity, the whole scene draws to a close with a familiar voice declaring, "This is my beloved Son; listen to him!" (οὗτός ἐστιν ὁ υἱός μου ὁ ἀγαπητός· ἀκούετε αὐτοῦ; 9:7).

---

[4] Cf. Marcus, *Mark 1–8*, 64, 255; Black, *Mark*, 105, 150.
[5] Despite suggestions to the contrary over the decades, it runs counter to Mark's entire narrative thus far to suppose that Peter's response is either inappropriate (à la James D. G. Dunn ["The Messianic Secret in Mark," *TynBul* 21 {1970}: 92–117) and Weeden, *Traditions*, 64–9) or unsatisfactory (Kingsbury, *Christology*, 91–2) in Jesus's view. Rather, with Marcus (*Mark 8–16*, 612), it makes far more sense in 8:30 (καὶ ἐπετίμησεν αὐτοῖς ἵνα μηδενὶ λέγωσιν περὶ αὐτοῦ) to suppose that Jesus simply desires his identity to be kept quiet for the time being, as (plainly) in 9:9.
[6] So, e.g., R. Holmes, "The Purpose of the Transfiguration," *JTS* 4 (1903): 543–47 (here, 546); Taylor, *Mark*, 392; Charles Edwin Carlston, "Transfiguration and Resurrection," *JBL* 80 (1961): 233–40 (here, 238); Terence L. Donaldson, *Jesus on the Mountain: A Study in Matthean Theology*, JSNTSup 8 (Sheffield: JSOT Press, 1985), 154; Hooker, *Mark*, 214–15; Gundry, *Mark*, 474; Donahue and Harrington, *Mark*, 268; Collins, *Mark*, 426; *contra* Black, *Mark*, 203.
[7] So already Origen, *Comm. Matt.* 12.31 (PG 13:1053–55); in modern scholarship, see esp., Morna Dorothy Hooker, *The Son of Man in Mark: A Study of the Background of the Term "Son of Man" and Its Use in St. Mark's Gospel* (Montreal: McGill University Press, 1967), 125–26; see also Pesch, *Markusevangelium*, 2:69; Gundry, *Mark*, 470; France, *Mark*, 346; Donahue and Harrington, *Mark*, 268, 273; Boring, *Mark*, 261; Collins, *Mark*, 426; Marcus, *Mark 8–16*, 635; Black, *Mark*, 203."

Both the words and the declaration itself are an obvious repetition of the divine pronouncement at Jesus's baptism, calling us back to that earlier pivotal moment like a case of narrative déjà vu:[8]

Mark 9:7	καὶ ἐγένετο φωνὴ ἐκ τῆς νεφέλης·
	οὗτός ἐστιν ὁ υἱός μου ὁ ἀγαπητός, ἀκούετε αὐτοῦ.
Mark 1:11	καὶ φωνὴ ἐγένετο ἐκ τῶν οὐρανῶν·
	σὺ εἶ ὁ υἱός μου ὁ ἀγαπητός, ἐν σοὶ εὐδόκησα.

Scholars generally acknowledge that Mark 9:7 likewise repeats the allusion to Ps 2:7 LXX (υἱὸς μου εἶ σύ) from 1:11.[9] We have merely switched from the second person to the third to suit the narrative situation: instead of addressing Jesus directly, the voice now addresses Peter, James, and John *about* Jesus.[10] Meanwhile, the allusion to Isa 42:1 has largely, if not entirely, dropped out and been replaced by Deut 18:15 LXX (the "prophet like Moses") instead—a point to which we will return.[11]

So in the larger scheme of Mark's narrative, we have here a repetition not only of the divine voice from Jesus's baptism (1:11) but also Ps 2:7. The importance of this fact should not be overlooked. As Bal observes, repeated frames of reference are one of the principal means of constructing a character's identity in a narrative; over the course of a narrative the most important information about the character is repeated every so often so "that they emerge more and more clearly."[12] Given that the speaker in 1:11 and 9:7 also happens to be God himself, Bal's point assumes double significance. Twice now, in the two most dramatic revelatory moments of the Gospel so far, Mark has identified Jesus as God's Son via God's own voice, echoing Ps 2:7. Such a pattern gives undeniable weight to Ps 2:7 in Mark's portrait of Jesus.

There is more to say about Ps 2:7's use in Mark 9:7, however. What, after all, are we to make of Ps 2:7 *within* the transfiguration scene (9:2-8)? Various interpreters

---

[8] Black (*Mark*, 204), in fact, notes a series of parallels between 1:1-11 and 9:2-8 besides the close symmetry of the constructions in 1:11 and 9:7, including a temporal indication, the presence of Elijah (at least figuratively, through John), a divine declaration and the motif of the *bat qol*, and the use of passives (e.g., μετεμορφώθη [9:2] and ὤφθη [9:4] vs. ἐβαπτίσθη [1:9] and σχιζομένους [1:10], indicating that Jesus is the recipient of a significant, revelatory action in each episode; cf. Collins, *Mark*, 425.

[9] Those who perceive the allusion to Ps 2:7 LXX in Mark 1:11 do so in 9:7 as well; to cite the entire list of names would therefore be redundant. But see, *inter alia*, Gundry, *Use*, 36-7; Steichele, *Sohn Gottes*, 161; Evans, *Mark 8:27-16:20*, 38; Watts, "Mark," in *CNTUOT*, 186; Janse, *Son*, 110-14. Curiously, Pesch (*Markusevangelium*, 2:76) suggests that Jesus would have heard Ps 2:7 (among other Scriptures) echoed in the words from the cloud even though he denies an allusion to Ps 2:7 in Mark 1:11.

[10] Cf. Schweizer, *Mark*, 182; Evans, *Mark 8:27-16:20*, 38; Moloney, *Mark*, 180; Black, *Mark*, 206; Bock, *Mark*, 251.

[11] So also Gnilka, *Markus*, 2:36; Pesch, *Markusevangelium*, 2:76; Steichele, *Sohn Gottes*, 167-81; Marcus, *Way*, 81; idem, *Mark 8-16*, 640; Collins, *Mark*, 426. Whether any trace of Isa 42:1 remains depends on whether one considers ἀγαπητός to be derived from that verse. Matthew 17:5, at any rate, retains Isa 42:1 alongside Deut 18:15: ὑτός ἐστιν ὁ υἱός μου ὁ ἀγαπητός, ἐν ᾧ εὐδόκησα· ἀκούετε αὐτοῦ; and ὁ ἐκλελεγμένος in Luke 9:35 (οὗτός ἐστιν ὁ υἱός μου ὁ ἐκλελεγμένος, αὐτοῦ ἀκούετε) probably also recalls from Isa 42:1.

[12] Bal, *Narratology*, 127-28. Cf. Trocmé (*Marc*, 36): 9:7 reinforces the certitude of 1:11.

have recognized that, as the climax of the pericope, the "voice from the cloud" logically "interprets all the major events that [precede] it"[13]—though only a few afford Ps 2:7 any actual weight in their exegesis.[14] Those that do, however, typically note the theme of enthronement.[15] Maria Horstmann, for instance, understands the statement οὗτός ἐστιν ὁ υἱός μου as a typical enthronement formula based on Ps 2:7.[16] Taking God's decree in 9:7 as her starting point, she concludes that the entire scene is modeled on Jewish patterns of enthronement so as to convey a vision of Jesus's enthronement as God's Messiah.[17]

In support of Horstmann's view, it is worth noting that Jesus's transfiguration, like Psalm 2, takes place on a mountaintop. Whereas in the psalm God establishes his king upon Zion, his "holy mountain" (ὄρος τὸ ἅγιον αὐτοῦ) and decrees, "You are my Son" (2:6-7), the voice from the cloud declares of Jesus, "This is my Son" (Mark 9:7) upon a "high mountain" (9:2). As Terrence Donaldson observes, "the use in 2 Pet 1.18 and *Apoc. Pet.* 15 of τὸ ἅγιον ὄρος, found also in Ps 2:6 and used frequently as an equivalent for Jerusalem/Zion, indicates that the earliest commentators on the tradition interpreted it in just this way."[18]

Even apart from Psalm 2, mountains (often either Zion or Sinai) frequently serve as the site of either God's throne (Pss 48:2; 99:1-5; 146:10; Jer 8:19; cf. Pss 68:15; 78:54) or

---

[13] So Marcus, *Way*, 81; and similarly Ernst Lohmeyer, "Die Verklärung Jesu nach dem Markus-Evangelium," *ZNW* 21 (1922): 185–215, esp. 186–87; H. C. Kee, "The Transfiguration in Mark: Epiphany or Apocalyptic Vision?," in *Understanding the Sacred Text: Essays in Honor of Morton S. Enslin on the Hebrew Bible and Christian Beginnings*, ed. J. H. P. Reumann (Valley Forge: Judson, 1972), 139.

[14] Despite the comment above, for instance, Marcus (*Way*, 80–93) focuses almost entirely on Mosaic motifs in his treatment of Mark 9:2-8, devoting less than a full paragraph to the presence or function of Ps 2:7. Most commentators evidence a similar practice.

[15] A number of ancient exegetes also associate Jesus's transfiguration with either his enthronement or kingship: e.g., Eusebius, *Comm. Luc.* 9 (*PG* 24:549); Hilary, *Trin.* 11.37 (*PL* 11:423–24); Chrysostom, *Theod. laps.* 1.11 (*PG* 47:291); John of Damascus, *Or. Trans.* 2 (*PG* 96:545).

[16] See Maria Horstmann, *Studien zur markinischen Christologie: Mk 8, 27-9, 13 als Zugang zum Christusbild des zweiten Evangeliums* (Münster: Aschendorff, 1969), 72–103.

[17] Horstmann, *Studien*, 90–6; cf. Harald Riesenfeld, *Jésus transfiguré, l'arrière-plan du récit évangélique de la transfiguration de Notre-Seigneur*, Acta 16 (København: Munksgaar, 1947), 68–9, 250–53. This typical, threefold enthronement formula (eleveation, presentation, and enthronement) was previously identified by Karl Heinrich Rengstorf, "Old and New Testament Traces of a Formula of the Judaean Royal Ritual," *NovT* 5 (1962): 229–44; as well as Joachim Jeremias (*Jesus' Promise to the Nations: The Franz Delitzsch Lectures for 1953*, trans. S. H. Hooke, SBT 24 [London: SCM Press, 1958], 38), who finds the same pattern in Matt 28:16-20; Phil 2:9-11; Heb 1:5-14; 1 Tim 3:16; and Otto Michel, "Der Abschluß des Matthäusevangeliums," *EvT* 10 (1950): 16–26. Ulrich B. Müller ("Die christologische Absicht des Markusevangeliums und die Verklärungsgeschichte," *ZNW* 64 [1973]: 159–93; esp. 185–87) argues that Mark 9:2-8 follows a similar enthronement formula (apotheosis, presentation, and enthronement), though he believes it to be of Hellenistic rather than Jewish origin. One is also reminded of Vielhauer's ("Erwägungen," 199–214) thesis that Mark 1:11; 9:7; and 15:39 are modeled on an Egyptian enthronement ritual. Although Vielhauer's proposal runs into particular difficulties (namely, the supposition of an Egyptian background (see Pesch, *Markusevangelium*, 1:97) the recognition of an ancient enthronement formula is consistent.

[18] Donaldson, *Jesus on the Mountain*, 148. Zion is described either as "the holy mountain" or God's "holy mountain" in Pss 3:4; 15:1; 43:3; 48:1; 87:1; 99:9; Isa 11:9; 27:13; 56:7; 57:13; 65:11, 25; 66:20; Jer 31:23; Ezek 20:40; 28:14; Dan 9:16, 20; Joel 2:1; 3:17; Obad 16; Zeph 3:11; Zech 8:3. It is also worth noting that 2 Pet 1:17 understands the transfiguration as Jesus receiving "honor" (τιμήν) and "glory" (δόξαν) from "the Majestic Glory" (τῆς μεγαλοπρεποῦς δόξης)—the language of enthronement.

that of his anointed king (Pss 2:6; 110:2; 132:11-18) throughout the Jewish Scriptures.[19] In prophetic literature, moreover, we read that "on that day" either YHWH (Isa 24:23; 52:7; Ezek 20:33, 40; Mic 4:6f.; Zech 14:8-11; cf. Isa 2:2-3; 11:9; 25:6-7) or his messianic king (Ezek 17:22-24; 34:23-31; Mic 5:2-4) will reign on Mount Zion."[20] The same trends continue in Second Temple literature, where the mountain is often the seat of God's throne (*Jub.* 1:17-29; *1 En.* 18:8; 24:2-25:6; cf. Tob. 13:11; *Sib. Or.* 3:716-720) and/or the place from where the Messiah will exercise his rule (*4 Ezra* 13; *2 Bar.* 40:1-4; cf. *Ps. Sol.* 17:23-51).

There are a number of hints, then, that Jesus's transfiguration has something to do with the idea of his enthronement as God's Messiah and that the reverberation of Ps 2:7 at the climax of this scene recalls the divine decree of enthronement itself, just as it did at Jesus's baptism (1:11). Yet there is more evidence to support this intuition than is typically realized. Mark's transfiguration scene is composed of several "richly allusive" threads recalling "various climactic events in sacred history" and simultaneously anticipating God's promised future.[21] Each of these threads lends to, and ultimately helps solidify, the impression that Jesus's transfiguration is essentially a prefiguration, or glimpse, of his cosmic enthronement.[22]

5.2 The Mountain Remembered: Echoes of Sinai in Mark 9:2-8

We begin with the mountain itself. Scholars since D. F. Strauss have recognized that Mark's transfiguration narrative contains a whole series of allusions to the theophany story in Exodus 24.[23] In the Exodus story, Moses and three companions ascend Mount

---

[19] For a thorough study of the mountain motif in Jewish tradition, see Donaldson, *Jesus on the Mountain*, 30–86.

[20] Donaldson, *Jesus on the Mountain*, 147.

[21] The words above are those of Hays (*Gospels*, 15) and Culpepper (*Mark*, 293), respectively. Hays continues: "[m]any of the key images in this mysterious narrative are drawn from Israel's Scriptures; indeed, a reader who fails to discern the significance of these images can hardly grasp Mark's message." Though Hays refers to Mark's Gospel as a whole, nowhere is his comment more appropos than in Mark 9:2-8.

[22] Donaldson (*Jesus on the Mountain*, 136) comments on the ages-old difficulty of unifying all of these threads: "the task of discovering a single interpretative key that will allow all of these associations and links to be seen as parts of an overall pattern has proven to be virtually impossible." I do not presume to solve this problem; rather, I suggest that, whatever else may be taking place in Mark 9:2-8, a proleptic glimpse of Jesus's enthronement is a prominent part of it.

[23] See, *inter alia*, David Friedrich Strauss, *The Life of Jesus: Critically Examined*, ed. Peter C. Hodgson, trans. George Eliot, Lives of Jesus Series (Philadelphia: Fortress, 1972), 544–45; Taylor, *Mark*, 386–88; Jeremias, "Μωυσῆς," *TDNT* 4:867 n. 228; Gnilka, *Markus*, 2:32; Pesch, *Markusevangelium*, 2:71; Bruce D. Chilton, "The Transfiguration: Dominical Assurance and Apostolic Vision," *NTS* 27 (1980): 115–24; Marcus, *Way*, 81–3. Though Strauss is perhaps most responsible for reviving this recognition in modern scholarship, there had been a widespread tradition associating the mountain of the transfiguration with Mt. Sinai from ancient times: see Dale C. Allison, *The New Moses: A Matthean Typology* (Minneapolis: Fortress, 1993), 243; cf. Gertrud Schiller, Iconography of Christian Art (trans. Janet Seligman; 2 vols; Greenwich: New York Graphic Society, 1972), 1:145–52. Attempts to downplay or deny the Exodus 24 parallels are few and unconvincing, but see Bultmann, *History*, 259–61; Kee ("Transfiguration," 138–39), who follows Bultmann; and John C. Poirier ("Jewish and Christian Tradition in the Transfiguration," *RB* 111 [2004]: 516–30), whose argument is rebutted by Craig A. Evans ("Zechariah in the Markan Passion Narrative," in *Biblical Interpretation in the Early Christian Gospels: Volume 1: The Gospel of Mark*, ed. T. R. Hatina, LNTS 304 [London/New York: T&T Clark, 2006], 66 n .7).

Sinai where they behold the God of Israel (v. 10); a cloud covers the mountain and, after six days, God calls to Moses from the cloud (v. 16). In Mark 9:2-8, by comparison, Jesus and three companions ascend a mountain after six days where they behold Jesus transfigured, and a voice from a cloud speaks to them. We can summarize the most important parallels as follows:[24]

Mark		**Exodus**
9:2a	six days (μετά ἡμέρας ἕξ/ἓξ ἡμέρας)[25]	24:16
9:2a	Jesus/Moses and three companions	24:1, 9
9:2b	ascend a mountain	24:9, 12-13, 15, 18
9:2b, 8	alone (μόνους/μόνος)	24:2
9:4	Moses appears	24:1-16
9:7b	a cloud (νεφέλη) overshadows/covers them	24:15-16, 18
9:7b	God speaks out of the cloud ([ἐκ] τῆς νεφέλης)	24:16

Intriguingly, Mark's most precise allusions, at the beginning and end of the pericope, are to Exod 24:16, which reads:[26]

καὶ κατέβη ἡ δόξα τοῦ θεοῦ ἐπὶ τὸ ὄρος τὸ Σινα, καὶ ἐκάλυψεν αὐτὸ ἡ νεφέλη ἓξ ἡμέρας· καὶ ἐκάλεσεν κύριος τὸν Μωυσῆν τῇ ἡμέρᾳ τῇ ἑβδόμῃ ἐκ μέσου τῆς νεφέλης.

Exod 24:16 LXX

Mark effectively frames his account of Jesus's transfiguration within the very climax of the Sinai theophany itself: the glory of the Lord descends, the cloud covers the mountain, and, at last, God speaks on the mountain. At least two inferences follow.

First, no one can easily deny the theophanic dimensions of the story.[27] As Moses and his companions once ascended the mountain and beheld the glory of the Lord, the disciples behold Jesus in his glory occupying the centerstage filled by the God of Israel in the Exodus story. The implications of this point for Markan Christology and,

---

[24] Similar list provided by Marcus, *Way*, 82. Many (including Marcus) also see an allusion to Moses's shining face in Exod 34:29 (εδόξασται ἡ ὄψις τοῦ χρώματος τοῦ προσώπου αὐτοῦ) in Jesus's glistening garments (στίλβοντα λευκὰ λίαν; Mark 9:3). Unlike Matt 17:2, however, which adds that Jesus's *face* "shone like the sun" (καὶ ἔλαμψεν τὸ πρόσωπον αὐτοῦ ὡς ὁ ἥλιος, τὰ δὲ ἱμάτια αὐτοῦ ἐγένετο λευκὰ ὡς τὸ φῶς), Mark's description of Jesus's clothing (rather than face) more closely resembles another background, as we will see below. See similarly John Paul Heil, *The Transfiguration of Jesus: Narrative Meaning and Function of Mark 9:2-8, Matt 17:1-8 and Luke 9:28-36*, AnBib 144 (Rome: Pontifical Biblical Institute, 2000), 79.

[25] Specific temporal markers are rare in Mark, which increases the suspicion that Mark has allusive motives in 9:2; see Pesch, *Markusevangelium*, 2:72; Marcus, *Mark 8–16*, 631.

[26] Cf. Collins (*Mark*, 417), who emphasizes Mark's allusions to Exod 24:16 in particular.

[27] As Evans (*Mark 8:27–16:20*, 35) states, YHWH's appearance to Moses in Exodus 24 is the "epochal epiphany" in all of Jewish salvation history. Cf. Gnilka, *Markus*, 2:32; Pesch, *Markusevangelium*, 2:72; Donahue and Harrington, *Mark*, 286; Watts, "Mark," in *CNTUOT*, 186. Even when God speaks in 9:7, it is to call all attention to his "Son."

indeed, *Theology*, should not be missed. Second, whatever its actual location may be, in a figurative sense, the mount of the transfiguration *is* Mount Sinai for Mark.

Both of these inferences are confirmed by the appearance of "Elijah together with Moses" (Ἡλείας σὺν Μωυσεῖ) in 9:4.[28] In 1 Kings 19:11-13, Elijah is told to ascend the same mountain where he hears God speak—not out of a cloud, but out of a storm, nevertheless.[29] Subsequent tradition regularly remembers Elijah as a "new Moses," often comparing the two figures precisely in terms of their mutual encounters with God on Sinai.[30] Allison connects the dots for us nicely: "Moses and Elijah, who both converse with the transfigured Jesus, are the only figures in the Jewish Bible of whom it is related that they spoke with God on Mount Sinai: so their presence together makes us think of that mountain. It beggars belief to entertain coincidence for all these parallels."[31] Likewise, by placing Jesus in conversation (συλλαλοῦντες) with these two figures at once, Mark reinforces the theophanic dimensions of the story supplied by Exodus 24 in the first place.

In Jewish tradition, in fact, Sinai was sometimes imagined to be the site of God's very throne (Pss 68:16-17; 97:1-3; *Ezek. Trag.* 68-69). Already in Exod 24:10, the imagery surrounding YHWH's appearance ("there was under his feet as it were a pavement of sapphire stone, like the very heaven for clearness") anticipates that of later throne visions, such as Ezek 1:26 (cf. *1 En.* 18:8). Indeed, there is even a tradition that Moses himself was enthroned by God as his vice-regent on Sinai.[32] Moreover, there is evidence that much of the significance of Sinai was later compared or even transferred

---

[28] As many others have observed, it is rather curious that Mark mentions Elijah before Moses (*contra* Matt 17:3 and Luke 9:30) given that Moses came first historically. John Paul Heil ("A Note on 'Elijah with Moses' in Mark 9, 4," *Bib* 80 [1999]: 115) argues that whenever Mark introduces a second figure with the preposition σύν, pride of place goes to the latter figure; cf. Cranfield, *Mark*, 291. Conversely, Marcus (*Way*, 83–4) and Moloney (*Mark*, 179) suggest that the priority of Elijah points toward the eschatological significance of the event at hand. In any case, Elijah (6:15; 8:28; 9:4-5, 11-13; 15:35-36; cf. 1:6) is no less significant than Moses (1:44; 7:10; 9:4-5; 10:3-4; 12:19, 26) throughout Mark's narrative as a whole.

[29] Traditionally, Sinai = Horeb; cf. "Sinai" in Exodus 19; 24; and 32 vs. "Horeb" in Deut 4:10; 5:2; 9:8; 18:16; 1 Kgs 8:9; 2 Chr 5:10; Ps 106:19; Mal 4:4.

[30] Like Moses, Elijah performs unparalleled signs (1 Kgs 17, 18:43-45), flees to the wilderness (19:1-4), spends forty days at the same mountain (19:8) before encountering God there (19:11-13), and later parts the Jordan as Moses parted the sea (2 Kgs 2:8). Elijah appears next to Moses again, with specific reference to Horeb, in Mal 3:22-23; Sirach 45–48, which compares the two figures as prophets par excellence; Josephus, *Ant.* 8.13.7; and b. Meg. 19b, both of which emphasize the parallel between Moses and Elijah by claiming that the cleft where God appeared to Elijah was the same cleft in the rock where he had appeared to Moses; *Deut. Rab.* 3.17, which follows Malachi by expecting the return of both figures in the final days; and *Pesiq. R.* 4.2, which compares the two on a number of points. Cf. John Gray, *I & II Kings: A Commentary* (Philadelphia: Westminster, 1970), 376; Simon J. De Vries, *1 Kings*, WBC 12 (Nashville: Thomas Nelson, 2003), 209–10; R. A. Carlson "Élie à l'Horeb," *VT* 19 (1969): 416–39; Donaldson, *Jesus on the Mountain*, 45; Marcus, *Way*, 83–4; Evans, *Mark 8:27– 16:20*, 36; Watts, "Mark," in *CNTUOT*, 187; Simon S. Lee, *Jesus' Transfiguration and the Believers' Transformation: A Study of the Transfiguration and Its Development in Early Christian Writings*, WUNT 2/265 (Tübingen: Mohr Siebeck, 2009), 19.

[31] Allison, *New Moses*, 244.

[32] See Wayne A. Meeks, *The Prophet-King: Moses Traditions and the Johannine Christology*, NovTSup 14 (Leiden: Brill, 1967), 181–96, 227–38; cf. Kee, "Transfiguration," 147; Marcus, *Way*, 84–9. This tradition is attested in *Ezek. Trag.* 68-82; Philo, *Vit. Mos.* 1:155-58; *Tanh. A* on Num 10:1-2.; *Mek.* 167; b. Zeb. 102a; *Gen. Rab.* 55.6; *Exod. Rab.* 2.6, 40.2; *Deut. Rab.* 2.7.

to Mount Zion as the two paradigmatic mountains in biblical salvation history from which God rules over his creation.[33]

Both Moses and Elijah were also expected to return in the last days, sometimes as forerunners of the Messiah himself.[34] Marcus is almost certainly correct, as such, that the appearance of "Elijah together with Moses" in 9:4 ensures that the entire event on the mountain would be understood eschatologically.[35] Indeed, an ancient Jewish reader might even suppose that the Messiah, too, stands on the horizon.[36] Symbolically, we may also say that this eschatological event appears to take place on the mount of God's abode.

Many treatments of Mark 9:2-8 stop here, as though the event were sufficiently explained as a recapitulation of Moses's experience on Sinai. Yet even the past stories of Moses and Elijah combined cannot account for all of the imagery and allusions contained in this scene, including Jesus's very transformation in 9:2-3 and the divine voice in 9:7. As Allison recognizes, unlike Matthew's account:

> In the Second the transfiguration is probably best understood in comparison with Mark's emphasis upon the passion and resurrection of the Son of man (cf. 8.27–9.1). This appears from the insistence on the cross (9.12); from the priority given to Elijah, who is identified with the Baptist, whose death was a premonition of that of Jesus himself (9.12); from the similarity between the transfiguration and Gethsemane, in that the witnesses are both identical (9.2; 14.33); and from the metamorphosis of Jesus in 9.2, which looks forward to the glory of the resurrection.[37]

Such emphases direct us, invariably, into the realm of apocalyptic literature.

---

[33] As Donaldson (*Jesus on the Mountain*, 45–6) notes, Zion functions as the "new Sinai" in a number of passages, including Isa 2:2f.: "[t]hus, just as the final redemption is often pictured as a new Exodus, so eschatological Zion, the goal of this Exodus, stands in these passages as a new Sinai. In the future Zion will be the place where the law is heard."; cf. Jon D. Levenson (*Sinai & Zion: An Entry into the Jewish Bible* [San Francisco: Harper & Row, 1987], 187–217) on biblical parallels between the two mountains generally. Psalm 97 offers a good example of this tendency; whereas the imagery in vv. 1-4 is plainly that of Sinai, recalling Exod 19:16-20 (see Zenger, *Psalms 2*, 472, 474), it is Zion that is named in v. 8. If Sinai is emblematic of the Mosaic covenant with Israel, Zion is emblematic of the later Davidic covenant. Both mountains have in common that God was thought to rule from them.

[34] Already Mal 3:22-23 expects Elijah (mentioned alongside Moses) ahead of the Day of the Lord; various rabbinic texts later present Elijah as the forerunner of the Messiah (cf. Mark 9:11-13; Matt 17:10-12); and, finally, one late text anticipates the return of Moses and Elijah together (*Deut. Rab.* 3.17). Cf. See similarly Schweizer, *Mark*, 183; Hooker, *Mark*, 216; France, *Mark*, 348; Moloney, *Mark*, 179; Watts, "Mark," in *CNTUOT*, 187; Lee, *Transfiguration*, 17–8; Dale C. Allison, Jr., "Elijah Must Come First," *JBL* 103 (1984): 256–58.

[35] Marcus, *Way*, 83–4.

[36] So Pesch, *Markusevangelium*, 2:74.

[37] Davies and Allison, *Matthew*, 2:685. Davies and Allison further explain that Matthew enhances Mark's allusions to the Exodus story and to Moses, in particular, so much so that "[t]he major theme of the epiphany story would seem to be Jesus's status as a new Moses." The most important changes are that: (1) Moses now comes before Elijah (17:3); (2) Jesus's "face" (τὸ πρόσωπον αὐτοῦ) now shines like the sun (17:2; cf. Exod 34:29); and (3) the cloud is described as "bright" (φωτεινή), recalling the Shekinah that filled the tabernacle in the wilderness. Thus, Matthew especially strengthens the parallels between Jesus and Moses (cf. Davies and Allison, *Matthew*, 2:687), which fits with Matthew's larger objective to portray Jesus as a new Moses (see Allison, *The New Moses*, passim).

5.3 Apocalyptic Topography and Radiant Garments: The Reinterpretation of Sinai in Mark 9:2-8

If the greatest number of commentators have emphasized the allusions to Exodus 24 in Mark 9:2-8, nearly as many have stressed the apocalyptic motifs scattered throughout the scene, including resonances with Daniel 7, and rightly so.[38] High mountains, clouds, heavenly voices, changed appearances, and bright, white clothing are all common features of apocalyptic visions.

To begin with, mountains—and *high* mountains in particular—often serve as sites of divine revelation both in the Jewish Scriptures and in subsequent apocalyptic literature.[39] For example, in *2 Bar.* 13:1 a heavenly voice calls to Baruch as he stands on Mount Zion: "And it happened after these things that I, Baruch, stood on Mount Zion (ὄρος Σιών) and behold, a voice came forth from high (φωνὴ ἐξῆλθεν ἐξ ὕψους) and spoke to me."[40] The connotations are much the same in the NT; in the few instances where high mountains occur, they serve as vantage points for supernatural revelations or insights.[41]

For his own part, Mark shows little interest in the precise geographic location of Jesus's transfiguration.[42] What matters is that it is a "high mountain" (ὄρος ὑψηλόν). As Malbon insightfully observes, topographical features in Mark "are more than mere stage settings for the dramatic action," but often bear a deeper, symbolic meaning in the narrative.[43] Such is the impression one gains here. The mountain of the transfiguration is a one of apocalyptic revelation: "an *axis mundi*, a conduit between earth and the divine realm," as Jamie Davies writes.[44]

---

[38] See, e.g., Maurice Sabbé, "La redaction du récit de la Transfiguration," in *La Venue du Messie*, ed. Edouard Massaux, RechBib 6 (Leuven: Leuven University Press, 1962), 65–100; Kee, "Transfiguration," 135–53; Donaldson, *Jesus on the Mountain*, 141–42; William Richard Stegner, "The Use of Scripture in Two Narratives of Early Jewish Christianity (Matthew 4.1-11; Mark 9.2-8)," in *Early Christian Interpretation of the Scriptures of Israel: Investigations and Proposals*, ed. Craig A. Evans and James A. Sanders, JSNTSup 148 (Sheffield: Sheffield Academic, 1997), 98–120; Evans, *Mark 8:27–16:20*, 35–6; Delbert Burkett, "The Transfiguration of Jesus (Mark 9:2-8): Epiphany or Apotheosis?," *JBL* 138 (2019): 413–32; Jamie Davies, "Apocalyptic Topography in Mark's Gospel: Theophany and Divine Invisibility at Sinai, Horeb, and the Mount of Transfiguration," *JTI* 14 (2020): 140–48.

[39] E.g., in Isa 40:9; Ezek 40:2; *1 En.* 18:6-16; 22:1; 25:1; 32:2; *T. Levi* 2:5; *4 Ezra* 13:6f.; *2 Bar.* 13:1; 2 Macc. 2:4-8; *Apoc. Zeph.* 3; *Apoc. Abr.* 12; *Mem. Marq.* 4:6; 5:3; Rev 21:10. The exact phrase ὄρος ὑψηλόν occurs in more than half of these examples (Isa 40:9; Ezek 40:2; *1 En.* 22:1; 25:1; 32:2; *T. Levi* 2:5; Rev 21:10). Cf. Donaldson, *Jesus on the Mountain*, 142; Boring, *Mark*, 261; Davies, "Apocalyptic Topography," 141.

[40] Author's translation. In addition to *2 Bar.* 13:1, the motif of a heavenly voice also occurs in Dan 8:16; *1 En.* 13:8; 18:6; and Rev 11:12.

[41] See Matt 4:8; 17:1; and Rev 21:10. Luke 9:28 omits ὑψηλόν, apparently finding it either unnecessary or geographically inaccurate.

[42] Cf. Cranfield, *Mark*, 289; Hooker, *Mark*, 215–16; Evans, *Mark 8:27–16:20*, 35; Collins, *Mark*, 421; Black, *Mark*, 203–04. Neither physical geography nor identifying the historic site appear to be Mark's concern.

[43] Elizabeth Struthers Malbon, *Narrative Space and Mythic Meaning in Mark* (Sheffield: Sheffield Academic, 1991), 50; cf. Davies, "Apocalyptic," 140–48.

[44] Davies, "Apocalyptic," 141. See similarly, Malbon, *Narrative Space*, 85; Hooker, *Mark*, 215–16; Donahue and Harrington, *Mark*, 268; Black, *Mark*, 203–04.

Clouds are also common in apocalyptic scenes, sometimes in connection with mountains.⁴⁵ For instance, *4 Ezra* 13:3-6 describes "the figure of one like a man" (a messianic figure in *4 Ezra*), who comes on the clouds of heaven (cf. Dan 7:13-14) and carves out a mountain for himself, which is later revealed to be Mount Zion in a section displaying the influence of Psalm 2.⁴⁶ Another important example for our purposes occurs in 2 Macc. 2:4-8, which promises that in the last days "the glory of the Lord and the cloud will appear" (ὀφθήσεται ἡ δόξα τοῦ κυρίου καὶ ἡ νεφέλη) again on Sinai and Zion as in the days of Moses and Solomon. The existence of such a tradition sheds some light on how first-century Jews would have understood Jesus's transfiguration: if the glory (shown on Jesus himself) and the cloud have returned, then the promises of the last days are being fulfilled.

Meanwhile, Jesus's transformation (μεταμορφώθη) itself and "gleaming, exceedingly white" (στίλβοντα λευκὰ λίαν) clothing in 9:2-3 resemble the bright, white garments worn by various heavenly figures in apocalyptic literature, including the glorified righteous, angels, the Ancient of Days, and still others.⁴⁷ H. C. Kee calls attention to the eschatological glorification of the righteous in such passages as Dan 12:3 and *2 Bar.* 51:1-3, in particular:⁴⁸

Dan 12:3   And those who are wise will shine like the brightness of the heavens, and those who lead many to righteousness like the stars of heaven forever and ever.

2 Bar. 51:1-3   ... their splendor shall be glorified in changes and the form of their beauty shall be turned into the light of their beauty that they may be able to acquire and receive the world which does not die.

Yet Jesus's appearance in Mark 9:3 reminds others especially of the description of the Ancient of Days/Great Glory in Dan 7:9 and *1 En.* 14:20:⁴⁹

---

⁴⁵ See Dan 7:13; Rev 14:14; 2 Macc. 2:4-8; *4 Ezra* 13:3f.

⁴⁶ See *4 Ezra* 13:31-37.

⁴⁷ See, e.g., the glorified righteous: Dan 12:3; *1 En.* 62:15; 106:2-6; *2 Bar.* 51:1-3; *4 Ezra* 7:97; 10:25; Rev 3:5; 4:4; 7:13-14; 19:14; cf. Matt 13:43; angels: Dan 10:5-6; *2 En.* 22:8-10; cf. *1 En.* 106:2-6; cf. Matt 28:3; Mark 16:5; Luke 24:4; John 20:12; the Ancient of Days: Dan 7:9; *1 En.* 14:20; and others: *T. Abr.* A 12:5; Rev 1:13-16. In view of such variety, it is misleading to identify such imagery too closely with any one being or category. Rather, changed appearances and bright, white garments appear to be indicative of glorified beings in general. Candida R. Moss ("The Transfiguration: An Exercise in Markan Accommodation," *BibInt* 12 [2004]: 69–89) has shown that gleaming, radiant garments are often worn by divine and otherworldly figures in Greco-Roman literature as well. While Mark's text displays no evidence that his account alludes to such literature, these examples do offer evidence of what radiant appearances signified to ancients at large.

⁴⁸ The translations below are Kee's (see "Transfiguration," 143–44).

⁴⁹ See Schweizer, *Mark*, 181; Hooker, *Mark*, 216; Evans, *Mark 8:27–16:20*, 36, Moloney, *Mark*, 178; Boring, *Mark*, 261; France, *Mark*, 351; Watts, "Mark," in *CNTUOT*, 186; cf. James D. G. Dunn, "The Danielic Son of Man in the New Testament," in *The Book of Daniel: Composition and Reception*, ed. John J. Collins and Peter W. Flint, 2 vols, VTSup 83 (Leiden/Boston: Brill, 2001), 2:533; Christopher Rowland and Christopher R. A. Morray-Jones, *The Mystery of God: Early Jewish Mysticism and the New Testament*, Compendia Rerum Iudaicarum Ad Novum Testamentum. Section III, Jewish Traditions in Early Christian Literature 12 (Leiden/Boston: Brill, 2009), 106, 106. See also Louis Francis Hartman, *The Book of Daniel*, AB 23 (Garden City, NY: Doubleday, 1978), 218; Collins, *Daniel*, 301; C. L. Seow, *Daniel* (Louisville: Westminster John Knox, 2003), 107.

Mark 9:3	His clothes became gleaming, exceedingly white such as no fuller on earth could so whiten them.
Dan 7:9	His cloak was white as snow and the hair of his head as pure white wool; his throne as the gleam of fire.
1 En. 14:20	His cloak was like the appearance of the sun and whiter than much snow.

All three passages, in fact, share elements of syntax and diction, including a twofold emphasis on the otherworldly radiance and whiteness of the person's garments, and a superlative emphasis on the latter. In Mark's case, the implication is that these qualities are divinely imparted.[50]

We will return to this comparison in due course. But already, one can see that various features of Mark's scene from the "high mountain" to Jesus's transformation, gleaming white garments, the cloud, and the heavenly voice that speaks from it indicate that what transpires on the mountain is an apocalyptic revelation of some sort.[51]

At times, however, interpreters have imposed a false alternative on Mark's text, as though Jesus's transfiguration must be *either* an apocalyptic vision *or* a recapitulation of the Sinai theophany from Exodus 24—but not both.[52] But such a dichotomy is both unnecessary and unwarranted. As Grant Macaskill has shown, "it is a characteristic feature of apocalyptic texts that their revelatory elements are developed by means of the interpretation of older texts and traditions."[53] This is precisely what appears to have taken place in Mark 9:2-8: Jesus's transfiguration is not simply a recapitulation of Exodus 24 with Jesus in the place of Moses, but an apocalyptic reformulation of that earlier event, anticipating the unfolding of God's promised future after the pattern of the sacred past. Upon closer inspection, there have, in fact, been a number of clues already as to precisely what future scene Mark 9:2-8 envisions.

Dan 7:9-14 and *1 En.* 14:8-23, meanwhile, have a definite literary relationship with one another, though scholars debate which text is the more primitive. While many argue for Daniel 7's dependence on *1 Enoch* 14, Stokes ("Throne Visions," 340–58) argues the opposite. John J. Collins's ((*Daniel*, Hermeneia [Minneapolis: Fortress, 1993], 300) conclusion may be the safest, however: "the direction of the influence cannot be established, but these texts are closely related"; cf. John Goldingay, *Daniel*, WBC 30 (Dallas: Word, 1989), 164; Daniel L. Smith-Christopher, *Daniel*, NIB 7 (Nashville: Abingdon, 1994), 103. Alternatively, Jonathan R. Trotter ("The Tradition of Throne Vision in the Second Temple Period: Daniel 7:9-10, 1 Enoch 14:18-23, and the Book of Giants (4Q530)," *RevQ* 25 [2012]: 451–66) argues against literary dependence in favor of the possibility that both texts reflect a common oral tradition.

[50] As Meyer (*Markus*, 109) previously observed, Mark's phrase "no fuller on earth ..." implies the heavenly luster of Jesus's garments.

[51] Cf. Donaldson, *Jesus on the Mountain*, 142.

[52] Most notably, Kee ("Transfiguration," 149), who is one of the few to dismiss the Exodus 24 allusions, arguing that Mark 9:2-8 is "not a theophany," but rather a "proleptic vision" of Jesus's glory to come.

[53] Grant Macaskill, "Apocalypse and the Gospel of Mark," in *The Jewish Apocalyptic Tradition and the Shaping of New Testament Thought*, ed. Benjamin E. Reynolds and Loren T. Stuckenbruck (Minneapolis: Fortress, 2017), 53–77, calling attention to an argument by Eibert J. C. Tigchelaar (*Prophets of Old and the Day of the End: Zechariah, the Book of Watchers, and Apocalyptic*, OTS 35 [Leiden/New York: Brill, 1996], 243–47); cf. Davies, "Apocalyptic," 143. In Tigchelaar's words (245), "revelation arises from tradition and interpretation." Tigchelaar (245) argues that the author of *1 En.* 6–11, for example, "created a new literary work by converting several traditions into a story with a new scope." We appear to witness a similar phenomenon in Mark 9:2-8.

5.4 Jesus in the Throne Room

The particular combination of images and motifs in Mark 9:2-8 points not only toward the broad genre of apocalyptic literature, but to the specific conventions of what is commonly known as a "throne vision" or "throne theophany": visions of the God of Israel seated on his throne in the cosmic throne room.[54] For example, God's throne is commonly pictured on top of a mountain, most often either Sinai or Zion, both in formal throne visions (Ps 97:1-3; *1 En.* 14:18; 18:8) and elsewhere.[55] Likewise, the heavenly throne is often surrounded by clouds (e.g., Ps 97:1-3; Dan 7:13; Ezek 1:26-28; *1 En.* 14:8; *2 En.* 29:3; cf. *4 Ezra* 13:3f.).

In every case, God's throne exudes splendor or radiance of some kind, such as that of fire, lightning, or precious stones and metals (Ps 97:1-4; Dan 7:9-10; Ezek 1:26-28; Esdr. 4:9; *1 En.* 14:8-23; 71:1-10; 90:20-27). It is worth glancing at a few of these examples, such as Psalm 97's depiction of God's throne on Zion (v. 8) in terms strikingly reminiscent of Sinai:

> *Clouds* and thick darkness are all around him; righteousness and justice are the foundation of his *throne*. *Fire* goes before him and consumes his adversaries all around. His *lightnings* light up the world; the earth sees and trembles.
>
> Ps 97:2-4

Perhaps the most extensive throne vision in the Jewish Scriptures, apart from Dan 7:9-14, is Ezekiel's dramatic vision out of a "stormy wind" and "great cloud" (1:4) by the river Chebar:

> And above the platform that was over their heads was the form of a *throne*, like *sapphire* in appearance; and above the form of the throne, a form like a human being on it, above. And I saw like the *gleam of metal*, the appearance of *fire* within it all around, from the appearance of his loins upward and from the appearance of his loins downward I saw the appearance of *fire* and *radiance* all around. Like the appearance of the rainbow in a *cloud* on a rainy day, such was the appearance of the *radiance* all around. This was the appearance of the form of the glory of YHWH.
>
> Ezek 1:26-28

---

[54] See, e.g., Christopher Rowland, "The Visions of God in Apocalyptic Literature," *JSJ* 10 (1979): 137-54; Richard Bauckham, "The Worship of Jesus in Apocalyptic Christianity," *NTS* 27 (1981): 322-41; Rowland and Morray-Jones, *Mystery*, 106. Strictly speaking, visions of God's throne are not limited to apocalyptic literature. One of the oldest depictions of God's throne occurs in Psalm 97 and we have observed that the vision in Ezek 1:26-28 echoes imagery already present in Exodus 24. Nevertheless, the motifs are both more common and more developed in later apocalyptic literature, where throne visions beome a type scene.

[55] E.g., Pss 48:2; 68:16-17; 99:1-5; 146:10; Jer 8:19; Isa 24:23; 52:7; Ezek 20:33, 40; Mic 4:6; Zech 14:8-11; Jud. 1.17-29; *1 En.* 24:2-25:6; cf. Tob. 13:11; *Sib. Or.* 3:716-720; *4 Ezra* 13:31f.; *Ezek. Trag.* 68-69. Additionally, in *1 En.* 25:3, the summit of a "high mountain" (τὸ ὄρος τὸ ὑψηλόν) is likened to "the throne of God" (θρόνου θεοῦ). On *4 Ezra* 13, see further below. The vision is not a typical throne vision, but it does appear to envision an enthronement, nevertheless.

The most elaborate of all such visions, however, occurs in *1 En.* 14:8-23. In these verses, Enoch sees the "Great Glory" (v. 20) seated on a "high throne" made of crystal (v. 18) in heaven, in a hall of "white marble" (vv. 9-10) surrounded by "clouds," (v. 8) "flashes of lightning," (vv. 8, 11, 17) and "encircling fire" (vv. 10-12, 17, 19, 21). Here, the various imagery found in other throne visions comes together in a vivid display.

Finally, whenever pictured, the one seated on the throne (e.g., the Ancient of Days in Dan 7:9 and the Great Glory in *1 En.* 14:20) appears in gleaming, often white, garments. Another important example of such imagery occurs in *T. Abr.* A 12:3-5, where Abraham sees Abel seated on the throne to dispense judgment:

> So we also followed the angels and came within that broad gate, and in between those two gates stood a throne terrible in appearance, of terrible crystal, gleaming like fire (ἐξαστράπτων ὡς πῦρ). And on it sat a wondrous man bright as the sun (ἡλιόρατος), like unto a son of God.

Although this particular vision is not of God himself, the same general imagery common to throne theophanies applies here as well. Wherever thrones are placed in heaven, brilliance, fire, and lightning gather around the one enthroned.

In summary, the particular array of apocalyptic imagery in Mark 9:2-8 (namely mountains, clouds, radiance or brilliance of some kind, and white garments) are all common motifs, or generic features, of throne visions. The shared similarities among the most extensive visions can be summarized as follows:

	Mark 9:2-8	Dan 7:9-14	*1 En.* 14:8-23	*1 En.* 90:20-27	Ps 97:1-6	Ezek 1:26-28
Radiance	•	•	•	•		•
Lightning			•		•	
Fire		•	•	•	•	•
White garments	•	•	•	•		
Mountains	•			•		
Clouds	•	•	•		•	•

As Christopher Rowland observes, not every motif is present on every occasion (with the exception of *1 Enoch* 14), but the overlapping features above are consistent enough to speak of something like a type scene.[56] Any of these motifs can also occur in contexts other than throne visions, of course, but it is the overlap of several motifs in Mark 9:2-8 and the other texts above that accounts for their "family resemblance."[57]

---

[56] Rowland, "Visions," 145.
[57] Here I refer to Ludwig Wittgenstein's concept of *Familienähnlichkeit*. As Wittgenstein (*PI*, §67) argues, the resemblances between members of a family consist not "in the fact that one fibre runs through the whole length, but in the overlapping of [various] fibres."

5.5 Jesus's Transfiguration and Daniel's Vision (7:9-14)

There are several clues that Mark's account of Jesus's transfiguration recalls one throne vision in particular: Dan 7:9-14. As noted above, the family resemblance between Mark 9:3; Dan 7:9; and *1 En.* 14:20 is especially strong; hence, Mark's description of Jesus's appearance reminds many interpreters of Dan 7:9. Watts, for example, suggests that:

> [t]he resemblance between Dan 7:9's Ancient of Days, whose 'clothing was as white as snow' and to whom the son of man comes on the clouds, and, in the context of the overshadowing cloud, Jesus' clothing, which is 'dazzling white,' confirms Jesus' self-designation that he is the glorious Son of Man (8:31).[58]

In point of fact, the specific wording στίλβοντα λευκὰ λίαν, though virtually unexplored in previous scholarship, supports this interpretive instinct. Semantically speaking, στίλβω refers to the "flash" of lightning, or "gleam" of stars or shining metals, and often functions as a synonym for the verbs ἀστράπτω and ἐξαστράπτω (meaning "to shine like stars" [ἀστήρ] or "flash like lightning").[59] In the LXX, it is used "almost always of the radiance of stars or the luster of metals."[60]

In the NT, στίλβω is a *hapax legomenon*. Matthew, by contrast, uses the more natural verb, λάμπω, to describe Jesus's shining face (17:2), while Luke (9:29) rather employs ἐξαστράπτων ("flashing like lightning"), which is reminiscent of throne theophanies like Ezek 1:26-28 and *1 En.* 14:8-23. There are two close precedents for Mark's usage in the LXX, however, which also account for the only other uses of στίλβω to refer to a someone's appearance in biblical literature: Ezek 40:3 and Dan 10:6. Both examples refer to heavenly beings whose appearance is said to be like "gleaming bronze" (χαλκοῦ στίλβοντος). The latter is worth quoting in full:

> And I lifted up my eyes and looked, and behold: a man clothed in linen, and his loins were girded with gold of Ophaz; his body was like beryl, and his face was like the sight of lightning (ἀστραπῆς), and his eyes as lamps of fire, and his arms and his legs as the sight of gleaming bronze (χαλκοῦ στίλβοντος), and the voice of his words as the voice of a multitude.
>
> Dan 10:5-6 LXX[61]

---

[58] Watts, "Mark," in *CNTUOT*, 186; see also, Hooker, *Mark*, 216; and Evans (*Mark 8:27–16:20*, 36), who comments: "Perhaps in his transformation we should understand that Jesus, as the 'son of man' in the presence of the Ancient of Days, has taken on some of God's characteristics." As we shall see, Evans strikes close to the mark.

[59] See LSJ, "στιλβαῖος," s. v.; L&N, "στίλβω," 1:175.

[60] BDAG, "στίλβω," s.v.; cf. Collins, *Mark*, 421. There are actually no exceptions to this rule in the LXX. See 1 Esd 8:56/Ezra 8:27; 1 Macc 6:39 (x2); Nah 3:3; Ep. Jer. 1:23; Ezek 21:15, 20, 33; 40:3; Dan 10:6; cf. Josephus, *Ant.* 8:68, 177, 185; and Philo, *Cher.* 1:22; *Her.* 1:224; *Decal.* 1:54.

[61] Notably, Dan 10:6 LXX exemplifies the connotation of "lightning" often implicit in the word στίλβω by connecting it with ἀστραπή just prior.

What makes Dan 10:6 LXX so intriguing vis-à-vis Mark 9:3 is that this very text is conflated with Dan 7:9 in Rev 1:13-15, which describes John's vision of Jesus, the glorified Son of Man:

> And in the midst of the lampstands [was] one like a son of man [cf. Dan 7:13], clothed with a long robe and with a golden sash around his chest. The hairs of his head were white, like white wool, like snow [cf. Dan 7:9]. His eyes were like the gleam of fire (φλὸξ πυρὸς), his feet were like burnished bronze (χαλκολιβάνῳ), refined in a furnace, and his voice was like the roar of many waters [cf. Dan 10:6].

Although Revelation does not employ the term στίλβοντος like Dan 10:6, the conflation of imagery from both passages, Dan 7:9 and 10:6, in application to the Son of Man is obvious.[62] Hence, Revelation offers evidence that the imagery of these two verses, though originally separate, were combined early on in application to Jesus as the exalted Son of Man. As Collins observes, the depiction of Jesus in Rev 1:13-15 is perhaps our closest analogue to his appearance in Mark 9:3.[63] It is not hard to imagine, then, that Mark has similarly conflated the language of Dan 7:9 and 10:6 in his own vision of Jesus as the exalted Son of Man.

There is other evidence besides the verbal clue provided by στίλβοντα linking Mark's account to Dan 7:9-14. Daniel—and Daniel 7, in particular—is after all a key text for Mark. The evangelist alludes directly to Dan 7:13 at least three times in the course of the Gospel, the first of which occurs with Jesus's prediction about the "Son of Man" who is coming with the "glory of his Father" and "the kingdom of God" (8:38–9:1), which the transfiguration scene seems intentionally positioned to fulfill. Mark has, as such, cued us to think of the scene in Dan 7:9-14 just as the journey up the mountain begins in 9:2. Yet we also encounter another mention of the "Son of Man" immediately *after* the transfiguration narrative in Mark 9:9:[64]

> And as they were coming down from the mountain, he charged them not to narrate [διηγήσωνται] what they saw to anyone until the Son of Man had risen from the dead.

As a result, Jesus's transfiguration is effectively bookeneded by references to the Son of Man, the first of which plainly alludes to Dan 7:13. It takes little imagination at this point for the reader to connect what happens in between to the foretold coming of the Son of Man.

Indeed, rather than fading into the background the Gospel afterward, Dan 7:13 assumes even greater importance as we draw nearer to Jesus's passion. In 13:26, Jesus

---

[62] Cf. Rowland, "Visions," 154; Rowland and Morray-Jones, *Mystery*, 106; Aune, *Revelation 1–5*, 94–5; Garrick V. Allen, "The Son of God in the Book of Revelation and Apocalyptic Literature," in *Son of God*, 57–8.
[63] See Collins, *Mark*, 422.
[64] Cf. Pesch (*Markusevangelium*, 2:70), who reads 9:9 as a comment on the meaning of 9:2-8: "geht es um eine Schau der Auferstehungsgestalt des Menschensohnes."

closely paraphrases Daniel's vision, promising again that people "will see the Son of Man coming on the clouds with great power and glory." In 14:62, he then quotes Dan 7:13 in combination with Ps 110:1, all the while elaborating on the alleged (and accepted) moniker "Messiah, Son of the Blessed" (14:61) at his trial before the Sanhedrin. Adela Collins, in fact, considers Dan 7:13 to be the likely source of *all* the Son of Man sayings in Mark—or, in other words, the very concept of the Son of Man in Mark.[65] In support of Collins's view, while the phrase "son of man" does occur elsewhere (e.g., Ps 8:4; Ezekiel; *1 En.* 48:2), Dan 7:13 is the only potential background to which Mark ever alludes, and he does so at key moments in the narrative. All told, the specific language used in Mark 9:3 along with the broader cues in the surrounding narrative suggest that what transpires on the mount of the transfiguration corresponds somehow to Daniel's vision in 7:9-14.

5.5.1 Daniel 7:9-14 Revisited: the Enthronement of the Son of Man

The vision described in Dan 7:9-14, then, consists of two principal images, the Ancient of Days seated on his throne (7:9-10) and the coming of the Son of Man (7:13-14), which form a single poem, interrupted in the middle by a brief "narrative ellipsis" in vv. 11-12:[66]

> I was looking
> when thrones were placed,
>   and the Ancient of Days sat,
> and his raiment was white as snow
>   and the hair of his head as pure white
>   wool;
> his throne as the gleam of fire,
>   its wheels burning fire.
> A river of fire was flowing before him;
> thousands of thousands were serving him
>   and myriad myriads stood before him.
> The court sat
>   and the scrolls were opened.
>   . . .

---

[65] See Adela Yarbro Collins, "The Influence of Daniel 7 on the New Testament," in Collins, *Daniel*, 90–123; idem, "Daniel 7 and Jesus," *JT* 93 (1989): 5–19; idem, "The Apocalyptic Son of Man Sayings," in *The Future of Early Christianity: Essays in Honor of Helmut Koester*, ed. B. A. Pearson (Minneapolis: Fortress, 1991), 220–28; idem, *Mark*, 186, 205, 402. Cf. Hooker, *Son of Man*, 192; Chrys C. Caragounis, *The Son of Man: Vision and Interpretation*, WUNT 38 (Tübingen: Mohr Siebeck, 1986), 174–211; Jonathan W. Lo, "The Contours and Functions of Danielic References in the Gospel of Mark," Ph.D. diss. (University of Edinburgh, 2012), 65 and *passim*. Hooker and Collins differ as to whether the Son of Man sayings in Mark should be traced back to Jesus himself, with Hooker answering in the negative and Collins in the affirmative, yet both agree that "Son of Man" in Mark ubiquitously recalls Daniel 7.

[66] So Collins, *Daniel*, 303. Seow (*Daniel*, 106) suggests that the vision of the heavenly court is presented in poetry in contrast to the scenes of earthly chaos.

> I was looking in visions of the night
> and lo, with the clouds of heaven
>   one like a son of man was coming,
> and he came to the Ancient of Days
>   and he was presented before him.
> And to him was given the rule, and the
>   honor, and the kingdom.
> And all the peoples, tribes, and languages
>   will serve him.
> His dominion is an everlasting dominion,
>   which shall never pass away,
> and his kingdom,
>   shall not be destroyed.
>
> Dan 7:9-10, 13-14 Θ[67]

The scene draws to a close Daniel's larger vision of four beasts, which represent four successive empires that cause chaos on earth. Against this backdrop, Dan 7:9-14 envisions God's dispensing of justice (v. 10), whereby he set right the course of history.

The setting depicted is not merely a courtroom, however, but the heavenly court of God's throne room.[68] (It is worth noting, in fact, that the fiery images surrounding the throne may recall traditional depictions of Sinai stemming from the Exodus narrative, which is to say that Dan 7:9-14 may locate God's throne on Sinai as do other texts and traditions.[69] It may not be an happenstance, as such, that the Sinai theophany and Daniel 7 appear blended together in Mark's transfiguration scene.) The precise justice that God dispenses is, moreover, is to enthrone the enigmatic "one like a son of man" (כבר אנש/ὡς υἱὸς ἀνθρώπου) who presents himself before him in v. 13. There are, after all, two thrones (כרסא/θρόνοι) placed in v. 9,[70] and while the Son of Man's enthronement is not explicitly stated, it is readily implied by the fact that he is given (a) dominion/authority (שלטן/ἡ ἀρχή), (b) glory (יקר/ἡ τιμή), and (c) the kingdom (מלכו/ἡ βασιλεία) so that "all peoples, nations, and languages might serve him."[71] Lastly, it is said of this

---

[67] I have relied on Theodotion's version of Daniel since Mark's allusions to Dan 7:13 (8:38; 13:26; 14:62) agree with Theodotion over the OG. Theodotion's translation is also notably closer to the MT.

[68] Hence, we read, "thrones were placed and the Ancient of Days took his seat." Collins (*Daniel*, 300) observes that, unlike the parallel vision in *1 En.* 14:8-23, Dan 7:9-14 never specifies the location of the throne, yet the imagery used would seem to indicate a cosmic or heavenly setting here, just as in *1 Enoch* (so also Montgomery, *Daniel*, 296). Both Goldingay (*Daniel*, 165) and Athalya Brenner-Idan (*Colour Terms in the Old Testament*, JSOTSup 21 [Sheffield: JSOT Press, 1982], 90, 93, 133) further observe that the Ancient of Days's clothing resembles descriptions of royal clothing in other literature (e.g., Esth 1:6; 8:15; *4 Ezra* 2:39-40 and other passages noted above).

[69] See Hartman, *Daniel*, 218; Goldingay, *Daniel*, 165; Collins, *Daniel*, 302. Sinai appears as a fiery mountain in Exod 19:18; 20:18; 24:17; Deut 4:36; Pss 97:3; 104:32; 144:5.

[70] *Contra* Montgomery (*Daniel*, 296), who states that "the plural is not to be stressed for only one took his seat," the vast majority of exegetes throughout the centuries have thought just the opposite (e.g., Collins, *Daniel*, 301).

[71] As Collins (*Daniel*, 301) states, the Son of Man "is given a kingdom, so it is reasonable to assume that he is enthroned." See similarly Stephen R. Miller, *Daniel*, NAC 18 (Nashville: Broadman & Holman, 1994), 207; Edward Adams, "The Coming of the Son of Man in Mark's Gospel," *TynBul* 56 (2005): 39–61.

Son of Man that "his dominion is an everlasting dominion, which shall never pass away, and his kingdom one that shall not be destroyed" (v. 14)—a refrain that has previously referred to God's own kingdom (Dan 2:44; 4:3).[72] It is clear, then, whose kingdom the Son of Man is given to rule (and who sets him on the throne).[73] Daniel 7:9-14 is not simply a vision of God seated on his throne, but of God's enthronement of the Son of Man as his vice-regent.

Thematically, this scene has clear affinities with Psalm 2. Both describe God's enthronement of his anointed king as his vice-regent in answer to the rebellion of the nations against his rule. As we have already seen and as we will presently see further, these affinities were not lost on subsequent readers (e.g., 4Q246) who appear to have conflated these texts in their visions of the days to come.

5.5.2 Daniel 7, the Enthronement of the Son of Man, and Psalm 2 in Tradition

The text of 4QAramaic Apocalypse (4Q246) is essentially a riff on Daniel 7. The extant text contains a number of plain allusions to Daniel, such as the phrase "His kingdom will be an eternal kingdom" in col. ii., line 5 (cf. 2:9).[74] Yet the figure described in 4Q246 is not called the "Son of Man," but "Son of God" and "Son of the Most-High." As we have seen, this language probably derives from Ps 2:7, making 4Q246 a case of inner-biblical interpretation between Daniel 7 and Psalm 2.[75]

In the *Similitudes of Enoch*, we find a more definite example of a similar pattern. Here, the "Son of Man," who is also called the "Chosen One" (45:3; 52:6; 53:6) and "Messiah" (48:10; 52:4), sits on the "throne of glory" in passages plainly dependent on Dan 7:9-14 (45:3; 55:4; 62:3, 5; cf. Matt 19:28).[76] Throughout the *Similitudes* the same throne is occupied by the "Head of Days" (the *Similitude's* equivalent of the "Ancient of Days").[77] In the *Similitudes*, then, the scene in Dan 7:9-14 becomes paradigmatic of the Messiah's enthronement on the Head of Days's own throne, or at least alongside him. It is within this same context that Dan 7:9-14 rubs shoulders with Psalm 2, on which *1 En.* 48:8-10 chiefly depends.[78]

While the *Similitudes* draw their Son of Man language from Dan 7:13 (with additional touches from 7:9), they draw their most explicit Messiah language from Psalm 2. Chapter 48 offers a prime example of the interaction between these two texts

---

[72] Cf. Ps 145:13, according to some mss. The authenticity of the line is questionable, yet some scholars believe it to be necessary to the psalm's structure; see Hossfeld, *Psalms 3*, 592–93.
[73] Michael Segal, "Who Is the 'Son of God' in 4Q246? An Overlooked Example of Early Biblical Interpretation," *DSD* 21.3 (2014): 289–312 (here, 292–93).
[74] See, e.g., Segal, "Who Is the 'Son of God,'" 289–312; Reinhard G. Kratz, "Son of God and Son of Man: 4Q246 in the Light of the Book of Daniel," in *Son of God*, 9–27.
[75] See Chapter 3; cf. Collins, "Son of God Text," in *Jesus to John*, 76–82.
[76] See Nickelsburg and Vanderkam's (*1 Enoch 2*, 155) comment on *1 En.* 46:1: "[t]he seer's brief account of his vision compresses and rewrites Dan 7:9 and 13."
[77] See *1 En.* 47:3; 60:2. 1 Enoch 62:2 is especially straightforward: "And the Lord of Spirits seated him [his Chosen One/the Son of Man] upon the throne of his glory."
[78] See Chapter 3.

in *1 Enoch*. The "Son of Man" is presented to the "Head of Days" in v. 2 and is shortly thereafter identified as the Lord's "Messiah" whom "the kings of the earth" have denied (vv. 8-10; cf. Ps 2:2):[79]

48:2 And in that hour that *Son of Man was named in the presence of* the Lord of Spirits, and his name, *before the Head of Days*....

[Dan 7:13]

48:8 In those days, downcast will be the face of *the kings of the earth*, and the strong who possess the land, because of the deeds of their hands ...

[Ps 2:2]

48:10 And on the day of their distress there will be rest on the earth, and before them they will fall and not rise, and there will be no one to take them with his hand and raise them, for they have denied *the Lord* of Spirits *and his Messiah*.[80]

[Ps 2:2]

Likewise, *4 Ezra* 13:1-13 envisages one "like the figure of a man," known elsewhere as the "Messiah" and God's "Son," who comes up out of the sea, flying with the clouds of heaven (cf. Dan 7:13).[81] Shortly thereafter, Ezra receives the interpretation of this vision: the man who came up from the sea is "he whom the Most-High has been keeping for many ages, who will himself deliver his creation" (v. 26) and is indeed God's "Son" (v. 32) who will stand atop Mount Zion (v. 35), from where he "will reprove the assembled nations" that gathered to make war against him (vv. 31-34). Again, the enthronement of the man-like figure/Son of God is not explicitly stated, but can be inferred. What is more: this interpretation of the Danielic Son of Man depends heavily on Psalm 2, as we saw in Chapter 1.[82] As in the *Similitudes*, the visions of Daniel 7 and Psalm 2 are thoroughly conflated.

Revelation 1-2 also intertwines Daniel 7 and Psalm 2 in its simultaneous portrayal of Jesus as Son of Man and Son of God. According to Garrick Allen, Revelation's depiction of Jesus as God's Son is entirely dependent on Psalm 2.[83] But when John first beholds Jesus and is told to write what he sees and "send it back to the seven churches" (1:11), he appears as the exalted Son of Man with imagery dependent on Dan 7:9-14 and 10:1-11, as we saw earlier (Rev 1:13-16). In 2:26-27, however, the

---

[79] See Chapter 3; cf. Nickelsburg and Vanderkam, *1 Enoch 2*, 167.
[80] Translations adapted from Nickelsburg and Vanderkam, *1 Enoch*, 62-3.
[81] See, e.g., *4 Ezra* 12:32: "this is the Messiah, whom the Most-High has kept until the end of days, who will arise from the offspring of David"; and 13:32: "then my Son will be revealed, whom you saw as a man coming up from the sea." Stone (*Fourth Ezra*, 397) comments that the Son of Man from Dan 7 in *4 Ezra* 13 "is interpreted as the Messiah, precreated and prepared in advance, who will deliver creation and direct those who are left"; cf. Collins, "The Apocalyptic Son of Man Sayings," 220-28; John J. Collins, "The Son of Man in First-Century Judaism," *NTS* 38 (1992): 448-66.
[82] Cf. Stone, *4 Ezra*, 397.
[83] Allen, "Son of God," 61. See also Chapter 3 of this study on Revelation's extensive use of Psalm 2.

letter to Thyatira closes with an allusion to Ps 2:7-9, promising to the faithful the same authority to rule over the nations with a "rod of iron" that Jesus himself has received from his Father. Even more to the point, in 2:18 Jesus identifies himself as "the Son of God" (ὁ υἱὸς τοῦ θεοῦ)—but with a description recalling that of the Son of Man from Rev 1:13-15 (ὁ ἔχων τοὺς ὀφθαλμοὺς [αὐτοῦ] ὡς φλόγα πυρός, καὶ οἱ πόδες αὐτοῦ ὅμοιοι χαλκολιβάνῳ), dependent on Dan 7:9 and 10:6.[84]

In various rabbinic texts, Dan 7:9 and 13 are the source of speculations that the Messiah/David/Son of David will be enthroned alongside God himself.[85] According to Rabbi Akiba, for instance, Dan 7:9 refers to two thrones: "one for [God], and one for David."[86] Likewise, *b. Sanh.* 96b identifies *Bar Naflé* ("Son of the Clouds," i.e., Daniel's "one like a son of man") as the "Messiah," and *b. Sanh.* 98a as the "Son of David." In this vein, we should not forget that Dan 7:13-14 explicitly interprets Ps 2:7 in *Midr. Ps.* 2.9. Once again, the text reads:

> *I will declare of the decree of the Lord. He said unto me: "Thou art My son"* (Ps. 2:7).... In the decree of the Writings it is written. *The Lord said unto my lord: "Sit thou at My right hand, until 1 make thine enemies thy footstool"* (Ps. 110:1), and it is also written *I saw in the night visions, and, behold, there came with the clouds of heaven one like unto a son of man, and he came even to the Ancient of days, and he was brought near before Him. And there was given him dominion, and glory, and a kingdom, that all the peoples, nations, and languages should serve him.*
>
> Dan. 7:13, 14

In a variety of ancient Jewish literature, then, we find a consistent understanding of (a) Dan 7:9-14 as an enthronement scene; (b) the Son of Man as the Messiah; (c) a close association between the images in Dan 7:9 and 13, which describe the figures who occupy the thrones; and (d) an intermeshing of Dan 7:9-14 and Psalm 2 (especially 2:7) owing to their shared eschatological vision.

5.5.3 Summary: Son of Man and Son of God

To state the obvious, "Son of Man" is not "Son of God." Nevertheless, we have just seen that these two figures were often conflated with each other in early Jewish literature. Seyoon Kim has, in fact, demonstrated that Mark appears to stand within this tradition.[87] Kim traces a pattern through all four Gospels, beginning with Mark, in which the Son of Man is, at least implicitly, also the Son of God.[88] Kim's first example is

---

[84] Cf. Allen, "Son of God," 53.
[85] See *b. Hag.* 14a-b; *b. Sanh.* 38b; 96b, 98a; *Exod. Rab.* 15:26; *Midr. Ps.* 72:2.
[86] See *b. Hag.* 14a-b; *b. Sanh.* 38b. See further the discussions in Maurice Casey, *Son of Man: The Interpretation and Influence of Daniel 7* (London: SPCK, 1979), 86–8. Alan F. Segal (*Two Powers in Heaven: Early Rabbinic Reports about Christianity and Gnosticism*, SJLA 25 [Leiden: Brill, 1977], 33–57) believes Dan 7:9 was at the center of the "two powers" controversy in rabbinic Judaism.
[87] See Seyoon Kim, *The "Son of Man" as the Son of God*, WUNT 30 (Tübingen: Mohr Siebeck, 1983).
[88] Kim (*Son of Man*, 1) makes Mark the starting point for his overall argument that "the Evangelists understood themselves [sic.] the Son of Man to be the Son of God and intended to present their unity."

no other text than Mark 8:38: Jesus declares that the Son of Man will come with the glory of *his Father*.[89]

As Kim recognizes, the basis of this identification in Mark, as in the various texts surveyed above, is that both the Son of Man and the Son of God were understood as the Davidic Messiah, just as Daniel 7 and Psalm 2 were both understood as enthronement texts.[90] The case is not that "Son of Man" *means* "Son of God," but rather that, in the eyes of both Mark and others, the Son of Man and the Son of God turn out to be the same person. Likewise, the enthronement of the Son of Man and the enthronement of the Son of God are not so disparate as one might assume.

5.6 Conclusions: Psalm 2 and the Son's Enthronement in Mark 9:2-8

We have now seen ample evidence to support the contention that Jesus's transfiguration in Mark envisions his enthronement on the mountain and that it alludes to Dan 7:9-14, in particular. Finally, we have observed that the eschatological visions of enthronement in Daniel 7 and Psalm 2 were conflated with one another in a variety of different texts earlier and later than Mark's Gospel. So when we return to the words of Ps 2:7 at the climax of Mark's scene, all indications are that Mark envisions the enthronement of God's royal Son, the Messiah, as his vice-regent who will establish his kingdom on earth.

The pairing of Ps 2:7 with Deut 18:15 (Προφήτην ἐκ τῶν ἀδελφῶν σου ὡς ἐμὲ ἀναστήσει Κύριος ὁ θεός σου σοί, αὐτοῦ ἀκούσεσθε) in Mark 9:7, in fact, supports this assessment. In context, Moses refers to his successor ("a prophet like me"), yet these words later assumed an eschatological interpretation in a number of Second Temple texts.[91] So there is little doubt, given the combination of Deut 18:15 with Ps 2:7 (and possibly Isa 42:1), that Mark 9:7 "present[s] the Messiah," just as the voice from heaven did in 1:11.[92] Hence, Jesus's transfiguration, properly understood, does indeed offer a confirmation of Peter's declaration in 8:29, as well as Jesus's own prediction in 8:38–9:1.

But what place does this scene finally occupy in Mark's story of Jesus as a whole, and how, in particular, does it relate to his baptism, which served as his messianic anointing in the Gospel narrative? To start, we may say that the transfiguration envisions Jesus's

---

[89] Ibid., 1, 88.
[90] Ibid., 1-3; 79-81, 99-102.
[91] See 4Q175 I, 5-8; 1QS IX, 10-11; 11Q13 II, 17-18; *T. Benj.* 9:2. According to Daniel Falk, "The Teacher of Righteousness in the sectarian scrolls is [also] modeled as a prophet like Moses"; see Falk, "Moses," in *EDSS* 577. Furthermore, H. C. Kee observes that "[t]he expectation of the eschatological prophet builds on Deut 18:15 and figures importantly at Qumran: 1QS IX, 10-11; 1QSª II, 11-12. Possibly the star, mentioned in CD VII, 15-20 (which is based on Num 24:17) is the One Who Teaches Rightly (1QS I, 11), forerunner of the unique prophet of the endtime. The prophet is directly mentioned in PssJosh 5-8 (= 4QTestim) in a passage which leads into a declaration about the star. The text from Num 24 is quoted in Stephen's sermon (Acts 7:37), where it is taken to refer to Jesus as the eschatological prophet"; see H. C. Kee, "Testaments of the Twelve Patriarchs," in *OTP* 1:827 n. 9b.
[92] So Pesch, *Markusevangelium*, 2:76; see similarly Gnilka, *Markus*, 2:36; Steichele, *Sohn Gottes*, 181, 188–89; Boring, *Mark*, 261–62; France, *Mark*, 355; Marcus, *Way*, 81, 85–6.

enthronement even more vividly than did 1:9-11. As dramatic as the rending of the heavens and descent of the Spirit were, the otherworldly radiance of the present scene arguably surpasses it. Jesus's glory has now been *seen* by others and they, too, have heard the divine decree. But the transfiguration is more than an intensification of the baptism scene. If Jesus's baptism acts as his royal anointing, then the transfiguration offers a proleptic glance at his enthroned state, or exaltation (cf. Rev 1:13-16). The notion that the transfiguration offers a "vision" of some kind or "prefigures" a future reality is both common and appropriate given the terms of the text, such as ὤφθη (v. 4) and εἶδον (vv. 8, 9).[93] What the disciples receive in 9:2-8 is seemingly a glimpse of a future that is not yet—one apparently linked to Jesus's resurrection in Mark's understanding.[94]

Yet, as Marcus observes, the greatest parallels are, paradoxically, with Jesus's passion.[95] Allison has traced a similar set of parallels, both similarities and contrasts, in Matthew, most of which also apply to Mark's account:[96]

The Transfiguration (Mark 9:2-8)	The Crucifixion (Mark 15:16-40)
Similarities	
"After six days" (9:2)	"When the sixth hour came" (15:33)
Three named onlookers (9:2)	Three named onlookers (15:40)
Jesus declared God's "Son" (9:7)	Jesus declared God's "Son" (15:39)
Contrasts	
Jesus takes others (9:2)	Jesus is taken by others (15:16, 22)
Elevation on a mountain (9:2)	Elevation on the cross (15:24, 27)
Private epiphany (9:2)	Public spectacle (15:29)
Light (9:3)	Darkness (15:33)
Garments illuminated (9:3)	Garments stripped off (15:20)
Jesus glorified (9:3-7)	Jesus shamed (15:16-20, 29-32)
Elijah appears (9:4)	Elijah does not appear (15:35-36)
Two saints beside Jesus (9:4-5)	Two criminals beside Jesus (15:27)
God exalts Jesus (9:7)	God abandons Jesus (15:34)

---

[93] Among ancient interpreters, see, e.g., Origen, *Cels.* 2.65 (*PG* 11:900); *Comm. Matt.* 12.43 (*PG* 13:1081–85); Eusebius, *Comm. Luc.* 9 (*PG* 24:549); Hilary, *Matt.* 17.2 (*PL* 9:1013b–1014b); Ambrose, *Enarrat. Ps.* 45.2 (*PL* 14:1187); Jerome, *Comm. Matt.* 3.17 (*PL* 26:121-124); Augustine, *Hom.* 28 (*PL* 38:490-93); and the earliest commentary on Mark: *Exp. Marc.* ad loc. (CChr 82). Among modern interpreters, see, e.g., Taylor, *Mark*, 386–88; Pesch, *Markusevangelium*, 2:69; Marcus, *Mark 8–16*, 633; Hays, *Gospels*, 62.

[94] Kee, "Transfiguration," 149; Pesch, *Markusevangelium*, 2:70.

[95] Marcus, *Mark 8–16*, 641.

[96] Allison, "Foreshadowing," 226–29. The chart here is a near reproduction of the chart that appears in pages 228–29 of Allison's book. Others who have since followed Allison's reading (which originally appears in Davies and Allison, *Matthew*, 2:706-07) include David E. Garland, *Reading Matthew: A Literary and Theological Commentary on the First Gospel* (London: SPCK, 1993), 183–84; Thomas G. Long, *Matthew*, WBC (Louisville, KY: Westminster John Knox, 1997), 194.

As Allison observes, placing the two scenes side by side "creates pictorial antithetical parallelism, something like a diptych in which the two plates have similar outlines but different colors. If one scene were sketched on a transparency and placed over the other, many of its lines would disappear."[97] So from the standpoint of Mark's narrative, what unfolds in 9:2-8 is not yet resolved, but awaits a certain fulfillment via Jesus's crucifixion. If this is true of the scene in general, it also true of Mark 9:7 in specific. Inasmuch as 9:7 anticipates 15:39, the full meaning of the words "This is my Son, the beloved; listen to him!" finally depends, however ironically, on the centurion's confession, "Truly, this man was the Son of God."

---

[97] Allison, "Foreshadowing," 229.

6

The Son in the Parable

The whole parable [of the Wicked Tenants] is apparently pure allegory.

Joachim Jeremias[1]

The son is the point on which the parable turns.

Klyne R. Snodgrass[2]

In between the transfiguration and passion narratives, the reader encounters the familiar term υἱὸς ἀγαπητός ("beloved son") once more in the Parable of the Wicked Tenants (Mark 12:1-12)—or, as Pesch names it, "The Parable of the Son's Murder."[3] This use of sonship language bears *de facto* importance within the narrative since it (a) comes from Jesus's own lips, and (b) echoes God's earlier pronouncements in 1:11 and 9:7. Nevertheless, the parable does not usually weigh heavily in studies of Mark's Son of God, nor do many interpreters connect it to the prior allusions to Psalm 2 in 1:11 and 9:7.

This chapter offers a corrective to both of these tendencies. First, I aim to show that in the narrative world of Mark's Gospel the υἱὸς ἀγαπητός in 12:6 is one and the same as the messianic "son" of Psalm 2. Second, within the Gospel, Jesus's parable acts a kind of *Schlüsseltext*—a story within a story (*mise en abyme*) that hints at the meaning of the whole as we approach the Gospel's final act. When these two points are held together, the Parable of the Wicked Tenants sheds significant light on the plot inherent to Jesus's sonship in Mark as a whole.

6.1 The Parable at a Glance: An Allegory Rooted in Israel's Scriptures

The Parable of the Wicked Tenants is one of the most studied of all Jesus's parables.[4] While we need not delve into all of its many interpretive issues in order to see its

---

[1] Joachim Jeremias, *The Parables of Jesus*, trans. S. H. Hooke (New York: Scribner, 1972), 70.
[2] Klyne R. Snodgrass, *The Parable of the Wicked Tenants: An Inquiry into Parable Interpretation*, WUNT 27 (Tübingen: Mohr Siebeck, 1983), 81.
[3] See Pesch, *Markusevangelium*, 2:213: "Das Gleichnis von der Tötung des Sohnes." Cf. Matthew Black ("The Christological Use of the Old Testament in the New Testament," *NTS* 18 [1971]: 1–14 [here, 13]): "the parable of the Rejected Son."
[4] For a useful summary of the issues and ongoing debates, see Klyne R. Snodgrass, "Recent Research on the Parable of the Wicked Tenants: An Assessment," *BBR* 8 (1998): 187–215; idem, *Stories with*

relationship to Psalm 2 and to the rest of Mark's narrative, it will be helpful to summarize some basic points before moving forward.

Despite Jülicher's categorical insistence that a parable is not an allegory, the present parable, in its present form, is an obvious example of just that.[5] The vineyard stands for Israel, its owner for God, the tenants for the Jewish authorities, the servants for the prophets of old, and the owner's beloved son for Jesus himself.[6] Identification of this *dramatis personae* depends on hearing the story's several intertextual allusions to Israel's Scriptures.

As is well-known, the parable takes its opening cues from Isaiah's "Song of the Vineyard" (5:1-7), which likens Israel to a vineyard planted by God, yet one that fails to bear good fruit.[7] The rich allusions to Isaiah's song (Mark 12:1 borrows no fewer

---

Intent, 2nd ed. (Grand Rapids: Eerdmans, 2018), 276–98. Snodgrass's earlier study (*The Parable of the Wicked Tenants*) is still the most thorough study of the parable. The most thorough commentary on Mark 12:1-12 is Evans, *Mark 8:27–16:20*, 210–40.

[5] In addition to most commentaries, see, e.g., John Drury, "The Sower, the Vineyard, and the Place of Allegory in the Interpretation of Mark's Parables," *JTS* 24 (1973): 367–79; J. D. M. Derrett, "Allegory and the Wicked Vinedressers," *JTS* 25 (1974): 426–32; Snodgrass, *Parable*, 13–26; Johannes C. de Moor, "The Targumic Background of Mark 12:1-12: The Parable of the Wicked Tenants," *JSJ* 29 (1998): 63–80; Arland J. Hultgren, *The Parables of Jesus: A Commentary* (Grand Rapids: Eerdmans, 2000), 357. Even Jeremias (*The Parables of Jesus*, trans. S. H. Hooke [New York: Scribner, 1972], 70), though he believes the parable had been allegorized at an earlier stage of tradition inherited by Mark, acknowledges that the parable in its present form is "pure allegory." In any case, Jülicher's (*Die gleichnisreden Jesu* [Freiburg: Mohr Siebeck, 1899], 1:49, 74) categorical distinction between parable and allegory has since fallen on hard times based on recognition that (a) Jülicher was reacting against the allegorizing tendencies of the early church, which are different than allegory itself; (b) his definition of allegory is too narrow in comparison to that of ancient rhetoricians such as Quintilian and Cicero; and (c) many of the rabbinic parables, which offer our closest parallels to Jesus's own are explicit allegories (e.g., *Midr. Tanḥ. Besh.* 4.7; *Midr. Tanḥ. Emor* 8.30); see, *inter alia*, Hans-Josef Klauck (*Allegorie und Allegorese in synoptischen Gleichnistexten* [Münster: Aschendorff, 1978]); Snodgrass (*Parable*, 13–26); and, more recently, Suk Kwan Wong (*Allegorical Spectrum of the Parables of Jesus* [Eugene, OR: Wipf & Stock, 2017]). Additionally, Matthew Black ("Die Gleichnisse als Allegorien," in *Gleichnisse Jesu: Positionen der Auslegung von Adolf Jülicher bis zur Formgeschichte*, ed. Wolfgang Harnisch, WF 366 [Darmstadt: Wissenschaftliche Buchgesellschaft, 1982], 262–80) observes that Jülicher actually admitted that certain parables (such as the present one) *are* allegories; he simply denied that they were parables of Jesus.

[6] A similar summary appears in Hugh Anderson (The Gospel of Mark, NCB [Grand Rapids: Eerdmans, 1981], 270) and many other commentaries.

[7] In addition to the major commentaries, see esp. Snodgrass, *Parable*, 47–8; Watts, *New Exodus*, 339–49; and Wim J. C. Weren, "The Use of Isaiah 5,1-7 in the Parable of the Tenants (Mark 12,1-12; Matthew 21,33-46)," *Bib* 79 (1998): 1–26. On the use of Isaiah 5 in 4Q500 and its relevance to Mark 12:1-12, including the possible more specific identification of the vineyard with the Jerusalem temple, see George J. Brooke, "4Q500 1 and the Use of Scripture in the Parable of the Vineyard," *DSD* 2 (1995): 268–94. On the question of whether Mark follows the LXX or MT version of Isa 5:1-7, see the debate between Craig A. Evans ("How Septuagintal Is Isa. 5:1-7 in Mark 12:1-9?," *NovT* 45 [2003]: 105–10) and John S. Kloppenborg ("Egyptian Viticultural Practices and the Citation of Isa 5:1-7 in Mark 12:1-9," *NovT* 44 [2002]: 134–59; idem, "Isa 5:1-7 LXX and Mark 12:1, 9, Again," *NovT* 46 [2004]: 12–19). For the image of Israel as a vineyard elsewhere in Scripture, see Deut 32:32; Ps 80:8-16; Isa 27:2-7; Jer 2:21; 12:10; Ezek 19:10-14; Hos 10:1. The image is also common in rabbinic parables, such as *Sipre Deut.* 312; *Tanḥ. Lev.* 7.6; *Exod. Rab.* 30.17; and *Midr. Prov.* 19:21. Yet, for reasons clarified just below, it is beyond doubt that the parable alludes specifically to Isa 5:1-7.

than eight terms from Isa 5:1-2 LXX)[8] frame the entire parable as a story about Israel's relation to God.[9]

Yet Jesus's parable quickly introduces characters not found in Isaiah, which change the tune considerably.[10] The "tenants" (γεωργοί) who first appear in 12:1 plainly represent Israel's leaders—"the chief priests, scribes, and elders" (οἱ ἀρχιερεῖς καὶ οἱ γραμματεῖς καὶ οἱ πρεσβύτεροι) from 11:28, who indeed recognize themselves in 12:12.[11] The owner's servants (δοῦλοι), on the other hand, recall the prophets of old, who are frequently described by the same term in the LXX and whose similar fates are recorded in numerous instances.[12] In the first half of the parable, then, Jesus expands Isaiah's original allegory about Israel and Israel's God into a retelling of Israel's rebellious history, albeit one that specifically lays the blame on Israel's unjust leaders.[13]

In keeping with the prior use of ὁ υἱός μου ὁ ἀγαπητός to refer to Jesus in 1:11 and 9:7, nearly all interpreters recognize that the allegory takes something of an autobiographical turn with the introduction of the owner's υἱὸς ἀγαπητός in 12:6.[14] The owner's son, whom he sends last (ἔσχατον) is killed and cast out of the vineyard just as Jesus is ultimately crucified outside the city of Jerusalem.[15] By inserting himself into the center of the parable Jesus reads his own fate into the climax of Israel's own story.[16]

---

[8] E.g., ἀμπελών, φυτεύω, περιτίθημι, φραγμός, ὀρύσσω, ὑπολήνιον (cf. προλήνιον), οἰκοδομέω, and πύργος. Additionally, Jesus's question in 12:9, τί [οὖν] ποιήσει ὁ κύριος τοῦ ἀμπελῶνος, recalls Isa 5:5 LXX: νῦν δὲ ἀναγγελῶ ὑμῖν τί ποιήσω τῷ ἀμπελῶνί μου.

[9] See similarly Snodgrass, *Parable*, 76.

[10] So Cranfield (*Mark*, 365): Jesus's parable "strikes in a different direction."

[11] As France (*Mark*, 456) observes, there is no indication that the location or audience has changed from the previous pericope (11:27-33); see similarly Pesch, *Markusevangelium*, 2:221; Gnilka, *Markus*, 2:142; Trocme, *Marc*, 296; Donahue and Harrington, *Mark*, 337; Boring, *Mark*, 328; Black, *Mark*, 250, 253. Watts (*New Exodus*, 342) also notes that "in fact, on all three occasions where Jesus has been confronted by authorities from Jerusalem (3:22ff, 7:14ff, and here), has response has been in parables."

[12] Cf. Boring, *Mark*, 329; Marcus, *Mark 8-16*, 803. Both δοῦλος and ἀποστέλλω are used of the prophets in 2 Chr 36:15; Jer 7:25-26; 25:4; Amos 3:7; Zech 1:6; cf. 1QpHab 2.9; 7.5. For references to the persecution and/or murder of the prophets, see 1 Kgs 18:4, 12-13; 19:10; 2 Chr 16:10; 24:20-22; 36:15-16; Neh 9:26; Jer 2:30; 20:2. In fact, the persecution and murder of the prophets had become something of a trope in Israel's memory by Jesus's day: see *Jub.* 1:12; *Liv. Proph.*, *passim*; Josephus, *Ant.* 10.38; Matt 23:34, 37; Luke 11:47, 49; 13:34. On prophetic martyrdom, see further H. A. Fischel, "Martyr and Prophet (A Study in Jewish Literature)," *JQR* 37 (1947): 265–80; O. H. Steck, *Israel Und Das Gewaltsame Geschick Der Propheten: Untersuchungen Zur Überlieferung Des Deuteronomistischen Geschichtsbildes Im Alten Testament, Spätjudentum Und Urchristentum*, WMANT 23 (Neukirchen-Vluyn: Neukirchener Verlag, 1967).

[13] So Black (*Mark*, 251): "Jesus is *not* singing the same old prophetic ballad of Israel's infertility in righteousness," but rather a variation on a theme, one might say.

[14] Focant (*Mark*, 474) states the point nicely: "The christological allusion is transparent, if the reader remembers that Jesus has been designated in this way by the heavenly voice from his baptism (1:11) and his transfiguration (9:7)"; cf. Legassé, *Marc*, 714. For others who recognize the intranarrative allusion to 1:11 and 9:7 in 12:6, see note 24 below.

[15] Cf. Gnlika, *Markus*, 2:147; Marcus, *Way*, 113; Donahue and Harrington, *Mark*, 339; France, *Mark*, 458; Boring, *Mark*, 331. Both Matthew (21:39) and Luke (20:15) reverse the order so that the son is first thrown out of the vineyard and *then* killed so as to bring the details of the parable into closer approximation with the actual events of Jesus's death.

[16] So also Hays (*Gospels*, 40): the parable "foreshadows the climax of [Israel's] plot in the fate of Jesus himself"; cf. Davies and Allison, *Matthew*, 3:178.

At last, the quotation of Ps 117:22-23 LXX in Mark 12:10-11 draws the parable to a conclusion in more ways than one. In the first place, it is widely acknowledged that the psalm quotation interprets the foregoing story in 12:1-9.[17] David Stern, followed by Snodgrass, helpfully compares these verses to a *nimshal* offering an explanation of the preceding *mashal*.[18] In particular, "the stone that the builders rejected" (λίθον ὃν ἀπεδοκίμασαν οἱ οἰκοδομοῦντες) corresponds to the murdered "beloved son" in 12:6-8: a connection that may even be signaled by the use of a traditional wordplay (*paranomasia*) between "son" (בן) and "stone" (אבן) already found in the Hebrew Scriptures and attested in multiple languages in the first century CE and afterward.[19] This understanding is further supported by the fact that the verb ἀποδοκιμάζω occurs in only one other instance in Mark: Jesus's first passion prediction in 8:31, where his rejection by the "elders, chief priests, and scribes" (cf. 11:28) interprets his death.[20]

Second, the quotation of Ps 117:22-23 also completes the allegory by foreshadowing not only Jesus's death, but also his vindication; as the psalm reads, "This one has become the head of the corner" (οὗτος ἐγενήθη εἰς κεφαλὴν γωνίας; cf. Mark 8:31; 9:31;

---

[17] There is debate as to whether 12:10-11 were part of the original parable (so Snodgrass, *Parable*, 95-7), already added to the version Mark inherited (so Hengel, "Gleichnis," 1; Gnilka, *Markus*, 2:142; Pesch, *Markusevangelium*, 2:213; Jeremias, *Parables*, 72-4; Marcus, *Way*, 112), or added by Mark himself (Trocme, *Marc*, 299), but none debate the interpretive function of these verses in the parable as it stands. Whatever the case may be, it is worth noting that there is no extant version of the parable without a quotation (see Matt 21:33-44; Luke 20:9-18) or at least an allusion (*Gos. Thom.* 66) to Ps 117:22 LXX.

[18] See David Stern, "Jesus' Parables from the Perspective of Rabbinic Literature," in *Parable and Story in Judaism and Christianity*, ed. Clemens Thoma et al., Studies in Judaism and Christianity (New York: Paulist, 1989), 66-7; idem, *Parables in Midrash: Narrative and Exegesis in Rabbinic Literature* (Cambridge: Harvard University Press, 1991), 197; Snodgrass, *Parable*, 96-7; idem, *Stories*, 276. On the relationship between *mashal* and *nimshal*, see further David Stern, "The Rabbinic Parable and the Narrative of Interpretation," in *The Midrashic Imagination: Jewish Exegesis, Thought, And history*, ed. Michael A. Fishbane (Albany: State University of New York Press, 1993), 78-95 (here, 79). Something akin to the *nimshal* can be found in many scriptural parables in the OT: e.g., Judg 9:7-20; 2 Sam 12:1-14; 14:1-17; 1 Kgs 20:35-43; 2 Kgs 14:8-10; Isa 5:1-7; Ezek 17:3-21; 19:1-14; 21:1-5; 24:3-14. The classic example is Nathan's comment, "You are the man!" in 2 Sam 12:7.

[19] See esp. Snodgrass, *Parable*, 113-18; as well as Carrington, *Mark*, 256; Black, "Christological," 12-4; Pesch, *Markusevangelium*, 2:222; Marcus, *Way*, 114; Moor, "Targumic," 75; Evans, *Mark 8:27-16:20*, 228-29; and others. Some, such as Hultgren (*Parables*, 363) object that the wordplay only works in Hebrew and would therefore "demands too much subtlety on the part of both the composer and the first hearers of the parable"; cf. France, *Mark*, 463. Yet, in addition to the Hebrew Scriptures (e.g., Exod 28:9-12, 17, 21; 39:6-7, 14; Josh 4:6-7; Lam 4:1-2; Isa 54:11-13; Zech 9:16), Snodgrass demonstrates that the wordplay is preserved in the Aramaic targums of Exodus 28 and 39; Joshua 4; and Isaiah 54. Importantly, *Tg. Ps.* 118:22 changes אבן to טליא . . . בניא דיש׳ ("the boy ... among the sons of Jesse"). Talmudic literature also attests the wordplay in b. Sem. 47b-48a. אבן is taken to refer to individuals several times in both the targums (*Tg.-Onq. Gen.* 49:24; *Tg. Exod.* 28:14, 16) and in rabbinic literature (*Shem. Rab.* 20.9; 46.2; *'Est. Rab.* 7.10; *'Ekah. Rab.* 4:1). Josephus (*War* 5.272) relates a story attesting the wordplay during the siege of Jerusalem. Finally, the same wordplay may underlie several other passages in the Gospels: see Matt 3:9; 4:3; 7:9; 21:15; and Luke 19:39-40. The evidence for a traditional wordplay between "son" and "stone" is sound, therefore.

[20] It is, in fact, probable, as Snodgrass (*Parable*, 101) demonstrates, that Mark 8:31 is essentially a paraphrase of Ps 117:22 LXX in the first place: "*The stone which the builders rejected*—i.e., 'It is necessary for the Son of Man to suffer and be rejected by the religious authorities and to be killed;'—*This has become the head of the corner*—i.e., '... to arise after three days.'" (italics original). See similarly Gnilka, *Markus*, 2:149; Marcus, *Way*, 114; Legassé, *Marc*, 718; Focant, *Mark*, 476; Standaert, *Marc*, 851.

10:33-34).²¹ Given that this exact verse refers to Jesus's resurrection elsewhere (Acts 4:11; Eph 2:20; 1 Pet 2:4-8; *Barn.* 6:2; 16:5), it is safe to assume that it serves the that function here.²² In its totality, then, Jesus's parable in Mark constitutes a miniaturized telling of his story as the climax of Israel's own story, which is accomplished from beginning to end through intertextual allusions to Israel's Scriptures and intratextual allusions to the rest of Mark's narrative at the same time.

6.2 The "Beloved Son" and Psalm 2

As noted in the introduction, only a few interpreters connect υἱὸς ἀγαπητός in 12:6 to Psalm 2 in any way.²³ Alternatively, some suggest a possible allusion to Genesis 22, where the same terminology refers to Isaac.²⁴ Yet virtually all interpreters recognize that υἱὸς ἀγαπητός chiefly recalls the use of the same words at Jesus's baptism (1:11) and transfiguration (9:7).²⁵ A number of scholars even suspect that Mark may have added ἀγαπητός himself precisely in order to conform 12:6 to 1:11 and 9:7.²⁶ The modifier is, in any case, absent from the parallel accounts in both Matt 21:37 and *Gos. Thom.* 65, and occurs in only these three instances in Mark.²⁷

---

²¹ John Dominic Crossan ("The Parable of the Wicked Husbandmen," *JBL* 90 [1971]: 451–65 [here, 454]) regards the psalm quotation in 12:10-11 as "an obvious necessity" in order for the allegory to work; cf. Pesch, *Markusevangelium*, 2:222; Gnilka, *Markus*, 2:148; Jeremias, *Parables*, 76; Snodgrass, *Parable*, 100–01; Marcus, *Way*, 114; France, *Mark*, 463; Hays, *Gospels*, 44.

²² See also Pesch, *Markusevangelium*, 2:222.

²³ Namely, Lövestam, *Son and Saviour*, 97; Matera, *Kingship*, 78; de Moor, "Targumic," 76; Watts, "Mark," in *CNTUOT*, 212–13; Kelli S. O'Brien, *The Use of Scripture in the Markan Passion Narrative*, LNTS 384 (London/New York: T&T Clark, 2010), 165; and Botner, *Son of David*, 157. Nevertheless, not one major commentary on Mark mentions any possible connection to Psalm 2 in 12:1-12. Snodgrass ("Recent Research," 199) does not even list Psalm 2 among the possible connections that have been considered by past interpreters.

²⁴ E.g., Kazmierski, *Jesus*, 53–6; Frank Stern, *A Rabbi Looks at Jesus' Parables* (Lanham, MD: Rowman & Littlefield, 2006), 119; Evans, *Mark 8:27–16:20*, 234–35; Marcus, *Mark 8–16*, 803; Hays, *Gospels*, 43. Botner (*Son of David*, 157) suggests that there has been actual "resistance" to seeing an allusion to Psalm 2 due to the methodological decision to privilege one intertext over another. In my view, "resistance" may be too strong of a word, but Botner is certainly correct that methodological presuppositions have caused Psalm 2 to be overlooked.

²⁵ E.g., Carrington, *Mark*, 255; Crossan, "Parable," 453; Gnilka, *Markus*, 2:143; Pesch, *Markusevangelium*, 2:221; Jeremias, *Parables*, 73; Hooker, *Mark*, 276; Marcus, *Way*, 113; Legassé, *Marc*, 714; Hultgren, *Parables*, 368; Evans, *Mark 8:27–16:20*, 234; Donahue and Harrington, *Mark*, 338; France, *Mark*, 458; Boring, *Mark*, 328; Focant, *Mark*, 474; Collins, *Mark*, 547; Standaert, *Marc*, 432; Iverson, "Jews, Gentiles, and the Kingdom of God," 319; Hays, *Gospels*, 42; Tania Oldenhage, "Spiralen Der Gewalt (Die Bösen Winzer)," in *Kompendium Der Gleichnisse Jesu*, ed. Ruben Zimmermann and Detlev Dormeyer (Gütersloh: Gütersloher, 2007), 352–66 (here, 356). A handful of interpreters, such as Malcolm F. Lowe ("From the Parable of the Vineyard to a Pre-Synoptic Source," *NTS* 28 [1982]: 257–63 [here, 257]) and Stern ("Jesus' Parables, 65) argue that the "beloved son" in 12:6 refers to John the Baptist rather than Jesus, but their suggestions have not caught on for obvious reasons; see Hultgren, *Parables*, 360.

²⁶ Klauck (*Allegorie*, 543), for instance, believes that this is Mark's one and only addition to the parable as he received it. See also Jeremias, *Parables*, 73; Gnilka, *Markus*, 2:143; Grundmann, *Markus*, 322–23; Snodgrass, *Parable*, 58; Marcus, *Way*, 114.

²⁷ Luke 20:13, on the other hand, reads τὸν υἱόν μου τὸν ἀγαπητόν, thus approximating the baptism pronouncement even more closely (cf. 3:22).

Yet to recall 1:11 and 9:7 is necessarily to recall Ps 2:7 on some level. At each of these prior moments in the narrative, the unique collocation ὁ υἱός μου ὁ ἀγαπητός reflects a fusion of the royal anointing language in Ps 2:7 and Isa 42:1; in the linguistic universe of Mark's Gospel, then, υἱὸς ἀγαπητός is synonymous with God's messianic son in Psalm 2.[28] Said differently, this is now the third time that Mark's audience has encountered υἱὸς ἀγαπητός, and in each of the prior instances these words echo Psalm 2.[29] It is possible to ignore these implications of υἱὸς ἀγαπητός only by reading Mark 12:6 in isolation from the foregoing narrative—an interpretive move that Mark, as we will see, implicitly rejects.

6.2.1 Reading Mark's Parable in Context: Echoes of Psalm 2 in and around Mark's Parable

There are a number of other reasons to make this identification in the vicinity of Mark 12:6. In its broader narrative setting, Jesus's parable answers the pair of questions voiced by the authorities (οἱ ἀρχιερεῖς καὶ οἱ γραμματεῖς καὶ οἱ πρεσβύτεροι) in 11:27-28: "By what authority are you doing these things? Or who gave you this authority to do these things?" (ἐν ποίᾳ ἐξουσίᾳ ταῦτα ποιεῖς; ἢ τίς σοι ἔδωκεν τὴν ἐξουσίαν ταύτην ἵνα ταῦτα ποιῇς;).[30] In the exchange that follows, Jesus initially responds by posing a counter-question, "Was the baptism of John from heaven or from men? Answer me" (τὸ βάπτισμα τὸ Ἰωάννου ἐξ οὐρανοῦ ἦν ἢ ἐξ ἀνθρώπων; ἀποκρίθητέ μοι).[31] Though subtle, the mention of John's baptism naturally recalls the reader to the earlier moment in 1:9-11 when the heavens were split and a voice from the heavens affirmed Jesus's identity as his beloved son. As Botner writes,

> Regardless of what the temple leaders know about John's baptism—the narrative is silent on this point—there is no question that, from the audience's perspective, John's baptism was the moment when the heavens were torn open and a voice declared, 'You are *my son, the beloved*, in whom I am well pleased' (Mark 1:11). Since the baptism is the narratival moment at which Mark's Jesus is identified from heaven as the son of God ... it seems significant that he chooses to raise this issue just prior to telling a story about a υἱὸς ἀγαπητός, 'beloved son,' whom a vineyard owner sent ἔσχατον, 'last of all' (cf. 1:14-15).[32]

---

[28] Here, I draw upon the Piercian concept of the "universe of discourse," discussed by Alkier (*Wunder und Wirklichkeit*, 74–9), which refers to the text-immanent world of discourse, including definitions of terms, established by each text within itself.

[29] To quote Boring (*Mark*, 328), "The reader will inevitably make this connection, [though] the characters in the story do not."

[30] See n. 11 above.

[31] The dialogue concludes in 11:33 with the authorities responding, "We do not know" (οὐκ οἴδαμεν), to which Jesus responds "Neither will I tell you by what authority I do these things" (οὐδὲ ἐγὼ λέγω ὑμῖν ἐν ποίᾳ ἐξουσίᾳ ταῦτα ποιῶ). The next words of Mark's Gospel are "he began to speak to them in parables" (12:1), thus presenting the parable that follows as an extension of the foregoing dialogue.

[32] Botner, *Son of David*, 157. On the likely eschatological force of ἔσχατον in Mark 12:6, see, *inter alia*, Pesch, *Markusevangelium*, 2:218; Collins, *Mark*, 547; and Marcus, *Mark 8–16*, 803. The latter maintains that "[i]n Christian biblical theology [and already in the LXX], this neuter adjective (here used adverbially) has become a technical term for the end of days"—a contention which he supports

Again, when the tenants in the parable identify the owner's υἱὸς ἀγαπητός as "the heir" (ὁ κληρονόμος) and conspire to kill him for his "inheritance" (κληρονομία) (12:7-8), we can hear further echoes of the language of Psalm 2: "The Lord said to me, 'You are my son (υἱός μου); today I have begotten you. Ask of me and I will give you the nations as your inheritance (δώσω σοι ἔθνη τὴν κληρονομίαν σου)'" (Ps 2:7-8 LXX).[33] In the psalm, moreover, the nations and rulers ultimately face destruction for their rebellion against God's son (2:9-12), as do the tenants in Jesus's parable (12:9). Yet the son himself is vindicated, just as the rejected son is vindicated in the parable (12:10-11).

6.2.2 The Rejected Stone (Ps 117:22 LXX) and the Davidic Identity of the "Beloved Son"

As we noted above, it is generally acknowledged that the rejected "stone" from Ps 117:22 LXX, quoted in Mark 12:10, interprets the "beloved son" in 12:6-8. This is not the first time Mark's audience has heard the words of this psalm, however. Previously, the crowds quoted Ps 117:25 LXX as Jesus rode into Jerusalem (11:9-10), where it was given an overtly Davidic interpretation: "*Hosanna! Blessed is the one who comes in the name of the Lord!* Blessed is the coming kingdom of our father, David! Hosanna in the highest!" (ὡσαννά· εὐλογημένος ὁ ἐρχόμενος ἐν ὀνόματι κυρίου· εὐλογημένη ἡ ἐρχομένη βασιλεία τοῦ πατρὸς ἡμῶν Δαυίδ· ὡσαννὰ ἐν τοῖς ὑψίστοις).[34] Given that this passage (11:1-11) is logically connected to the events in 11:27-12:12, it seems unlikely that the reader should disregard the Davidic interpretation of the "the one who comes in the name of the Lord" when considering the identity of the rejected "stone" a short time later.[35]

In point of fact, although the "stone" in Ps 118:22 can be identified with a number of different figures in later Jewish literature, it is overwhelmingly associated with David.[36] For instance, in the Cairo Genizah fragment of the "Song of David," which probably dates to the first century CE, the "rejected cornerstone" is taken to be an eschatological descendant of David whom God appointed to be "king of all nations forever" (*CšD* I,

---

with examples from Num 24:14; Deut 4:30; 32:20; Isa 2:2; Jer 30:24 [37:24 LXX]; Dan 10:14; 2 Tim 3:1; Heb 1:2; Jas 5:3; 2 Pet 3:3; cf. 1 Cor 15:26, 45, 52; 1 Pet 1:5, 20; 1 John 2:18; Jude 18; cf. 1Qsa 1:1; 1QpHab 2:5-6; 9:6; 4QFlor I 1:15, 19.

[33] So also Lövestam, *Son and Saviour*, 97; Matera, *Kingship*, 78; O'brien, *Use of Scripture*, 165; Watts, "Mark," in *CNTUOT*, 213; Botner, *Son of David*, 157.

[34] Matthew 21:9 strengthens the Davidic reference to Jesus by having the crowd exclaim "Hosanna to the Son of David!"; while Luke 19:38 contains a more veiled messianic reference, reading, "Blessed is the King who comes in the name of the Lord"; and John 12:13 identifies "the one who comes [ὁ ἐρχόμενος] in the name of the Lord" as "the King of Israel" (ὁ βασιλεὺς τοῦ Ἰσραήλ).

[35] See Botner, *Son of David*, 155–56. As Botner (156) concludes, "since the audience already knows that 'the one who comes [ὁ ἐρχόμενος] in the name of the Lord' (Ps 117:26 LXX) is messiah son of David (cf. 10:46-11:10), there can be little doubt that 'the stone [λίθον] that the builders rejected' (Ps 117:22 LXX) is too."

[36] Other referents include Abraham (*Pirqe R. El.* 24); Jacob (*Midr. Ps.* 118:20); and Israel (*Esth. Rab.* 7.10; *Midr. Ps.* 118:21); for further discussion, see Snodgrass, *Parable*, 98–9.

18-23).³⁷ The targums consistently associate the "stone" with David, as in *Tg. Ps.* 118:22, which interprets the stone as "the *child* (טלי) the builders abandoned [who] was among the sons of Jesse (ביני בניא דישי) [who] was worthy to be appointed king and ruler."³⁸ So also do various rabbinic texts (*b. Pesaḥ* 119a; *Exod. Rab.* 37:1).³⁹ Midrash Psalm 118:20 initially interprets the "stone" as Israel, yet the following verse (118:21) sees the promise of Ps 118:22 fulfilled by "David, king of Israel." *Midrash Psalm* 118:10-12, furthermore, associates the psalm with the eschatological war against Gog and Magog and even mentions Ps 2:1, which was widely associated with the same conflict.⁴⁰ Since Psalm 118 appears to have been sung on the eve of the Passover during the Second Temple period, one may plausibly venture, as Watts does, that the psalm "with its focus on the temple and Zion as the goal of the new exodus, became a communal anticipation of Israel's eschatological redemption under a royal Davidide."⁴¹

In any case, that Mark voices a Davidic interpretation of Psalm 118 not long prior to the quotation in 12:10-11 suggests that he shares the general Davidic and messianic interpretations above. Insofar as the rejected "stone" interprets the "beloved son" in 12:6, we should understand the one to be David's eschatological heir along with the other—that is to say, as one and the same figure as God's anointed "son" in Ps 2:7.⁴²

---

³⁷ On the date of the "Songs of David," see G. W. Lorein and E. van Staalduine-Sulman ("Songs of David," in *Old Testament Pseudepigrapha: More Noncanonical Scriptures*, ed. Richard Bauckham, James R. Davila, and Alexander Panayotov [Grand Rapids; Cambridge: Eerdmans, 2013], 257–62), who conclude that "an origin during in the latter period of the Qumran community seems a valid option." Just prior to the lines cited above, the text alone alludes to Ps 89:4, which is a sister text to Psalm 2 in the tradition of the Davidic king's sonship stemming from 2 Sam 7:12-14. Lorein and Staalduine–Sulman ("Song," 261) observe that this text also has parallels to *Ps. Sol.* 17, which contains multiple allusions to Psalm 2; and 4Q174, which offers a messianic interpretation of both 2 Sam 7:12-14 and Psalm 2.

³⁸ See also *Tg. Zech.* 4:7, which translates הָאֶבֶן as "his [the Lord's] anointed" (משיחיה); *Tg. Zech.* 6:12-13, in which the Davidic Messiah rebuilds the temple; *Tg. Zech.* 10:4, which again interprets the "cornerstone" (פנה) as "his king … his anointed" (משיחיה … מלכיה); and *Tg. Isa.* 28:16, which interprets the "stone" (אבן) as the Davidic King enthroned on Zion. According to Watts ("Mark," in *CNTUOT*, 213), "Psalm 118 thus becomes a celebration of David's inexorable accession to the throne."

³⁹ There is evidence of possible messianic interpretation among rabbinic texts, as well. In *Tanḥ. B Tol.* 20, the stone in Dan 2:34-35 (also associated here with Ps 121:1-2; Isa 52:7; Dan 7:13; and Zech 4:7) is "the King Messiah" (cf. *Tanḥ. A Tem.* 7; *Num. Rab.* 13.14), which is given a similar interpretation and compared to the stone from Ps 118:22 in *Esth. Rab.* 7.10, albeit without a reference to the Messiah in the latter text; see Craig A. Evans, "Daniel in the New Testament: Visions of God's Kingdom," in *The Book of Daniel: Composition and Reception*, ed. John J. Collins and Peter W. Flint, vol. 2 of VTSup 83 (Leiden/Boston: Brill, 2001), 490–527 (here, 507–10); Watts, "Mark," in *CNTUOT*, 213.

⁴⁰ Cf. *y. Ber.* 2:3; *Midr. Ps.* 26:6; *Pesiq. Rab.* 51:7. Other texts associate Psalm 118 with eschatological events such as the coming of the Messiah (*y. Ber.* 2:3; *b. Pesah* 119a; *Pesiq Rab.* 36:1; *Midr. Ps.* 118:22); the restoration of Jerusalem (*Pesiq. Rab Kah.* 17:5; *Lev. Rab.* 37:4); the rebuilding of the temple (*y. Ber.* 2:3); and the world to come (*Pesiq. Rab Kah.* 27:5; *Midr. Ps.* 26:6). See also Marcus, *Way*, 115; Watts, "Mark," in *CNTUOT*, 207.

⁴¹ Watts, "Mark," in *CNTUOT*, 207. On the "Egyptian Hallel" and the practice of singing Psalm 118 before the Passover, see *t. Sukkah* 3:2; *m. Pesaḥ* 10:6; *b. Ber.* 56a. See further the discussion in Zenger, *Psalms 3*, 178–79, 236; idem, "The Composition and Theology of the Fifth Book of Psalms, Psalms 107–145," *JSOT* 23 (1998): 77–102 (here, 91–2); and Jutta Schröten (*Entstehung, Komposition Und Wirkungsgeschichte Des 118. Psalms*, BBB 95 (Weinheim: Beltz Athenäum, 1995).

⁴² Ps 118 and Ps 2 do occasionally appear together elsewhere, as in Acts 4:11, 25-28, which aligns the "builders" in Ps 118:22 (4:11) with the "rulers" in Ps 2:1-2 (4:26), and likewise understands both the rejection of the stone and the plotting of the peoples against the Lord's Messiah as the crucifixion of Jesus. See also Justin, *Dial.* 122, 126 (PG 6:760, 769), where Justin quotes Ps 2:6-9 and, not long afterward, identifies the "stone" of Ps 118:22 as "the Son of God."

6.2.2 A Familiar Story: Mark 12:1-12 in Retrospect

When we glance back at Mark 12:1-12 in retrospect, the plot of the parable as a whole displays a certain similarity to the plot of Psalm 2: God's messianic son is rejected by the rulers who, indeed, rebel against God himself (Mark 12:1-8/Ps 2:1-3); yet, the son is ultimately vindicated and exalted above the same rulers (Mark 12:10-11/Ps 2:6-8, 10), who face destruction for their malice (Mark 12:9/Ps 2:5, 9-12).[43] As in the psalm, so in the parable: the son's vindication in the face of opposition represents the climax of Israel's own story. These connections are strengthened by the fact that "the chief priests, scribes, and elders" (οἱ ἀρχιερεῖς καὶ οἱ γραμματεῖς καὶ οἱ πρεσβύτεροι) represented by the tenants in the parable are identified with Ps 2:2's "rulers" (οἱ ἄρχοντες) elsewhere in the NT, including Mark 15:1.[44] There is also a thematic similarity between the conclusion of this episode in 12:12 ("And they sought to seize him, but they were afraid of the crowd...") and Mark's earlier comment in 3:6 ("And the Pharisees went out and immediately made counsel with the Herodians in order that they might destroy him"; cf. 15:1).[45] As we have seen, the earlier comment contains its own probable allusion to Ps 2:1-2.

Overall, Mark's prior use of υἱὸς ἀγαπητός to refer to God's messianic son in 1:11 and 9:7, the narrative context that introduces the parable, additional echoes of Psalm 2's language within the parable, the implicit identification of the "beloved son" as the Davidic Messiah via Mark's use of Ps 117 LXX, and the broadly similar plots of the parable and the psalm all suggest that we should hear echoes of Psalm 2's son-of-God language informing Jesus's parable. That is to say, Mark's implicit use of υἱὸς [θεοῦ] in the parable conforms to the same pattern as his use of υἱὸς [θεοῦ] up to this point.

6.3 A Story within a Story: Mark's Parable as *Mise en Abyme*

Precisely in its allegorical and christological features, however, Jesus's parable resembles not only Psalm 2, but Mark's Gospel as a whole. To summarize (and add to) what we have observed so far, "beloved son" (υἱὸς ἀγαπητός) recalls what is arguably the most pivotal identity of Jesus in the Gospel up to this point, having been conferred and reiterated by God himself at two major turning points in the narrative (1:11; 9:7). At the same time, it foreshadows themes and events still to come, such as the high priest's question in 14:61 (σὺ εἶ ὁ χριστὸς ὁ υἱὸς τοῦ εὐλογητοῦ;), which leads directly to Jesus's condemnation and death, and the centurion's climactic statement, ἀληθῶς οὗτος ὁ ἄνθρωπος υἱὸς θεοῦ ἦν (15:39).[46] As these two instances bear out, Jesus's identity as God's Son is closely linked to the circumstances of his death.

Likewise, that the "beloved son's" murder in the parable stands for Jesus's own crucifixion is confirmed by the details of 12:8: καὶ λαβόντες ἀπέκτειναν αὐτὸν καὶ

---

[43] So also O'brien, *Use of Scripture*, 165; Watts, "Mark," in *CNTUOT*, 213.
[44] See also Matt 26:3, 57; 27:1; 28:11-12; Luke 22:66; Acts 4:5 and the discussion in Chapter 2.
[45] So also Focant, *Mark*, 477.
[46] Cf. Cranfield, *Mark*, 368; Snodgrass, *Parable*, 99; France, *Mark*, 461.

ἐξέβαλον αὐτὸν ἔξω τοῦ ἀμπελῶνος ("And seizing him, they killed him and threw him out of the vineyard"). Just as the beloved son in the parable is thrown out of the vineyard, Jesus will be crucified outside Jerusalem (cf. 15:22).[47] Although the details of 12:6-8 may not have much "historical verisimilitude," as Collins observes, they display a great deal of verisimilitude to the events of the Gospel itself.[48] The foreshadowing of the passion throughout the parable, in fact, leads Pesch to suspect that Mark constructed the parable to reflect a pre-Markan passion narrative.[49] (One need not necessarily agree with Pesch's conclusions, moreover, to accept the premises.)

In any case, the parable is thematically aligned with Jesus's passion predictions (8:31; 9:31; 10:33-34) by their common use of Ps 117:22-23 LXX. In one sense, the whole parable serves as another such prediction, albeit in story form. Finally, the reaction of the authorities in 12:12 reminds one, generally, of the pervasive opposition to Jesus from authorities throughout the Gospel, and specifically recalls 3:6 while foreshadowing 15:1.[50]

In brief, Jesus, the beloved (and messianic) Son of God is rejected and murdered by Israel's leaders; yet he will ultimately be vindicated and exalted over those who rejected him. This sentence, more or less, captures the plot of the parable and the Gospel alike. Something of this sort has already been observed by Ernst van Eck, in fact, who argues that Mark 12:1-12 contains the plot of Mark's Gospel "in a nutshell."[51]

6.3.1 Mark's Parable and Mise en Abyme

Although Markan scholarship has never, to my knowledge, identified it as such, this mirroring of the story within the story is a textbook example of the literary phenomenon known as *mise en abyme*: "a work within another work which in one way or another resembles the outer work (or part of it)."[52] The effect is often likened to a "Chinese box"

---

[47] See again Gnlika, *Markus*, 2:147; Marcus, *Way*, 113; Donahue and Harrington, *Mark*, 339; France, *Mark*, 458; and Boring, *Mark*, 331, among others. To be fair, Mark does not tell us that Jesus is crucified outside Jerusalem, but one may infer that this detail was part of the tradition Mark inherited; cf. John 19:20; Heb 13:12.

[48] Collins, *Mark*, 546. See similarly, France, *Mark*, 460.

[49] Pesch, *Markusevangelium*, 2:213.

[50] Cf. Mark 2:6, 16, 18, 24; 7:1, 5; 8:11, 15; 8:1; 9:14; 10:2; 10:33; 11:18, 27; 12:13; 12:38; 14:43; 53; 15:1. Rhoads, Dewey, and Michie (*Mark as Story*, 77-97) observe that "conflict" on a variety of planes, ranging from the cosmic to the political, is one of the defining characteristics of Mark's plot. Such conflict is primarily the result of Jesus instantiating the kingdom of God on earth.

[51] Ernst Van Eck, "A Narratological Analysis of Mark 12:1-12: The Plot of the Gospel of Mark in a Nutshell," HTS 45 (1989): 778–800. Van Eck (792) defines the plot of Mark this way: "Jesus Christ as Son of God, in accordance with the will of God, but with the aid of the Jewish leaders, had to suffer. Jesus, however, announces at his resurrection that true life follows suffering which culminated at the cross." He finds this same plot woven into the Parable of the Wicked Tenants.

[52] Irene J. F. de Jong, "The Shield of Achilles: From Metalepsis to Mise En Abyme," *Ramus* 40 (2011): 1–14 (here 10). The term was first coined by André Gide (*Journals: 1889-1913*, trans. Justin O'brien [Urbana: University of Illinois Press, 2000], 30–1) and subsequently developed by Lucien Dällenbach (*Le récit spéculaire: essai sur la mise en abyme* [Paris: Seuil, 1977].). Dällenbach's book remains the only full-length study of *mise en abyme*, though the topic is widely studied in current literary journals. *Mise en abyme* is a subset of "embedded narrative" or "frame narrative" (see Bal, *Narratology*, 57, 135–36; Mieke Bal and Eve Tavor, "Notes on Narrative Embedding," *Poetics Today* 2 [1981]: 41–59) defined precisely by the mirroring of the embedding narrative by the embedded.

or a "Russian doll": the inner story duplicates features of the outer story.[53] Turning to an example from classic literature will help to illustrate how this technique actually works.

One of the most well-known examples of *mise en abyme* occurs in Shakespeare's *Hamlet* when the Prince of Denmark himself stages a play depicting the murder of a king whose poisoner afterward takes the dead king's wife as his own, thus rehearsing the actual events of *Hamlet*.[54] The stated purpose of Hamlet's play, which he appropriately names "The Mousetrap," is to trap the conscience of his uncle, Claudius, and so reveal his guilt in his father's murder.[55] Yet Shakespeare hints at another purpose of this play-within-a-play as well. The "purpose of playing," Hamlet instructs the players,

> is to hold, as 'twere, the mirror up to nature, to show virtue
> her own feature, scorn her own image, and the very age and
> body of the time his form and pressure.[56]

The players will "tell all," in other words (3.2.147). The part sheds light on the meaning of the whole. So when the player-queen declares:

> Such love needs be treason in my breast.
> In second husband let me be accurst;
> None wed the second but who kill'd the first...[57]

the reader understands that she not only *alludes to* but *interprets* as "treason" the actual queen's complicity in her husband's murder, and even pronounces a curse on her marriage to Claudius. When the play is done, Hamlet tellingly declares to Horatio:

> For thou dost know, O Damon dear,
>   This realm dismantled was
> Of Jove himself; and now reigns here
>   A very, very pajock.[58]

By identifying the "realm dismantled" as Jove's own, he signifies that it is the "real" world and suggests that the play-world reflects the real world by imitating it in the manner of a scarecrow ("pajock").[59] To this Horatio replies, "You might have rimed" (3.2.291). At second glance, then, Hamlet's play also mirrors the outer play thematically.

---

[53] William Nelles, "Stories within Stories: Narrative Levels and Embedded Narrative," *Studies in the Literary Imagination* 25 (1992): 79–96 (here 79).
[54] See Shakespeare, *Hamlet*, 3.2.
[55] 3.2.245.
[56] 3.2.19-22.
[57] 3.2.185-187.
[58] 3.2.287-290.
[59] "And now reigns here//a very, very pajock" is probably an instance of double entendre, referring to Claudius as both a scarecrow of the true king, Hamlet's father, and a scarecrow (or copy) of the murderer in the play. In this case, the lines between the two realms are blurred in both directions: the world of the Mousetrap reflects Hamlet's own world, but the reigning king is also a mere reflection of the play-murderer.

The relationship between the world ("realm") of "the Mousetrap" and Hamlet's own is obscured, just as the relationship between Hamlet himself and the "antic disposition" he puts on (1.5.180) is ultimately obscured (cf. 3.4.187-188).

The play-within-the-play thus serves to explain the primary (or outer) story by mirroring it. This is the usual effect, and purpose, of *mise en abyme* according to Peter Brooks: "framed narration in general offers a way to make explicit and dramatize the motive for storytelling."[60] Ann Jefferson similarly states that *mise en abyme* functions as "a condensed image of the overall design and the theme of a narrative."[61] Precisely in the manner of a mirror, the secondary narrative, or inner story, reflects the meaning of the primary story, albeit in a condensed form, allowing for easier discernment.

The technique was hardly invented by Shakespeare, however. *Mise en abyme* was also a common feature of ancient storytelling. Examples include the shield of Achilles in the *Illiad* (18.478-608), the three songs of Demodocus in the *Odyssey* (book 8), three separate oracles in Sophocles's *Oedipus Tyrannus*, and Socrates's tale of Meroe's enchantments in Apuleius's *Metamorphoses* (1.9-10).[62] According to William Nelles, the phenomenon is "so widespread among the narrative literature of all cultures and periods as to approach universality."[63] Notably, Dällenbach observed in his original study of *mise en abyme* that the technique is not limited to fictional narratives either.[64] In more recent years, David Bosworth has highlighted the use of *mise en abyme* in biblical Hebrew narrative, specifically in Genesis 38; 1 Samuel 25; 1 Kings 13; and 2 Kings 23.[65]

The purpose of this brief excursus into literary criticism, however, is not simply to call attention to interesting similarities between Mark and classic literature, but rather to consider the purpose of *mise en abyme* itself. As we have seen above, *mise*

---

[60] Peter Brooks (*Reading for the Plot: Design and Intention in Narrative* [Cambridge: Harvard University Press, 1984], 259) quoted in Nelles, "Stories within Stories," 91; see similarly Moshe Ron, "The Restricted Abyss: Nine Problems in the Theory of Mise En Abyme," *Poetics Today* 8 (1987): 417–38 (here 419). Bal (*Narratology*, 135–36) maintains that embedded narratives may have one of two purposes: the embedded narrative *either* explains the primary story *or* mirrors it. Yet Nelles ("Stories within Stories," 79-96) offers an important corrective to Bal's work by demonstrating that *mise en abyme* inevitably performs both functions at once.

[61] Ann Jefferson, "'Mise En Abyme' and the Prophetic in Narrative," *Style* 17 (1983): 196–208 (here 196–97).

[62] For studies of each of these examples, see, respectively, de Jong, "Shield," 1–14; Yoav Rinon, "'Mise En Abyme' and Tragic Signification in the 'Odyssey': The Three Songs of Demodocus," *Mnemosyne* 59 (2006): 208–25; Ann Jefferson, "'Mise En Abyme' and the Prophetic in Narrative," *Style* 17 (1983): 196–208 (here 201–03); and Paul Murgatroyd, "Embedded Narrative in Apuleius' 'Metamorphoses' 1.9-10," *Museum Helveticum* 58 (2001): 40–6.

[63] Nelles, "Stories within Stories," 79. Other famous examples include *One Thousand One Nights*; and the "Mad Trist" in Edgar Allen Poe's "The Fall of the House of Usher." The former is a series of frame stories from beginning to end, but on the six hundred and second night, in particular, the king hears a story that is essentially his own and "comprises all the others too"; see Jorge Luis Borges, "Partial Magic in the Quixote," in *Labyrinths*, ed. Donald A. Yates and James E. Irby (Harmondsworth: Penguin, 1970), 230.

[64] Dällenbach, *Le récit*, 16–7; cf. Rinon, "Mise en abyme," 209 n. 5.

[65] David A. Bosworth, *The Story Within a Story in Biblical Hebrew Narrative*, CBQMS 45 (Washington, DC: Catholic Biblical Association, 2008). As the review by David Cotter ("*Review of The Story within a Story in Biblical Hebrew Narrative [CBQMS 45]*, by David Bosworth, *CBQ* 72 [2010]: 561–63) indicates, Bosworth's study raises various questions for further study, but provides a useful first exploration of *mise en abyme* in biblical narrative.

en abyme holds up a mirror to the outer narrative in order to reveal something of its meaning. So, in *Hamlet*, "the Mousetrap" not only reflects the events of the outer play, but alludes to the gradual blurring of the real versus the feigned in Hamlet's own mind and character. The shield of Achilles, fashioned in the poem by Hephaestus, allows the Homeric narrator to allude to himself as an artist and, likewise, model what should be our own response to his art.[66] The songs of Demodocus successively exemplify various aspects of the *Odyssey* from "the inner-epic dialogue of the *Odyssey* with the *Iliad*," to some of the main themes and motifs of the work (namely, "adultery, shame, anger and cunning"), to the overarching emphasis of the *Iliad-Odyssey* as a whole (an implicit contrast between faithfulness and unfaithfulness).[67] Again, Socrates's tale encapsulates and foreshadows the whole plot of *Metamorphoses*.[68] The story of Judah and Tamar in Genesis 38 parallels the larger story of Joseph and his brothers (Genesis 37-50) in such a way that the line "she is more righteous than I" (38:26) ultimately embodies Joseph's relation to his brothers as well.[69]

As a plot-moving device, *mise en abyme* also serves a second function: to build a sense of anticipation not unlike the effect of prophesy. As Jefferson observes, *mise en abyme* often exercises a prophetic voice in narrative by foreshadowing the end before it happens.[70] This quality is readily obvious in the case of Mark 12:1-12 since, to the degree that Jesus allegorically refers to his own fate, the parable is essentially an instance of prophesy belonging, as we have seen above, with the earlier passion predictions in 8:31; 9:31; 10:33-34.

6.3.2 The Parable in the Gospel: Peering into the Mirror

In Mark, then, I contend that "the Parable of the Wicked Tenants" (or "Parable of the Rejected Son") not only offers a condensed image of the overall plot of the Gospel, which foreshadows the end ahead of time, but suggests how we ought to understand the larger narrative. Accordingly, the death and subsequent vindication of the "beloved son" is the main thing: what Mark's narrative chiefly concerns. As in the parable, furthermore, the son's death and vindication together serve as the climax in the story of Israel's own relationship to God. But for those who grasp the significance of the scriptural language in 12:10-11 (and 12:6-8!), Mark's story is also given a decidedly Davidic interpretation: it is as the Davidic Messiah Son of God that Jesus is rejected and killed by the rulers, yet exalted by God in spite of their rejection.

The inclusion of this parable within Mark's narrative as a veritable *mise en abyme* ultimately commends the relative importance of the particular themes and motifs that appear there to the Gospel as a whole. Highlighting the "beloved son" (υἱὸς ἀγαπητός), for example, solidifies for the reader that this particular identity of Jesus that was

---

[66] So de Jong, "Shield," 10.
[67] See Rinon, "Mise en abyme," 209, 211, 217–22.
[68] Murgatoyd, "Embedded Narrative," 40-6
[69] Bosworth, *Story within the Story*, 49–50.
[70] Jefferson, "Mise en abyme," 196–208. Jefferson (206) concludes that *mise en abyme* "differs [from other forms of prolepsis] only in having an additional, non-chronological function as an illuminator of overall theme and design."

pronounced by God himself on two previous occasions (1:11; 9:7) is indeed pivotal to the larger story at hand. To the extent that "beloved son" here recalls the connotations of Psalm 2, which it acquired vis-à-vis 1:11 and 9:7, the parable also confirms the psalm's significance as backstory for Mark's own story of Jesus. Simply put, it is *this* identity of Jesus, υἱὸς ἀγαπητός, informed by Psalm 2, that the evangelist now singles out in the middle of the story within the story. This, in turn, suggests that Mark's Gospel really is (among other things) the story of Psalm 2's actualization in the earthly career of Jesus of Nazareth: the story of an earlier story unfolding in a particular person and life.

6.4 Summary: The Death of God's Son Foreshadowed

Far from inconsequential, then, the parable in Mark 12:1-12 offers substantial insight into the meaning of Jesus's divine sonship in Mark's Gospel. Although few interpreters have connected υἱὸς ἀγαπητός (12:6) with Psalm 2, within the linguistic parameters of Mark's narrative, such language invariably recalls the prior allusions to Ps 2:7 at Jesus's baptism (1:11) and transfiguration (9:7)—an inference supported by further linguistic and thematic echoes throughout the parable and its narrative context. All of these factors together suggest that, from the perspective of the Markan narrative, the beloved son in 12:6, like the beloved son in 1:11 and 9:7, is the messianic son of Psalm 2, invested with the entire plot of the psalm as well.

Within the overarching design of Mark's Gospel, Jesus's parable appears to serve as a kind of *Schlüsseltext*: a *mise en abyme* condensing the larger narrative to a point and highlighting its most important features for our notice. When these two points are taken together, the parable offers a significant confirmation of what has been argued up to this point: that Psalm 2 informs Jesus's identity as God's Son in Mark's Gospel, and so also the meaning of the story as a whole.

Yet Jesus's parable not only recalls his charter as God's "beloved son" from earlier portions of the narrative, but likewise foreshadows the fate of God's Son to come in the Gospel's conclusion. As we will see shortly, Jesus's identity as God's Son vis-à-vis Psalm 2 is indeed closely linked, however ironically, with his death.

7

Part 1: The Son of God on the Cross

And the Angel says to them again, "Fear not." I do not say to the soldiers, "fear not," but to you. As for them, let them be afraid, so that, having learned by trial, they may bear witness and say, "Truly this was the Son of God"; but you ought not be afraid, "for perfect love casts out fear." "Go, tell His disciples that He is risen; and the rest." And they depart with joy, yet fearfully. Is this also written? Yes, so says the Second Psalm, which narrates the passion of Christ, "Serve the Lord with fear, and rejoice in Him with trembling." Rejoice on account of the risen Lord; but with trembling, because of the earthquake, and the angel who appeared as lightning.

Cyril of Jerusalem, *Catechesis* 14.13

When the Gospel of Mark places in the mouth of the Gentile captain the confession of the Son of God, still the υἱὸς τοῦ θεοῦ here cannot be understood in the sense of a confession to the Jewish Messiah. Instead, we see clearly that for the evangelist [ὁ] υἱὸς τοῦ θεοῦ was here the great formula in which the nature of Jesus Christ was summarized for the faith of the Gentile Christian community.

Wilhelm Bousset, *Kyrios Christos*, 95

In the previous chapters, we have seen that Mark's son-of-God language consistently takes its cue from Psalm 2, thus presenting Jesus as the Davidic Messiah enthroned by God at the turn of the ages. We have also seen that the preceding narrative has, in various ways, foreshadowed the death of God's Son even while simultaneously anticipating his exaltation. Now, in this final chapter, we will explore how Mark's passion narrative and, in particular, the centurion's confession gives decisive shape to his gospel of the Son of God and surprisingly fulfills the vision of Psalm 2 in a single breath.

Although Jesus is referred to as God's Son only twice in Mark's passion narrative, both instances are indispensable to the story he tells. The first amounts to the charge against Jesus that leads to his condemnation (14:61), while the second, the centurion's confession upon Jesus's death (15:39), is arguably the climax of the entire Gospel. Together, these two instances effectively frame Jesus's crucifixion, almost as though the centurion's confession were an answer to the high priest's question.[1]

---

[1] Cf. Kingsbury, *Christology*, 131.

Accordingly, my approach here is twofold. First, I trace Mark's use of Psalm 2 alongside the general theme of kingship in the passion narrative, which begins in 14:61 and paves the way for a particular understanding of 15:39. Second, I turn my focus to the centurion's confession directly with a special emphasis on the question of how the words of this Roman officer align with Mark's preceding narrative of Jesus's sonship. Only then will we be able to perceive what it finally means for Mark to call Jesus the Son of God.

7.1 Are You the Messiah Son of God? (Mark 14:61-62)

After an inconclusive round of questioning concerning Jesus's alleged threat to destroy the temple (14:55-60), the trial before the Sanhedrin reaches its zenith when the high priest asks, σὺ εἶ ὁ χριστὸς ὁ υἱὸς τοῦ εὐλογητοῦ (14:61).[2] In response, Jesus unambiguously answers, ἐγώ εἰμί (14:62).[3] Since εὐλογητός serves as a circumlocution for God, the question is effectively, "Are you the Messiah Son of God?"[4] The juxtaposition of "Messiah" and "Son of God," as such, raises further questions about the relationship between the two epithets per the high priest's understanding.

Perhaps the most obvious reading, given the apposition of ὁ χριστός and ὁ υἱός, is that the two terms are more or less synonymous.[5] Yet Marcus observes that there are two types of apposition: *non-restrictive* (wherein the two appositives are more or less

---

[2] The link between the earlier allegations and the question in 14:61 falls outside the scope of this study, but Taylor (*Mark*, 567) intriguingly posits that it may be the concept of the messianic temple builder found in, e.g., *1 En.* 90:29; *4 Ezra* 9:38-10:27; *Tg. Isa.* 53:5. Taylor suggests that "Jesus made the Messianic claim that He would establish the new Temple [cf. 14:58] .... If one takes this view, it becomes at once intelligible that the high priest presses Jesus for an answer." Likewise, one can understand why the high priest turns suddenly from the temple to Jesus's messianic claim; cf. Pesch, *Markusevnagelium*, 2:436-37; Donald Senior, *The Passion of Jesus in the Gospel of Mark*, The Passion Series 2 (Wilmington, DE: Glazier, 1984), 93; Brown, *Death*, 1:464; Bock, *Mark*, 355.

[3] Some interpreters (e.g., Taylor, *Mark*, 568; Evans, *Mark 8:27–16:20*, 450) support the variant σὺ εἶπας ὅτι ἐγώ εἰμι attested in Θ *f*13 565. 700. 2542s and Origen (cf. Matt 26:64; Luke 22:70), supposing it more likely that a scribe would change an ambiguous reply to an explicit one than that Matthew and Luke would alter the explicit statement in 14:62. Yet, as Marcus (*Mark 8–16*, 1005-06) observes, the variant is poorly attested and it is just as likely that a later scribe assimilated Mark 14:62 to agree with Matthew and Luke; see similarly Collins, *Mark*, 696. Moreover, the boldness of ἐγώ εἰμι fits the unabashed reply that follows. Matthew accounts for the discrepancy in tone between σὺ εἶπας and the ensuing quotations only by adding the phrase πλὴν λέγω ὑμῖν. See further Renatus Kempthorne, "The Marcan Text of Jesus' Answer to the High Priest (Mark XIV 62)," *NovT* 19 (1977): 197–208; and Brown, *Death*, 1:489.

[4] See Taylor, *Mark*, 467; Evans, *Mark 8:27–16:20*, 449; Marcus, *Mark 8–16*, 1004; and especially Israel Abrahams, *Studies in Pharisaism and the Gospels: First and Second Series*, Library of Biblical Studies (New York: Ktav, 1967), 2:212. The adjective ברוך for the name of God is ubiquitous in rabbinic literature, though it typically appears in the form of an appendix: הקדוש ברוך הוא, but המברוך is used alone in *y. Ber.* 55a; *y. Sanh.* 2b:1; *m. Ber.* 7:3. Collins (*Mark*, 704) also notes Philo's reference to God, τῷ πάντα μακαρίῳ, in *Somn.* 2.130. In the NT, εὐλογητός always refers to God, with the possible exception of Rom 9:5, which may refer to Christ: see Luke 1:68; Rom 1:25; 2 Cor 1:3; 11:31; Eph 1:3; 1 Pet 1:3.

[5] So, e.g., Evald Lövestam, "Die Frage des Hohenpriesters [Mark 14, 61 par Matth 26, 63]," *SEÅ* 26 (1961): 94–5; Juel, *Messiah and Temple*, 82, 110–11; and Bock (*Mark*, 355), who comments: "[a]s a Jew, [the high priest] is not thinking of God having a son in any other sense."

synonymous) and *restrictive* (wherein the second appositive adds essential specificity the first).[6] In his estimation, Mark 14:61 is an example of the latter, implying a higher, "quasi-divine" Messiah (i.e., Messiah Son of God) rather than a mundane Messiah (i.e., Messiah Son of David).[7] Marcus's argument suffers from a critical difficulty, however, in that there is no precedent for an elevated "Messiah Son of God" of the sort that he proposes. By contrast, we have repeatedly seen son-of-God language refer to the Davidic Messiah in dependence on both 2 Sam 7:14 and, especially, Ps 2:7.[8] So while ὁ χριστός ὁ υἱὸς τοῦ εὐλογητοῦ may well be restrictive, as Marcus suggests, the high priest seemingly asks Jesus *precisely* whether he is the Davidic Messiah as opposed to some other.[9]

In all probability, then, the apposition of Messiah and Son of God in 14:61 originates from the similar juxtaposition of ὁ χριστός and υἱός μου in Ps 2:2, 7: the only scriptural text to pair the two terms, and the basis for the identification of the Messiah as God's Son elsewhere in Jewish literature.[10] Especially when we consider that all of Mark's son-of-God language thus far has also evoked Psalm 2, the high priest's question naturally makes us think again of the psalm.[11]

Indeed, the wording of Mark 14:61 noticeably recalls several past instances in the narrative, such as the similar apposition of χριστός and υἱὸς θεοῦ in 1:1 (Ἰησοῦ Χριστοῦ υἱοῦ θεοῦ),[12] and two prior declarations of Jesus's sonship, including God's pronouncement via Ps 2:7 at Jesus's baptism:

1:11   σὺ εἶ ὁ υἱός μου
3:11   σὺ εἶ ὁ υἱὸς τοῦ θεοῦ
14:61   σὺ εἶ ὁ χριστὸς ὁ υἱὸς τοῦ εὐλογητοῦ.

So then, the intranarrative cues of Mark's Gospel suggest that we should understand the "Son" in 14:61 to be precisely the same Son of God announced in 1:1, anointed by God at the baptism (1:11), recognized by the demons (3:11), and so forth: that is, the

---

[6] See Joel Marcus, "Mark 14:61: 'Are You the Messiah-Son-of-God?'" *NovT* 31 (1989): 125–41.
[7] Marcus, "Mark 14:61," 138–41.
[8] So Evans (*Mark 8:27–16:20*, 448): "it is doubtful that the high priest made this distinction. To be the Messiah, son of David, was to be in some sense the 'son of God' (as in 2 Sam 7:12-14; Ps 2:2, 7)."
[9] As Marcus ("Mark 14:61," 130–35) himself notes, there were, after all, non-Davidic messiah figures in some strands of Jewish expectation, such as the priestly Messiah (e.g., the Messiahs of Aaron and Israel in 1QS 9.11; or the Messiah ben Joseph in *b. Sukkah* 52a). Notably, when the latter distinguishes between the Messiah Son of David and the Messiah son of Joseph it alludes to Ps 2:8 in reference to the Messiah, Son of David.
[10] Recall the discussion in Chapter 2.
[11] Cf. O'brien, *Use*, 106–07, 155–66; Botner, *Son of David*, 179. David R. Catchpole (*The Trial of Jesus: A Study in the Gospels and Jewish Historiography from 1770 to the Present Day*, SPB 18 [Leiden: Brill, 1971], 98–100) observes that a number of earlier interpreters also made this connection, including Elija Grünebaum and Carsten Wilke, *Die Sittenlehre Des Judenthums Andern Bekenntnissen Gegenüber: Nebst Dem Geschichtlichen Nachweise Über Die Entstehung Und Bedeutung Des Pharisaismus Und Dessen Verhältniss Zum Stifter Der Christlichen Religion*, 2nd ed., Deutsch-Jüdische Autoren Des 19. Jahrhunderts 1 (Strassburg: Schneider, 1878), 274; Kaufmann Kohler, *The Origins of the Synagogue and the Church* (New York: Macmillan, 1929), 230. Gnilka (*Markus*, 2:281) thinks here of 2 Sam 7:14 and 4Q174, but Psalm 2 and 2 Sam 7:14 are closely related in tradition, as 4Q174 attests.
[12] So Taylor, *Mark*, 152; Kingsbury, *Christology*, 14, 98; Matera, *Christology*, 8.

messianic son enthroned by God in Psalm 2. Jesus's response, in fact, powerfully reinforces this suggestion.

7.1.1 Jesus's Response (14:62)

Following his initial affirmation, Jesus elaborates by aligning the Messiah Son of God with the Danielic Son of Man (Dan 7:13) and the enthroned lord in Ps 110:1 (109:1 LXX):[13]

Mark 14:62	καὶ ὄψεσθε τὸν υἱὸν τοῦ ἀνθρώπου ἐκ δεξιῶν καθήμενον τῆς δυνάμεως καὶ ἐρχόμενον μετὰ τῶν νεφελῶν τοῦ οὐρανοῦ.
Dan 7:13 Θ	καὶ ἰδοὺ ἐπὶ τῶν νεφελῶν τοῦ οὐρανοῦ ὡς υἱὸς ἀνθρώπου ἤρχετο καὶ ὡς παλαιὸς ἡμερῶν παρῆν καὶ οἱ παρεστηκότες παρῆσαν αὐτῷ.
Ps 109:1 LXX	ὁ κύριος τῷ κυρίῳ μου *κάθου ἐκ δεξιῶν μου ἕως ἂν θῶ τοὺς ἐχθρούς σου ὑποπόδιον τῶν ποδῶν σου*.

Neither of the Scriptures Jesus cites mentions God's Son or the Messiah, of course. Yet we have seen that Dan 7:13-14 appears alongside Psalm 2 elsewhere in texts that conflate the enthronement of the Son of Man in Dan 7:13-14 with that of God's Son in Psalm 2 (e.g., 4Q246; *1 En.* 46–48; *4 Ezra* 13; *Midr. Ps.* 2.9). As it happens, another text that sometimes appears alongside Dan 7:13-14 and Psalm 2 in such contexts is Ps 110:1 (109:1 LXX).

For instance, Hengel observes that Dan 7:13 has influenced numerous visions of the Messiah's enthronement in the *Similitudes of Enoch* (45:3; 46:1; 48:3-7; 55:4; 62:2-7; 69:29).[14] But what the author of the *Similitudes* found "missing in Daniel"—namely, an explicit description of enthronement—he supplied from Ps 110:1 (see *1 En.* 51:3; 55:4; 61:8; 62:2).[15] As Hengel notes, Dan 7:13-14 and Ps 110:1 share a number of themes besides that of enthronement, including the "subjugation of the kingdoms of the world, the judgement over kings and peoples and the everlasting character of [the ruler's] dominion," and the "transference of divine authority," so the two texts naturally coalesce.[16] Adding Psalm 2 back into the mix, we can chart the *Similitudes's* allusions to all three texts as follows:

---

[13] See similarly Botner, *Son of David*, 179. This is not the first time that Jesus has applied these Scriptures to himself in Mark, of course. Jesus previously applied Dan 7:13 to himself in 8:38 and 13:26; and Ps 110:1 in 12:36. In the latter instance, he plainly interprets Ps 110:1 messianically.

[14] Hengel, "'Sit at My Right Hand!,'" 182–86.

[15] So Hengel, "'Sit at My Right Hand,'" 185–86; cf. Johannes Theisohn, *Der auserwählte Richter: Untersuchungen z. traditionsgeschichtl. Ort d. Menschensohngestalt d. Bilderreden d. Äthiopischen Henoch*, SUNT 12 (Göttingen: Vandenhoeck und Ruprecht, 1975), 96–8; Matthew Black, "The Messianism of the Parables of Enoch: Their Date and Contribution to Christological Origins," in *The Messiah*, 150–56; Helge Kvanvig, "The Son of Man in the Parables," in *Enoch and the Messiah Son of Man: Revisiting the Book of Parables*, ed. Gabriele Boccaccini (Grand Rapids: Eerdmans, 2007), 189–93; Nickelsburg and Vanderkam, *1 Enoch*, 2:262; and Bernardo Cho, *Royal Messianism and the Jerusalem Priesthood in the Gospel of Mark*, LNTS 607 (T&T Clark, 2019), 66.

[16] Hengel, "'Sit at My Right Hand,'" 182, 185.

1 Enoch	Scriptural Allusions
45:3	Dan 7:13
46:1	Dan 7:13
48:3-7	Dan 7:13
48:8-10	Ps 2:2
51:3	Ps 110:1
52:4	Ps 2:8, 10
55:4	Ps 110:1
61:8	Ps 110:1
62:2	Ps 110:1
62:3-7	Dan 7:13
69:29	Dan 7:13

The *Similitudes* thus conflate these three texts as visions of the Messiah's future enthronement. Yet the *Similitudes* are not the only text to do so. Indeed, Ps 110:1 and Psalm 2 also appear alongside one another in early Christian literature beginning with Heb 1:3-5 and 5:5-6.[17]

But the most striking example of all is that of *Midr. Ps.* 2.9, portions of which have already been quoted in previous chapters. The relevant portion here reads:

> I will declare of the decree of the Lord. He said unto me: "You are My son" (Ps 2:7)....
> In the decree of the Writings it is written, "The Lord said unto my lord: 'Sit at My right hand, until I make your enemies your footstool' (Ps 110:1), and it is also written, "I saw in the night visions, and, behold, there came with the clouds of heaven one like a son of man, and he came even to the Ancient of Days, and he was brought near before Him. And there was given him dominion, and glory, and a kingdom, that all the peoples, nations, and languages should serve him" (Dan 7:13-14).[18]

Here Ps 110:1 and Dan 7:13-14 are conflated with one another (cf. Mark 14:62) in a comment on Ps 2:7. Given that this triumvirate texts already appears in the *Similitudes*, their appearance together in the midrash is not novel within Judaism. But the conflation of the former two in elaboration on the latter is telling. In its entirety, *Midr. Ps.* 2.9 cites prooftexts for Ps 2:7 from each portion of the Tanak: from the Torah, Exod 4:22; from the Prophets, Isa 42:1 and 52:13; and from the Writings, Ps 110:1 and Dan 7:13-14. That these two texts, which also partner with Psalm 2 elsewhere, were chosen from the Writings suggests that their association was, by that time, traditional. In any case, a comparison with the *Similitudes* confirms that the conflation of Dan 7:13 and Ps 110:1 (as well as their association with Psalm 2) predates the NT; it is a tradition attested in it rather one created by it.[19]

---

[17] See, e.g., *1 Clem.* 36; Justin, *1 Apol.* 40 (*PG* 6:388–89); Eusebius, *Comm. Ps. 2* (*PG* 23:88), who quotes Ps 110:1 as a gloss on Ps 2:6; and Cassiodorus, *Comm. Ps. 2* (*PL* 70:38c), who quotes Ps 110:1 as a gloss on Ps 2:7. Both psalms comprise classic statements of Jesus's exaltation in the NT; cf. Gnilka, *Markus*, 2:281.

[18] Translation adapted from Braude, *Midrash Psalms*.

[19] *Contra* Norman Perrin, "Mark xiv.62: The End Product of a Christian Pesher Tradition?" *NTS* 12 (1966): 150–55. As the title of his article suggests, Perrin believes the conflation of Dan 7:13 and Ps

It is not happenstance, then, that Jesus aligns the "Messiah Son of God" with Dan 7:13-14 and Ps 110:1; he was neither the first nor the last to do so. Whatever the claims of the "corrective Christology" school, it would appear that, from Mark's perspective, the Son of Man is in fact the Son of God, insofar as both terms refer to the Davidic Messiah.[20] Moreover, the decision to explicate "Messiah Son of God" by way of these two Scriptures all but confirms its dependence on Psalm 2 in 14:61.

7.1.2 Summary: Psalm 2 and Mark 14:61-62

At least three observations bear pointing out before we move forward. First, Son of God still takes its definition from Psalm 2 in Mark's passion narrative as elsewhere in the Gospel. Second, Jesus's identity as the Messiah Son of God stands at the forefront of Mark's trial and crucifixion narrative from its beginning. Third, just as Mark's use of Psalm 2's sonship language up to this point has routinely evoked the psalm's theme of enthronement, so here we find Psalm 2's Messiah Son of God aligned with two distinct enthronement texts, Dan 7:13 and Ps 110:1. It would seem, then, that the theme of enthronement looms large over Mark's passion narrative as well.

7.2 Are You the King of the Jews? (Mark 15:1-15)

We do not encounter "Son of God" again until the centurion's confession in 15:39. Yet it would be a mistake to suppose that Mark abandons the motifs so central to 14:61-62 in the meantime. As we shall see, neither "Son of God" nor Psalm 2 vanish in Mark 15 so much as they merge into the language of kingship.

Mark 15 begins, in fact, with a probable allusion to Ps 2:1-2:

> "And first thing in the morning, having held counsel together (συμβούλιον ποιήσαντες), the chief priests along with the elders and the scribes and the whole council bound Jesus, led him away, and handed him over to Pilate."

As previously noted, the phrase συμβούλιον ποιήσαντες appears to be a gloss on συνήχθησαν in Ps 2:2 LXX (οἱ βασιλεῖς τῆς γῆς καὶ οἱ ἄρχοντες συνήχθησαν ἐπὶ τὸ αὐτὸ κατὰ τοῦ κυρίου καὶ κατὰ τοῦ χριστοῦ αὐτοῦ).[21] There is no need to recount the entire argument for a second time.[22] To summarize, this curious phrase and its cognates

---

110:1 to be the product of an early Christian pesher, but the evidence above (and below) suggests that it is more likely a Jewish tradition inherited by the NT; cf. Bock, *Mark*, 356; Evans, *Mark 8:27-16:20*, 450–51.

[20] So Kim, "*Son of Man*," passim. See also the earliest commentary on Mark (*Exp. Marc. ad. loc.* [CChr 82]): "The priest interrogates the Son of God, but Jesus replies 'the Son of Man' ... in order that we may understand that the Son of God is the same as the Son of Man."

[21] See also Albert Barnes, *Notes on the New Testament: Matthew and Mark*, ed. Robert Frew, Barnes' Notes IX (Grand Rapids: Baker, 1987), 38; Pesch, *Markusevangelium*, 1:195, 2:456. Pesch does not mention Psalm 2 directly in his comments on Mark 15:1, but refers the reader back to his comments on 3:6 where he entertains the possibility of an allusion to Psalm 2 in 3:6 and 15:1 alike.

[22] See Chapter 4.

never appear outside the Gospels and later literature citing them, where they consistently serve as a gloss on συνήχθησαν in Ps 2:2.²³ Both Origen and Chrysostom use Mark's expression, συμβούλιον ποιήσαντες, interchangeably with συνήχθησαν and Matthew's συμβούλιον λάβοντες, which the former also regards as an allusion to Ps 2:2.²⁴

When we consider that Christianity generally associated Ps 2:1-2 with the collusion between the Jewish leaders (ἀρχιερεῖς/ἄρχοντες) and Pilate in the first place, the linguistic clue provided συμβούλιον ποιήσαντες makes it altogether likely that Mark's account of Jesus's trial begins with an allusion to Psalm 2: the rulers "take counsel together against the Lord and his Messiah."²⁵ Just as early interpreters often linked Ps 2:2 to the transfer of Jesus from one set of authorities to another, so Mark 15:1 recounts the transition from one trial proceeding to another.²⁶

7.2.1 The King of the Jews and the Son of God (Mark 14:61 and 15:2)

In the very next verse Pilate's question, σὺ εἶ ὁ βασιλεὺς τῶν Ἰουδαίων, likewise, exhibits a kind of synonymous parallelism with the high priest's question, σὺ εἶ ὁ χριστὸς ὁ υἱὸς τοῦ εὐλογητοῦ, from 14:61.²⁷ This similarity is, in fact, only one in a series of parallels between the two trial scenes:²⁸

14:53, 55, 60-62	15:1-5
Jesus is led to the high priest, where all the chief priests, elders, scribes, and the whole council were gathered together (vv. 53, 55).	"Having held counsel together, the chief priests, elders, scribes, and the whole council led Jesus away to Pilate."
And the high priest asked Jesus ...	And Pilate asked him ...

---

²³ Cf. συμβούλιον ἐδίδουν in Mark 3:6; συμβούλιον ἔλαβον/λάβοντες in Matt 12:14; 22:15; 27:1-2, 7; 28:12; and see further Origen, *Hom. Ps. ad loc.* (*PG* 12:1102b); Theodoret, *Comm. Ps. ad loc.* (*PG* 80:874d); Athanasius, *Ep. Fest.* 11 (*PG* 26:1411); Leontius, *Hom.* 6 (CChr 17).

²⁴ Origen *Comm. John*, 28.12.112, 118 (*PG* 14:709, 712); Chrysostom *Hom. Matt.*, 86, 90 (*PG* 58:761, 787).

²⁵ Cf. Matt 26:3-4, 57; Luke 22:63-23:43; Acts 4:25-29; Hippolytus, *Frag. Gen.* 49.5 (*PG* 10:793); Tertullian, *Marc.* 3.22; 4.39, 42; 5.3, 4, 17 (*PL* 2:349b-464a); Origen, *Princ.* 3.3 (*PG* 11:315-16); *Comm. Matt.* 12:1; 13:9 (*PG* 13:976, 1117c); Eusebius, *Comm. Ps.* 2.2 (*PG* 23:81); Athanasius, *Ep. fest.* 11 (*PG* 26:1411); Chrysostom, *Hom. Matt.* 36 (*PG* 57:415c); Diodore, *Comm. Ps.* 2 (CChr 6); Augustine, *Cons.* 3.16.53 (*PL* 34:1191); *Faust.* 13.7 (*PL* 42:285); *Serm. Dom.* 21.72 (*PL* 34:1265); Theodoret, *Comm. Ps.* 2 (*PG* 80:871) and others noted in Chapter 2.

²⁶ See, e.g., Dieter Lührmann, "Markus 14:55-64: Christologie und Zerstörung des Tempels im Markusevangelium," *NTS* 27 (1981): 457-74; Brown, *Death*, 1:631-32; Boring, *Mark*, 417. The participial phrase συμβούλιον ποιήσαντες is probably *resumptive*, renewing the main trial narrative after the brief excursus recounting Peter's denials in 14:66-72. The phrase refers back to the council's decision from the night before (14:53-65), so joining the two interrogations into one; see similarly Pesch, *Markusevangelium*, 2:455-56; A. N. Sherwin-White, *Roman Society and Roman Law in the New Testament* (Grand Rapids: Baker, 1981), 44-5; Evans, *Mark 8:27-16:20*, 475.

²⁷ See similarly Gnilka, *Markus*, 2:299-300; Pesch, *Markusevangelium*, 2:437; Edwards, *Mark*, 458; Boring, *Mark*, 418; Black, *Mark*, 316.

²⁸ Cf. Georg Braumann, "Markus 15:2-5 und Markus 14:55-64," *ZNW* 52 (1961): 273-78; Gerhard Schneider, "Gab es eine vorsynoptische Szene 'Jesus vor dem Synedrium'?" *NovT* 12 (1970): 22-39; Matera, *Kingship*, 7; Boring, *Mark*, 418.

οὐκ ἀπεκρίνατο οὐδέν	οὐκ ἀπεκρίνατο οὐδέν;
But he was silent and gave no answer.	But Jesus no longer answered at all.
Again the high priest asked him, σὺ εἶ ὁ χριστὸς ὁ υἱὸς τοῦ εὐλογητοῦ;	And Pilate asked him, σύ εἶ ὁ βασιλεὺς τῶν Ἰουδαίων;
And Jesus said, "I am . . ."	And Jesus answered him, "You say so."

Like the resumptive συμβούλιον ποιήσαντες, these parallels invite us to connect the two proceedings, including the two charges: ὁ χριστὸς ὁ υἱὸς τοῦ εὐλογητοῦ and ὁ βασιλεὺς τῶν Ἰουδαίων.

The connection is more than rhetorical, in fact. As many have observed, the question with which Jesus's trial begins in Mark 15 effectively equals the question with which the previous trial ended, for if χριστός and υἱὸς θεοῦ (as well as βασιλεὺς Ἰσραήλ in 15:32) are characteristically Jewish designations for Israel's king, ὁ βασιλεὺς τῶν Ἰουδαίων is a typical Roman designation for the same.[29] So Pilate's question in 15:2 is essentially a Roman restatement of the charge from 14:61 (cf. Luke 23:2).[30]

In this way, ὁ βασιλεὺς τῶν Ἰδουαίων assumes the connotations of ὁ χριστός ὁ υἱὸς τοῦ θεοῦ from 14:61-62 in the narrative going forward. In terms of Mark's narrative, ὁ βασιλεὺς τῶν Ἰδουαίων *is* ὁ χριστός ὁ υἱὸς τοῦ θεοῦ. On a further note, Jesus is tried as χριστός, υἱός, and βασιλεύς in 14:61 and 15:2: the very three terms applied to Israel's king in Ps 2:2, 6, 7 LXX (and there alone). Though a possible coincidence, it is also possible that we see here one more hint of Psalm 2's influence in Mark's passion narrative.

7.2.2 A King's Trial (Mark 15:1-15)

Thereafter, ὁ βασιλεὺς τῶν Ἰουδαίων becomes Jesus's predominant designation throughout the remainder of Mark 15.[31] All told, Jesus is called βασιλεύς six times in thirty verses: more than in any chapter of the NT besides John 19.[32] When viewed as a sequence, these occurrences are nothing short of redundant:[33]

---

[29] See, e.g., Taylor, *Mark*, 579; Gnilka, *Markus* 2:299; Gundry, *Mark*, 924; Evans, *Mark 8:27-16:20*, 478; Marcus, *Mark 8-16*, 1027, 1033. In the NT, the title occurs almost exclusively on the lips of Roman characters, with the singular exception of the magi in Matt 2:2. (John 19:21 could be seen as an exception but for the fact that the chief priests are only quoting what Pilate has written on the titulus.) Historically, Rome had previously granted this very title to both Alexander Jannaeus and Herod the Great (see Josephus, *War* 1.14.4; *Ant.* 14.36, 15.373). Yet when Herod's son, Antipas, petitioned Rome for the same title, he was promptly exiled to Gaul instead (*Ant.* 18.8.2). See also E. Mary Smallwood, *The Jews under Roman Rule: From Pompey to Diocletian: A Study in Political Relations*, SJLA 20 (Leiden: Brill, 1981), 56, 74-6; 191.

[30] Cf. Marcus, *Mark 8-16*, 1033.

[31] Cf. Matera, *Kingship*, 4.

[32] Jesus is referred to as "king" seven times in John 19:3, 12, 14, 15, 19, 21; four times in Matt 27:11, 29, 37, 42); and four times in Luke 23:2, 37.

[33] Cf. Collins, *Mark*, 719. Furthermore, whereas Matthew and Luke each include the full title, ὁ βασιλεὺς τῶν Ἰουδαίων, only once in their trial narratives (Matt 27:11; Luke 23:3), Mark has Pilate pronounce the full title three times in 15:2, 9, 12. And whereas Matthew, perhaps more plausibly, has Pilate refer to Jesus as "Jesus *who is called* Christ" (Ἰησοῦν τὸν λεγόμενον χριστόν) in 27:17, 22, Mark contains no such qualifiers so that Pilate instead calls Jesus "the King of the Jews" outright in 15:9, 12.

Part 1: The Son of God on the Cross   151

15:2   σὺ εἶ ὁ βασιλεὺς τῶν Ἰουδαίων;
15:9   θέλετε ἀπολύσω ὑμῖν τὸν βασιλέα τῶν Ἰουδαίων;
15:12   τί οὖν ποιήσω τὸν βασιλέα τῶν Ἰουδαίων;[34]
15:18   χαῖρε, βασιλεῦ τῶν Ἰουδαίων
15:26   καὶ ἦν ἡ ἐπιγραφὴ τῆς αἰτίας αὐτοῦ ἐπιγεγραμμένη· ὁ βασιλεὺς τῶν Ἰουδαίων
15:32   ὁ χριστὸς ὁ βασιλεὺς Ἰσραὴλ καταβάτω

In contrast to the other Gospels, moreover, Mark never has Jesus called a "king" prior to his trial in Mark 15.[35] As a result, Jesus's kingship is bound to his passion in Mark's Gospel as in no other.[36] The evangelist is emphatic that Jesus is tried and crucified as a king.[37]

On a historical level, this makes good sense. As is well-documented, under Roman law, the claim to be a king other than Caesar constituted an assault on the emperor's majesty (*crimen laesae maiestatis*) punishable by death, often by crucifixion in particular.[38] Hence, Mark, like each of the evangelists, depicts Jesus crucified by Rome as a would-be rival to Caesar.[39]

The remark could be "contemptuous," as Taylor (*Mark*, 582) thinks, but it may also be a slight rhetorical play by Mark to make Pilate ironically state the truth and so remind the reader that this is in fact Jesus's true identity (so Swete, *St. Mark*, 371; Jerry Camery-Hoggatt, *Irony in Mark's Gospel: Text and Subtext* [Cambridge/New York: Cambridge University Press, 1991], 174; and Fowler, *Let the Reader Understand*, 159). Collins (*Mark*, 719) suggests that "Mark narrates the story in this way in order to construct a scene in which the people of Jerusalem have a choice between Jesus and Barabbas and all that each signifies" and similarly suspects that Mark's narrative aims lie behind the phrasing of 15:9.

[34] Some mss of Mark 15:12 (including ℵ C K 𝔐 and others) read τί οὖν θέλετε ποιήσω ὃν λέγετε τὸν βασιλέα τῶν Ἰουδαίων. The vast majority of witnesses, however, support the reading above.
[35] Cf. Matt 2:2; 21:5; 25:34, 40; Luke 19:38; John 1:49; 12:13, 15.
[36] Cf. Juel, *Messiah and Temple*, 64–72 and *passim*.
[37] So Matera, *Kingship*, 136.
[38] On the penalty of crucifixion for claiming to be a king, see Paulus, *Sent.* 5.21.3 and Petronius, *Sat.* 53.3. Most likely, Pilate's question in 15:2 (cf. 9, 12, 26) reflects the charge of *perduellio* ("sedition") or *crimen laesae maiestatis* ("the crime of injured majesty"): see, e.g., Brown, *Death*, 1:719; C. W. Chilton, "The Roman Law of Treason under the Early Principate," *JRS* 45 (1955): 73–81; Larry R. Overstreet, "Roman Law and the Trial of Christ," *BSac* 135 (1978): 323–32; David W. Chapman and Eckhard J. Schnabel, *The Trial and Crucifixion of Jesus: Texts and Commentary*, WUNT 344 (Tübingen: Mohr Siebeck, 2015), 221. According to Ulpian (Dig. 48.4.1), *crimen laesae maiestatis* originally referred to any crime "against the Roman people or against their safety." Cicero (*Inv.* 2.17.53) similarly defines this crime as "a lessening of the dignity or greatness or authority of the people or of those to whom the people have given authority." But as the emperor increasingly became synonymous with the state, this category of crimes came to include virtually any insult to the emperor imaginable, or even, as Paulus (*Sent.* 5.21.3) records, consulting a soothsayer "about the life of the emperor." Although the *Digesta* and Paulus are both later than the Gospels, a number of ancient authors note that such decrees were already issued by Augustus and (even more so) Tiberius: see Cassius Dio, *Hist.* 56.27, 59.1-6; Seneca, *Ben.* 3.26; Tacitus, *Ann.* 1.72-73; and Suetonius, *Tib.* 58. See further S. P. Scott, "The Digest or Pandects—Book XLVIII. Title IV: On the Julian Law Relating to the Crime of Lesse Majesty," in *The Civil Law, Including the Twelve Tables, the Institutes of Gaius, the Rules of Ulpian, the Opinions of Paulus, the Enactments of Justinian, and the Constitutions of Leo*; Vol. XI (Cincinnati: The Central Trust Company, 1932), 28; Arthur Keaveney and John A. Madden, "The Crimen Maiestatis under Caligula: The Evidence of Dio Cassius," *ClQ* 48 (1998): 316–20.
[39] See, e.g., Pesch, *Markusevangelium*, 2:457; Gundry, *Mark*, 924; Marcus, *Mark 8–16*, 1027, 1034; also E. P. Sanders, *Jesus and Judaism* (Philadelphia: Fortress, 1985), 294. As A. N. Sherwin-White (*Roman*

Yet, on a narrative level, Jesus's characterization as βασιλεύς also continues to advance the connotations of Davidic messianism inherited from ὁ χριστὸς ὁ υἱὸς τοῦ εὐλογητοῦ in 14:61.[40] This connection ultimately becomes explicit in 15:32: ὁ χριστὸς ὁ βασιλεὺς Ἰσραὴλ. Far from abandoning Psalm 2's motifs of divine sonship, messianism, and enthronement, then, Mark's focus on kingship, led off by allusions to Psalm 2, has the conspicuous effect of suggesting that Jesus goes to the cross precisely as the royal Messiah Son of God.

7.3 Irony and Parodic Enthronement in Mark 15:16-32

Mark's portrayal of Jesus as king, as such, relies heavily on irony. As Juel recognizes, "[t]he irony in the passion story works because the reader possesses information not available to the characters in the story."[41] So while Pilate lobs ὁ βασιλεύς against Jesus as a criminal charge rather than a confession of faith, he nevertheless states what the reader has known to be true since the Gospel's opening verse (1:1). Pilate, that is to say, speaks truer than he knows.[42] As Mark 15 progresses, the irony intensifies. In Mark 15:16-32 Jesus is called βασιλεύς in three more instances, all rife with dramatic irony.

Society and Roman Law in the New Testament [Grand Rapids: Baker, 1981], 1–32) observes, the trial narratives closely align with what we know of provincial trial proceedings. Non-citizens (*peregrini*) were typically tried outside the normal parameters of the legal system (i.e., *extra-ordinem*), meaning no formal accusers, juries, or barristers were required. Instead, charges were brought by independent accusers (*delatores*) to the provincial governor (cf. Pliny, *Ep*. 10.97.1), who functioned as the sole judiciary with the authority to conduct his own investigation (*cognito*). As holder of the *imperium*, the governor likewise possessed the authority to pass whatever sentence he saw fit, including death (cf. Josephus, *War* 2.8.1; *Ant*. 18.1.1; Pliny, *Ep*. 10.30.1; Dig. 1.18.8-9). See also Josef Blinzler, *The Trial of Jesus: The Jewish and Roman Proceedings against Jesus Christ Described and Assessed from the Oldest Accounts* [Westminster, MD: Newman, 1959], 170–71; Brown, *Death*, 1:716; Overstreet, "Roman Law," 325–28. Accordingly, in Mark, independent accusers (the Jewish leaders) bring Jesus before Pilate (15:1), who interrogates him (15:2-5) and sentences him (15:15) per the usual process.

One gains the same basic picture from the other Gospel accounts. Sherwin-White (*Roman Society*, 32–9) notes that Luke, in particular, "is remarkable in that his additional materials—the full formulation of the charges before Pilate, the reference to Herod, and the proposed acquittal with admonition—are all technically correct [per the Roman legal process]." Thus, Luke is the most specific about the charges against Jesus: "We found this man inciting (διαστρέφοντα) our nation and forbidding us to pay taxes to Caesar and saying that he himself is Christ, a king" (23:2). The claim of kingship likewise figures prominently in John 18:28–19:30; but, like Luke, John adds certain details that reinforce the picture above, such as in John 19:12: "If you release this man, you are not *Caesar's friend* (φίλος τοῦ Καίσαρος); everyone who makes himself a king opposes Caesar." As both Sherwin-White (*Roman Law*, 47) and Winter (*Divine Honours*, 70) note, *Caesaris amicus* was a *terminus technicus* of political significance (cf. Philo, *Flacc*. 2.40). So John makes explicit what is implicit in the Synoptics: that loyalty to the emperor is the central question at stake in Jesus's trial; see also Brown, *Death*, 1:723–59, 787–861.

[40] Cf. Matera, *Kingship*, 29; Black, *Mark*, 316.
[41] Juel, *Messianic Exegesis*, 94. Notably, Juel (95) goes on to state that "[i]n the account of Jesus' crucifixion, it is the words and phrases from the psalms that perform this function."
[42] See similarly Swete, *St. Mark*, 371; Taylor, *Mark*, 582; Jerry Camery-Hoggatt, *Irony in Mark's Gospel: Text and Subtext* (Cambridge/New York: Cambridge University Press, 1991), 174; Fowler, *Let the Reader Understand*, 159.

7.3.1 "Hail, King of the Jews! (Mark 15:16-20)

First, in 15:16-20, Mark depicts the soldiers engaged in a typical "mock coronation" ritual familiar to us from various ancient sources.[43] The soldiers lead Jesus into the courtyard ("which," Mark specifically notes, "is the *praetorium*" [ὅ ἐστιν πραιτώριον]), where they summon the entire cohort (σπεῖρα), clothe him in purple, crown him with a makeshift diadem of twisted thorns, and salute him, Χαῖρε, βασιλεῦ τῶν Ἰουδαίων, before kneeling in mock-obeisance and striking him with a reed, meant to resemble a scepter.[44] When they have finished mocking him (καὶ ὅτε ἐνέπαιξαν), Mark tells us, they strip him of his parodic garments and return him to his own clothes (v. 20).

As the ancient parallels demonstrate, the intent behind such rituals was to satirize those deemed to have usurped their rightful place in society, often as a prelude to execution. Hence, Jesus, a would-be king, is hailed (Χαῖρε) as though he were Caesar himself. As T. E. Schmidt observes, many of the details in Mark 15:16-20 specifically parallel those of a Roman triumph.[45] In this case, Jesus is not only mocked as a would-be king, but likened to the emperor himself on his way to the cross.

In point of fact, Marcus has demonstrated that crucifixion itself was intentionally construed to parody exaltation and/or enthronement.[46] As Marcus notes, mimicry was a common feature of Roman punishments, which, in any case, aimed to make an

---

[43] See similarly Pesch *Markusevangelium*, 2:470–71; Gnilka, *Markus*, 2:306–08; Gundry, *Mark*, 940–42; Evans, *Mark 8:27–16:20*, 490; Marcus, *Mark 8–16*, 1045–48; Bock, *Mark*, 367. Remarkably similar scenes are recounted in Philo, *Flac.* 6.36-39 (recounting the mock coronation of Carabbas, a poor derelict, whom the people enthrone, crown, with a papyrus, clothe with a dormat, and salute as king in mockery); 4 *Macc.* 6:1-30 (recounting the mock coronation of Eleazar prior to his execution for defying Antiochus IV); Josephus, *War* 4.3.8 (on the mock-installation of Phannias son of Samuel as high priest); and Dio Cassius 64.20-21 (describing the mockery of Emperor Vitellius prior to his execution by his own soldiers).

[44] Cf. Philo, *Flac.* 6:36-39.

[45] See T. E. Schmidt, "Mark 15:16-32: The Crucifixion Narrative and the Roman Triumphal Procession," *NTS* 41 (1995): 1–18. Schmidt observes similar practices surrounding the triumphs of various emperors such as crowning the emperor with a laurel wreath and clothing him in purple garments, and the characteristic salute "*Ave, Caesar!*" in a variety of texts including Suetonius, *Calig.* 19.3 (Gaius, 40 CE); Dio Cassius 62.4.3 (Nero, 66 CE); Tac. *Hist.* 2.59 (Vitellius, 68 CE); Joseph. *War* 7.5.4 (Vespasian and Titus, 71 CE). Schmidt moreover suggests that the wording of Mark 15:16-18 may even be formulaic; "in one text after another the triumphator is introduced clad in, consecutively, a ceremonial purple robe and a crown" (7). Examples include Livy, *Epit.* 10.7.9, 30.15.11; Dio Cassius 62.4.3-6.2, 62.20.2-6; Dionysius of Halicarnassus 5.47.2-3; Suetonius, *Tib.* 17, *Ner.* 25; and Plutarch, *Aem.* 34.4 among others. It should be noted that although triumphs were once held for victorious generals during the era of the Republic, from 20 BCE onward the triumph was the "exclusive privilege of the emperor," celebrating his accession to the throne (see Schmidt, "Mark 15:16-32," 4; and H. S. Versnel, *Triumphus: An Inquiry into the Origin, Development and Meaning of the Roman Triumph* (Leiden: Brill, 1970).

[46] Joel Marcus, "Crucifixion as Parodic Exaltation," *JBL* 125 (2006): 73–87. Marcus, along with Justin Meggitt ("Laughing and Dreaming at the Foot of the Cross: Context and Reception of a Religious Symbol," in *Modern Spiritualities: An Inquiry*, ed. Laurence Brown et al. Westminster College-Oxford: Critical Studies in Religion [Amherst, NY; Oxford: Prometheus Books, 1997], 63–70); idem ("Artemidorus and the Johannine Crucifixion," *JHC* 5 [1998]: 203–08), observes that crucifixion is strangely associated with ideas of social promotion in a number of texts. In his book of dream exegesis, for example, Artemidorus (*Oneirocritica* 2.53) maintains that "it is also auspicious for a poor person [to dream of crucifixion]. For a crucified person is raised high and nourishes many..."

example of the victim.⁴⁷ Quintilian is explicit on this point: "[e]very punishment has less to do with the offense than with the example ... [so] when we [Romans] crucify criminals the most frequent roads are chosen, where the greatest number of people can look and be seized by this fear."⁴⁸ The twisted logic behind the spectacle was that the lowly (*humilior*) person who presumed to usurp the position of the high (*altior*) would be raised up in a parody of the higher status he dared to claim.⁴⁹ Again, Dio Chrysostom expresses this very point when describing the mock coronation of a prisoner about to be "hanged" (ἐκρέμασαν):⁵⁰

> They take one of their prisoners ... who has been condemned to death, set him upon the king's throne, give him the royal apparel, and permit him to give orders, to drink and carouse, and to dally with the royal concubines during those days ... but after that they strip and scourge him and then hang him. Now what do you suppose this is meant to signify and what is the purpose of this Persian custom? Is it not to show that foolish and wicked men frequently acquire this royal power and title and then after a season of wanton insolence come to a most shameful and wretched end? ... Therefore, O perverse man, do not attempt to be king before you have attained wisdom."⁵¹

---

⁴⁷ See not only Marcus ("Crucifixion," 80), but also Florence Dupont (cited in Carlin A. Barton, *The Sorrows of the Ancient Romans: The Gladiator and the Monster* [Princeton: Princeton University Press, 1993], 137): "Imitation, not in the Greek sense of representation (mimesis), but in the sense of mimic buffoonery, the play of the comic double and of mirroring, was a fundamental component of Roman culture"; and Richard A. Bauman, *Crime and Punishment in Ancient Rome* (London/New York: Routledge, 1996), 68–9, 75–6, 182 n. 37.

⁴⁸ *Decl.* 274.

⁴⁹ Marcus, "Crucifixion," 77–8. Crucifixion was, after all, typically the punishment of rebellious slaves, insurrectionists, would-be kings, and enemies of the state—i.e., those who sought to elevate themselves above their station—as made clear in Cicero, *Rab. Perd.* 3.10; 4.12; 5.15-16; *Verr.* 2.5.168. On this point, see further Martin Hengel, *Crucifixion in the Ancient World and the Folly of the Message of the Cross* (Philadelphia: Fortress, 1977), 28–37; Gerald O'Collins ("Crucifixion," *ABD* 1:1208; John Granger Cook, *Crucifixion in the Mediterranean World* (Tübingen: Mohr Siebeck, 2014), 65; and David W. Chapman, *Ancient Jewish and Christian Perceptions of Crucifixion* (Grand Rapids: Baker Academic, 2010), 82; and Tom Thatcher, "I Have Conquered the World," in *Empire in the New Testament*, ed. Stanley E. Porter and Cynthia Long Westfall, MNTSS 10 (Eugene, Or: Pickwick, 2011), 146.

⁵⁰ Dio may well refer to crucifixion here. The verb κρεμάω/κρεμάννυμι properly refers to "hanging up" high, "suspending," or even "crucifying" a person, as in Plutarch, *Caes.* 2 (see LSJ, s.v., κρεμάννυμι). The manner of execution Dio refers to therefore belongs the larger category of "suspension" punishments, of which crucifixion was one (see Gunnar Samuelsson, *Crucifixion in Antiquity: An Inquiry into the Background and Significance of the New Testament Terminology of Crucifixion*, WUNT 2/310 [Tübingen: Mohr Siebeck, 2011], *passim*.

⁵¹ *Orat.* 4.67-70 (trans. Cohoon, LCL). As Marcus observes, interpreters have frequently noted the parallels between the passage above and the Gospel passion narratives; see, e.g., Hugo Grotius, *Annotationes in Novum Testamentum Volume II: Ad Matth. XIV–XXVIII* (Groningen: W. Zuidema, 1827), 354; Vernon K. Robbins, *Jesus the Teacher: A Socio-Rhetorical Interpretation of Mark* (1984; reprint, Minneapolis: Fortress, 1992), 189–91; Robert L. Brawley, "Resistance to the Carnivalization of Jesus: Scripture in the Lucan Passion Narrative," *Sem* 69–70 (1995): 37–8. Cf. James G. Frazer, *The Golden Bough: A Study in Magic and Religion*, Part 6, The Scapegoat (London: Macmillan, 1913), 413–14.

It follows, then, that if the ritual in 15:16-20 is intended as Jesus's mock coronation ceremony, the crucifixion serves as the parodic enthronement itself.

Yet "[t]he danger of parody," as Marcus writes, "is that it may turn into reality."[52] With Marcus, I submit that this is precisely what happens in Mark's passion narrative.[53] Though the rulers mock and deride, they unwittingly declare again and again what the reader knows to be true. As a result, "the mockery that has transformed kingship into a joke encounters a sharper mockery that unmasks it, so that the derision of kingship is itself derided and true royalty emerges through the negation of the negation."[54]

7.3.2 The King on Zion's Hill: Psalm 2 and the Titulus in Mark 15:26

The discussion of parodic enthronement above leads us naturally to the *titulus* above the cross. As Mark recounts, "The inscription of the charge against him was written, 'The King of the Jews'" (ἦν ἡ ἐπιγραφὴ τῆς αἰτίας αὐτοῦ ἐπιγεγραμμένη· ὁ βασιλεὺς τῶν Ἰουδαίων).[55] Many interpreters in history besides Marcus and Schmidt have viewed the *titulus* as the epitome of dramatic irony in the passion narratives, boldly declaring the reality behind the parody.[56]

As we saw in Chapter 2, many ancient interpreters in fact saw in the *titulus* the fulfillment of one or more of the royal psalms, including Ps 2:6 LXX: ἐγώ δὲ κατεστάθην βασιλεὺς ὑπ᾽ αὐτοῦ ἐπὶ Σιων ὄρος τὸ ἅγιον αὐτοῦ.[57] In his commentary, Bede applies this interpretation to Mark 15:26 directly:

---

[52] Marcus, "Crucifixion," 86. Marcus (87), in fact, offers a historical example of such from Silius Italicus (*Punica* 2.344): "I was looking on when he hung high upon the tree and saw Italy from his lofty cross" (cf. Mark 15:39 par.).
[53] See also Schmidt, "Mark 15:16-32," 18.
[54] Marcus, "Crucifixion," 87.
[55] Cf. Matt 27:37; Luke 23:38; John 19:19. Perhaps as a testament to its perceived significance, the reported content of the *titulus* grows over the course of the Gospel tradition.
[56] See, e.g., *Exp. Marc.* 15:26 (CChr 82); Bede, *Exp. Marc.* IV.1430-41; Albertus Magnus, *Enarr. Marc.* 15:26; Lapide, *Commentaria*, 3:29; Calvin, *Harmony*, 302; Trapp, *Commentary*, 329; and more recently, Carl Daniel Peddinghaus, "Die Entstehung der Leidensgeschichte: Eine traditionsgeschichtliche und historische Untersuchung des Werdens und Wachsens der erzählenden Passionstradition bis zum Entwurf des Markus. [1. 2]" (PhD diss, Heidelberg, 1966), 160-5; Grundmann, *Markus*, 314; Matera, *Kingship*, 61-2. According to Niclas Förster ("Der titulus crucis: Demütigung der Judäer und Proklamation des Messias," *NovT* 56 [2014]: 113-33) this has been the usual understanding of Mark's *titulus* throughout the history of Christian interpretation; indeed, earlier scholarship sometimes doubted the historicity of the inscription precisely because of its loaded theological significance within the narrative (so Bultmann, *History*, 272; Ernst Haenchen, "History and Interpretation in the Johannine Passion Narrative," *Int* 24 [1970]: 198-219; Heinz-Wolfgang Kuhn, "Jesus Als Gekreuzigter In Der Frühchristlichen Verkündigung Bis Zur Mitte Des 2. Jahrhunderts," *ZTK* 72 [1975]: 1-46). More recently, however, both Förster (above), and Paul L. Maier ("The Inscription on the Cross of Jesus of Nazareth," *Hermes* 124 [1996]: 58-75) have argued in favor of its historicity.
[57] See Ferda, "Matthew's Titulus," 565-66. Citing Ps 2:6, see Origen, *Comm. Matt.* 130 in *Origenes Werke*, 11:267; Augustine, *Tract. Ev. Jo.*, 115, 117 (*PL* 35:1939, 1946); Serm. 218.5 (*PL* 38:1085); Bede, *Exp. Marc.* IV.1430-41 (CChr 120); Pseudo-Cyprian, *De duobus montibus Sina et Sion* 9.1-2 (*PL* 4:950-51); Cassiodorus, *Expl. Ps.* 2 (*PL* 70:38); *Gloss. ord.* on Mark 15:26; (see Walahfrid Strabo et al., *Bibliorum sacrorum cum glossa ordinaria* [Venice: Publisher unknown, 1603], 647); Albertus Magnus, *Enarrat. Jo.*, in *Opera Omnia*, vol. 24, ed. Auguste Borgnet (Paris: Ludovicum Vives, 1899), 657; Thomas Aquinas, *Super Evangelium S. Matthaei: Lectura*, ed. P. Raphaelis Cai (Turin: Marietti, 1951), 363; R. A. Torrey, *The Treasury of Scripture Knowledge* (Peabody, MA: Hendrickson, 2019),

The titulus placed above the cross, on which was written, "King of the Jews," shows that not even by killing him could they manage not to have him as king. Hence in the psalm it is sung, "I have been made king by him on Zion, his holy mountain [Ps 2:6]." . . . through the cross, he does not lose his claim to be king, but confirms and reinforces his rule.[58]

Yet, as Tucker Ferda observes, this reading has dropped entirely from the modern commentary tradition.[59] This oversight may be due in part to a preoccupation with verbal parallels in modern scholarship.[60] Yet, as Holly Carey has shown, recollections of earlier biblical scenes in narrative often depend on parallel circumstances: that is circumstances that seem to repeat themselves.[61] This appears to have been the logic of the past interpreters who saw symbolized in the *titulus* a fulfillment of Ps 2:6, in which the king is enthroned on Zion. As we have seen, a similar allusion to Ps 2:6 appears to underlie *4 Ezra* 13:35-36 where Ezra sees God's "son," the "Messiah," standing "atop Mount Zion."[62]

In view of the prominent role Psalm 2 plays elsewhere in Mark's Gospel, including in the passion narrative, we should consider seriously the possibility that earlier interpreters captured and preserved an allusion already present in Mark's narrative.[63] If so, the dramatic reversal of parody suggested by Marcus, Schmidt, and many others in history involves an allusion to no other verse than Ps 2:6. Though the ruling powers gather against the Lord's Messiah in mockery and derision (cf. Ps 2:1-3), the joke is finally on them; for (Mark implies) the king really has been enthroned on Zion.

7.3.3 The Messiah, the King of Israel (Mark 15:32)

As Jesus hangs on the cross, the chief priests and the scribes below mock him in terms that recall their earlier charge against him: ὁ χριστὸς ὁ βασιλεὺς Ἰσραὴλ καταβάτω νῦν ἀπὸ τοῦ σταυροῦ, ἵνα ἴδωμεν καὶ πιστεύσωμεν (15:32; cf. 14:61). The recollection is seemingly confirmed by the fact that their comments just beforehand similarly recall

---

627. Citing other royal psalms, see *Exp. Marc.* 15:26 (CChr 82), citing Ps 110:1; Augustine, *Enarrat. Ps.* 46.4 (PL 36:526); Cassiodorus, *Exp. Ps.* 15, 20, 46 (PL 70:112, 147, 333); and others cited by Ferda.

[58] Bede, *Exp. Marc.* IV.1430-41 (CChr 120). Bede quotes the Vulgate version of Ps 2:6, *Ego autem constitutus sum rex ab eo super Sion, montem sanctum ejus*, which follows the LXX. A portion of the Latin passage translated above is also identical to an excerpt from Augustine, *Serm.* 218.5 (PL 38:1085), so Bede is plainly dependent on Augustine here.

[59] See Ferda, "Matthew's Titulus," 566. Ferda writes of Matthew specifically, "this reading has, for reasons I know not, dropped completely from Matthew commentaries"; but the same is true of all the Gospels.

[60] See the recent discussion by David Allen, "The Use of Criteria," in *Methodology*, 129-141. Allen reviews various lists of criteria beginning with Richard Hays's original list of seven. Although verbal repetition is only one of Hays's seven criteria (and only one of the criteria suggested by other scholars since) it is the one most often prioritized above all others.

[61] Carey, *Jesus' Cry*, 41-3. See also Brown, "Metalepsis," in *Exploring Intertextuality*, 29-42; and Smith, "The Use of Criteria: A Proposal from Relevance Theory," in *Methodology*, 142-54 (esp. 145).

[62] See Chapter 2.

[63] See similarly Ferda ("Matthew's Titulus," 568-71) concerning Matthew's Gospel. Most of the allusions to Psalm 2 that Ferda observes in Matthew are already present in Mark.

Jesus's threat to destroy the temple (15:29; cf. 14:58). The irony here is thinly veiled in such comments as, "he saved others, [but] he cannot save himself" (15:31). Mark thus prompts the reader to recall the many past scenes in which Jesus indeed saved others as well as, perhaps, his own predictions of his impending death and resurrection—reasons, that is, to "see and believe."

Significantly, ὁ χριστός here becomes synonymous with ὁ βασιλεύς. In this way, Mark not only circles back to the charge from 14:61-62 (ὁ χριστὸς ὁ υἱὸς τοῦ εὐλογητοῦ [θεοῦ]), but confirms its connection to ὁ βασιλεὺς in 15:2. And while the third epithet, υἱὸς θεοῦ, does not appear just yet, it is worth noting that it does so swiftly upon Jesus's death in the very next pericope (15:33-39), when the centurion declares, ἀληθῶς οὗτος ὁ ἄνθρωπος υἱὸς θεοῦ ἦν.

7.4 Part 1 Summary

In summary, we have seen that (1) Mark's son-of-God language continues to take its cue from Psalm 2 in the passion narrative as throughout the Gospel as a whole. (2) Though disguised, as it were, "Son of God" does not disappear from the passion narrative after 14:61 so much as it is (in a manner consistent with Psalm 2) restyled as ὁ βασιλεύς, which bears the connotations of Messiah Son of God through the rest of Mark 15. (3) Finally, the entirety of Mark 15 up to this point ironically portrays Jesus's crucifixion as his enthronement while also continuing to sound echoes of Psalm 2 in 15:1 and possibly 15:26, thus exerting a kind of "contextual pressure" on our interpretation of the centurion's confession that bids us to hear it in the same vein.[64] Without further ado, then, we turn to the centurion's words themselves.

---

[64] Eco, *Semiotics*, 117–18.

Part 2: The Centurion's Confession (Mark 15:39)

The centurion's confession is arguably the climax not only of 15:33-39, but of Mark's entire Gospel.[65] In its immediate context, it occurs as the apogee in a series of apocalyptic events surrounding Jesus's death. First, in 15:33, we read that "darkness came over the whole land" (σκότος ἐγένετο ἐφ᾽ ὅλην τὴν γῆν) from the sixth hour until the ninth: an allusion to the "day of the Lord" in Amos 8:9-10 and possibly Exod 10:21-23 as well.[66] Then, following the cry of dereliction (v. 34; cf. Ps 21:1 LXX), offer of sour wine (v. 36; cf. Ps 68:21 LXX), and an eschatologically loaded comment about the coming of Elijah (vv. 35-36),[67] Jesus utters a loud cry (φωνὴν μεγάλην) and breathes his last (ἐξέπνευσεν) (v. 37). With hardly so much as a pause, Mark then tells us that "the temple veil was torn from above to below" (καὶ τὸ καταπέτασμα τοῦ ναοῦ ἐσχίσθη εἰς δύο ἀπ᾽ ἄνωθεν ἕως κάτω) and "when the centurion who was standing opposite him saw that in this he breathed his last, he said, 'Truly, this man was Son of God'" (Ἰδὼν δὲ ὁ κεντυρίων ὁ παρεστηκὼς ἐξ ἐναντίας αὐτοῦ ὅτι οὕτως ἐξέπνευσεν εἶπεν· ἀληθῶς οὗτος ὁ ἄνθρωπος υἱὸς θεοῦ ἦν) (15:38-39).[68]

As many have inferred, the rending of the veil suggests an act of divine revelation running exactly parallel to the rending of the heavens at Jesus's baptism (1:10).[69] It follows, as such, that the centurion's confession is itself the result a revelatory insight (cf. 1:11).[70]

In the Gospel as a whole, then, the centurion becomes the first human character to declare of Jesus what God originally declared at his baptism (1:11), with which

---

[65] See, *inter alia*, Gnilka, *Markus*, 2:324-25; Matera, *Kingship*, 128-34; Philip G. Davis, "Mark's Christological Paradox," *JSNT* 35 (1989): 3-18; Hooker, "Good News," 165-80; and especially Gamel, *Mark 15:39*, passim.
[66] See, e.g., Grundmann, *Markus*, 315; Boring, *Mark*, 430; Marcus, *Mark 8-16*, 1053-054; and the excellent treatment in Allison, *Studies in Matthew*, 79-106. The darkness at noon is probably intended to evoke both the eschatological Day of the Lord (cf. Joel 2:1-2, 10, 30-31) and a repetition of the exodus event.
[67] See, e.g., Kent Brower, "Elijah in the Markan Passion Narrative," *JSNT* 5 (1983): 85-101.
[68] Despite the practice of many modern translations, ἄνωθεν and κάτω are not attested for "top" and "bottom" apart from Matt 27:53 and Mark 15:38 (see TLG; LSJ "ἄνωθεν," s.v.; "κάτω," s.v.; nor BDAG "ἄνωθεν," s.v.; "κάτω," s.v.). Both words typically denote *directionality* rather than extremities. Mark's phrase, as such, further implies the divine origin of the action, also implied by the passive ἐσχίσθη.
[69] See esp. Harry L. Chronis, "The Torn Veil: Cultus and Christology in Mark 15:37-39," *JBL* 101 (1982): 97-114; Daniel Gurtner, "The Rending of the Veil and Markan Christology: 'Unveiling' the 'ΥΙΟΣ ΘΕΟΥ' (Mark 15:38-39)," *BibInt* 15 (2007): 292-306..
[70] See esp. Gamel, *Mark 15.39*, 115-72.

15:39 forms part of an *inclusio*.⁷¹ Likewise, his confession completes the sequence of Mark's "architectonic acclamations" of Jesus's sonship⁷² and even offers the Gospel's final evaluation of Jesus's identity, coinciding with his death.⁷³ Taken at face value, the centurion's confession appears to be a triumphant acclamation of Jesus's identity from a most unlikely character, communicating a profound reversal after the darkness and mockery surrounding the cross.

7.5 The Problem(s) of a Centurion's Confession

At second glance, however, the centurion's confession poses a number of questions for the interpreter including whether or not he speaks sincerely, what he means by υἱὸς θεοῦ in the first place, and how a centurion can possibly mean by υἱὸς θεοῦ anything like what God means in Mark 1:11—namely, that Jesus is the royal Messiah, anointed by God to instantiate his kingdom on earth per Ps 2:7. Bousset captured the essence of this final problem long ago:

> When the Gospel of Mark places in the mouth of the *Gentile captain* the confession of the Son of God, still the υἱὸς τοῦ θεοῦ here cannot be understood in the sense of a confession to the *Jewish Messiah*. Instead, we see clearly that for the evangelist [ὁ] υἱὸς τοῦ θεοῦ was here the great formula in which the nature of Jesus Christ was summarized for the faith of the Gentile Christian community.⁷⁴

One need not accept Bousset's conclusions above in order to grasp the problem he identifies: namely, the virtual impossibility of a Roman centurion confessing Jesus to be the Jewish Messiah—or, one might add, that any first-century person would have supposed that he did.⁷⁵ Owing no doubt to the incredible nature of what he says, the authenticity of the centurion's confession has been challenged from a number of angles over the years, corresponding to the questions above. Each of these questions must be considered if we are to ascertain how Mark 15:39 completes Mark's portrayal of Jesus as God's Son.

---

⁷¹ Cf. Kingsbury, *Jesus Christ*, 34–7; idem, *Christology*, 152.
⁷² Marcus, *Mark 8–16*, 1059; cf. Gamel (*Mark 15:39*, 4): "15:39 marks the end of the Christological tension present throughout Mark."
⁷³ Cf. Lohmeyer, Markus, 437; Taylor, *Mark*, 597–98.
⁷⁴ Bousset, *Kyrios Christos*, 95 (emphasis added); See also Hooker ("Good News," 175–76) who recognizes something of the same problem when she writes that "Although a Roman centurion could hardly have used these words with the significance that Mark gave them, they echo the words of the heavenly voice in 1:11 and 9:7, and as though to ensure that we see the connection, Mark links the centurion's confession with the statement that the temple curtain was torn in two, using the same verb that he used in 1:10 of the tearing apart of the heavens."
⁷⁵ Swete's (*Mark*, 388) suggestion that the centurion "borrowed the words [υἱὸς θεοῦ] from the Jewish priests (v. 31)" is surely special pleading (in *Mark*, unlike Matt 27:40, the chief priests do not even call Jesus "Son of God" at the cross); yet even so Swete goes on to state that the centurion "could scarcely have understood them in the Messianic sense." Collins (*Mark*, 767) also grasps something of this problem when she states that "If … the cultural and social likelihood of the centurion's being a Gentile is taken seriously, the noun phrase would not have the meaning 'king of the Jews' or 'messiah' for such a character."

7.5.1 The Sincerity of the Centurion's Confession

In recent decades, some have questioned whether the centurion's words should be construed as a "confession" at all. Earl S. Johnson, for one, maintains that the traditional reading of Mark 15:39 "could not have provided a credible narrative for Mark's readers" based on their familiarity with "a centurion's typical role and reputation."[76] Others, too, find it more likely that the centurion's remark is a sarcastic one belonging "with the other ironic statements at the foot of the cross about who Jesus is,"[77] or that it is altogether ambiguous.[78] Precisely in view of the preceding mockery, such objections must be taken seriously. On closer inspection, however, Mark's narrative commends a different interpretation.

As Gamel has recently shown, Mark is actually remarkably careful throughout the trial and crucifixion narratives to label derisive speech and actions as such. Indeed, the evangelist "has consistently alerted his readers to every instance when an action that might appear as respectful or even honouring is, in fact, mockery."[79] When we come to the centurion's words in 15:39, however, there are no indicators of mockery. Instead, the opposite is true: there are multiple indications in 15:39 that Mark means for us to hear the centurion's declaration as a sincere one.

First, Kelly Iverson observes that, without exception, every use of ἀληθῶς/ἀλήθεια/ἀληθής in Mark indicates sincere or truthful speech (see 5:33; 12:14, 32; 14:70).[80] To those who have been following the narrative up to this point, the use of ἀληθῶς thus offers a meaningful clue as to how one ought to receive 15:39.

---

[76] Earl S. Johnson, Jr., "Is Mark 15.39 the Key to Mark's Christology," *JSNT* 31 (1987): 3–22 (here 8, 13).

[77] Johnson, "Key," 16. Cf. Myers, *Binding*, 393; Juel, *Master of Surprise*, 74; Sharyn Echols Dowd, *Reading Mark: A Literary and Theological Commentary on the Second Gospel*, RNTC (Macon: Smyth & Helwys, 2000), 162; Mark S. Goodacre, *The Case against Q: Studies in Markan Priority and Synoptic Problem* (Harrisburg: Trinity, 2001), 160 n. 28; Richard A. Horsley, *Hearing the Whole Story: The Politics of Plot in Mark's Gospel* (Louisville: Westminster John Knox Press, 2001), 252.

[78] So Fowler, *Let the Reader Understand*, 207; Whitney T. Shiner, "The Ambiguous Pronouncement of the Centurion and the Shrouding of Meaning in Mark," *JSNT* 22 (2000): 3–22; Black, *Mark*, 333; Laura C. Sweat, *The Theological Role of Paradox in the Gospel of Mark*, LNTS 492 (London/New York: Bloomsbury, 2013), 143–44.

[79] Gamel, *Mark 15.39*, 28. E.g., (1) Mark summarizes the entire mock coronation ceremony in 15:16-20 with the comment καὶ ὅτε ἐνέπαιζαν αὐτῷ (v. 20); (2) when the passersby wag their heads and taunt Jesus to save himself and "come down from the cross," Mark specifies that ἐβλασφήμουν αὐτὸν (15:29-30); (3) immediately afterward, Mark states that ὁμοίως καὶ οἱ ἀρχιερεῖς ἐμπαίζοντες πρὸς ἀλλήλους μετὰ τῶν γραμματέων (v. 31); then (4) Mark states again in v. 32 that οἱ συνεσταυρωμένοι σὺν αὐτῷ ὠείδιζον αὐτόν. One could also consider the incident in 15:34-36, in which the bystanders offer Jesus sour wine to drink on the basis of an apparent misunderstanding of Jesus's cry. Though the intent of this act might initially seem ambiguous, the scene likely alludes to Ps 68:22 LXX ("they gave me poison for food, and for my thirst they gave me sour wine to drink"). In this case, this episode is also marked as one of mockery (so Gamel, *Mark 15.39*, 29–35).

[80] Iverson, "Confession," 335; see also Gamel, *Mark 15:39*, 36–7. Examples include Mark 5:33, where the expression πᾶσαν τὴν ἀλήθειαν refers to telling "the whole truth"; 12:32, where the expression ἐπ' ἀληθείας again refers to the truthfulness of Jesus's own speech, specifically his correct identification of Israel's foremost commandment, the Shema (Deut 6:4); 14:70, in which, although directed at Peter in the act of denying Jesus, ἀληθῶς plainly indicates an accurate, truthful observation on part of the bystanders: "*Certainly* you are one of them, for you are also a Galilean." Mark 12:14 is more complicated since the phrases ἀληθής and ἐπ' ἀληθείας are embedded within an attempt by Jesus's opponents to trap him, but the comment itself, "we know that you are *sincere; with integrity* you teach the way of God," is obviously a truthful one. In Mark's usage, therefore, ἀληθ- language consistently characterizes truthful speech, including, on three occasions, Jesus's own speech.

Second, Iverson also demonstrates that the centurion's confession bears the characteristics of what Whitney Shiner calls an "applause line": a line in ancient rhetoric crafted to illicit a strong "affiliative response" from the audience.[81] Shiner identifies three characteristics that typically mark occasions for audience applause in ancient performances and oratory, namely (a) the reinforcement of key values, (b) the use of stylized language, and (c) placement at the conclusion of a scene or at natural breaks in the narrative.[82] By comparison, the centurion's statement displays all three characteristics: (a) it reinforces the central identity of Jesus throughout the narrative as a whole; (b) "[t]he repetition of /o/, /os/, and /ō/ sounds creates a rhythmical quality that draws further attention to the significance of the pronouncement";[83] and (c) the centurion's words mark the conclusion of the death scene in 15:33-39, with 15:40-41 providing a brief transition to Jesus's burial (15:42-47).[84]

Finally, it is noteworthy that not one interpreter prior to the twentieth century (including Matthew and Luke) appears to have read the centurion's comment as sarcasm.[85] To the contrary, earlier interpreters universally regarded his words as a sincere confession, however ironic, symbolizing Jesus's ultimate triumph, just as Iverson suggests they would have done.[86] So, despite the seeming plausibility of Johnson's argument, close attention to Mark's narrative suggests that the centurion's confession is an instance of *dramatic* irony rather than mockery.[87]

7.5.2 υἱὸς θεοῦ ἦν: The Grammar of the Centurion's Confession

To affirm that the centurion appears to be sincere, however, is not yet to determine what he actually confesses. Capitalizing on the fact that υἱὸς θεοῦ lacks the article in Mark 15:39 (a departure from Mark's usual convention elsewhere, though cf. 1:1), Ezra

---

[81] Iverson, "Confession," 343; drawing on the work of Whitney T. Shiner, *Proclaiming the Gospel: First-Century Performance of Mark* (Harrisburg, PA: Trinity Press International, 2003), 153–70; idem, "Applause and Applause Lines in the Gospel of Mark," in *Rhetorics and Hermeneutics: Wilhelm Wuellner and His Influence*, ed. James D. Hester and David Hester, Emory Studies in Early Christianity 9 (New York: T&T Clark, 2004), 129–44.

[82] Shiner (*Proclaiming*, 154–56) examines discussions of applause in Lucian, *Pro imag.* 4; Seneca (the Elder), *Contr.* 7.4.10; Seneca (the Younger), *Ep.* 108.8-9; Quintilian, *Inst.* 5.13.42; 8.5.2-3, 13-14; 12.9.8; Cicero, *De. or.* 3.50.196; *Or. Brut.* 50.168; 63.214-19; Plutarch, *Rect. rat. aud.* 41d; and Tacitus, *Dial.* 20, 22, all of whom discuss various reasons why audiences might applaud a certain line, as well as techniques that can be used to gain applause.

[83] Iverson, "Confession," 343–44. Shiner himself makes similar arguments about the rhythmical quality produced by the repetition of "ou" sounds in Mark 1:1; see Shiner, *Proclaiming*, 162. In addition to this quality, we may note the use of ἀληθῶς, discussed above and the use of σχίζω in the previous verse (15:38), which helps create an inclusio between 15:38-39 and 1:10-11 as two more examples of heightened stylization.

[84] So Hooker, *Mark*, 379; Iverson, "Confession," 344; Gamel, *Mark 15:39*, 41.

[85] Matt 27:54 removes any ambiguity by tying the centurion's confession to the preceding signs in vv. 51-53. Luke 23:47 alters the content of the confession significantly, but nonetheless portrays it in an unambiguously positive light.

[86] See Section 7.7 below.

[87] So Collins, *Mark*, 769. On the important distinction between *verbal irony* (i.e., mockery or sarcasm within a story) and *dramatic irony* (an ironic twist on the level of the story as a whole), see Iverson, "Confession," 331 n. 8.

Gould and others around the end of the nineteenth century opined that the centurion understands Jesus to be "not *the* Son of God, but *a* son of God, a hero after the heathen conception."[88] On the surface, Gould's view has the advantage of taking both grammar and the centurion's pagan background seriously.

Yet as E. C. Colwell demonstrated, definite predicate nominatives preceding the verb (e.g., υἱὸς θεοῦ ἦν) *usually* lack the article.[89] The lack of the article, therefore, does not necessarily indicate an indefinite reading. Forty years late, Philip B. Harner clarified that such constructions are primarily *qualitative* in force, rather than definite or indefinite.[90] Thus, the proper inference in Mark 15:39 is not that the centurion specifies either that Jesus is *a* son of God or *the* son of God, but that he attributes the *connotations* of υἱὸς θεοῦ to Jesus (whatever those might be).[91]

An even greater problem for Gould's interpretation, however, is that the generic phrase υἱὸς θεοῦ does not appear to have been used to describe semi-divine figures in the ancient world.[92] As Hengel explains, given the polytheistic nature of the pantheon, in which there were many gods, semi-divine heroes and demigods tended to be known as "son of Zeus," or some other god, rather than simply "son of god," which would only beg the question: which god?[93] Whatever the centurion claims about Jesus in Mark 15:39, then, the idea that he hails Jesus as a pagan hero is not so tenable as Gould and others once assumed.

7.6 The Son of God in the Roman World

By contrast, there was precisely one figure in the Roman world known as the "son of [a] god": namely, the emperor. As noted in the introduction of this book, Bousset and the early *religionsgeschichtliche Schule* originally treated the emperor cult as one more

---

[88] Gould, *Mark*, 295. See similarly Heinrich August Wilhelm Meyer, *Kritisch Exegetisches Handbuch Über Das Evangelium Des Matthäus*, 5th ed., KEK 1 (Göttingen: Vandenhoeck und Ruprecht, 1864), 602–03; G. F. Maclear, *The Gospel According to St. Mark: With Notes and Introduction* (Cambridge: Cambridge University Press, 1877), 182; similarly Swete, *St. Mark*, 388; Alfred Plummer, *The Gospel According to St. Mark* (Cambridge: Cambridge University Press, 1914), 361. Variations of this view can also be found among more recent interpreters, such as Shiner ("Ambiguous," 4).

[89] E. C. Colwell, "A Definite Rule for the Use of the Article in the Greek New Testament," *JBL* 52 (1933): 12–21; Colwell's rule has sometimes been misquoted and/or misapplied to state that anarthrous predicate nominatives preceding the verb are always definite (the fallacy of assuming the converse). But while this misapplication has been rightly challenged, Colwell's *actual* rule has never been disproven.

[90] Philip B. Harner, "Qualitative Anarthrous Predicate Nouns: Mark 15:39 and John 1:1," *JBL* 92 (1973): 75–87.

[91] In Harner's ("Qualitative," 81) own words, "The word-order of [Mark 15:39] suggests that he was primarily concerned to say something about the meaning of Jesus' sonship rather than designate him as 'a' son or 'the' son of God at this point."

[92] See already Henry Alford (*Alford's Greek Testament: An Exegetical and Critical Commentary* [Grand Rapids: Guardian Press, 1976], 1:209) in direct response to Meyer: "When Meyer says that he must have used them in a heathen sense, meaning *hero* or *demigod*, we must first be shewn that '*Son of God*' was ever so used."

[93] Hengel, *Son of God*, 30; cf. Collins, "The Son of God among Greeks and Romans," 86–7; Gamel, *Mark 15.39*, 49. Peppard ("Son of God in Gentile Contexts," in *Son of God*, 138 n. 11) helpfully adds, "[t]here is a misconception 'son of god' was a common title. In fact, though divine sonship ideology

example of Hellenisitic "divine man" language and so afforded it little attention in its own right.⁹⁴ Yet more recent scholarship has recognized the emperor's designation *divi filius*/θεοῦ υἱός as an independent phenomenon with its own relevance to the NT.⁹⁵ The history behind this epithet is worth retracing at some length as a means of reconstructing an important facet of Mark's cultural encyclopedia.

7.6.1 Imperator Caesar Divi filius Augustus

The well-known story of Augustus's claim to divine sonship begins with the deification of his adoptive father, Julius Caesar, who had already received divine honors in his lifetime.⁹⁶ Following Caesar's death in 44 BCE, Octavian, along with his fellow triumvirs Marc Antony and Lepidus, compelled the senate to recognize his divinity formally.⁹⁷ He was officially deified by the senate as Divus Julius on January 1, 42 BCE.⁹⁸ Thereafter (41 BCE), Octavian began to refer to himself as *divi filius*, short for *divi Iuli filius* ("son of the deified Julius"). He had already worn this epithet for fourteen years by the time

---

as a grounding for claims to kingship was fairly common and claims of divine ancestry or election by specific named gods was too (e.g., 'son of Hercules'), the bare title 'son of god' in Greek, without a name for the deity, was applied almost exclusively to emperors (Augustus and successors) and Jesus." These claims are confirmed by a TLG search, which produces *zero* examples of υἱὸς θεοῦ (or any near equivalent) used in such a way.

⁹⁴ See Bousset, *Kyrios Christos*, 93–7. Even Hengel (*Son of God*, 30) quickly dismisses the emperor's designation as "son of god" as one more example within the Hellenistic world with no apparent relevance to the New Testament. One notable exception, however, is Deissmann (*Light from the Ancient East*, 342), who suggests that "there arises a polemical parallelism between the cult of the emperor and the cult of Christ, which makes itself felt where [Septuagint or Gospel terminology] happen to coincide [with imperial concepts] which sounded the same or similar."

⁹⁵ E.g., Winter (*Divine Honours*, 67–71) argues that the emperor's claim to be the son of a god posed a serious challenge for Christians who proclaimed Jesus to be *the* Son of God. Peppard (*Son of God*, 4, 46–9, and *passim*) similarly argues that Octavian's designation "son of a god" was unavoidable in the ancient world and gave rise to an inevitable contrast for the early Christians between Jesus and the emperor. Evans (*Mark 8:27–16:20*, 510) and Winn (*Purpose*, *passim*) go so far as to suggest that Mark presents Jesus as a counter-emperor to Vespasian (cf. Peppard, *Son of God*, 132–33). Gamel (*Mark 15.39*, 50–5) is less interested in the implicit contrast between Jesus and the emperor, but nevertheless believes that the imperial title served as a ready-at-hand model for Mark's readers of the kind of divine ruler that Jesus is.

⁹⁶ Lily Ross Taylor (*The Divinity of the Roman Emperor* [New York: Arno, 1975], 58–77) argues that Caesar intended to establish a divine monarchy in his lifetime "influenced chiefly by the traditions of the Hellenistic monarch handed down from the empire of Alexander" (58), which he encountered during his time in Egypt; cf. Stefan Weinstock, *Divus Julius* (Oxford: Clarendon, 1971), *passim*; Karl Galinsky, *Augustan Culture: An Interpretive Introduction* (Princeton: Princeton University Press, 1996), 312; Zsuzsanna Várhelyi, "Imperial Cult, Roman," *OEAGR* 4:54. In addition to claiming descent from Venus, Caesar was honored with a statue of him bearing the inscription *Deo Invicto* ("to the unconquered god") in 45 BCE, and was even called "Jupiter Julius" by the Senate during the final months of his life. See Dio, *Hist.* 43.45.3; 44.6.4; Cicero, *Att.* 12.45.3; 13.28.3.

⁹⁷ Dio, *Hist.* 47.18.4; cf. Várhelyi, "Imperial Cult," 4:55. In one of the uncannier accidents of history, a comet streaked across the sky for seven days during the games thrown by Octavian to celebrate Caesar's apotheosis; see Pliny, *Nat.* 2.93-94; Suetonius, *Jul.* 88; Horace, *Odes* 1.12.47; and the discussions in Taylor, *Divinity*, 90–91; S. R. F. Price, *Rituals and Power: The Roman Imperial Cult in Asia Minor* (Cambridge/New York: Cambridge University Press, 1984), 72.

⁹⁸ Plutarch, *Caes.*, 67.4; Weinstock, *Divus*, 399; Price, *Rituals and Power*, 72.

the senate conferred upon him the honorific Augustus (27 BCE),[99] at which time his full title became *Imperator Caesar Divi filius Augustus* or, in Greek, Αὐτοκράτωρ Καῖσαρ Θεοῦ υἱός Σεβαστός.[100] As his cognomen, *divi filius* effectively functioned like a nickname reminding everyone of his divine authority.[101] As Lily Ross Taylor observes in her classic study, "Octavian at any rate allowed no one to forget his connection with Caesar and with Caesar's divine ancestors. He signed himself henceforth *divi filius*, son of god, in his official name and he issued coins with representations of Aeneas carrying Anchises from Troy."[102]

Although no emperor after Augustus bore the precise name *divi filius*, Rome's first emperor had established a pattern for his successors, who instead often styled themselves "son of the god Augustus" (*divi Augusti filius*/Θεοῦ Σεβαστοῦ υἱός).[103] Caligula, Claudius, Nero, and others even designated themselves gods on earth.[104] So while Tae Hun Kim is probably correct that the precise designation υἱὸς θεοῦ would have evoked the memory of Augustus in specific (as, indeed, every subsequent emperor sought to evoke his memory in general), the epithet also became associated the office of the emperor more generally.[105]

[99] Meret Bochum Strothmann, "Augustus," BNP 2:364; Victor Ehrenberg and A. H. M. Jones, *Documents Illustrating the Reigns of Augustus & Tiberius* (2nd ed. Oxford: Clarendon, 1976), 32; cf. Adela Yarbro Collins, "The Worship of Jesus and the Imperial Cult," in *The Jewish Roots of Christological Monotheism: Papers from the St. Andrews Conference on the Historical Origins of the Worship of Jesus*, ed. Carey C. Newman, James R. Davila, and Gladys S. Lewis, JSJSup 63 (Leiden/Boston: Brill, 1999), 253; Várhelyi, "Imperial Cult," 55.

[100] Várhelyi, "Imperial Cult," 55; Collins, "Imperial Cult," 254. For numismatic and epigraphic evidence see further Stefan Weinstock, *Divus Julius*, plate 29, coin no. 12; and Ehrenberg and Jones, *Documents*, no. 108 (91), no. 105 (93). Other stylings of Augustus's name include ἡ Καίσαρος κράτησις θεοῦ υἱοῦ, "The mastery of Caesar, son of God" (P.Ryl. 601; *PSI* 1150); *Imperator Caesar divi filius Augustus*, "Emperor Caesar Augustus, son of god" (*SB* 401; BGU 628); Καίσαρος θεοῦ υἱὸς αὐτοκράτωρ, Caesar, son of god, Emperor" (P.Teb. 382); Καίσαρος αὐτοκράτωρ θεοῦ υἱὸς Ζεὺς ἐλευθέριος Σεβαστός, "Emperor Caesar, son of God, Zeus the liberator, Augustus" (P.Oslo. 26; *SB*8824); Αὐτολράτορα Καίσαρα θεοῦ υἱὸν θεὸν Σεβαστὸν Ἰάσης γῆς καὶ θαλάσσης ἐπόπτην, "The Emperor, Caesar, son of god, the god Augustus, the overseer of every land and sea" (*IGR* 1:901; cf. *IGR* 4:309, 315); θεοῦ Καίσ[α] | ρος θεοῦ υἱοῦ Σεβαστοῦ Σωτῆρος Ἐλευθερίου, "Caesar, son of god, Augustus, Savior, Liberator (SEG XI 922–23).

[101] See Ronald Syme, "Imperator Caesar: A Study in Nomenclature," in *Augustus*, ed. J. C. Edmondson, Edinburgh Readings on the Ancient World. (Edinburgh: Edinburgh University Press, 2009), 40–59; as well as Galinsky, *Augustan Culture*, 319; Kim, "Υἱός Θεοῦ," 237; Collins, "Imperial Cult," 256.

[102] Taylor, *Divinity*, 106. For further examples of letters in which Augustus describes himself as *divi filius*, see Winter, *Divine Honours*, 67–8.

[103] As Winter (*Divine Honours*, 67) notes, "all the remaining Julio-Claudian emperors, Tiberius, Gaius, Claudius and Nero, were also addressed, or designated themselves in official decrees as 'a son of a god [i.e., Augustus].'" See, e.g., *IGRR* 3.933 = *OGI* 2.583.

[104] In contrast to Tiberius and Germanicus, Caligula notoriously deified himself during his own lifetime (e.g., νέωι θεῶι, "new god" [*IGR* 4:1094]); thus, he did not use any variant of *divi filius*/θεοῦ υἱός; yet even Caligula referred to himself as Σεβαστοῦ υἱὸν νέον Ἄρη ("Son of Augustus, a new Ares") (*CIA* 3:444). Claudius likewise deified himself, but not entirely apart from a connection to Augustus: θεὸς Κλαύδιος ("Claudius, god") (*PSI* 1235; P.Oxy. 713); θεὸς Καίσαρ ("Caesar, god") (P.Oxy. 808; P.Oxy. 1021); θεὸς Σεβαστός ("Augustus, god") (P.Mich. 244). Nero, on the other hand, styled himself τὸν υἱὸν τοῦ μεγίστου θεῶν ("the son of the greatest of the gods") (*IM* 157b). See further the discussions in Winter, *Divine Honours*, 214–21; and Peppard, "Son of God in Gentile Contexts," in *Son of God*, 138–48.

[105] Kim ("Υἱός Θεοῦ," 221–41 [here, 240]) stresses that the epithet *divi filius* referred exclusively to Augustus himself. But while Kim is correct that *divi filius* continues to bear special reference to Augustus wherever it appears in the nomenclature of later emperors, it also acquires a lasting connection with the person and office of the emperor in general; see Collins, "Imperial Cult," 254; Várhelyi, "Imperial Cult," 4:55-6.

In Mark 15:39, then, both "the circumstances" (i.e., that the speaker is a Roman centurion) "and diction" of the anarthrous υἱὸς θεοῦ "are consistent with features of the Roman imperial cult," as Kim observes.[106] Notably, some manuscripts of Mark 15:39, including the majority of old Latin manuscripts, even reverse the word order so that it matches the usual word order of the imperial designation, θεοῦ υἱὸς (cf. Matt 27:54).[107]

7.6.2 A Pervasive Ideology

Classical scholars in recent years have often stated that there was no such thing as the imperial cult *per se*—that is, as a cultic institution independent of Rome's larger religio-political matrix. Instead, the emperor's cult was simply one facet of Rome's civic religion in general.[108] So Simon Price: "the imperial cult, along with politics and diplomacy, constructed the reality of the Roman empire."[109] One should not, as such, imagine that the emperor's title, *divi filius*, occurred only sparingly throughout the empire. Rather, as Fronto states, the emperor was *usquequaque ubique* ("on all occasions, everywhere").[110]

Research over the last thirty years has revealed the spread of Roman imperial ideology to the furthest reaches of the empire, both east and west, including Asia, North Africa, Syria, and even Judea via a wealth of material and literary evidence.[111] According to Peppard, "Modern scholars estimate that between 25,000 and 50,000 portraits of

---

[106] Kim, "Υἱός Θεοῦ" 223.
[107] See D 565 *l* 844 it ff2; additionally, 1071 reads θεοῦ υἱὸς ἦν ὁ ἄνθρωπος οὗτος. According to Franz Joseph Dölger (*ΙΧΘΥΣ: Das Fischsymbol in frühchristlicher Zeit*, 3 vols [Münster: Aschendorff, 1910], 1:403–05), the most probable explanations for the reading θεοῦ υἱὸς are either that it reflects the language of the imperial cult or its use in the acronym Ἰησοῦ Χριστοῦ Θεοῦ Υἱὸς Σωτήρ. See similarly Collins, "Son of God Among Greeks and Romans," 96; idem, *Mark*, 768. On the other hand, it is also possible that these mss. have assimilated the centurion's confession to match Matt 27:54 (cf. Matt 14:33 and 27:43, which reads θεοῦ εἰμι υἱός).
[108] Karl Galinsky, *Augustus: Introduction to the Life of an Emperor* (New York: Cambridge University Press, 2012), 169.
[109] Price, *Rituals and Power*, 71; also cited by Galinsky, *Augustus*, 170. Cf. Mary Beard, John North, and S. R. F. Price (*Religions of Rome*, 2 vols [Cambridge/New York: Cambridge University Press, 1998], 1:360), who caution that the imperial cult is often exaggerated precisely insofar as it is imagined to be an independent religious entity. Rather, the worship of the *divi* had its place within Rome's broader civic religion.
[110] Ep. 4.12; also cited by Peppard, "Son of God in Gentile Contexts," in *Son of God*, 137. See also Winter (*Divine Honours*, 1): "imperial cultic phenomena were all-pervasive and inescapable."
[111] See Paul Zanker, *The Power of Images in the Age of Augustus* (Ann Arbor: University of Michigan Press, 1988), 297–333; Galinsky, *Augustan Culture*, 323–33; Clifford Ando, *Imperial Ideology and Provincial Loyalty in the Roman Empire* (Berkeley: University of California Press, 2000), *passim*; Richard Gordon, "The Roman Imperial Cult and the Question of Power," in *The Religious History of the Roman Empire: Pagans, Jews, and Christians*, ed. John North and S. R. F. Price, Oxford Readings in Classical Studies. (New York: Oxford University Press, 2011), 37–70; and the essays in "Part IV: The Impact of Augustus in the Roman Provinces" of Edmondson (ed.), *Augustus*, 419–82. On Judea specifically see especially Monika Bernett, *Der Kaiserkult in Judäa unter den Herodiern und Römern: Untersuchungen zur politischen und religiösen Geschichte Judäas von 30 v. bis 66 n. Chr*, WUNT 203 (Tübingen: Mohr Siebeck, 2007). In addition to the coins and inscriptions noted above, see the discussions of imperial coinage in Ando, *Ideology*, 215–28; and Carlos F. Noreña, "The Communication of the Emperor's Virtues," *JRS* 91 (2001): 146–68. As Peppard (*Son of God*, 91) aptly explains, "Coins were by far the most abundant, reliable, and portable means of imperial news and values.... Furthermore, coins were uniquely effective at controlling a message–it was quite against the interest of their recipients to deface their texts and images." For further discussions of Imperial Rome's material culture, see Zanker, *Images, passim*; Justin J. Meggitt, "Taking the Emperor's Clothes

Augustus existed in the Roman Empire—about one portrait for every 1,000–2,000 people," which is to say, "there were as many portraits of Augustus *per capita* then as there are Christian churches *per capita* now in the United States."[112] Peppard suggests that "[t]o get a sense of how widespread the *imago* of Augustus was, we might imagine seeing him in the place of every church in an American neighborhood or city."[113]

A striking example of the rhetoric surrounding the emperor occurs in the calendar inscription from Priene (modern-day Turkey). The relevant portion reads:

> Since Providence, which has ordered all things of our life, has eagerly and most zealously mustered the perfect culmination for our lives by giving us Augustus, whom she filled with virtue for the benefit of humankind, sending him as a savior [σωτήρ], both for us and those after us, that he might end war and set all things in order; and since Caesar, when he appeared, surpassed the hopes of all those who had anticipated good tidings [εὐαγγέλια], not only surpassing all benefactors before him, but not even leaving those to come any hope of surpassing him; and since the birthday of the god [Augustus] was the beginning for the world of the good tidings that came by reason of him [ἦρξεν δὲ τῶι κόσμωι τῶν δι'αὐτὸν εὐαγγελίων ἡ γενέθλιος τοῦ θεοῦ]. . . . Therefore, with good fortune and deliverance, it was decreed by the Greeks in Asia, that the New Year for all cities should begin on 23 September, which is the birthday of Augustus.[114]

As previously noted, this inscription contains a number of parallels with Mark's incipit (1:1). Not only is Caesar hailed as "god" and "savior," but his birth is described as the beginning of "the good tidings" for the world—the "soteriological" telos of history, one might say.[115] Mark may not have known this particular inscription, of course, but neither this inscription nor its rhetoric were unique.[116]

First-century Palestine was not free from the influence of the emperor's cult either.[117] Archaeological evidence suggests that Herod the Great was a strong supporter

---

Seriously: The New Testament and the Roman Emperor," in *The Quest for Wisdom: Essays in Honour of Philip Budd*, ed. Christine E. Joynes (Cambridge: Orchard Academic, 2002), 143–69; and Andrew Wallace-Hadrill, *Rome's Cultural Revolution* (New York: Cambridge University Press, 2008); idem, *Augustan Rome*, 2nd ed. (New York: Bloomsbury Academic, 2018).

[112] Peppard, *Son of God*, 91.
[113] Ibid., 91.
[114] Translation adapted from Galinsky, *Augustus*, 162. For the Greek text see *OGIS* 458.
[115] "Soteriological" is Galinsky (*Augustan Culture*, 313)'s own characterization of Rome's claims about Augustus here and elsewhere.
[116] See Edmondson ("Introduction to Part IV: The Impact of Augustus in the Roman Provinces," in *Augustus*, 420): "This is just one isolated example of the many profound changes that affected the lives of the fifty million or so inhabitants of the Roman Empire during the age of Augustus." Likewise, as Beard, North, and Price (*Relgions*, 1:4) state, no two calendars were exactly the same, but they are all recognizable as variations on the same theme. Most of those calendars that have survived come from Italy and date to the age of Augustus. The calendar itself was a document of religious importance since it served as the schedule of Roman rituals and festivals.
[117] See esp. Bernett, *Kaiserkult, passim*; idem, "Roman Imperial Cult in the Galilee: Structures, Functions, and Dynamics," in *Religion, Ethnicity and Identity in Ancient Galilee: A Region in Transition*, ed. Jürgen Zangenberg, Harold W. Attridge, and Dale B. Martin, WUNT 210 (Tübingen: Mohr Siebeck,

of the cult. As an example, some years after he was named "king of the Jews" by Antony and Octavian, Herod helped build the city of Nicopolis to commemorate Octavian's victory at Actium.[118] Subsequently, Herod Hellenized and renamed the city of Samaria "Sebaste" in honor of Augustus.[119] "Of even greater significance than increasing the size of the city," writes Mary Smallwood,

> was the establishment of the imperial cult, a facet of the policy of Hellenization which Herod pursued wherever and whenever he could: a temple of Augustus in a large precinct stood conspicuously on the summit of the hill in the centre of the city—an engineering feat, incidentally, of some magnitude.[120]

Following Sebaste came Caesarea, also named for Augustus, which had a temple dedicated to the emperor's cult complete with ominous statues of Augustus and Roma, and a third temple dedicated to Augustus near Banias, which would later become Caesarea Philippi.[121] After the completion of Caesarea (a project of ten years or more), Herod decreed a festival to be held in Augustus's honor every four years.[122] Although Herod was cautious enough not to institute the emperor's cult in Jerusalem itself, even there he established a four-yearly festival honoring Augustus, linked to the cult.[123]

Furthermore, Joan Taylor has analyzed numismatic and epigraphic evidence demonstrating that, like Herod, Pontius Pilate was also an ardent promoter of the emperor's cult in Judea, including Jerusalem itself.[124] Taylor's findings are consistent with Beard, North, and Price's comment that "in the provinces emperor and governor filled the role occupied in Italy by the *pontifices*"; thus, it was the provincial governor's responsibility to supervise "religious matters along essentially *Roman* guidelines."[125]

The simple but important point to state, then, is that no matter where Mark and his intended audience were located in the ancient world, whether Rome, Syria, or anywhere else within the boundaries of the empire, they cannot have escaped familiarity with

---

2007), 337–56. Bernett ("Imperial Cult," 337) observes that scholars have "never ignored" the existence of the imperial cult in Herodian Palestine, but have never previously made it a "topic of historical analysis in its own right," either.

[118] Smallwood, *Roman Rule*, 56, 70. See Josephus, *Ant.* 15.195-201; *War* 1.391-95.

[119] Josephus, *Ant.* 25.292-93, 296-98; *War* 1.403; see Smallwood, *Roman Rule*, 77; and further Bernett, *Kaiserkult*, 66–97.

[120] Smallwood, *Roman Rule*, 78.

[121] Josephus, *Ant.* 15.331-41, 363-64; *War* 1.404-06, 408-15; See Bernett, *Kaiserkult*, 98–125.

[122] Smallwood, *Roman Rule*, 79.

[123] Smallwood, *Roman Rule*, 84. See also Winter, *Divine Honours*, 96-8 on Herod's promotion of the cult.

[124] Joan E. Taylor, "Pontius Pilate and the Imperial Cult in Roman Judaea," *NTS* 52 (2006): 555–82. Taylor examines bronze coins minted in Jerusalem by Pilate between 29 and 31 CE, which bear images closely associated with the imperial cult (the *lituus* and the *simpulum*). One coin dated to 31 was still in the process of being manufactured. Additionally, Taylor provides a thorough analysis of the famed "Pilate Inscription" from Caesarea, the last line of which should probably be restored to read *divi Augusti filius* ("son of the deified Augustus"). These two pieces of material evidence, along with the account in Philo, suggest that Pilate was an active promoter of the imperial cult. On Pilate's promotion of the imperial cult in general, see also Bernett, *Kaiserkult*, 200.

[125] Beard, North, and Price, *Religions*, 1:321. See also Philo's account (*Legat.* 199-205) of Pilate setting up shields bearing images associated with the imperial cult in Jerusalem.

Rome's imperial rhetoric, including the emperor's title "son of god." As Peppard reminds us, the emperor was, after all, "the most famous 'son of God' in the Roman world."[126]

7.6.3 The Centurion in First-Century Perspective

Per Johnson's earlier point, then, we should consider what expectations Mark's audience would have had of the centurion himself. As often noted, centurions formed the backbone of the Roman army both by serving as a bridge between the common soldiers and higher ranks, and by maintaining discipline throughout the ranks.[127] Their reputation was one of unswerving loyalty.[128] Under Augustus and his successors centurions were, in fact, responsible for ensuring the army's loyalty to the emperor at large.[129] For this reason, commissions were sometimes approved by the emperor himself, while others were approved by the provincial governor.[130] Tacitus, however, scorns the idea of a general selecting his own centurions.[131]

Like all soldiers, centurions took a formal oath of loyalty known as the *sacramentum*, punishable by death if violated.[132] In the Imperial era, the *sacramentum* "mentioned the emperor by name and bound the soldiers to him by ties of personal loyalty and obedience to his instructions."[133] As such, the oath almost certainly would have included the very words *divi filius* for those emperors whose name and title included some variation of them.[134] All legions, likewise, carried *imagos imperatoris* ("images of

---

[126] Peppard, *Son of God*, 4.
[127] See C. E. Brand, *Roman Military Law* (Austin: University of Texas Press, 1968), 51; Michael Grant, *The Army of the Caesars* (New York: Scribner's, 1974), 19–20; cf. J. Brian Campbell, "Centurio," in BNP 3:127; Henry Michael Denne Parker and Geoffrey Walter Richardson, "Centurio," in *OCD*, 298–99.
[128] See, e.g., Tacitus, *Ann.* 1.23.4; 1.24.3.
[129] Grant, *Army*, 19–20, 73–5. Julius Caesar had depended heavily on his centurions not only for the efficiency of his army, but for their loyalty to himself. Augustus subsequently formalized this trend. As Brian Dobson ("The Significance of the Centurion and the 'Primipilaris' in the Roman Army and Administration," *ANRW* 2.1.395–97, 432) explains, Octavian emerged "well aware how much his power depended on the loyalty of his army, and how great a part in maintaining control over that army the centurions played" (395). Accordingly, he instituted a fixed term of service, and a gratuity of land or money guaranteed by the emperor himself, in addition to opening up the possibility of promotion to equestrian rank upon retirement. "The logic is unquestionable: ... they owed everything to the emperor" (397).
[130] Juvenal, *Satires*, 14.193; see also Grant, *Army*, 74; G. R. Watson, *The Roman Soldier*, Aspects of Greek and Roman Life (London: Thames & Hudson, 1969), 87. In most cases, promotions to the rank of centurion came only after 16–20 years of service in the legions or the praetorian guard (see Dobson, "Significance," 403–04).
[131] *Ann.* 3.49.
[132] On the *sacramentum* as the most sacred of all Roman oaths, see Brand, *Military*, 91; Grant, *Army*, 159; J. B. Campbell, *The Emperor and the Roman Army, 31 BC–AD 235* (New York: Oxford University Press, 1984), 23–5. The exact wording of the *sacramentum* has not survived, but its content is preserved by both Polybius 6.21 and Livy 22.38.
[133] Campbell, *Emperor*, 25.
[134] Campbell (*Emperor*, 130) notes that emperors were regularly known throughout the army by their cognomina; cf. Syme ("Imperator Caesar," in *Augustus*, 40–59): illustrious persons were frequently known by their cognomina. In the case of Augustus, his adoption of *divi filius* as a cognomen was hardly accidental. According to Taylor (*Divinity*, 57–78), soldiers also took religious oaths to the emperor, praising him as either a god or the son of a god. Even in the Christian period, Vegetius (*Ep. Mil.* 2.5) records that soldiers swore an oath to the Trinity and "to the majesty of the emperor, for when the emperor has taken the name of Augustus, *as if it were to a present and bodily god, faithful* allegiance must be rendered" (quoted in Galinsky, *Augustan Culture*, 316 [emphasis added]).

the emperor"), to which they made religious observances.¹³⁵ According to Tertullian, soldiers "venerated the standards, swore by the standards, set the standards before all the gods."¹³⁶ Even if Tertullian exaggerates, both Josephus and Dio also record religious observances for the emperor among Roman soldiers.¹³⁷ Moreover, the Roman military calendar shows a "large number of festivals devoted to the reigning emperor and his deified ancestors," even to the point of eclipsing the other gods.¹³⁸ In short, soldiers were far more entrenched than most in the emperor's cult, and centurions even more so than most soldiers. It seems inevitable, then, that a centurion's first association with the words υἱὸς θεοῦ would be with the emperor.

7.6.4 Summary

To summarize: (1) the emperor was the one figure in the ancient Roman world widely known as "son of god"; (2) such language permeated every corner of the empire; and (3) centurions were tightly bound to this "confession." Finally, we may add that Mark and his audience knew all of these facts far better than modern scholars, not as a matter of book knowledge, but as realities of day-to-day life. The most natural assumption, therefore, is that the centurion's confession, υἱὸς θεοῦ ἦν borrows from the language of the emperor's cult.¹³⁹

That is not to suggest, of course, that the centurion proclaims Jesus to be the emperor. Such a statement would manifestly absurd given the circumstances (Jesus having just died on a Roman cross). Rather, I suggest that the centurion confesses in the only language available to him what he has, by divine revelation, come to see (ἰδών) as the truth (ἀληθῶς), that Jesus is in reality what Rome claimed Caesar to be: the rightful ruler of the world on whom all its hopes and salvation rest.¹⁴⁰ In this respect, the centurion's words constitute a virtual shift of "allegiance," as Evans suggests, and, so, a true confession.¹⁴¹ In the most ironic moment of the Gospel so far, the centurion effectively bows the knee to the crucified Jewish Messiah.

---

¹³⁵ Campbell, *Emperor*, 96–7; cf. Tacitus (*Ann.* 1.39), who records that statues of the emperor were kept in the camp temple.

¹³⁶ *Apol.* 16.8.

¹³⁷ Josephus, *War* 6.316; Dio 40.18.

¹³⁸ Campbell, *Emperor*, 99.

¹³⁹ Recall Eco, *Role*, 31–33. All narrative contexts invariably "blow up" (or activate) certain frames within the reader's cultural encyclopedia and "narcotize" others. On the one hand, Mark's entire narrative up to this point activates Psalm 2; on the other hand, the very identity of the speaker, a Roman centurion, in 15:39 activates an altogether different frame of reference (i.e., the imperial title). The effect of Mark's narrative at this point is thus to create something akin to what Ricoeur (*Oneself*, 141) calls "discordant concordance": the "synthesis of the heterogeneous," created by a "competition between a demand for concordance," on the one hand, "and the admission of discordances," on the other.

¹⁴⁰ In addition to the various references above, if one wishes to gain a sense of the sorts of salvific and even eschatological hopes Rome regularly attached to Caesar's status as *divi filius*, one ultimately need only read Virgil's *Aeneid* (6.791-798): "this in truth is he whom you so often hear promised you, Augustus Caesar, son of a god, who will again establish a golden age in Latium amid fields once ruled by Saturn; he will advance his empire beyond the Garamants and Indians to a land which lies beyond our stars, beyond the path of year and sun, where sky-bearing Atlas wheels on his shoulders the blazing star-studded sphere" (trans. Fairclough, LCL).

¹⁴¹ Evans, *Mark 8:27–16:20*, 510.

7.7 Excursus: A History of Irony

In point of fact, dramatic irony is how most interpreters in history have understood the centurion's confession. Cranfield speaks for many modern interpreters when he states that, whatever the centurion meant personally, his words amount to "an unwitting proclamation of the truth. For *Mark* it is clearly important that at this point, whether intentionally or unintentionally, the truth was publicly declared."[142] Like Pilate and even the *titulus* above the cross, the centurion says more than he knows. In literary terms, this move is akin to what Aristotle called a περιπέτεια: a sudden overthrow or turning point at a pivotal moment in a narrative.[143] Whereas Jesus is steadily mocked throughout Mark 15, the centurion's confession signifies a dramatic reversal that turns the previous mockery on its head: in Marcus's words, the moment when parody becomes reality.

This is, in fact, how virtually all exegetes prior to the nineteenth century understood the centurion's words. Matthew Henry, for instance, maintained that the meaning of the centurion's confession lies in its contrast with the previous mockery, for "God can maintain and assert the honour of a truth when it seems to be crushed and run down."[144] Henry goes on to emphasize the special irony bound up in the centurion's identity as a Roman soldier "who knew not the scriptures which were now fulfilled."[145] Hugo Grotius suggests that the centurion's confession is a symbol and foreshadowing of the Romans' obedience to Christ.[146] So too our earliest commentary on Mark: the point of the centurion's confession is that "[t]he Gentile people confesses!"[147] These ideas and others can already be found in Calvin's *Commentary on a Harmony of the Evangelists*. In Calvin's estimation:

> the Evangelists mention this circumstance respecting [the centurion] for the purpose of heightening their description of [Jesus as the Son of God]: for it is

---

[142] Cranfield, *Mark*, 460. Just prior to this remark, Cranfield states: "What exactly *the centurion* meant by υἱὸς θεοῦ we cannot be sure. Quite possibly he used the term in a Gentile sense—'demi-god,' 'hero.'"; cf. Taylor, *Mark*, 597. While we have seen that Cranfield's own guess is almost certainly incorrect, in light of more recent scholarship, his intuition that the centurion speaks more truly than he knows remains valid.

[143] See Aristotle, *Poetics*, 1.1452a22–29; Lausberg, *Handbook*, §1212. Though περιπέτεια is most often a turn for the worst, it is not always so. According to Andreas Mehl (*Roman Historiography: An Introduction to Its Basic Aspects and Development*, Blackwell Introductions to the Classical World 11 [Malden, MA: Wiley-Blackwell, 2011], 20), περιπέτεια "became a customary and favorite rhetorical means for Roman historians from the time of Lucius Calpurnius Piso [c. 105–43 BCE]."

[144] Matthew Henry, *Matthew Henry's Commentary on the Whole Bible* (Peabody: Hendrickson, 2009), 5:350, commenting on Matt 27:54. See similarly Henry's comments on Mark 15:39: "Our Lord Jesus, even in the depth of his suffering and humiliation, was the Son of God, and was declared to be so *with power*" (*Commentary*, 5:457). All italics are Henry's.

[145] Ibid., 5:350. See similarly Matthew Poole, *A Commentary on the Holy Bible* (Edinburgh; Carlisle, PA: Banner of Truth Trust, 1962), 3:142; John Gill, *Gill's Commentary* (Grand Rapids: Baker, 1980), 5:398; and Theodor Zahn, *Das Evangelium des Matthäus* (Wuppertal: R. Brockhaus, 1984), 717.

[146] Hugo Grotius, *Annotation on the New Testament*, 577 on Matt 27:54.

[147] *Exp. Marc.* 15:39 (CChr 82).

Part 2: *The Centurion's Confession (Mark 15:39)* 171

wonderful that an irreligious man, who had not been instructed in the Law, and was ignorant of true religion, should form so correct a judgment from the signs which he beheld.[148]

For Calvin, then, the irony of the centurion's confession, owing precisely to his cultural and religious identity, is the very point of its telling in the Gospel narratives.

Yet such thinking was hardly new even in the sixteenth century. Aphrahat had already stated the basic point centuries earlier: "His preachers came out of the People that persecuted Him."[149] Jerome, moreover, highlights the sharp irony of the fact that the centurion makes his confession "before the cross, in the very scandal of the Passion."[150] That a crucifixion is of all occasions the least likely for such a confession is not lost on Jerome; to the contrary, he sees it as the very significance of the episode.

One of the most intriguing comments of all comes from Augustine's *De Consensu evangelistarum*. As the title of the work suggests, Augustine attempts to reconcile differences between Matthew, Mark, and Luke. When commenting specifically on the contrast between δίκαιος in Luke's version of the confession (23:47) and υἱὸς θεοῦ/ θεοῦ υἱός in Mark and Matthew, Augustine offers the following suggestions: "it may be the case that the centurion did not really understand Him to be the Only-begotten, equal with the Father; but that he called Him the Son of God simply because he believed Him to be a righteous man, as many righteous men have been named sons of God."[151] In essence, Augustine suggests that we are dealing with a case of divinely-ordained dramatic irony, which manifests itself in the contrast between the centurion's own understanding and the service into which his words are pressed within the Gospel passion narratives.[152] The centurion, as such, speaks truer than he knows. Again, Matthew Henry espouses a similar logic: "'Surely,' thinks [the centurion], 'this must be some divine person, highly beloved of God.' This he expresses by such words as denote his eternal generation as God, and his special designation to the office of Mediator, *though he meant not so*."[153]

These few examples demonstrate that earlier (including ancient) readers, were just as aware of the *prima facie* unlikelihood and, hence, irony of the centurion's confession as any modern reader. But for the first eighteen centuries of interpretation, this irony was universally regarded as the very point; the evangelists did not report the centurion's words because they were ordinary but because they were *extra*ordinary.

---

[148] Jean Calvin, *Commentary on a Harmony of the Evangelists, Matthew, Mark, and Luke*, vol. 3, trans. William Pringle, *Calvin's Commentaries* 17 (Grand Rapids: Baker, 1989), 326.

[149] Aphrahat, *Dem.* 21.20 (*PS* 1:982; trans. *NPNF* 13:400). Cf. Leo the Great, *Serm.* 68.3 (*PL* 54:375a); Hilary, *Comm. Matt.* 33.7 (*PL* 9:1075b); Bede, *Exp. Marc.* IV.1594-1601 (CChr 120); Pseudo-Jerome, *Comm. Marc., ad loc.* (*PL* 30:640a); Theophylact, *Comm. Marc., ad loc.* (*PG* 123:671d); Albertus Magnus, *Enarrat. Marc.*, 742; Cornelius Cornelii à Lapide, *Commentaria in Scripturam Sacram*, ed. Augustine Crampon (Paris: Ludovicus Vives, 1868), 15:637.

[150] Jerome, *Comm. Matt., ad loc.* (*PL* 26:214a).

[151] Augustine, *Cons.*, 20.57 (*PL* 34:1193–94). Augustine may be influenced here the scriptural tradition of designating the righteous "sons of God" (e.g., Gen 6:2, 4; Deut 14:1; Isa 63:8; Sir 4:10; Wis 2:18), since it is difficult to locate any Greco-Roman tradition thereof.

[152] See similarly Juan de Maldonado, *A Commentary on the Holy Gospels*, trans. George John Davie, Catholic Standard Library (London: J. Hodges, 1888), 2:568; and Lapide, *Commentaria*, 637.

[153] Henry (*Commentary*, 5:457) on Mark 15:39, italics added.

7.8 The Centurion's Confession and the Fulfillment of Psalm 2

At the very point at which we perceive the likely meaning of his words vis-à-vis the emperor, the centurion's confession is, in fact, astonishingly reminiscent of the outcome anticipated in Psalm 2. A representative of the reigning world empire bows the knee to God's Son, the Messiah, just as in Ps 2:7-8, we read:

> I will tell the Lord's decree: He said to me, "You are my Son! Today I have begotten you. Ask of me, and *I will give you the nations as your inheritance* and the ends of the earth as your possession."

In the confession of a Roman officer from the foot of the cross, the Son symbolically begins to inherit the nations: "[t]he Gentile people confesses."[154] In recent years, Richard Hays has also recognized a profound connection between the centurion's confession and Psalm 2. As Hays writes,

> the centurion not only answers the question, "Who really is the Son of God?" but does so precisely by unwittingly echoing Psalm 2, the very psalm that proclaims the futility of the efforts of kings and nations to conspire "against the Lord and his anointed" (LXX: κατὰ τοῦ κυρίου καὶ κατὰ τοῦ χριστοῦ αὐτοῦ; Ps 2:2). The Gentile outsider, the solider who had been the tool of "the kings of the earth" to plot the death of the Lord's anointed, now joins the heavenly voice in naming Jesus, the crucified Messiah, as God's true Son. The dramatic irony of this paradoxical reversal ... is felt only by the reader who hears the reprise of the scriptural intertext from Psalm 2:7.[155]

The reprise to which Hays refers has, of course, been the subject of much of this book. First heard in 1:11, "You are my Son," the echo of YHWH's royal decree in Ps 2:7 resounds in each of the two prior architectonic acclamations of Jesus's sonship in Mark (cf. 9:7) leading up to the third in 15:39. The reader who has recognized this pattern thus far is automatically encouraged to think of Ps 2:7 in Mark 15:39 as well. As Gamel states, it is finally hard to imagine that "the centurion means something different than the heavenly voice in 1.11 and 9.7, something other than the demons in [3.11 and] 5.7 and the high priest in 14.61"—that is, something apart from the narrative arc that began at Jesus's baptism.[156] In fact, Mark powerfully signals to us that we should do just the opposite.

---

[154] *Exp. Marc.* 15:39 (CChr 82).
[155] Hays, *Gospels*, 96. See also Nenad Božović ("Ps 2,7-8 im Narrativ des Markusevangeliums," in *Christ of the Sacred Stories*, ed. Predrag Dragutinović et al., WUNT 2/453 [Tübingen: Mohr Siebeck, 2017], 325–45) who also argues that the schema of Ps 2:7-8 underlies Mark 15:39 as well as 1:11 and 9:7. According to Božović, however, the chief connection between Mark 15:38-39 and Psalm 2 is actually the rending of the temple veil in 15:38, which ostensibly fulfills Ps 2:8 insofar as it suggests unrestricted access to God among all the nations. Though I agree with Božović's assessment that Psalm 2 informs all three of Mark's architectonic acclamations of Jesus's sonship (1:11; 9:7; 15:39) on some level, I find this specific argument less convincing.
[156] Gamel, *Mark 15.39*, 48. To borrow a term from Samuel Taylor Coleridge (*Biographia Literaria*, ed. James Engell and W. Jackson Bate, reprint ed., The Collected Works of Samuel Taylor Coleridge 7 [Princeton: Princeton University Press, 1985], 140, 195), there is an esemplastic quality to Mark's use of son-of-God language that implies a unified meaning.

7.8.1 The Inclusio of Mark 1:10-11 and 15:38-39 Revisited

It is just here that we must revisit the *inclusio* formed by Mark 1:10-11 and 15:38-39, which bids us to recall God's pronouncement in 1:11 in particular. As we have seen the rending (ἐσχίσθη) of the temple veil followed by the centurion's confession, "Truly, this man was the Son of God," distinctly mirrors the rending (σχιζομένους) of the heavens at Jesus's baptism, followed by God's pronouncement, "You are My Son." Mark, that is, deliberately recalls our attention to this earlier moment in the narrative, when Jesus was first introduced to us as God's Son, so as to hear the centurion's confession in the light of God's original pronouncement.[157] To do so, however, is also to hear the centurion's confession in the light of the royal decree of Ps 2:7, from which the words of the heavenly voice derive. If we Mark's *inclusio* seriously, then, he has effectively told us that we are meant to hear the centurion's confession in the light of Psalm 2.

In Mark 1:11, after all, God speaks not merely to recall but to *enact* the royal decree from the psalm, thereby anointing Jesus as his messianic vice-regent, who will inherit the nations and establish his reign on earth. Now, at the opposite end of the Gospel, the centurion's confession signifies that the fulfillment of that royal anointing, Jesus's enthronement, has indeed taken place. As Tannehill observes, the use of the past tense (ἦν) indicates that there is a "retrospective" quality to the centurion's confession, reminding us that his words are, after all, a reflection on what has taken place just beforehand: namely, Jesus's death on the cross.[158] That is to say that, while the centurion doubtless did not mean to imply so much himself, for the reader familiar with the backstory of Psalm 2 in Mark's Gospel, his words signify that Jesus has indeed been enthroned as God's Messiah on the cross; hence, the Son ironically begins to inherit the nations.

7.8.2 A Final Voice from History

We have seen previously that many early interpreters read Ps 2:8 as a prophecy of the Gentiles' faith in Christ regardless.[159] Some even held that Ps 2:7-9 specifically anticipated Christ's triumph over the Romans and his superiority to the emperor personally.[160] But it is Cyril of Jerusalem who actually implies some sort of linkage between the centurion's confession and Psalm 2:

---

[157] To recall Quintilian (*Inst.* 9.3.34) once more, this is the very purpose of an *inclusio*: *respondent primis et ultima*. Cf. C. Clifton Black ("The Kijé Effect: Revenants in the Markan Passion Narrative," in *Modern and Ancient Literary Criticism of the Gospels: Continuing the Debate on Gospel Genre(s)*, ed. Robert Matthew Calhoun, David P. Moessner, and Tobias Nicklas [Tübingen: Mohr Siebeck, 2020], 290–91), who identifies 15:39 as one of a variety of instances in which Mark's passion narrative recalls earlier moments in the narrative, specifically 1:11.

[158] Tannehill, "Narrative Christology," 88.

[159] See *1 Clem.* 36; Justin, *Dial.* 122 (PG 6:760); Tertullian, *Marc.* 3.20, 4.25, 39, 5.17 (PL 2:349b, 423a, 457c, 464a); Irenaeus, *Haer.* 4.21 (PG 7:1045), Cyril of Jerusalem, *Cat.* 12.18 (PG 33:748); Chrysostom, *Catech. Illum.* 1.4 (PG 49:227); Augustine, *Fid.* 7 (PL 40:176), *Faust.* 12.43 (PL 42:277), *Tract. Ev. Jo.* 115, 117 (PL 35:1939, 1946); Theodoret, *Ep. 146* (PG 83:1395).

[160] So Eusebius, *Hist. eccl.* 3.8.11 (PG 20:240); Cyril of Jerusalem, *Cat.* 12.18 (PG 33:748); see also Augustine's interpretation of Ps 2:11 in *Ep.* 93.3.9, 185.5.19 (PL 33:325, 891).

And the Angel says to them again, "Fear not." I do not say to the soldiers, "fear not," but to you. As for them, let them be afraid, so that, having learned by trial, they may bear witness and say, "*Truly this was the Son of God*"; but you ought not be afraid, "for perfect love casts out fear." "Go, tell His disciples that He is risen; and the rest." And they depart with joy, yet fearfully. Is this also written? Yes, so says the Second Psalm, which narrates the passion of Christ, "*Serve the Lord with fear, and rejoice in Him with trembling.*" Rejoice on account of the risen Lord; but with trembling, because of the earthquake, and the angel who appeared as lightning.[161]

Like many other ancient interpreters, Cyril considers Psalm 2 to be a virtual transcript of Jesus's passion. In this vein he pairs Matt 27:54 (cf. Mark 15:39), "Truly, this was the Son of God," alongside Ps 2:11, "Serve the Lord with fear, and rejoice in Him with trembling." Though the connection between the two passages is far from obvious, Cyril apparently links the two by associating the trembling mentioned in the psalm with the earthquake that accompanies the centurion's confession in Matt 27:51-54. Thus, Cyril associates the centurion's confession with the outcome in Psalm 2, particularly Ps 2:11, where the nations are enjoined to serve the Lord through submission to his Son. This interpretation not only agrees with other early interpretations of the centurion's confession and Psalm 2 alike, but with the interpretation of Mark 15:39 offered here.

But, moreover, given the obscurity of the connection, it is hard to imagine that the mere occurrence of "trembling" in Ps 2:11 really accounts for Cyril's association of this verse with the centurion's confession. Rather, one suspects that Cyril's interpretation rests in a long-established tradition of associating Psalm 2 with Jesus's passion in general, including, as it were, the centurion's confession. As Cyril himself hints, the real justification for his interpretation is that the second psalm "narrates the passion of Christ."

7.9 Conclusions

In this final chapter, we began by observing that Mark's use of son-of-God language in the passion narrative follows the trend of the Gospel as a whole by taking its cue from Psalm 2. In 14:61-62, it is Jesus's alleged identity as the Messiah Son of God (cf. Ps 2:2, 7) that sets the stage for the trial and crucifixion narratives, including his ironic depiction as "the king of the Jews," in Mark 15, which begins with another allusion to Ps 2:1-2. The undercurrents of Davidic messianism via Psalm 2 remain active throughout Mark 15, which portrays Jesus's crucifixion as his actual enthronement wherein parody has become reality.

All of this, in turn, bears significantly on our hearing on the final acclamation of Jesus's sonship in Mark (and yet the first by a human being) when the centurion declares, "Truly, this man was the Son of God" (15:39). Although the centurion himself likely borrows the language of the emperor's cult familiar to him, within the contours

---

[161] Cyril of Jerusalem, *Cat.* 14.13 (*PG* 33.841a).

of Mark's narrative his words ultimately complete the vision of Psalm 2 that has coursed through Mark's entire portrayal of Jesus as the Son of God: the Son begins to inherit the nations (Ps 2:7-8). That is to say, the centurion's confession signals to the scripturally attuned reader that Jesus has indeed been enthroned as God's Messiah, who will instantiate his reign and bring forth his justice on earth. But the most shocking implication of all is that all of this has occurred through Jesus's death on the cross.

In her commentary, Collins speaks of the divine pronouncement at Jesus's baptism as an "actualization" of Ps 2:7.[162] I suggest that this assessment is correct insofar as it goes. In retrospect, however, just as the baptism is only the beginning of the journey that ends at the cross, it is not merely Jesus's baptism that signifies an actualization of Ps 2:7, but Jesus's entire earthly career, culminating with his crucifixion, that ironically signifies the actualization of the second psalm as a whole.

---

[162] Collins, *Mark*, 150.

Conclusions

I began this study by asking why Mark's "Son of God," though arguably the most important identity of Jesus in the Gospel narrative, has been so little studied, and by simultaneosly contending that there is more at stake in Mark's portrayal of Jesus as God's Son than past scholarship has typically inferred. While the answers to this initial question inevitably reduce to various preconceived notions about what "Son of God" means as a title, I suggest that Mark's dynamic depiction of "the gospel of Jesus Christ, Son of God" from baptism to crucifixion indeed tells a story. In particular, I have argued that, for Mark, the Son of God is precisely the messianic "son" described in Psalm 2; and that Mark's Gospel, as such presents the earthly career of Jesus as the actualization of Psalm 2, wherein God overcomes the chaos of the world by enthroning his Messiah as his vice-regent on earth, whose rule amounts to salvation.

In Chapter 2, then, I began by retracing the story of Psalm through ancient Jewish and Christian tradition—i.e., the tradition Mark inherited and the one of which he was an early member. Psalm 2 emerges as a coronation hymn celebrating the enthronement of the Davidic king as God's answer to the tumult and chaos of human history, which exerted a powerful influence in early Jewish sources, where it is almost universally interpreted messianically. Significantly, Psalm 2 also emerges as the *locus classicus* for the identification of the Davidic Messiah as the Son of God. Early Christian tradition, in turn, universally associated the psalm with Jesus as the Davidic Messiah, transferring the entirety of the psalm's inherent plot and eschatological hopes to the person of Christ. Messianology thus becomes Christology. Moreover, already in the NT, the psalm is widely associated not only with Jesus's sonship and enthronement, but also with his death and resurrection.

After laying this necessary foundation, the rest of the book from Chapters 3–7 traces the actual influence of Psalm 2 on Mark's portrayal of Jesus as God's Son from his baptism to his crucifixion. So, in Chapter 3 I began by observing that God's introduction of Jesus into the narrative as his Son via Ps 2:7 (1:11) both portrays his baptism as his royal anointing and, furthermore, sets the parameters for our understanding of "Son of God" in the narrative going forward. Moreover, observing Mark's broader use of Scripture in the prologue alongside the tendencies of other Jewish literature suggests that the larger context of the psalm is not incidental to the evangelist. From the start of the Gospel, then, to be God's son is to be the royal messianic son of Psalm 2.

Following on the heels of Chapter 3, Chapter 4 demonstrated how Jesus begins to realize the implications of his royal anointing via Psalm 2 through his disestablishment of Satan's kingdom. It is this paradigm that best explains why the demons highlight his identity as the Son of God, in particular (3:11; 5:7). Following these episodes, the repetition of the allusion to Ps 2:7 at Jesus's transfiguration (Chapter 5) powerfully reinforces its importance for defining what it means to be God's Son in Mark. Likewise, the transfiguration advances the royal themes of Psalm 2 from Jesus's baptism by offering a proleptic glimpse of Jesus's messianic enthronement. As Mark's narrative turns toward Jesus's passion, the Parable of the Vineyard (Chapter 6) uniquely encapsulates the Gospel as a whole as a *mise en abyme*, complete with echoes of Psalm 2 accompanying Jesus's self-characterization as the "beloved son" who is rejected and killed, yet exalted in the end.

But the meaning of Jesus's identity as God's Son in Mark ultimately hinges on the climactic moment of the centurion's confession, which accompanies his death on the cross in 15:39. Despite the *prima facie* unlikelihood that the centurion's confession has anything to do with Psalm 2, both the continued echoes of Psalm 2 throughout Mark's passion narrative (beginning with the high priest's question in 14:61) and the *inclusio* between 1:10-11 and 15:38-39 suggest that Mark means us to hear his confession precisely in the light of the psalm, which has defined "Son of God" up to this point. So while the centurion likely borrows the words υἱὸς θεοῦ from the language of the emperor's cult (thus conveying supreme authority to rule with soteriological overtones), his confession ironically completes the arc of Psalm 2 in Mark's Gospel: the Son begins to inherit the nations (cf. Ps 2:7-8). In this way, the centurion's confession also signals that Jesus has, ironically, been enthroned as God's Messiah, vice-regent who will instantiate his reign on earth, precisely and only through his death on the cross.

This interpretation, of course, begs the obvious question of how one who is dead can possibly be said to have been enthroned or to reign over anything; indeed, it is more typically Jesus's resurrection that is associated with his enthronement in early Christian tradition (e.g., Acts 13:33). To this excellent question I should respond that the resurrection implicitly plays this role in Mark as well. It is a mistake to suppose, as some do, that the resurrection plays no part in Markan theology simply because we do not see the risen Jesus himself, but only his empty tomb and the angel declaring that he is risen, in 16:5-7.[1] To the contrary, from the moment of Jesus's first prediction of his death in 8:31, he also predicts his resurrection in the same sentence. The cross and the resurrection are indissolubly linked to one another in this Gospel as throughout the NT as a whole. The Son of Man (and God) suffers and dies only to rise again after three days (cf. 9:31; 10:33-34), just as Jesus anticipates his resurrection from the dead in 9:9, in the immediate wake of his transfiguration, and predicts the same on the eve of his death in 14:28. Ultimately, there is not one mention of the cross apart from the resurrection outside of the account of the crucifixion itself in Mark's Gospel. In 16:6-7, then, the angel's declaration at the tomb that Jesus is risen and has gone ahead of his disciples to Galilee is not an afterthought, but a reminder and a fulfillment of Jesus's words from a few days earlier (14:28). As the cross presupposes the resurrection

---

[1] See similarly Botner, *Son of David*, 174–88.

throughout Mark, so also does the triumph of the cross signified by the centurion's confession. Jesus is enthroned through his death on the cross, but he reigns as the Risen Lord.

In the end, however, Mark is nothing if not a theologian of the cross. Like so much else in this Gospel, the light of the resurrection is left for us to find by way of the cross in Mark 15. As so many Markan interpreters over the decades and even centuries have observed, it is Jesus's suffering, culminating in the cross, that constitutes Mark's distinct theological emphasis. Thus even Jesus's kingship, even his *glory*, is inextricably bound to the cross. And so, though the resurrection is assuredly presupposed, it is the crucifixion that signifies the actual moment of Jesus's coronation as God's Messiah for Mark. One might say that Jesus's resurrection-reign is here the consequence of his crucifixion-coronation.

Others, meanwhile, may find the emphasis on ironic exaltation and the triumph of the cross to sound more Johannine than Markan. Here my response is twofold. First, however Johannine such ideas may be, I suggest that they are also Markan. The ironic glory of the cross has, perhaps, been too narrowly identified as a specifically Johannine one in the past. Second, an increasing number of scholars are now reassessing the once widely maintained divide between John and the Synoptics.[2] If Mark and John appear to share a common interpretation of Jesus's death, that need not come as a great surprise to us. It may be that we have here a case of John making overt what he found implied in the Synoptics.[3] The gulf between Mark and John, in turn, may not be a theological one as much as a stylistic one: the hidden versus the revealed (cf. Mark 4:22). The conclusion of a book is hardly the place to take up such arguments, of course, but I submit that if the old paradigm appears to be challenged by the present thesis, then perhaps it needs to be challenged.

Finally, I suggested from the outset of this study that, for Mark, to call Jesus the "Son of God" is not merely to assign an early christological title to him so much as to imply the mission and accomplishments of the Christ—i.e., the gospel in shorthand (cf. 1:1). Through Mark's consistent evocation of Psalm 2 in his identification of Jesus as God's Son, that is what we have finally witnessed. For Mark, to be the Son of God is to be the royal Messiah who triumphs over the powers opposed to God's rule and instantiates God's reign on earth, so saving the world precisely by his

---

[2] See, e.g., Udo Schnelle, "Johannes Und Die Synoptiker," in *The Four Gospels 1992: Festschrift Frans Neirynck*, ed. Frans van Segbroeck, BETL 100 (Leuven: Leuven University Press, 1992), 3:1799–1814; James W. Barker, *John's Use of Matthew*, Emerging Scholars (Minneapolis: Fortress, 2015); Dale C Allison, Jr., "Reflections on Matthew, John, and Jesus," in *Jesus Research: The Gospel of John in Historical Inquiry. The Third Princeton-Prague Symposium on Jesus Research: Princeton 2016*, ed. Charlesworth, James H. and Pruszinski, Jolyon G. R., JCTCRSS 26 (London/New York: T&T Clark, 2019), 47–68; and the essays in Eve-Marie Becker, Helen K. Bond, and Catrin H. Williams, eds., *John's Transformation of Mark* (London/New York: T&T Clark, 2021).

[3] See Helen Bond, "The Triumph of the King: John's Transformation of Mark's Account of the Passion," in *John's Transformation of Mark*, 251–67. According to Bond (266), "we see John drawing out themes already present in Mark and heightening their dramatic quality—both the motifs of kingship and triumph, for example can be found in Mark."

rule. All of this, Mark tells us, Jesus accomplished through the cross. So while this study bears a variety of implications for Mark's use of Scripture, Markan soteriology, Mark's engagement with the political sphere, his upending of traditional power dynamics via a Messiah who loses his life in order to conquer and save the world, and much more, it is chiefly a book about the gospel according to Mark—the Gospel, that is, of the Son of God.

Bibliography

Abrahams, Israel. *Studies in Pharisaism and the Gospels: First and Second Series*. Library of Biblical Studies. New York: Ktav, 1967.
Achtemeier, Paul J. "The Origin and Function of the Pre-Marcan Miracle Catenae." *JBL* 91 (1972): 198–221.
Adams, Edward. "The Coming of the Son of Man in Mark's Gospel." *TynBul* 56 (2005): 39–61.
Ahearne-Kroll, Stephen P. *The Psalms of Lament in Mark's Passion: Jesus' Davidic Suffering*. SNTSMS 142. Cambridge/New York: Cambridge University Press, 2007.
Albl, Martin C. "The Testimonia Hypothesis and Composite Citations." *Composite Citations in Antiquity. Volume 1: Jewish, Graeco-Roman, and Early Christian Uses*. Edited by Sean A. Adams and Seth Ehorn. LNTS 525. New York: T&T Clark, 2015.
Alexander, Loveday. "What Is a Gospel?" Pages 13–33 in *The Cambridge Companion to the Gospels*. Edited by Stephen C. Barton. Cambridge/New York: Cambridge University Press, 2006.
Alford, Henry, ed. *Alford's Greek Testament: An Exegetical and Critical Commentary*. 4 vols Grand Rapids: Guardian Press, 1976.
Alkier, Stefan. "Intertextualität-Annäherungen an ein texttheoretisches Paradigma." Pages 1–26 in *Heiligkeit und Herrschaft: Intertextuelle Studien zu Heligkeitsvorstellungen und zu Psalm 110*. Edited by Dieter Sänger. Neukirchen-Vluyn: Neukirchener, 2003.
Alkier, Stefan. *Wunder und Wirklichkeit in den Briefen des Apostels Paulus: ein Beitrag zu einem Wunderverständnis jenseits von Entmythologisierung und Rehistorisierung*. WUNT 134. Tübingen: Mohr Siebeck, 2001.
Allen, David. "The Use of Criteria: The State of the Question." Pages 129–41 in *Methodology in the Use of the Old Testament in the New: Context and Criteria*. Edited by David Allen and Steve Smith. LNTS 597. London/New York: T&T Clark, 2020.
Allison, Jr., Dale C. *Constructing Jesus: Memory, Imagination, and History*. Grand Rapids: Baker, 2010.
Allison, Jr., Dale C. "Elijah Must Come First." *JBL* 103 (1984): 256–58.
Allison, Jr., Dale C. "Foreshadowing the Passion." Pages 217–35 in *Studies in Matthew: Interpretation Past and Present*. Grand Rapids: Baker, 2005.
Allison, Jr., Dale C. "Reflections on Matthew, John, and Jesus." Pages 47–68 in *Jesus Research: The Gospel of John in Historical Inquiry. The Third Princeton-Prague Symposium on Jesus Research: Princeton 2016*. Edited by Charlesworth, James H. and Pruszinski, Jolyon G. R. JCTCRSS 26. London; New York: T&T Clark, 2019.
Allison, Jr., Dale C. *Studies in Matthew: Interpretation Past and Present*. Grand Rapids: Baker Academic, 2005.
Allison, Jr., Dale C. *The Intertextual Jesus: Scripture in Q*. Harrisburg, PA: Trinity Press International, 2000.
Allison, Jr., Dale C. *The New Moses: A Matthean Typology*. Minneapolis: Fortress, 1993.
Allison, June W. "ΠΑΡΑΣΚΕΥΗ: Process-Product Ambiguity in Thucydides VI." *Hermes* 109 (1981): 118–23.

Alonso Schökel, Luis, and Cecilia Carniti. *Salmos: traducción introducciones y comentario*. Nueva Biblia Española. Estella: Editorial Verbo Divino, 1992.
Alt, Albrecht. "Jesaja 8,23–9,6. Befreiungsmacht und Krönungstag." Pages 29–49 in *Festschrift Alfred Bertholet zum 80. Geburtstag gewidmet*. Edited by Walter Baumgartner. Tübingen: Mohr Siebeck, 1950.
Alter, Robert. *The Art of Biblical Narrative*. Rev. & Updated ed. New York: Basic Books, 2011.
Ando, Clifford. *Imperial Ideology and Provincial Loyalty in the Roman Empire*. Berkeley: University of California Press, 2000.
Annen, Franz. *Heil für die Heiden: zur Bedeutung u. Geschichte d. Tradition vom besessenen Gerasener (Mk 5, 1-20 parr.)*. FTS 20. Frankfurt am Main: Knecht, 1976.
Aristotle. *The Works of Aristotle*. Translated by Thomas Taylor. Vol. 4. Frome, Somerset: Prometheus Trust, 2000.
Atherton, Catherine. "Apollonius Dyscolus and the Ambiguity of Ambiguity." *ClQ* 45 (1995): 441–73.
Atilius Fortunatianus. *Fortunatianus Aquileiensis Commentarii in Evangelia*. CSEL 103. Berlin: De Gruyter, 2017.
Atkinson, Kenneth. *An Intertextual Study of the Psalms of Solomon: Pseudepigrapha*. SBEC 49. Lewiston, NY: E. Mellen, 2001.
Atkinson, Kenneth. *I Cried to the Lord: A Study of the Psalms of Solomon's Historical Background and Social Setting*. JSJSup 84. Leiden/Boston: Brill, 2004.
Attardo, Salvatore. "Irony as Relevant Inappropriateness." Pages 135–70 in *Irony in Language and Thought: A Cognitive Science Reader*. Edited by Raymond W. Gibbs, Jr. and Herbert L. Colston. New York: Taylor & Francis Group, 2007.
Attridge, Harold W. *The Epistle to the Hebrews: A Commentary on the Epistle to the Hebrews*. Hermeneia. Philadelphia: Fortress, 1989.
Attridge, Harold W. "The Psalms in Hebrews." Pages 197–212 in *The Psalms in the New Testament*. Edited by Steve Moyise and Maarten J. J. Menken. NTSI. London: T&T Clark, 2004.
Auerbach, Erich. "Figura." Pages 65–113 in *Time, History, and Literature: Selected Essays of Erich Auerbach*. Edited by James I. Porter, Translated by Jane O. Newman. Reprint ed. Princeton: Princeton University Press, 2016.
Auerbach, Erich. *Mimesis: The Representation of Reality in Western Literature*. Princeton: Princeton University Press, 2003.
Auerbach, Erich. *Time, History, and Literature: Selected Essays of Erich Auerbach*. Edited by James I. Porter Translated by Jane O. Newman. Reprint ed. Princeton: Princeton University Press, 2016.
Augustine. *Basic Writings of Saint Augustine*. Edited by Whitney Jennings Oates Translated by J. G. Pilkington. Vol. 1. Grand Rapids: Baker, 1980.
Augustine. *Confessions*. Edited by John E. Rotelle Translated by Maria Boulding. 6th ed. Vol. 1 of *Works of Saint Augustine: A Translation for the 21st Century* 1. Hyde Park: New City, 2011.
Augustine. *The Works of Saint Augustine: A Translation for the 21st Century*. Edited by John E. Rotelle. Translated by Edmund Hill. New York: New City, 2001.
Aune, David E. "Christian Prophecy and the Messianic Status of Jesus." *The Messiah: Developments in Earliest Judaism and Christianity*. Edited by James H. Charlesworth. Minneapolis: Fortress, 1992.
Aune, David E. *The New Testament in Its Literary Environment*. Philadelphia: Westminster, 1987.

Aune, David E. *Revelation*. WBC 52a–b. Dallas: Word, 1997.
Aus, Roger David. *The Wicked Tenants and Gethsemane: Isaiah in the Wicked Tenants' Vineyard, and Moses and the High Priest in Gethsemane: Judaic Traditions in Mark 12:1-9 and 14:32-42*. ISFCJ. Scholars Press, 1996.
Austin, J. L. *How to Do Things with Words*. 2nd ed. The William James Lectures. Oxford: Clarendon, 1975.
Bächli, Otto. "Was habe ich mit Dir zu schaffen?: Eine formelhafte Frage im A.T. und N.T." *TZ* 33 (1977): 69–80.
Bal, Mieke. *Narratology: Introduction to the Theory of Narrative*. Translated by Christine van Boheemen. 3rd ed. University of Toronto Press, 2009.
Bal, Mieke, and Eve Tavor. "Notes on Narrative Embedding." *Poetics Today* 2 (1981): 41–59.
Barker, James W. *John's Use of Matthew*. Emerging Scholars. Minneapolis: Fortress, 2015.
Barr, James. *The Semantics of Biblical Language*. Oxford: Oxford University Press, 1961.
Barrett, C. K. *A Critical and Exegetical Commentary on the Acts of the Apostles*. 2 vols ICC 44. Edinburgh: T&T Clark, 1994.
Barrett, C. K. *The Gospel According to St. John: An Introduction with Commentary and Notes on the Greek Text*. 2nd ed. Philadelphia: Westminster Press, 1978.
Barth, Gerhard. "Matthew's Understanding of the Law." Pages 58–164 in *Tradition and Interpretation in Matthew*. Edited by Günther Bornkamm, Heinz Joachim Held, and Gerhard Barth, Translated by P. Scott. NTL. London: SCM Press, 1963.
Barton, Carlin A. *The Sorrows of the Ancient Romans: The Gladiator and the Monster*. Princeton, NJ: Princeton University Press, 1993.
Bates, Matthew W. "A Christology of Incarnation and Enthronement: Romans 1:3-4 as Unified, Nonadoptionist, and Nonconciliatory." *CBQ* 77 (2015): 107–127.
Bauckham, Richard. "Jesus and the Wild Animals." Pages 3–21 in *Jesus of Nazareth: Lord and Christ: Essays on the Historical Jesus and New Testament Christology*. Edited by Joel B. Green and Max Turner. Grand Rapids: Eerdmans, 1994.
Bauckham, Richard. "Markan Christology According to Richard Hays: Some Addenda." *JTI* 11 (2017): 21–36.
Bauckham, Richard. "The Worship of Jesus in Apocalytic Christianity." *NTS* 27 (1981): 322–41.
Bauckham, Richard, James R. Davila, and Alexander Panayotov, eds. *Old Testament Pseudepigrapha: More Noncanonical Scriptures*. Vol. 1. Grand Rapids/Cambridge: Eerdmans, 2013.
Bauernfeind, Otto. *Die Worte der Dämonen im Markusevangelium*. BWA(N)T. Stuttgart: Kohlhammer, 1927.
Bauman, Richard A. *Crime and Punishment in Ancient Rome*. London/New York: Routledge, 1996.
Bayer, Hans F. *Das Evangelium Des Markus*. Historisch Theologische Auslegung, Neues Testament. Witten: SCM R. Brockhaus; Giessen: Brunnen, 2008.
Beard, Mary, John North, and S. R. F. Price. *Religions of Rome*. 2 vols Cambridge/New York: Cambridge University Press, 1998.
Becker, Eve-Marie, Helen K. Bond, and Catrin H. Williams, eds. *John's Transformation of Mark*. London/New York: T&T Clark, 2021.
Becking, Bob. "'Wie Töpfe sollst du sie zerschmeissen': mesopotamische Parallelen zu Psalm 2:9b." *ZAW* 102 (1990): 59–79.
Bede. *Bedae Venerabilis Opera*. Edited by Charles Williams Jones and David Hurst. CChr 118A, etc. Turnholti: Typographi Brepols, 1955.

Bengel, Johann Albrecht. *Gnomon Novi Testamenti: In Quo Ex Nativa Verborum vi Simplicitas, Profunditas, Concinnitas, Salubritas Sensuum Coelestium Indicatur.* 4th ed. Tübingen: Sumptibus L. F. Fues, 1850.

Berlin, Adele, Marc Zvi Brettler, and Jewish Publication Society, eds. *The Jewish Study Bible.* 2nd ed. New York: Oxford University Press, 2014.

Bernett, Monika. *Der Kaiserkult in Judäa unter den Herodiern und Römern: Untersuchungen zur politischen und religiösen Geschichte Judäas von 30 v. bis 66 n. Chr.* WUNT 203. Tübingen: Mohr Siebeck, 2007.

Bernett, Monika. "Roman Imperial Cult in the Galilee: Structures, Functions, and Dynamics." Pages 315–36 in *Religion, Ethnicity and Identity in Ancient Galilee: A Region in Transition.* Edited by Jürgen Zangenberg, Harold W. Attridge, and Dale B. Martin. WUNT 210. Tübingen: Mohr Siebeck, 2007.

Best, Ernest. *Mark: The Gospel as Story.* Edinburgh: T&T Clark, 1983.

Best, Ernest. *The Temptation and the Passion: The Markan Soteriology.* 2nd ed. Cambridge: Cambridge University Press, 1990.

Betz, Hans Dieter. "Gottmensch II." *RAC* 12 (1982): 234–312.

Betz, Hans Dieter. "Jesus as Divine Man." *Jesus and the Historian* (1968): 114–33.

Betz, Otto. "Probleme Des Prozesses Jesu." *ANRW* 25:566–647.

Betz, Otto. "The Temple Scroll and the Trial of Jesus." *SwJT* 30 (1988): 5–8.

Bieler, Ludwig. *Theios Anēr: Das Bild Des "Göttlichen Menschen" in Spätantike Und Frühchristentum.* Wien: O. Höfels, 1935.

Black, C. Clifton. *Mark.* ANTC. Nashville: Abingdon, 2011.

Black, C. Clifton. "Was Mark a Roman Gospel?" *ExpTim* 105 (1993): 36–40.

Black, C. Clifton. "The Kijé Effect: Revenants in the Markan Passion Narrative," Page 273–306 in *Modern and Ancient Literary Criticism of the Gospels: Continuing the Debate on Gospel Genre(s).* Edited by Calhoun, Robert Matthew, David P. Moessner, and Tobias Nicklas. WUNT 451. Tübingen: Mohr Siebeck, 2020.

Black, Matthew. "Die Gleichnisse als Allegorien." Pages 262–80 in *Gleichnisse Jesu: Positionen der Auslegung von Adolf Jülicher bis zur Formgeschichte.* Edited by Wolfgang Harnisch. WF 366. Darmstadt: Wissenschaftliche Buchgesellschaft, 1982.

Black, Matthew. "The Christological Use of the Old Testament in the New Testament." *NTS* 18 (1971): 1–14.

Blackburn, Barry. *"Theios Aner" and the Markan Miracle Traditions: A Critique of the "Theios Aner" Concept as an Interpretative Backround of the Miracle Traditions Used by Mark.* WUNT 2/40. Tübingen: Mohr Siebeck, 1991.

Blass, Friedrich, Albert Debrunner, and Robert W. Funk. *A Greek Grammar of the New Testament and Other Early Christian Literature.* Chicago: University of Chicago Press, 1961.

Blenkinsopp, Joseph, ed. *Isaiah 40-55: A New Translation with Introduction and Commentary.* AB 19a. New York: Doubleday, 2002.

Bligh, P. H. "A Note on Huios Theou in Mark 15.39." *ExpTim* 80 (1968): 51–3.

Blinzler, Josef. *The Trial of Jesus: The Jewish and Roman Proceedings against Jesus Christ Described and Assessed from the Oldest Accounts.* Westminster, MD: Newman, 1959.

Boccaccini, Gabriele, ed. *Enoch and the Messiah Son of Man: Revisiting the Book of Parables.* Grand Rapids: Eerdmans, 2007.

Bock, Darrell L. "Jewish Expressions in Mark 14.61-62 and the Authenticity of the Jewish Examination of Jesus." *JSHS* 1 (2003): 147.

Bock, Darrell L. *Mark.* NCBC. New York: Cambridge University Press, 2015.

Bock, Darrell L. *Proclamation from Prophecy and Pattern: Lucan Old Testament Christology*. JSOTSup 12. Sheffield: JSOT Press, 1987.
Bond, Helen K. *The First Biography of Jesus: Genre and Meaning in Mark's Gospel*. Grand Rapids: Eerdmans, 2020.
Boobyer, G. H. *St. Mark and the Transfiguration Story*. Edinburgh: T&T Clark, 1942.
Borges, Jorge Luis. "Partial Magic in the Quixote." Pages 223–31 in *Labyrinths*. Edited by Donald A. Yates and James E. Irby. Harmondsworth: Penguin, 1970.
Boring, M. Eugene. *Matthew. NIB* 8. Nashville: Abingdon, 1995.
Boring, M. Eugene. *Mark: A Commentary*. NTL. Louisville, KY: Westminster John Knox Press, 2006.
Boring, M. Eugene. "Markan Christology: God-Language for Jesus?" *NTS* 45 (1999): 451–71.
Boring, M. Eugene. *Truly Human/Truly Divine: Christological Language and the Gospel Form*. St. Louis: CBP, 1984.
Boring, M. Eugene, Klaus Berger, and Carsten Colpe, eds. *Hellenistic Commentary to the New Testament*. Nashville: Abingdon, 1995.
Bosworth, David A. *The Story Within a Story in Biblical Hebrew Narrative*. CBQMS 45. Washington, DC: Catholic Biblical Association, 2008.
Botner, Max. *Jesus Christ as the Son of David in the Gospel of Mark*. SNTSMS 174. Cambridge: Cambridge University Press, 2019.
Botner, Max. "The Messiah Is 'the Holy One': Ὁ Ἅγιος Τοῦ Θεοῦ as a Messianic Title in Mark 1:24." *JBL* 136 (2017): 417–33.
Botner, Max. "The Role of Transcriptional Probability in the Text-Critical Debate on Mark 1:1." *CBQ* 77 (2015): 467–80.
Botner, Max. "What Has Mark's Christ to Do with David's Son? A History of Interpretation." *CRBS* 16 (2017): 50–70.
Bousset, Wilhelm. *Kyrios Christos: A History of the Belief in Christ from the Beginnings of Christianity to Irenaeus*. Waco, Texas: Baylor University Press, 2013. Translation of *Kyrios Christos: Geschichte des Christusglaubens von den Anfängen des Christentums bis Irenaeus*. Göttingen: Vandenhoeck & Ruprecht, 1913.
Bovon, François. *Luke*. 3 vols Minneapolis: Fortress, 2002–12.
Božović, Nenad. "Ps 2,7-8 im Narrativ des Markusevangeliums." Pages 325–45 in *Christ of the sacred stories*. Edited by Predrag Dragutinović, Tobias Nicklas, Kelsie G. Rodenbiker, and Vladan Tatalović. WUNT 2/453. Tübingen: Mohr Siebeck, 2017.
Brand, Clarence E. *Roman Military Law*. Austin: University of Texas Press, 1968.
Braude, William G., ed. *Pesikta Rabbati; Discourses for Feasts, Fasts, and Special Sabbaths*. YJS 18. New Haven: Yale University Press, 1968.
Braude, William G., ed. *The Midrash on Psalms*. 2 vols YJS 13. New Haven/London: Yale University Press, 1976.
Braumann, Georg. "Markus 15:2-5 und Markus 14:55-64." *ZNW* 52 (1961): 273–78.
Brenner-Idan, Athalya. *Colour Terms in the Old Testament*. JSOTSup 21. Sheffield: JSOT Press, 1982.
Bretscher, Paul G. "Exodus 4:22-23 and the Voice from Heaven." *JBL* 87 (1968): 301–11.
Briggs, Charles A., and Emilie Grace Briggs. *A Critical and Exegetical Commentary on the Book of Psalms*. ICC 19. New York: Scribner's, 1906.
Broadhead, Edwin K. *Naming Jesus: Titular Christology in the Gospel of Mark*. JSNTSup 175. Sheffield: Sheffield Academic, 1999.
Brooke, George J. "4Q500 1 and the Use of Scripture in the Parable of the Vineyard." *DSD* 2 (1995): 268–94.

Brooke, George J. *Exegesis at Qumran: 4Q Florilegium in Its Jewish Context*. JSOTSup 29. Sheffield: JSOT Press, 1985.
Brooks, Peter. *Reading for the Plot: Design and Intention in Narrative*. Cambridge: Harvard University Press, 1984.
Brown, Jeannine K. "Metalepsis." Page 33 in *Exploring Intertextuality: Diverse Strategies for New Testament Interpretation of Texts*. Edited by B. J. Oropeza and Steve Moyise. Eugene, OR: Cascade, 2016.
Brown, Jeannine K. *Scripture as Communication: Introducing Biblical Hermeneutics*. Grand Rapids: Baker Academic, 2007.
Brown, Raymond E. *The Death of the Messiah: From Gethsemane to the Grave: A Commentary on the Passion Narratives in the Four Gospels*. 2 vols New York: Doubleday, 1994.
Brown, Raymond E., ed. *The Gospel According to John: Introduction, Translation, and Notes*. 2nd ed. AB 29. Garden City: Doubleday, 1979.
Bruce, F. F. *The Gospel of John*. Grand Rapids: Eerdmans, 1983.
Brueggemann, Walter. *Isaiah*. 2 vols Louisville: Westminster John Knox, 1998.
Bryan, Christopher. *A Preface to Mark: Notes on the Gospel in Its Literary and Cultural Settings*. New York: Oxford University Press, 1993.
Buitenwerf, Rieuwerd. *Book III of the Sibylline Oracles and Its Social Setting*. SVTP 17. Leiden/Boston: Brill, 2003.
Bultmann, Rudolf. *The Gospel of John: A Commentary*. Translated by G. R. Beasley-Murray. Philadelphia: Westminster, 1971.
Bultmann, Rudolf. *The History of the Synoptic Tradition*. Translated by John Marsh. rev. ed. Oxford: Blackwell, 1963. Translation of *Die Geschichte der synoptischen Tradition*. Göttingen: Vandenhoeck & Ruprecht, 1931.
Bultmann, Rudolf. *Theology of the New Testament*. Translated by Kendrick Grobel. 2 vols New York: Scribner's, 1955.
Bundy, Walter E. "Dogma and Drama in the Gospel of Mark." Pages 70–94 in *New Testament Studies*. Edited by E. P. Booth. New York: Abingdon-Cokesbury, 1942.
Burchard, Christoph. "Markus 15 34." *ZNW* 74 (2009): 1–11.
Burdon, Christopher. "'To the Other Side': Construction of Evil and Fear of Liberation in Mark 5.1-20." *JSNT* 27 (2004): 149–67.
Burkett, Delbert. "The Transfiguration of Jesus (Mark 9:2-8): Epiphany or Apotheosis?" *JBL* 138 (2019): 413–32.
Burkill, T. A. "Mark 3:7-12 and the Alleged Dualism in the Evangelist's Miracle Material." *JBL* 87 (1968): 409–17.
Burridge, Richard A. *What Are the Gospels? A Comparison with Graeco-Roman Biography*. 2nd ed. Grand Rapids: Eerdmans, 2004.
Buse, Ivor. "The Markan Account of the Baptism of Jesus and Isaiah LXIII." *JTS* 7 (1956): 74–5.
Cahill, Michael, ed. *Expositio Evangelii Secundum Marcum*. CChr 82. Turnholti: Brepols, 1997.
Cahill, Michael, ed. *The First Commentary on Mark: An Annotated Translation*. New York: Oxford University Press, 1998.
Caird, G. B. *A Commentary on the Revelation of St. John the Divine*. BNTC. London: Black, 1966.
Caird, G. B. "Expository Problems: The Transfiguration." *ExpTim* 67 (1956): 291–94.

Calvin, Jean. *Commentary on a Harmony of the Evangelists, Matthew, Mark, and Luke*. Translated by William Pringle. Vol. 3 of *Calvin's Commentaries* 17. Grand Rapids: Baker, 1989.
Calvin, Jean. *Commentary on the Psalms*. Translated by David C. Searle. Edinburgh; Carlisle, PA: Banner of Truth Trust, 2009.
Camery-Hoggatt, Jerry. *Irony in Mark's Gospel: Text and Subtext*. Cambridge/New York: Cambridge University Press, 1991.
Campbell, Constantine R. *Basics of Verbal Aspect in Biblical Greek*. Grand Rapids: Zondervan, 2008.
Campbell, Constantine R. *Verbal Aspect, the Indicative Mood, and Narrative: Soundings in the Greek of the New Testament*. SBG 13. New York: Peter Lang, 2007.
Campbell, J. B. *The Emperor and the Roman Army, 31 BC-AD 235*. New York: Oxford University Press, 1984.
Caneday, A. B. "Christ's Baptism and Crucifixion: The Anointing and Enthronement of God's Son." *SBJT* 83 (2004): 70–85.
Caneday, A. B. "Mark's Provocative Use of Scripture in Narration: 'He Was with the Wild Animals and Angels Ministered to Him.'" *BBR* 9 (1999): 19–36.
Caragounis, Chrys C. *The Son of Man: Vision and Interpretation*. WUNT 38. Tübingen: Mohr Siebeck, 1986.
Carey, Holly J. *Jesus' Cry from the Cross: Towards a First-Century Understanding of the Intertextual Relationship between Psalm 22 and the Narrative of Mark's Gospel*. LNTS 398. London/New York: T&T Clark, 2009.
Carlson, R. A. "Élie à l'Horeb." *VT* 19 (1969): 416–39.
Carlston, Charles Edwin. "Transfiguration and Resurrection." *JBL* 80 (1961): 233–40.
Carroll, John T. *Luke: A Commentary*. NTL. Louisville: Westminster John Knox, 2012.
Carter, Warren. "Cross-Gendered Romans and Mark's Jesus: Legion Enters the Pigs (Mark 5:1-20)." *JBL* 134 (2015): 139–55.
Casey, Maurice. *Son of Man: The Interpretation and Influence of Daniel 7*. London: SPCK, 1979.
Casey, Maurice. *The Solution to the "Son of Man" Problem*. LNTS 343. London/New York: T&T Clark, 2007.
Catchpole, David R. "Answer of Jesus to Caiaphas: Matt 26:64." *NTS* 17 (1971): 213–26.
Catchpole, David R. *The Trial of Jesus: A Study in the Gospels and Jewish Historiography from 1770 to the Present Day*. SPB 18. Leiden: Brill, 1971.
Chapman, David W., and Eckhard J. Schnabel. *The Trial and Crucifixion of Jesus: Texts and Commentary*. WUNT 344. Tübingen: Mohr Siebeck, 2015.
Charlesworth, James H. [MEPR2] "From Messianology to Christology: Problems and Prospects." Pages 3–35 in *The Messiah: Developments in Earliest Judaism and Christianity*. Minneapolis: Fortress, 1992.
Charlesworth, James H. *Jesus within Judaism: New Light from Exciting Archaeological Discoveries*. New York: Doubleday, 1988.
Charlesworth James H., ed. *The Dead Sea Scrolls: Hebrew, Aramaic, and Greek Texts with the English Translations*. PTSDSSP. Tübingen; Louisville: Mohr Siebeck; Westminster John Knox, 1994.
Charlesworth, James H., ed. *The Old Testament Pseudepigrapha*. 2 vols Peabody, MA: Hendrickson, 2013.
Charlesworth, James H., and Darrell L. Bock, eds. *Parables of Enoch: A Paradigm Shift*. JCTCRSS 11. London: T&T Clark, 2013.
Chatman, Seymour Benjamin. *Story and Discourse: Narrative Structure in Fiction and Film*. Ithaca, NY: Cornell University Press, 1980.

Chevallier, Max-Alain. *L'Esprit et le Messie dans le bas-judaïsme et le Nouveau Testament*. Études d'histoire et de philosophie religieuses 49. Paris: Presses Universitaires de France, 1958.
Childs, Brevard S. *Isaiah*. Louisville: Westminster John Knox, 2001.
Chilton, Bruce D. "The Transfiguration: Dominical Assurance and Apostolic Vision." *NTS* 27 (1980): 115–24.
Chilton, Bruce D. *Jesus' Baptism and Jesus' Healing: His Personal Practice of Spirituality*. Harrisburg, Pa: Trinity Press International, 1998.
Chilton, Bruce D. *A Galilean Rabbi and His Bible: Jesus' Use of the Interpreted Scripture of His Time*. London: SPCK, 1984.
Chilton, Bruce D. "Greek Testament, Aramaic Targums, and Questions of Comparison." *Aramaic Studies* 11 (2013): 225–51.
Chilton, Bruce, and Darrell L. Bock, eds. *A Comparative Handbook to the Gospel of Mark: Comparisons with Pseudepigrapha, the Qumran Schrolls, and Rabbinic Literature*. The New Testament Gospels in Their Judaic Contexts 1. Leiden: Brill, 2010.
Chilton, C. W. "The Roman Law of Treason under the Early Principate." *JRS* 45 (1955): 73–81.
Cho, Bernardo. *Royal Messianism and the Jerusalem Priesthood in the Gospel of Mark*. LNTS 607. T&T Clark, 2019.
Chronis, Harry L. "The Torn Veil: Cultus and Christology in Mark 15:37-39." *JBL* 101 (1982): 97–114.
Chronis, Harry L. "To Reveal and to Conceal: A Literary-Critical Perspective on 'the Son of Man' in Mark." *NTS* 51 (2005): 459–81.
Clifford, Richard J. *Psalms 1-72*. AOTC. Nashville: Abingdon, 2002.
Cockerill, Gareth Lee. *The Epistle to the Hebrews*. NICNT. Grand Rapids: Eerdmans, 2012.
Coggins, R. J., and Michael A. Knibb. *The First and Second Books of Esdras*. CBC. Cambridge/New York: Cambridge University Press, 1979.
Cohn, Dorrit, and Lewis S. Gleich. "Metalepsis and Mise En Abyme." *Narrative* 20 (2012): 105–14.
Cole, Robert L. *Psalms 1-2: Gateway to the Psalter*. HBM 37. Sheffield: Sheffield Phoenix, 2012.
Coleridge, Samuel Taylor. *Biographia Literaria*. Edited by James Engell and W. Jackson Bate. Reprint ed. The Collected Works of Samuel Taylor Coleridge 7. Princeton: Princeton University Press, 1985.
Collins, Adela Yarbro. "Daniel 7 and Jesus." *JT* 93 (1989): 5–19.
Collins, Adela Yarbro. "Establishing the Text: Mark 1:1." Pages 111–25 in *Texts and Contexts: Biblical Texts in Their Textual and Situational Contexts*. Edited by Tord Fornberg and David Hellholm. Olso/Copenhagen/Stockholm/Boston: Scandinavian University Press, 1995.
Collins, Adela Yarbro. "Is Mark's Gospel a Life of Jesus? The Question of Genre." Pages 1–38 in *The Beginning of the Gospel: Probings of Mark in Context*. Minneapolis: Fortress, 1992.
Collins, Adela Yarbro. *Mark: A Commentary*. Hermeneia. Minneapolis: Fortress, 2007.
Collins, Adela Yarbro. "Mark and His Readers: The Son of God among Greeks and Romans." *HTR* 93 (2000): 85–100.
Collins, Adela Yarbro. "Mark and His Readers: The Son of God among Jews." *HTR* 92 (1999): 393–408.
Collins, Adela Yarbro. "Mark's Interpretation of the Death of Jesus." *JBL* 128 (2009): 545–54.

Collins, Adela Yarbro. "Narrative, History, and Gospel." *Semeia* 43 (1988): 145–53.
Collins, Adela Yarbro. "The Apocalyptic Son of Man Sayings." Pages 220–28 in *The Future of Early Christianity: Essays in Honor of Helmut Koester*. Edited by Helmut Koester, Birger A. Pearson, A. Thomas Kraabel, George W. E. Nickelsburg, and Norman R. Petersen. Minneapolis: Fortress, 1991.
Collins, Adela Yarbro. "The Charge of Blasphemy in Mark 14.64." *JSNT* 26 (2004): 379–401.
Collins, Adela Yarbro. "The Origin of the Designation of Jesus as 'Son of Man.'" *HTR* 80 (1987): 391–407.
Collins, Adela Yarbro. "The Worship of Jesus and the Imperial Cult." Pages 234–57 in *The Jewish Roots of Christological Monotheism: Papers from the St. Andrews Conference on the Historical Origins of the Worship of Jesus*. Edited by Carey C. Newman, James R. Davila, and Gladys S. Lewis. JSJSup 63. Leiden/Boston: Brill, 1999.
Collins, Adela Yarbro, and John J. Collins. *King and Messiah as Son of God: Divine, Human, and Angelic Messianic Figures in Biblical and Related Literature*. Grand Rapids: Eerdmans, 2008.
Collins, John J. "A Messiah Before Jesus?" *Christian Beginnings and the Dead Sea Scrolls*. Edited by John J. Collins and Craig A. Evans. Grand Rapids: Baker Academic, 2006.
Collins, John J. "Jesus, Messianism, and the Dead Sea Scrolls." Pages 100–134 in *Qumran-Messianism: Studies on the Messianic Expectations in the Dead Sea Scrolls*. Edited by James H. Charlesworth, Hermann Lichtenberger, and Gerbern S. Oegema. Tübingen: Mohr Siebeck, 1998.
Collins, John J. "The Background of the 'Son of God' Text." *BBR* 7 (1997): 51–61.
Collins, John J. *The Scepter and the Star: Messianism in Light of the Dead Sea Scrolls*. 2nd ed. Grand Rapids: Eerdmans, 2010.
Collins, John J. "The Son of God Text from Qumran." Pages 76–82 in *From Jesus to John: Essays on Jesus and New Testament Christology in Honour of Marinus de Jonge*. Edited by Martinus C. De Boer. JSNTSup 84. Sheffield: JSOT, 1993.
Collins, John J. "The Son of Man in First-Century Judaism." *NTS* 38 (1992): 448–66.
Collins, John J. "The Works of the Messiah." *DSD* 1 (1994): 98–112.
Colwell, E. C. "A Definite Rule for the Use of the Article in the Greek New Testament." *JBL* 52 (1933): 12–21.
Conzelmann, Hans. *Acts of the Apostles*. Translated by James Limburg, A. Thomas Kraabel, and Donald H. Juel. Hermeneia. Philadelphia: Fortress, 1987.
Conzelmann, Hans. "History and Theology in the Passion Narratives of the Synoptic Gospels." *Int* 24 (1970): 178–97.
Cooke, Gerald. "The Israelite King as Son of God." *ZAW* 73 (1961): 202–25.
Cotter, David. Review of *Review of The Story within a Story in Biblical Hebrew Narrative (CBQMS 45)*, by David Bosworth. *CBQ* 72 (2010): 561–63.
Craigie, Peter C. *Psalms 1–50*. WBC 19. Waco: Word, 1983.
Cramer, J. A. *Catenae in Evangelia S. Matthaei et S. Marci, Ad Fidem Codd. MSS*. Oxonii: E. Typographeo Academico, 1840.
Cranfield, C. E. B. *The Gospel According to Saint Mark: An Introd. and Commentary*. Cambridge: University Press, 1959.
Cranfield, C. E. B. "The Structure of the Apocalypse of 'Son of God' (4Q246)." Pages 151–58 in *Emanuel: Studies in Hebrew Bible, Septuagint, and Dead Sea Scrolls in Honor of Emanuel Tov*. Edited by Shalom M. Paul. VTSup 94. Leiden: Brill, 2003.
Crossan, John Dominic. "The Parable of the Wicked Husbandmen." *JBL* 90 (1971): 451–65.

Croy, N. Clayton. "Where the Gospel Text Begins: A Non-Theological Interpretation of Mark 1:1." *NovT* 43 (2001): 105–27.
Cullmann, Oscar. *Die Tauflehre des Neuen Testaments Erwachsenen- und Kindertaufe*. ATANT 12. Zürich: Zwingli, 1948.
Cullmann, Oscar. *The Christology of the New Testament*. Rev. ed. NTL. Philadelphia: Westminster Press, 1963.
Culpepper, R. Alan. *Mark*. SHBC 20. Macon, GA: Smyth & Helwys, 2007.
Curtis, Adrian, ed. *Oxford Bible Atlas*. 4th ed. Oxford/New York: Oxford University Press, 2007.
Dahl, Nils Alstrup, and Donald Juel. *Jesus the Christ: The Historical Origins of Christological Doctrine*. Minneapolis: Fortress Press, 1991.
Dahood, Mitchell J. *Psalms I: 1–50: Introduction, Translation, and Notes*. AB 16a. Garden City, NY: Doubleday, 1966.
Dahood, Mitchell J. *Psalms 2: 51–100: Introduction, Translation, and Notes*. AB 16b. Garden City, NY: Doubleday, 1966.
Dällenbach, Lucien. *Le récit spéculaire: essai sur la mise en abyme*. Paris, 1977.
Dalman, Gustaf Hermann. *Die Worte Jesu: mit Berücksichtigung des Nachkanonischen Jüdischen Schrifttums und der Armäischen Sprache*. Leipzig: J. C. Hinrichs'sche, 1898.
Dalman, Gustaf Hermann. *The Words of Jesus: Considered in the Light of Post-Biblical Jewish Writings and the Aramaic Language*. Translated by D. M. Kay. Edinburgh: T&T Clark, 1902.
Daly, Robert J. "The Soteriological Significance of the Sacrifice of Isaac." *CBQ* 39 (1977): 45–75.
Davidsen, Ole. *The Narrative Jesus: A Semiotic Reading of Mark's Gospel*. Aarhus, Denmark: Aarhus University Press, 1993.
Davies, Jamie. "Apocalyptic Topography in Mark's Gospel: Theophany and Divine Invisibility at Sinai, Horeb, and the Mount of Transfiguration." *JTI* 14 (2020): 140–48.
Davies, P. R., and B. D. Chilton. "The Aqedah: A Revised Tradition History." *CBQ* 40 (1978): 514–46.
Davies, W. D., and Dale C. Allison. *A Critical and Exegetical Commentary on the Gospel According to Saint Matthew*. 3 vols ICC 40. London/New York: T&T Clark, 2004.
Davis, Philip G. "Mark's Christological Paradox." *JSNT* 35 (1989): 3–18.
Day, John, ed. *King and Messiah in Israel and the Ancient Near East: Proceedings of the Oxford Old Testament Seminar*. JSOTSup 270. Sheffield, England: Sheffield Academic Press, 1998.
Deissmann, Gustav Adolf. *Light from the Ancient East: The New Testament Illustrated by Recently Discovered Texts of the Graeco-Roman World*. Translated by Lionel R. M. Strachan. New and completely revised. London: Hodder and Stoughton, 1927. Translated from *Licht Vom Osten: Das Neue Testament Und Die Neuentdeckten Texte der Hellenistisch Römischen Welt*. Tübingen: J. C. B. Mohr, 1908.
Deppe, Dean B. *Theological Intentions of Mark's Literary Devices: Markan Intercalations, Frames, Allusionary Repetitions, Narrative Surprises, and Three Types of Mirroring*. Eugene, OR: Wipf & Stock, 2015.
Derrett, J. Duncan M. "Allegory and the Wicked Vinedressers." *JTS* 25 (1974): 426–32.
Derrett, J. Duncan M. "Contributions to the Study of the Gerasene Demoniac." *JSNT* 2 (1979): 2–17.
Derrett, J. Duncan M. "Legend and Event: The Gerasene Demoniac: An Inquest into History and Liturgical Projection." Pages 63–73 in *Studia Biblica 1978*. Edited by Elizabeth A. Livingstone. JSNTSup 2. Sheffield: University of Sheffield Press, 1979.

Derrett, J. Duncan M. "Spirit-Possession and the Gerasene Demoniac." *Man* 14 (1979): 286-93.
Derrett, J. Duncan M. *The Making of Mark: The Scriptural Bases of the Earliest Gospel.* 2 vols Shipston-on-Stour: Drinkwater, 1985.
Dewey, Joanna. "Mark as Interwoven Tapestry: Forecasts and Echoes for a Listening Audience." *CBQ* 53 (1991): 221-36.
Dewey, Joanna. "Oral Methods of Structuring Narrative in Mark." *Int* 43 (1989): 32-44.
Dewey, Joanna. "The Gospel of Mark as an Oral-Aural Event: Implications for Interpretation." Pages 145-63 in *The New Literary Criticism and the New Testament.* Edited by Elizabeth Struthers Malbon and Edgar V. McKnight. JSNTSup 109. Sheffield: Sheffield Academic, 1994.
Dewey, Joanna. "The Literary Structure of the Controversy Stories in Mark 2:1-3:6." *JBL* 92 (1973): 394-401.
Dewey, Joanna. *The Oral Ethos of the Early Church: Speaking, Writing, and the Gospel of Mark.* Eugene, OR: Wipf & Stock, 2013.
Dibelius, Martin. "Herodes Und Pilatus." *ZNW* 16 (1915): 113-26.
Diodore. *Diodore of Tarsus: Commentary on Psalms 1-51.* Translated by Robert C. Hill. WGRW 9. Atlanta: SBL Press, 2005.
Diodore, and Jean-Marie Olivier. *Diodori Tarsensis Commentarii in Psalmos.* CChr 6. Turnhout: Leuven: Brepols; University Press, 1980.
Doble, Peter. "The Psalms in Luke-Acts." Pages 83-117 in *The Psalms in the New Testament.* Edited by Steve Moyise and Maarten J. J. Menken. NTSI. London: T&T Clark, 2004.
von Dobschütz, Ernst. "Zur Erzählerkunst des Markus." *ZNW* 27 (1928): 193-98.
Dobson, Brian. ""The Significance of the Centurion and the 'Primipilaris' in the Roman Army and Administration." *ANRW* 1:395-433.
Dodd, C. H. *Historical Tradition in the Fourth Gospel.* Cambridge: Cambridge University Press, 1989.
Domeris, W. R. "The Holy One of God as a Title for Jesus." *Neot* 19 (1985): 9-17.
Donahue, John R. "A Neglected Factor in the Theology of Mark." *JBL* 101 (1982): 563-94.
Donahue, John R., and Daniel J. Harrington. *The Gospel of Mark.* SP 2. Collegeville, MN: Liturgical, 2002.
Donaldson, Terence L. *Jesus on the Mountain: A Study in Matthean Theology.* JSNTSup 8. Sheffield: JSOT Press, 1985.
Dormandy, Richard. "The Expulsion of Legion: A Political Reading of Mark 5:1-20." *ExpTim* 111 (2000): 335-37.
Dormeyer, Detlev. *Das Markusevangelium.* Darmstadt: Wissenschaftliche Buchgesellschaft, 2005.
Dormeyer, Detlev. *Das Markusevangelium Als Idealbiographie von Jesus Christus, Dem Nazarener.* SBB 43. Stuttgart: Katholisches Bibelwerk, 1999.
Dormeyer, Detlev. "Mk 1,1-15 als Prolog des ersten idealbiographischen Evangeliums von Jesus Christus." *BibInt* 5 (1997): 181-211.
Dowd, Sharyn Echols. *Reading Mark: A Literary and Theological Commentary on the Second Gospel.* Macon, GA: Smyth & Helwys, 2000.
Draisma, Sipke (ed.). *Intertextuality in Biblical Writings: Essays in Honour of Bas van Iersel.* Peeters, 1989.
Drury, John. "The Sower, the Vineyard, and the Place of Allegory in the Interpretation of Mark's Parables." *JTS* 24 (1973): 367-79.
Duling, Dennis C. "The Promises to David and Their Entrance into Christianity—Nailing down a Likely Hypothesis*." *NTS* 20 (1973): 55-77.

Dunn, James D. G. "Messianic Ideas and Their Influence on the Jesus of History." Pages 365–81 in *The Messiah: Developments in Earliest Judaism and Christianity*. Edited by James H. Charlesworth. Minneapolis: Fortress, 1992.

Dunn, James D. G. *Christology in the Making: A New Testament Inquiry into the Origins of the Doctrine of the Incarnation*. 2nd ed. London: SCM, 1989.

Dunn, James D. G. "The Danielic Son of Man in the New Testament." Pages 528–49 in *The Book of Daniel: Composition and Reception*. Edited by John J. Collins and Peter W. Flint. Vol. 2 of VTSup 83. Leiden/Boston: Brill, 2001.

Dupont, Jacques. "Filius Meus Es Tu. L'interprétation du Ps. II 7, dans le Nouveau Testament." *RSR* 35 (1948): 522–42.

Eaton, John H. *Kingship and the Psalms*. 2nd ed. Sheffield: JSOT Press, 1986.

Eaton, John H. *The Psalms: A Historical and Spiritual Commentary*. London: T&T Clark, 2003.

Eckey, Wilfried. *Das Markusevangelium: Orientierung Am Weg Jesu; Ein Kommentar*. 2nd ed. Neukirchen-Vluyn: Neukirchener, 2008.

Eco, Umberto. *A Theory of Semiotics*. Indiana University Press, 1979.

Eco, Umberto. *Interpretation and Overinterpretation*. Edited by Stefan Collini. Cambridge: Cambridge University Press, 1992.

Eco, Umberto. *Semiotics and the Philosophy of Language*. Bloomington: Indiana University Press, 1986.

Eco, Umberto. *The Limits of Interpretation*. Bloomington; Indianapolis: Indiana University Press, 1990.

Edwards, James R. "Markan Sandwiches. The Significance of Interpolations in Markan Narratives." *NovT* 31 (1989): 193–216.

Edwards, James R. *The Gospel According to Mark*. PNTC. Grand Rapids: Eerdmans; Leicester: Apollos, 2002.

Edwards, Timothy M. *Exegesis in the Targum of the Psalms: The Old, the New, and the Rewritten*. First Gorgias Press ed. Gorgias Dissertations 28. Piscataway, NJ: Gorgias Press, 2007.

Egger, Wilhelm. *Frohbotschaft und Lehre: d. Sammelberichte d. Wirkens Jesu im Markusevangelium*. FTS 19. Frankfurt am Main: Knecht, 1976.

Egger, Wilhelm. "Die Verborgenheit Jesu in Mk 3:7-12." *Bib* 50 (1969): 466–90.

Ehrman, Bart D. *The Orthodox Corruption of Scripture: The Effect of Early Christological Controversies on the Text of the New Testament*. Updated and with a new afterword. New York: Oxford University Press, 2011.

Ehrman, Bart D. "The Text of Mark in the Hands of the Orthodox." *LQ* (1991): 143–56.

Eliot, T. S. *T. S. Eliot: Collected Poems, 1909-1962*. New York: Harcourt Brace, 1991.

Elliott, J. K. "Mark 1.1-3—A Later Addition to the Gospel?" *NTS* 46 (2000): 584–88.

Engnell, Ivan. *Studies in Divine Kingship in the Ancient Near East*. 2nd ed. Oxford: B. Blackwell, 1967.

Enslin, Morton S. "The Artistry of Mark." *JBL* 66 (1947): 385–99.

Epstein, Isadore, ed. *The Babylonian Talmud*. Quincentenary ed. Vol. 1. London: Soncino, 1978.

Ermakov, Arseny. "The Holy One of God in Markan Narrative." *HBT* 36 (2014): 159–84.

Ernst, Josef. *Das Evangelium Nach Markus*. 6th ed. RNT. Regensburg: Pustet, 1981.

Ernst, Josef. *Markus: ein theologisches Portrait*. Düsseldorf: Patmos, 1987.

Evans, Craig A. "How Septuagintal Is Isa. 5:1-7 in Mark 12:1-9?" *NovT* 45 (2003): 105–10.

Evans, Craig A. "A Note on the 'First-Born Son' of 4Q369." *DSD* 2 (1995): 185–201.

Evans, Craig A. "Are the 'Son' Texts at Qumran 'Messianic'? Reflections on 4Q369 and Related Scrolls," Pages 100–134 in *Qumran-Messianism: Studies on the Messianic Expectations in the Dead Sea Scrolls*. Edited by James H. Charlesworth, Hermann Lichtenberger, and Gerbern S. Oegema. Tübingen: Mohr Siebeck, 1998.

Evans, Craig A. "Daniel in the New Testament: Visions of God's Kingdom." Pages 490–527 in *The Book of Daniel: Composition and Reception*. Edited by John J. Collins and Peter W. Flint. Vol. 2 of VTSup 83. Leiden/Boston: Brill, 2001.

Evans, Craig A. *Mark 8:27-16:20*. WBC 34b. Nashville: Thomas Nelson Publishers, 2001.

Evans, Craig A. "Mark's Incipit and the Priene Calendar Inscription: From Jewish Gospel to Greco-Roman Gospel." *JGRChJ* 1 (2000): 67–81.

Evans, Craig A. "Zechariah in the Markan Passion Narrative." Pages 64–80 in *Biblical Interpretation in Early Christian Gospels*. Edited by T. R. Hatina. Vol. 1 of LNTS 304. London/New York: T&T Clark, 2006.

Ferda, Tucker S. "Matthew's Titulus and Psalm 2's King on Mount Zion." *JBL* 133 (2014): 561–81.

Ferda, Tucker S. "Naming the Messiah: A Contribution to the 4Q246 'Son of God' Debate." *DSD* 21 (2014): 150–75.

Ferda, Tucker S. "The Soldiers' Inscription and the Angel's Word: The Significance of 'Jesus' in Matt." *NovT* 55 (2013): 221–31.

Ferguson, Anthony. "The Elijah Forerunner Concept as an Authentic Jewish Expectation." *JBL* 137 (2018): 127–45.

Fischel, H. A. "Martyr and Prophet (A Study in Jewish Literature)." *JQR* 37 (1947): 265–80.

Fitzmyer, Joseph A. "4Q246: The 'Son of God' Document from Qumran." *Bib* 74 (1993): 153–74.

Fitzmyer, Joseph A. "Contribution of Qumran Aramaic to the Study of the New Testament." *NTS* 20 (1974): 382–407.

Fitzmyer, Joseph A. "Crucifixion in Ancient Palestine, Qumran Literature, and the New Testament." *CBQ* 40 (1978): 493–513.

Fitzmyer, Joseph A. "More about Elijah Coming First." *JBL* 104 (1985): 295–96.

Fitzmyer, Joseph A. "Some Observations on the 'Genesis Apocryphon.'" *CBQ* 22 (1960): 277–91.

Fitzmyer, Joseph A. *The Acts of the Apostles: A New Translation with Introduction and Commentary*. AB 31a. New York: Doubleday, 1998.

Fitzmyer, Joseph A. *The Gospel According to Luke (I-IX): Introduction, Translation, and Notes*. AB 28a–28b. Garden City, NY: Doubleday, 1981.

Flusser, David. *Judaism and the Origins of Christianity*. Jerusalem: Magnes Press, 1988.

Focant, Camille. *The Gospel According to Mark: A Commentary*. Translated by Leslie Robert Keylock. Eugene, OR: Pickwick, 2012. Translation of *L'évangile selon Marc*. Commentaire biblique: nouveau testament 2. Paris: Cerf, 2004.

Förster, Niclas. "Der titulus crucis: Demütigung der Judäer und Proklamation des Messias." *NovT* 56 (2014): 113–33.

Fowler, Alastair. *Kinds of Literature: An Introduction to the Theory of Genres and Modes*. Cambridge: Harvard University Press, 1982.

Fowler, Robert M. *Let the Reader Understand: Reader-Response Criticism and the Gospel of Mark*. Minneapolis: Fortress, 1991.

France, R. T. *The Gospel of Mark: A Commentary on the Greek Text*. NIGTC. Grand Rapids: Eerdmans, 2002.

Frankfort, Henri. *Kingship and the Gods: A Study of Ancient Near Eastern Religion as the Integration of Society & Nature.* Phoenix ed. An Oriental Institute Essay. Chicago: University of Chicago Press, 1978.

Frei, Hans W. *The Eclipse of Biblical Narrative; a Study in Eighteenth and Nineteenth Century Hermeneutics.* New Haven: Yale University Press, 1974.

Frei, Hans W. *The Identity of Jesus Christ: The Hermeneutical Bases of Dogmatic Theology.* Eugene, OR: Wipf & Stock, 2000.

Fuller, Reginald H. *The Foundations of New Testament Christology.* New York: Scribner, 1965.

Fuller, Reginald H. *The Mission and Achievement of Jesus: An Examination of the Presuppositions of New Testament Theology.* Chicago: Alec R. Allenson, 1956.

Funk, Robert W. "The Wilderness." *JBL* 78 (1959): 205–14.

Galinsky, Karl. *Augustan Culture: An Interpretive Introduction.* Princeton: Princeton University Press, 1996.

Galinsky, Karl. *Augustus: Introduction to the Life of an Emperor.* New York: Cambridge University Press, 2012.

Gamel, Brian K. *Mark 15:39 as a Markan Theology of Revelation: The Centurion's Confession as Apocalyptic Unveiling.* LNTS 458. London/New York: Bloomsbury T&T Clark, 2017.

García Martínez, Florentino. "Messianic Hope in the Qumran Writings." Pages 159–89 in *The People of the Dead Sea Scrolls: Their Writings, Beliefs and Practices.* Edited by Florentino García Martínez and Julio Trebolle Barrera. STDJ 30. Leiden: Brill, 1995.

García Martínez, Florentino. "The Eschatological Figure of 4Q246." Pages 162–79 in *Qumran and Apocalyptic: Studies on the Aramaic Texts from Qumran.* STDJ 9. New York: Brill, 1992.

Garland, David E. *Reading Matthew: A Literary and Theological Commentary on the First Gospel.* London: SPCK, 1993.

Garrett, Susan R. *The Temptations of Jesus in Mark's Gospel.* Grand Rapids: Eerdmans, 1998.

Gathercole, Simon J. *The Preexistent Son: Recovering the Christologies of Matthew, Mark, and Luke.* Grand Rapids: Eerdmans, 2006.

Genest, Hartmut, ed. *Christi Leidenspsalm: Arbeiten zum 22. Psalm; Festschrift zum 50. Jahr des Bestehens des Theologischen Seminars "Paulinum" Berlin.* Neukirchen-Vluyn: Neukirchener, 1996.

Gerhardsson, Birger. *The Testing of God's Son. (Matt. 4: 1-11 & Par.): An Analysis of an Early Christian Midrash.* ConBNT 2. Lund: Gleerup, 1966.

Gero, Stephen. "'My Son the Messiah': A Note on 4 Esr 7:28-29." *ZNW* 66 (1975): 264–67.

Gibson, Jeffrey B. "Jesus' Wilderness Temptation According to Mark." *JSNT* 53 (1994): 3–34.

Gide, André. *Journals: 1889-1913.* University of Illinois Press, 2000.

Gill, John. *Gill's Commentary.* 6 vols Grand Rapids: Baker, 1980.

Gillingham, S. E. *A Journey of Two Psalms: The Reception of Psalms 1 and 2 in Jewish and Christian Tradition.* Oxford, United Kingdom: Oxford University Press, 2013.

Globe, Alexander. "The Caesarean Omission of the Phrase 'Son of God' in Mark 1:1." *HTR* 75 (1982): 209–18.

Gnilka, Joachim. *Das Evangelium nach Markus.* 2 vols *EKKNT* 2. Zürich; Neukirchen-Vluyn: Benziger; Neukirchener, 1978.

Goldingay, John. *A Critical and Exegetical Commentary on Isaiah 56-66.* ICC 24. London: Bloomsbury, 2014.

Goldingay, John. *Daniel.* WBC 30. Dallas: Word, 1989.

Goldingay, John. *Psalms*. 3 vols Grand Rapids: Baker Academic, 2006.
Goldsmith, Dale. "Acts 13:33-37: A Pesher on II Samuel 7." *JBL* 87 (1968): 321-24.
Goodacre, Mark S. *The Case against Q: Studies in Markan Priority and Synoptic Problem*. Harrisburg: Trinity, 2001.
Gordon, Richard. "The Roman Imperial Cult and the Question of Power." Pages 37-70 in *The Religious History of the Roman Empire: Pagans, Jews, and Christians*. Edited by John North and S. R. F. Price. Oxford Readings in Classical Studies. New York: Oxford University Press, 2011.
Gould, Ezra Palmer. *A Critical and Exegetical Commentary on the Gospel According to St. Mark*. ICC 27. New York: Scribner's, 1896.
Grant, Michael. *The Army of the Caesars*. New York: Scribner's, 1974.
Green, Joel B. *The Gospel of Luke*. NICNT. Grand Rapids: Eerdmans, 1997.
Grotius, Hugo. *Annotationes in Novum Testamentum Volume II: Ad Matth. XVI-XXVIII*. Groningen: W. Zuidema, 1827.
Grundmann, Walter. *Das Evangelium Nach Markus*. THKNT 2. Berlin: Evangelische Verlagsanstalt, 1989.
Grünebaum, E., and Carsten Wilke. *Die Sittenlehre Des Judenthums Andern Bekenntnissen Gegenüber: Nebst Dem Geschichtlichen Nachweise Über Die Entstehung Und Bedeutung Des Pharisaismus Und Dessen Verhältniss Zum Stifter Der Christlichen Religion*. 2nd ed. Deutsch-Jüdische Autoren Des 19. Jahrhunderts 1. Strassburg: Schneider, 1878.
Guelich, Robert A. *Mark 1-8:26*. WBC 34a. Dallas: Word, 1989.
Guelich, Robert A. "'The Beginning of the Gospel': Mark 1:1-15." *BR* 27 (1982): 5-15.
Guillemette, Pierre. "Mc 1,24 est-il une formule de défense magique?" *ScEs* 30 (1978): 81-96.
Gundry, Robert H. *The Use of the Old Testament in St. Matthew's Gospel: With Special Reference to the Messianic Hope*. NovTSup 18. Leiden: Brill, 1967.
Gundry, Robert H. *Mark: A Commentary on His Apology for the Cross*. Grand Rapids: Eerdmans, 1993.
Gunkel, Hermann. *Einleitung in Die Psalmen*. Göttinger Handkommentar Zum Alten Testament. Göttingen: Vandenhoeck & Ruprecht, 1933.
Gurtner, Daniel. "The Rending of the Veil and Markan Christology: 'Unveiling' the ΥΙΟΣ ΘΕΟΥ (Mark 15:38-39)." *BibInt* 15 (2007): 292-306.
Gurtner, Daniel. "The Veil of the Temple in History and Legend." *JETS* 49 (2006): 97-114.
Haenchen, Ernst. *Der Weg Jesu: Eine Erklärung des Markus-Evangeliums und der kanonischen Parallelen*. Berlin: Töpelmann, 1966.
Haenchen, Ernst. "History and Interpretation in the Johannine Passion Narrative." *Int* 24 (1970): 198-219.
Haenchen, Ernst. *John: A Commentary on the Gospel of John*. Hermeneia. Philadelphia: Fortress, 1984.
Haenchen, Ernst. *The Acts of the Apostles: A Commentary*. Philadelphia: Westminster, 1971.
Hahn, Ferdinand. *Christologische Hoheitstitel: Ihre Geschichte im Frühen Christentum*. 5th ed. Göttingen: Vandenhoeck & Ruprecht, 1995.
Hahn, Ferdinand. *The Titles of Jesus in Christology: Their History in Early Christianity*. London: Lutterworth, 1969.
Ḥakham, 'Amos. *Sefer Tehilim* ספר תהלים. Torah, Nevi'im, Ketuvim 'im perush "Da'at Miḳra." Jerusalem: Mossad Harav Kook, 1979.
Hare, Douglas R. A. *Mark*. Louisville: Westminster John Knox, 1996.
Harner, Philip B. "Qualitative Anarthrous Predicate Nouns: Mark 15:39 and John 1:1." *JBL* 92 (1973): 75-87.

Hartman, Lars. *Markus evangeliet. Kommentar till Nya testamentet 2a–2b*. Stockholm: EFS-förlaget, 2004.
Hartman, Louis Francis. *The Book of Daniel*. AB 23. Garden City, NY: Doubleday, 1978.
Harvey, W. J. *Character and the Novel*. Ithaca, NY: Cornell University Press, 1965.
Hatina, Thomas R. *In Search of a Context: The Function of Scripture in Mark's Narrative*. SSEJC 8. London/New York: Sheffield Academic Press, 2002.
Hays, Richard B. *Echoes of Scripture in the Gospels*. Waco: Baylor University Press, 2016.
Hays, Richard B. *Echoes of Scripture in the Letters of Paul*. New Haven: Yale University Press, 1989.
Hays, Richard B., Stefan Alkier, and Leroy A Huizenga, eds. *Reading the Bible Intertextually*. Waco: Baylor University Press, 2015.
Head, Peter. "A Text-Critical Study of Mark 1.1: The Beginning of the Gospel of Jesus Christ." *NTS* 37 (1991): 621–29.
Hedrick, Charles W. "The Role of 'Summary Statements' in the Composition of the Gospel of Mark: A Dialog with Karl Schmidt and Norman Perrin." *NovT* 26 (1984): 289–311.
Heil, John Paul. "A Note on 'Elijah with Moses' in Mark 9,4." *Bib* 80 (1999): 115.
Heil, John Paul. "Jesus with the Wild Animals in Mark 1:13." *CBQ* 68 (2006): 63–78.
Heil, John Paul. *The Death and Resurrection of Jesus: A Narrative-Critical Reading of Matthew 26-28*. Minneapolis: Fortress, 1991.
Heil, John Paul. *The Transfiguration of Jesus: Narrative Meaning and Function of Mark 9:2-8, Matt 17:1-8 and Luke 9:28-36*. AnBib 144. Rome: Pontifical Biblical Institute, 2000.
Hengel, Martin. *Crucifixion in the Ancient World and the Folly of the Message of the Cross*. Philadelphia: Fortress, 1977.
Hengel, Martin. *Judaism and Hellenism: Studies in Their Encounter in Palestine during the Early Hellenistic Period*. Translated by John Bowden. London: SCM, 1974.
Hengel, Martin. "'Sit at My Right Hand!'" Pages 119–26 in *Studies in Early Christology*. Edinburgh: T&T Clark, 1995.
Hengel, Martin. *Studies in Early Christology*. Edinburgh: T&T Clark, 1995.
Hengel, Martin. *The Son of God: The Origin of Christology and the History of Jewish-Hellenistic Religion*. Translated by John Bowden. Eugene, OR: Wipf & Stock, 2007. Translation of *Der Sohn Gottes: die Entstehung der Christologie und die jüdisch-hellenistische Religionsgeschichte*. Tübingen: J. C. B. Mohr, 1975.
Henry, Matthew. *Matthew Henry's Commentary on the Whole Bible*. Vol. 5. Peabody, MA: Hendrickson, 2009.
Hill, Robert C., trans. *Theodoret of Cyrus: Commentary on the Psalms, 1-72*. FC 101. Washington, D.C.: Catholic University of America Press, 2000.
Hollander, John. *The Figure of Echo: A Mode of Allusion in Milton and After*. Berkeley: University of California Press, 1981.
Hollenbach, Paul W. "Jesus, Demoniacs, and Public Authorities: A Socio-Historical Study." *JAAR* 49 (1981): 567–88.
Holtzmann, Heinrich Julius. *Das messianische Bewusstsein Jesu: ein Beitrag zur Leben-Jesu-Forschung*. Tübingen: Mohr Siebeck, 1907.
Hooker, Morna D. "Good News about Jesus Christ, the Son of God." Pages 165–80 in *Mark as Story: Retrospect and Prospect*. Edited by Kelly R. Iverson and Christopher W. Skinner. RBS 65. Atlanta: SBL, 2011.
Hooker, Morna D. *The Gospel According to St. Mark*. Peabody: Hendrickson, 1993.

Hooker, Morna D. "'Who Can This Be?' The Christology of Mark's Gospel." Pages 79–99 in *Contours of Christology in the New Testament*. Edited by Richard N. Longenecker. Grand Rapids: Eerdmans, 2005.
Hooker, Morna D. *Jesus and the Servant: The Influence of the Servant Concept of Deutero-Isaiah in the New Testament*. London: SPCK, 1959.
Hooker, Morna D. *The Message of Mark*. London: Epworth, 1983.
Hooker, Morna D. *The Son of Man in Mark: A Study of the Background of the Term "Son of Man" and Its Use in St. Mark's Gospel*. Montreal: McGill University Press, 1967.
Horbury, William. *Jewish Messianism and the Cult of Christ*. London: SCM, 1998.
Horbury, William. "The Messianic Associations of 'The Son of Man.'" *JTS* 36 (1985): 34–55.
Horsley, Richard A. *Hearing the Whole Story: The Politics of Plot in Mark's Gospel*. Louisville: Westminster John Knox Press, 2001.
Horsley, Richard A., Jonathan A. Draper, John Miles Foley, and Werner H. Kelber, eds. *Performing the Gospel: Orality, Memory, and Mark*. Minneapolis: Fortress, 2006.
Horstmann, Maria. *Studien zur markinischen Christologie: Mk 8, 27-9, 13 als Zugang zum Christusbild des zweiten Evangeliums*. Münster: Aschendorff, 1969.
Hossfeld, Frank-Lothar, and Erich Zenger. *Psalms 2: A Commentary on Psalms 51-100*. Hermeneia. Minneapolis: Fortress, 2005.
Huizenga, Leroy Andrew. *The New Isaac: Tradition and Intertextuality in the Gospel of Matthew*. NovTSup 131. Leiden/Boston: Brill, 2009.
Hultgren, Arland J. *The Parables of Jesus: A Commentary*. Grand Rapids: Eerdmans, 2000.
Humphrey, Robert L. *Narrative Structure and Message in Mark: A Rhetorical Analysis*. SBEC 60. Lewiston, NY: E. Mellen, 2003.
Huntress, Erminie. "'Son of God' in Jewish Writings Prior to the Christian Era." *JBL* 54 (1935): 117–23.
Ibn Ezra, Abraham ben Meïr, and M. Friedländer. *The Commentary of Ibn Ezra on Isaiah*. Society of Hebrew Literature, Publications. London: N. Trübner, 1873.
Incigneri, Brian J. *The Gospel to the Romans: The Setting and Rhetoric of Mark's Gospel*. BibInt 65. Leiden/Boston, MA: Brill, 2003.
Iverson, Kelly R. "A Centurion's 'Confession': A Performance-Critical Analysis of Mark 15:39." *JBL* 130 (2011): 329–50.
Iverson, Kelly R. "Jews, Gentiles, and the Kingdom of God: The Parable of the Wicked Tenants in Narrative Perspective (Mark 12:1-12)." *BibInt* 20 (2012): 305–35.
Iverson, Kelly R. "Orality and the Gospels: A Survey of Recent Research." *CRBS* 8 (2009): 71–106.
Iverson, Kelly R., Christopher W. Skinner, and Society of Biblical Literature, eds. *Mark as Story: Retrospect and Prospect*. RBS 65. Atlanta: SBL, 2011.
Jackson, Howard M. "The Death of Jesus in Mark and the Miracle from the Cross." *NTS* 33 (1987): 16–37.
Janse, Sam. *You Are My Son: The Reception History of Psalm 2 in Early Judaism and the Early Church*. Leuven: Peeters, 2009.
Jefferson, Ann. "'Mise En Abyme' and the Prophetic in Narrative." *Style* 17 (1983): 196–208.
Jeremias, Joachim. *Jesus' Promise to the Nations: The Franz Delitzsch Lectures for 1953*. Translated by S. H. Hooke. SBT 24. London: SCM, 1958.
Jeremias, Joachim. *The Parables of Jesus*. Translated by S. H. Hooke. New York: Scribner, 1972.
Jervell, Jacob. *Die Apostelgeschichte*. KEK 3. Göttingen: Vandenhoeck & Ruprecht, 1998.
Jervell, Jacob. *The Theology of the Acts of the Apostles*. New Testament Theology. New York: Cambridge University Press, 1996.

Jipp, Joshua W. "Ancient, Modern, and Future Interpretations of Romans I:3-4: Reception History and Biblical Interpretation." *JTI* 3 (2009): 241–59.
Johnson, Earl S. "Mark 15,39 and the So-Called Confession of the Roman Centurion." *Bib* 81 (2000): 406–13.
Johnson, Earl S. "Is Mark 15.39 the Key to Mark's Christology." *JSNT* 31 (1987): 3–22.
Johnson, Luke Timothy. *The Gospel of Luke*. SP 3. Collegeville, MN: Liturgical, 1991.
Johnson, Nathan C. "Romans 1:3-4: Beyond Antithetical Parallelism." *JBL* 136 (2017): 467–90.
Jong, Irene J. F. de. "The Shield of Achilles: From Metalepsis to Mise En Abyme." *Ramus* 40 (2011): 1–14.
Juel, Donald. *A Master of Surprise: Mark Interpreted*. Minneapolis: Fortress, 1994.
Juel, Donald. *Messianic Exegesis: Christological Interpretation of the Old Testament in Early Christianity*. Philadelphia: Fortress, 1988.
Juel, Donald. *Messiah and Temple: The Trial of Jesus in the Gospel of Mark*. SBLDS 31. Missoula: Scholars, 1977.
Jülicher, Adolf. *Die gleichnisreden Jesu*. Freiburg: Mohr Siebeck, 1899.
Kazmierski, Carl R. *Jesus, the Son of God: A Study of the Markan Tradition and Its Redaction by the Evangelist*. FB 33. Würzburg: Echter, 1979.
Keaveney, Arthur, and John A. Madden. "The Crimen Maiestatis under Caligula: The Evidence of Dio Cassius." *ClQ* 48 (1998): 316–20.
Keck, Leander E. "Mark 3:7-12 and Mark's Christology." *JBL* 84 (1965): 341–58.
Keck, Leander E. "The Introduction to Mark's Gospel." *NTS* 12 (1966): 352–70.
Keck, Leander E. "Toward the Renewal of New Testament Christology." *NTS* 32 (1987): 362–77.
Kee, H. C. "The Transfiguration in Mark: Epiphany or Apocalyptic Vision?" Pages 135–53 in *Understanding the Sacred Text: Essays in Honor of Morton S. Enslin on the Hebrew Bible and Christian Beginnings*. Edited by J. H. P. Reumann. Valley Forge: Judson, 1972.
Kee, H. C. "The Terminology of Mark's Exorcism Stories." *NTS* 14 (1968): 232–46.
Keel, Othmar. *Die Welt der altorientalischen Bildsymbolik und das Alte Testament: am Beispiel der Psalmen*. 5th ed. Göttingen: Vandenhoeck & Ruprecht, 1996.
Keener, Craig S. *The Gospel of John: A Commentary*. 2 vols Peabody, MA: Hendrickson, 2010.
Kelber, Werner H. *The Oral and the Written Gospel: The Hermeneutics of Speaking and Writing in the Synoptic Tradition, Mark, Paul, and Q*. Bloomington: Indiana University Press, 1997.
Kempthorne, Renatus. "The Marcan Text of Jesus' Answer to the High Priest (Mark XIV 62)." *NovT* 19 (1977): 197–208.
Kennedy, Joel. *The Recapitulation of Israel: Use of Israel's History in Matthew 1:1-4:11*. WUNT 2/257. Tübingen: Mohr Siebeck, 2008.
Kenyon, Frederic G., and A. W. Adams. *The Text of the Greek Bible*. 3rd ed. London: Duckworth, 1975.
Kermode, Frank. "Anteriority, Authority, and Secrecy: A General Comment." *Semeia* 43 (1988): 155–67.
Kermode, Frank. *The Genesis of Secrecy: On the Interpretation of Narrative*. Cambridge: Harvard University Press, 1979.
Kertelge, Karl. *Die Wunder Jesu im Markusevangelium: eine redaktions-geschichtliche Untersuchung*. München: Kösel, 1970.
Kertelge, Karl. *Markusevangelium*. NEchtB 2. Würzburg: Echter, 1994.

Kim, Seyoon. *The "Son of Man" as the Son of God*. WUNT 30. Tübingen: Mohr Siebeck, 1983.
Kim, Tae Hun. "The Anarthrous Υἱός Θεοῦ in Mark 15,39 and the Roman Imperial Cult." *Bib* 79 (1998): 221–41.
Kingsbury, Jack Dean. *Jesus Christ in Matthew, Mark, and Luke*. Philadelphia: Fortress, 1981.
Kingsbury, Jack Dean. *The Christology of Mark's Gospel*. Philadelphia: Fortress, 1989.
Kingsbury, Jack Dean. "The Developing Conflict between Jesus and the Jewish Leaders in Matthew's Gospel: A Literary-Critical Study." *CBQ* 49 (1987): 57–73.
Kingsbury, Jack Dean. "The 'Divine Man' as the Key to Mark's Christology—The End of an Era?" *Int* 35 (1981): 243–57.
Kister, Menahem. "Son(s) of God: Israel and Christ: A Study of Transformation, Adaptation, and Rivalry." Pages 188–224 in *Son of God: Divine Sonship in Jewish and Christian Antiquity*. Edited by Garrick V. Allen, Kai Akagi, Paul Sloan, and Madhavi Nevader. University Park, PA: Eisenbrauns, 2019.
Kittel, Gerhard, and Gerhard Friedrich, eds. Theological Dictionary of the New Testament. Translated by Geoffrey W. Bromiley. 10 vols Grand Rapids: Eerdmans, 1964–1976.
Klauck, Hans-Josef. *Allegorie und Allegorese in synoptischen Gleichnistexten*. Münster: Aschendorff, 1978.
Kloppenborg, John S. "Isa 5:1-7 LXX and Mark 12:1, 9, Again." *NovT* 46 (2004): 12–19.
Kloppenborg, John S. *Q, the Earliest Gospel: An Introduction to the Original Stories and Sayings of Jesus*. Louisville: Westminster John Knox Press, 2008.
Kloppenborg, John S. *Reading Viticulture: The Social Context of the Parable of the Tenants in Mark and Thomas*. Vol. 44. Institute for Antiquity and Christianity. Claremont, CA: Institute for Antiquity and Christianity, 2002.
Kloppenborg, John S. "Variation in the Reproduction of the Double Tradition and an Oral Q?" *ETL* 83 (2007): 53–80.
Klostermann, Erich. *Das Markusevangelium*. 4th ed. HNT 3. Tübingen: Mohr Siebeck, 1950.
Koch, Dietrich-Alex. *Die Bedeutung der Wundererzählungen für die Christologie des Markusevangeliums*. BZNW 42. Berlin/New York: De Gruyter, 1975.
Koester, Craig R., ed. *Hebrews: A New Translation with Introduction and Commentary*. AB 36. New York: Doubleday, 2001.
Koester, Craig R., ed. *Revelation: A New Translation with Introduction and Commentary*. AB 38a. New Haven: Yale University Press, 2014.
Koester, Helmut, Birger A. Pearson, A. Thomas Kraabel, George W. E. Nickelsburg, and Norman R. Petersen, eds. *The Future of Early Christianity: Essays in Honor of Helmut Koester*. Minneapolis: Fortress, 1991.
Kohler, Kaufmann. *The Origins of the Synagogue and the Church*. New York: Macmillan, 1929.
Köhler, Ludwig, Walter Baumgartner, Johann Jakob Stamm, and M. E. J. Richardson. *The Hebrew and Aramaic Lexicon of the Old Testament*. Leiden/Boston: Brill, 2001.
Kramer, Werner R. *Christ, Lord, Son of God*. SBT 50. London: SCM, 1966.
Kramer, Werner R. *Psalms 1-59: A Commentary*. Minneapolis: Augsburg, 1988.
Krieg, Robert A. *Story-Shaped Christology: The Role of Narratives in Identifying Jesus Christ*. Theological Inquiries. New York: Paulist Press, 1988.
Kristeva, Julia. *Desire in Language: A Semiotic Approach to Literature and Art*. European Perspectives. New York: Columbia University Press, 1980.
Kristeva, Julia. *Revolution in Poetic Language*. New York: Columbia University Press, 1984.

Kristeva, Julia. *[Sēmeiōtikē] Recherches pour une sémanalyse*. Paris: Points, 1969.
Kugel, James. "4Q369 'Prayer of Enosh' and Ancient Biblical Interpretation." *DSD* 5 (1998): 119–48.
Kuhn, Heinz-Wolfgang. "Jesus Als Gekreuzigter in Der Frühchristlichen Verkündigung Bis Zur Mitte Des 2. Jahrhunderts." *ZTK* 72 (1975): 1–46.
Kuhn, Karl A. "The 'One like a Son of Man' Becomes the 'Son of God.'" *CBQ* 69 (2007): 22–42.
Kümmel, W. G. "Das Gleichnis von den Bösen Weingärtnern (Mark 12, 1-9)." Pages 120–31 in *Aux sources de la tradition chrétienne: mélanges offerts à M. Maurice Goguel à l'occasion de son soixante-dixième anniversaire*. Edited by J. J. von Allmen, P. Bonnard, Oscar Cullmann, E. Jacob, J. L. Leuba, E. Mauris, R. Mehl, and Ch. Senft. Neuchâtel: Delachaux & Niestlé, 1950.
Kvanvig, Helge. "The Son of Man in the Parables." Pages 179–215 in *Enoch and the Messiah Son of Man: Revisiting the Book of Parables*. Edited by Gabriele Boccaccini. Grand Rapids: Eerdmans, 2007.
La Gioia, Fabio. *Marco: analisi narrativa del Vangelo più antico*. Collana Logos. Todi: Tau editrice, 2019.
Lane, William L., ed. *The Gospel According to Mark: The English Text with Introduction, Exposition, and Notes*. NICNT 2. Grand Rapids: Eerdmans, 1974.
Lapide, Cornelius Cornelii à. *Commentaria in Scripturam Sacram*. Edited by Augustine Crampon. Vol. 15. Paris: Ludovicus Vives, 1868.
Lapide, Cornelius Cornelii à. *The Great Commentary of Cornelius à Lapide*. Translated by W. F. Cobb. Catholic Standard Library 3. London: J. Hodges, 1876.
Larsen, Matthew D. C. *Gospels before the Book*. New York: Oxford University Press, 2018.
Lau, Markus. "Die Legio X Fretensis Und Der Besessene von Gerasa Anmerkungen Zur Zahlenangabe 'Ungefähr Zweitausend' (Mk 5,13)." *Bib* 88 (2007): 351–64.
Lausberg, Heinrich. *Handbook of Literary Rhetoric: A Foundation for Literary Study*. Edited by David E. Orton and R. Dean Anderson Translated by Matthew T. Bliss, Annemiek Jansen, and David E. Orton. Leiden/Boston: Brill, 1998.
Lawrence, William Witherle. "The Play Scene in 'Hamlet.'" *The Journal of English and Germanic Philology* 18 (1919): 1–22.
Lee, Aquila H. I. *From Messiah to Preexistent Son: Jesus' Self-Consciousness and Early Christian Exegesis of Messianic Psalms*. WUNT 2/192. Tübingen: Mohr Siebeck, 2005.
Lee, Simon S. *Jesus' Transfiguration and the Believers' Transformation: A Study of the Transfiguration and Its Development in Early Christian Writings*. WUNT 2/265. Tübingen, Germany: Mohr Siebeck, 2009.
Légasse, S. *L'Evangile de Marc*. 2 vols Paris: Cerf, 1997.
Leim, Joshua E. *Matthew's Theological Grammar: The Father and the Son*. WUNT 2/402. Tübingen: Mohr Siebeck, 2015.
Lentzen-Deis, Fritzleo. *Die Taufe Jesu nach den Synoptikern: Literarkritische und gattungsgeschichtliche Untersuchungen*. FTS 4. Frankfurt: Knecht, 1970.
Levenson, Jon D. *Sinai & Zion: An Entry into the Jewish Bible*. San Francisco: Harper & Row, 1987.
Levinsohn, Stephen H. *Discourse Features of New Testament Greek: A Coursebook on the Information Structure of New Testament Greek*. 2nd ed. Dallas: SIL International, 2000.
Lewis, C. S. *The Weight of Glory*. San Francisco: HarperOne, 2001.

Lightfoot, R. H. *History and Interpretation in the Gospels: The Bampton Lectures 1934.* London: Hodder and Stoughton, 1935.
Lightfoot, R. H. *The Gospel Message of St. Mark.* London: Oxford University Press, 1962.
Lindars, Barnabas. *New Testament Apologetic: The Doctrinal Significance of the Old Testament Quotations.* London: SCM Press, 1973.
Lohmeyer, Ernst. *Das Evangelium des Markus: Übersetzt und Erklärt.* KEK 2. 11th ed. Göttingen: Vandenhoeck & Ruprecht, 1951.
Lohmeyer, Ernst. "Die Verklärung Jesu nach dem Markus-Evangelium." *ZNW* 21 (2009): 185–215.
Lohmeyer, Ernst. *Galiläa und Jerusalem.* Göttingen: Vandenhoeck & Ruprecht, 1936.
Lohmeyer, Ernst. *Gottesknecht Und Davidsohn.* FRLANT 43. 2nd ed. Göttingen: Vandenhoeck & Ruprecht, 1953.
Long, Thomas G. *Matthew.* Louisville, KY: Westminster John Knox, 1997.
Longenecker, Bruce W. *2 Esdras.* Guides to Apocrypha and Pseudepigrapha. Sheffield: Sheffield Academic Press, 1995.
Lorein, G. W., and E. van Staalduine-Sulman. "Songs of David." Pages 257–67 in *Old Testament Pseudepigrapha: More Noncanonical Scriptures.* Edited by Richard Bauckham, James R. Davila, and Alexander Panayotov. Grand Rapids; Cambridge: Eerdmans, 2013.
Louw, J. P., and Eugene A. Nida, eds. *Greek-English Lexicon of the New Testament: Based on Semantic Domains.* New York: United Bible Societies, 1988.
Lövestam, Evald. "Die Frage Des Hohenpriesters [Mark 14, 61 Par Matth 26, 63]." *SEÅ* 26 (1961): 94–5.
Lövestam, Evald. *Son and Saviour: A Study of Acts 13, 32-37, with an Appendix, "Son of God" in the Synoptic Gospels.* ConBNT 18. Lund: Gleerup, 1961.
Lowe, Malcolm F. "From the Parable of the Vineyard to a Pre-Synoptic Source." *NTS* 28 (1982): 257–63.
Lüdemann, Gerd. *Early Christianity According to the Traditions in Acts: A Commentary.* Translated by John Bowden. Minneapolis: Fortress, 1989.
Lüdemann, Gerd. *The Acts of the Apostles: What Really Happened in the Earliest Days of the Church.* Amherst, NY: Prometheus, 2005.
Lührmann, Dieter. *Das Markusevangelium.* HNT 3. Tübingen: Mohr Siebeck, 1987.
Lührmann, Dieter. "Markus 14:55-64: Christologie und Zerstörung des Tempels im Markusevangelium." *NTS* 27 (1981): 457–74.
Lust, Johann. "Gog." *DDD* 1:373–375.
Lust, Johann. "Magog." *DDD* 1:535–537.
Luz, Ulrich. "Das Geheimnismotiv und die markinische Christologie." *ZNW* 56 (2009): 9–30.
Macaskill, Grant. "Matthew and the Parables of Enoch." Pages 218–29 in *Parables of Enoch: A Paradigm Shift.* Edited by James H. Charlesworth and Darrell L. Bock. JCTCRSS 11. London: T&T Clark, 2013.
MacIntyre, Alasdair. *Whose Justice? Which Rationality?* Notre Dame: University of Notre Dame Press, 1988.
Maclear, G. F. *The Gospel According to St. Mark: With Notes and Introduction.* Cambridge: Cambridge University Press, 1879.
Magnus, Albertus. *Commentarii in Psalmos.* Edited by S. Borgnet. Opera Omnia 7. Paris, 1894.
Magnus, Albertus. *Enarrationes in Matthaeum (XXI-XXVIII)—In Marcum.* Edited by Auguste Borgnet. Opera Omnia 21. Paris: Ludovicus Vives, 1894.

Maier, Paul L. "The Inscription on the Cross of Jesus of Nazareth." *Hermes* 124 (1996): 58–75.
Malbon, Elizabeth Struthers. "Echoes and Foreshadowings in Mark 4-8 Reading and Rereading." *JBL* 112 (1993): 211–30.
Malbon, Elizabeth Struthers. *Mark's Jesus: Characterization as Narrative Christology*. Waco: Baylor University Press, 2009.
Malbon, Elizabeth Struthers. "Narrative Criticism: How Does the Story Mean?" Pages 27–45 in *Mark and Method: New Approaches in Biblical Studies*. Edited by Janice Capel Anderson and Stephen D. Moore. Philadelphia: Fortress, 1992.
Malbon, Elizabeth Struthers. *Narrative Space and Mythic Meaning in Mark*. New York: Harper & Row, 1986.
Malbon, Elizabeth Struthers. "The Christology of Mark's Gospel: Narrative Christology and the Markan Jesus." Pages 33–48 in *Who Do You Say That I Am? Essays on Christology*. Edited by Mark Allan Powell and David R. Bauer. Louisville: Westminster John Knox, 1999.
Maldonado, Juan de. *A Commentary on the Holy Gospels*. Translated by George John Davie. Catholic Standard Library. London: J. Hodges, 1888.
Mansfeld, J. "Ambiguity in Empedocles B17, 3-5: A Suggestion." *Phronesis* 17 (1972): 17–39.
Marcus, Joel. "Crucifixion as Parodic Exaltation." *JBL* 125 (2006): 73–87.
Marcus, Joel. *John the Baptist in History and Theology*. Columbia: University of South Carolina Press, 2018.
Marcus, Joel. "Mark 14:61: 'Are You the Messiah-Son-of-God?'" *NovT* 31 (1989): 125–41.
Marcus, Joel. *Mark 1–8: A New Translation with Introduction and Commentary*. AB 27a. New York: Doubleday, 2000.
Marcus, Joel. *Mark 8–16: A New Translation with Introduction and Commentary*. AB 27b. New York: Doubleday, 2012.
Marcus, Joel. "The Jewish War and the Sitz Im Leben of Mark." *JBL* 111 (1992): 441–62.
Marcus, Joel. *The Way of the Lord: Christological Exegesis of the Old Testament in the Gospel of Mark*. Louisville: Westminster/John Knox Press, 1992.
Marshall, I. Howard. "Son of God or Servant of Yahweh?—A Reconsideration of Mark I. 11." *NTS* 15 (1969): 326–36.
Marshall, I. Howard. *The Acts of the Apostles: An Introduction and Commentary*. TNTC. Grand Rapids: Eerdmans, 1980.
Martin, Ralph P. *Mark*. Knox Preaching Guides. Atlanta: Knox, 1982.
Marzolph, Ulrich. *The Arabian Nights Reader*. Wayne State University Press, 2006.
Masson, Charles. "La Transfiguration de Jésus (Marc 9:2-13)." *RTP* 14 (1964): 1–14.
Matera, Frank J. *New Testament Christology*. Louisville: Westminster John Knox, 1999.
Matera, Frank J. *Passion Narratives and Gospel Theologies: Interpreting the Synoptics through Their Passion Stories*. Eugene, OR: Wipf & Stock, 2001.
Matera, Frank J. *The Kingship of Jesus: Composition and Theology in Mark 15*. SBLDS 66. Chico, CA: Scholars, 1982.
Matera, Frank J. "The Prologue as the Interpretative Key to Mark's Gospel." *JSNT* 34 (1988): 3–20.
Mauser, Ulrich. *Christ in the Wilderness: The Wilderness Theme in the Second Gospel and Its Basis in the Biblical Tradition*. SBT 39. Naperville, IL: Allenson, 1963.
Mays, James Luther. *Psalms*. Interpretation. Louisville: Westminster John Knox, 1994.
McCann, Jr., J. Clinton. *The Book of Psalms: Introduction, Commentary, and Reflections*. NIB 4. Nashville: Abingdon, 1996.
McCasland, S. Vernon. "The Demonic 'Confessions' of Jesus." *JR* 24 (1944): 33–6.

McGuckin, John Anthony. *The Transfiguration of Christ in Scripture and Tradition.* SBEC 9. Lewiston, NY: Edwin Mellen, 1986.
Meeks, Wayne A. *The Prophet-King: Moses Traditions and the Johannine Christology.* NovTSup 14. Leiden: Brill, 1967.
Meggitt, Justin J. "Artemidorus and the Johannine Crucifixion," *JHC* 5 (1998): 203–08.
Meggitt, Justin J. "Laughing and Dreaming at the Foot of the Cross: Context and Reception of a Religious Symbol," in *Modern Spiritualities: An Inquiry*, ed. Laurence Brown et al. Westminster College-Oxford: Critical Studies in Religion (Amherst, NY; Oxford: Prometheus Books, 1997), 63–70.
Meggitt, Justin J. "Taking the Emperor's Clothes Seriously: The New Testament and the Roman Emperor." Pages 143–69 in *The Quest for Wisdom: Essays in Honour of Philip Budd*. Edited by Philip J. Budd and Christine E. Joynes. Cambridge: Orchard Academic, 2002.
Melville, Herman, and Carl F. Hovde. "Introduction." Pages xv–xli in *Moby-Dick*. New York: Barnes & Noble Classics, 2003.
Mercier, Robert. *L'Évangile Pour Que Vous Croyiez: Le Quatrième Évangile.* Collection Gratianus. Montréal: Wilson & Lafleur, 2010.
Mettinger, Tryggve N. D. *King and Messiah: The Civil and Sacral Legitimation of the Israelite Kings.* ConBOT 8. Lund: LiberLäromedel/Gleerup, 1976.
Metzger, Bruce M. *A Textual Commentary on the Greek New Testament.* London: UBS, 1971.
Meyer, Heinrich August Wilhelm. *Kritisch Exegetisches Handbuch über das Evangelium des Matthäus.* 5th ed. KEK 1. Göttingen: Vandenhoeck und Ruprecht, 1864.
Michaelis, Wilhelm. *Zur Engelchristologie Im Urchristentum: Abbau Der Konstruktion Martin Werners.* ATANT 1. Basel: Heinrich Majer, 1942.
Michaels, J. Ramsey. *The Gospel of John.* NICNT. Grand Rapids: Eerdmans, 2010.
Michel, Otto. "Der Abschluß des Matthäusevangeliums." *EvT* 10 (1950): 16–26.
Milgrom, Jacob. "Florilegium: A Midrash on 2 Samuel and Psalms 1-2." Pages 248–63 in *The Dead Sea Scrolls: Hebrew, Aramaic, and Greek Texts with the English Translations.* Edited by James H. Charlesworth. PTSDSSP 6b. Tübingen/Louisville: Mohr Siebeck; Westminster John Knox, 1994.
Milik, J. T. "Les Modèles Araméens Du Livre d'Esther Dans La Grotte 4 De Qumrân." *RevQ* 15 (1992): 321–406.
Millar, Fergus. *The Roman Near East, 31 B.C.–A.D. 337.* Cambridge: Harvard University Press, 1993.
Miller, Stephen R. *Daniel.* NAC 18. Nashville: Broadman & Holman, 1994.
Mitchell, David C. *The Message of the Psalter: An Eschatological Programme in the Book of Psalms.* JSOTSup 252. Sheffield: Sheffield Academic, 1997.
Mohr, Till Arend. *Markus- Und Johannespassion: Redaktions- Und Traditionsgeschichtliche Untersuchung Der Markinischen Und Johanneischen Passionstradition.* ATANT 70. Zürich: Theologischer, 1982.
Moj, Marcin. "Sandwich Technique in the Gospel of Mark." *BibAn* 8 (2018): 363–77.
Moloney, Francis J. *Mark: Storyteller, Interpreter, Evangelist.* Peabody: Hendrickson, 2004.
Moloney, Francis J. *The Gospel of Mark: A Commentary.* Peabody, MA: Hendrickson, 2002.
Mommsen, Theodor, Paul Krueger, and Alan Watson, eds. *The Digest of Justinian.* Philadelphia, Pa: University of Pennsylvania Press, 1985.
Montgomery, James A. *A Critical and Exegetical Commentary on the Book of Daniel.* ICC 27. Edinburgh: T&T Clark, 1959.

de Moor, Johannes C. "The Targumic Background of Mark 12:1-12: The Parable of the Wicked Tenants." *JSJ* 29 (1998): 63–80.
Moore, Stephen D. *Literary Criticism and the Gospels: The Theoretical Challenge.* New Haven: Yale University Press, 1989.
Moscicke, Hans M. "The Gerasene Exorcism and Jesus' Eschatological Expulsion of Cosmic Powers: Echoes of Second Temple Scapegoat Traditions in Mark 5.1-20." *JSNT* 41 (2019): 363–83.
Moss, Candida R. "The Transfiguration: An Exercise in Markan Accommodation." *BibInt* 12 (2004): 69–89.
Motyer, Stephen. "The Rending of the Veil: A Markan Pentecost?" *NTS* 33 (1987): 155–57.
Moule, C. F. D. *The Origin of Christology.* Cambridge/New York: Cambridge University Press, 1977.
Moule, C. F. D. "Christology and the Synoptic Problem: An Argument for Markan Priority." *The JTS* 49 (1998): 739–41.
Mowinckel, Sigmund. *Psalmenstudien.* 2 vols Amsterdam: P. Schippers, 1961.
Mowinckel, Sigmund. *The Psalms in Israel's Worship.* Translated by D. R. Ap-Thomas. 2 vols Oxford: Blackwell, 1962.
Müller, Ulrich B. "Die christologische Absicht des Markusevangeliums und die Verklärungsgeschichte." *ZNW* 64 (1973): 159–93.
Murgatroyd, Paul. "Embedded Narrative in Apuleius' 'Metamorphoses' 1.9-10." *Museum Helveticum* 58 (2001): 40–6.
Myers, Ched. *Binding the Strong Man: A Political Reading of Mark's Story of Jesus.* Maryknoll, NY: Orbis, 1988.
Nelles, William. *Frameworks: Narrative Levels and Embedded Narrative.* Wipf & Stock, 2020.
Nelles, William. "Stories within Stories: Narrative Levels and Embedded Narrative." *Studies in the Literary Imagination* 25 (1992): 79–96.
Nickelsburg, George W. E. *Jewish Literature between the Bible and the Mishnah: A Historical and Literary Introduction.* 2nd ed. Minneapolis: Fortress, 2005.
Nickelsburg, George W. E., and James C. VanderKam. *1 Enoch: A Commentary on the Book of 1 Enoch.* Minneapolis: Fortress, 2012.
Noegel, Scott P. "Phoenicia, Phoenicians." *DOTHB*, 792–98.
Nolan, Brian M. *The Royal Son of God: The Christology of Matthew 1-2 in the Setting of the Gospel.* OBO 23. Fribourg: Éditions universitaires; Göttingen: Vandenhoeck & Ruprecht, 1979.
Nolland, John. *Luke.* WBC 35c. Dallas: Word, 1989.
Noreña, Carlos F. "The Communication of the Emperor's Virtues." *JRS* 91 (2001): 146–68.
Novakovic, Lidija. *Messiah, the Healer of the Sick: A Study of Jesus as the Son of David in the Gospel of Matthew.* WUNT 2/170. Tübingen: Mohr Siebeck, 2003.
Novenson, Matthew V. *Christ among the Messiahs: Christ Language in Paul and Messiah Language in Ancient Judaism.* New York: Oxford University Press, 2012.
O'Brien, Kelli S. *The Use of Scripture in the Markan Passion Narrative.* LNTS 384. London/New York: T&T Clark, 2010.
Oden, Thomas C. *The African Memory of Mark: Reassessing Early Church Tradition.* Downers Grove: IVP Academic, 2011.
Oegema, Gerbern S. *The Anointed and His People: Messianic Expectations from Maccabees to Bar Kochba.* JSPSup 27. Sheffield: Sheffield Academic Press, 1998.

Oegema, Gerbern S., James H. Charlesworth, and Society for New Testament Studies, eds. *The Pseudepigrapha and Christian Origins: Essays from the Studiorum Novi Testamenti Societas*. JCTCRSS 4. New York: T&T Clark, 2008.

Oldenhage, Tania. "Spiralen Der Gewalt (Die Bösen Winzer)." Pages 352–66 in *Kompendium Der Gleichnisse Jesu*. Edited by Ruben Zimmermann and Detlev Dormeyer. Gütersloh: Gütersloher, 2007.

Otto, Eckart. "Psalm 2 in neuassyrischer Zeit. Assyrische Motive in der judäischen Königsideologie." Pages 335–49 in *Textarbeit. Studien zu Texten und ihrer Rezeption aus dem ALten Testament und der Umwelt Israels. Festschrift für Peter Weimar*. Edited by Klaus Kiesow and Thomas Meurer. AOAT 294. Münster: Ugarit, 2003.

Otto, Eckart, and Erich Zenger, eds. *"Mein Sohn Bist Du" (Ps 2,7): Studien Zu Den Königspsalmen*. SBS 192. Stuttgart: Katholisches Bibelwerk, 2002.

Overstreet, Larry R. "Roman Law and the Trial of Christ." *BSac* 135 (1978): 323–32.

Owen, John. *The Works of John Owen*. Edited by W. H. Goold. 16 vols London: Banner of Truth Trust, 1965.

Parker, D. C. *Codex Sinaiticus: The Story of the World's Oldest Bible*. London: British Library, 2010.

Parsons, Mikeal C., and Michael W. Martin. *Ancient Rhetoric and the New Testament: The Influence of Elementary Greek Composition*. Waco, Texas: Baylor University Press, 2018.

Peddinghaus, Carl Daniel. "Die Entstehung der Leidensgeschichte: Eine traditionsgeschichtliche und historische Untersuchung des Werdens und Wachsens der erzählenden Passionstradition bis zum Entwurf des Markus. [1. 2]." PhD diss, Heidelberg, 1966.

Peirce, Charles S. "On the Algebra of Logic." *Collected Papers of Charles Sanders Peirce, Edited by Charles Hartshorne and Paul Weiss*. Vol. 3. Edited by Charles Hartshorne, Paul Weiss, and Arthur W. Burks. Cambridge: Harard University Press, 1931.

Peppard, Michael. *The Son of God in the Roman World: Divine Sonship in Its Social and Political Context*. New York: Oxford University Press, 2011.

Perrin, Norman. "Mark Xiv.62: The End Product of a Christian Pesher Tradition?" *NTS* 12 (1966): 150–55.

Perrin, Norman. "The Christology of Mark: A Study in Methodology." *JR* 51 (1971): 173–87.

Perrin, Norman. *What Is Redaction Criticism?* Philadelphia: Fortress, 1969.

Perry, Menahem, and Meir Sternberg. "The King through Ironic Eyes: Biblical Narrative and the Literary Reading Process." *Poetics Today* 7 (1986): 275–322.

Person, Raymond F. "The Ancient Israelite Scribe as Performer." *JBL* 117 (1998): 601–09.

Pesch, Rudolf. *Das Markusevangelium*. 2 vols HThKNT 2. Freiburg: Herder, 1976–1977.

Pesch, Rudolf. *Die Apostelgeschichte*. 2 vols *EKKNT* 5. Zürich; Neukirchen-Vluyn: Benziger; Neukirchener, 1986.

Petersen, Allan Rosengren. *The Royal God: Enthronement Festivals in Ancient Israel and Ugarit?* JSOT 259. Sheffield: Sheffield Academic Press, 1998.

Plummer, Alfred. *The Gospel According to St. Mark*. Cambridge: Cambridge University Press, 1914.

Poirier, John C. "Jewish and Christian Tradition in the Transfiguration." *RB* 111 (2004): 516–30.

Pomykala, Kenneth. *The Davidic Dynasty Tradition in Early Judaism: Its History and Significance for Messianism*. EJL 7. Atlanta, GA: Scholars, 1995.

Poole, Matthew. *A Commentary on the Holy Bible*. Vol. 3. Edinburgh; Carlisle, PA: Banner of Truth Trust, 1962.
Powell, Mark Allan. "Toward a Narrative-Critical Understanding of Mark." *Int* 47 (1993): 341–46.
Powell, Mark Allan. *What Is Narrative Criticism?* Guides to Biblical Scholarship. Minneapolis: Fortress, 1990.
Powell, Mark Allan, Barry L. Bandstra, and HarperCollins (Firm), eds. *The Harper Collins Bible Dictionary*. 3rd ed. New York: HarperOne, 2011.
Poythress, Vern S. "Is Romans 1:3-4 a Pauline Confession After All?" *ExpTim* 87 (1976): 180–83.
Price, S. R. F. *Rituals and Power: The Roman Imperial Cult in Asia Minor*. Cambridge/New York: Cambridge University Press, 1984.
von Rad, Gerhard. "Das judäische Königsritual." *TLZ* 72 (1947): 211–16.
Reimarus, Hermann Samuel. *Fragments*. Edited by Charles H. Talbert Translated by R. S. Fraser. Lives of Jesus Series. London: SCM, 1971.
Rengstorf, Karl Heinrich. "Old and New Testament Traces of a Formula of the Judaean Royal Ritual." *NovT* 5 (1962): 229–44.
Reploh, Karl-Georg. *Markus, Lehrer der Gemeinde: eine redaktionsgeschichtliche Studie zu den Jüngerperikopen des Markus-Evangeliums*. SBM 9. Stuttgart: Katholisches Bibelwerk, 1969.
Resseguie, James L. "Point of View." Pages 79–96 in *How John Works: Storytelling in the Fourth Gospel*. Edited by Douglas Estes and Ruth Sheridan. RBS 86. Atlanta: SBL Press, 2016.
Reynolds, Benjamin E. "The 'One Like a Son of Man' According to the Old Greek of Daniel 7,13-14." *Bib* 89 (2008): 70–80.
Rhoads, David M., Joanna Dewey, and Donald Michie. *Mark as Story: An Introduction to the Narrative of a Gospel*. 3rd ed. Minneapolis: Fortress, 2013.
Richardson, Alan. *An Introduction to the Theology of the New Testament*. New York: Harper, 1959.
Ricoeur, Paul. "Interpretative Narrative." *The Book and the Text: The Bible and Literary Theory*. Edited by Regina M. Schwartz. Cambridge/Oxford: Blackwell, 1990.
Ricoeur, Paul. *Oneself as Another*. Chicago: University of Chicago Press, 1992.
Ridderbos, Herman N. *The Gospel According to John: A Theological Commentary*. Grand Rapids: Eerdmans, 1997.
Riesenfeld, Harald. *Jésus transfiguré, l'arrière-plan du récit évangélique de la transfiguration de Notre-Seigneur*. Acta 16. København: E. Munksgaar, 1947.
Rindge, Matthew S. "Reconfiguring the Akedah and Recasting God: Lament and Divine Abandonment in Mark." *JBL* 131 (2012): 755–74.
Rinon, Yoav. "'Mise En Abyme' and Tragic Signification in the 'Odyssey': The Three Songs of Demodocus." *Mnemosyne* 59 (2006): 208–25.
Roberts, Alexander, and James Donaldson, eds. *The Ante-Nicene Fathers*. Repr. 10 vols Peabody: Hendrickson, 1994.
Roberts, J. J. M. "Mowinckel's Enthronement Festival: A Review." *The Book of Psalms: Composition and Reception*. Edited by Peter W. Flint, Patrick D. Miller, Aaron Brunell, and Ryan Roberts. VTSup 99. Leiden/Boston: Brill, 2005.
Roberts, J. J. M. "The Old Testament's Contribution to Messianic Expectations." Pages 39–51 in *The Messiah: Developments in Earliest Judaism and Christianity*. Edited by James H. Charlesworth. Minneapolis: Fortress, 1992.

Roskam, Hendrika Nicoline, ed. *The Purpose of the Gospel of Mark in Its Historical and Social Context.* NovTSup 114. Leiden/Boston: Brill, 2004.
Ron, Moshe. "The Restricted Abyss: Nine Problems in the Theory of Mise En Abyme." *Poetics Today* 8 (1987): 417–38.
Ross, Allen P. *A Commentary on the Psalms.* Grand Rapids: Kregel Academic & Professional, 2011.
Rouwhorst, Gerard, and Marcel Poorthuis. "'Why Do the Nations Conspire': Psalm 2 in Post-Biblical Jewish and Christian Traditions." Pages 425–53 in *Empsychoi Logoi — Religious Innovations in Antiquity.* Edited by Alberdina Houtman, Albert de Jong, and Magda Misset-Van de Weg. AJEC 73. Leiden: Brill, 2008.
Rowe, C. Kavin. *World Upside Down: Reading Acts in the Graeco-Roman Age.* Oxford/New York: Oxford University Press, 2009.
Rowe, C. Kavin. *Early Narrative Christology: The Lord in the Gospel of Luke.* Berlin: de Gruyter, 2006.
Rowe, Robert D. *God's Kingdom and God's Son: The Background to Mark's Christology from Concepts of Kingship in the Psalms.* AGJU 50. Leiden/Boston: Brill, 2002.
Rowland, Christopher. "The Visions of God in Apocalyptic Literature." *JSJ* 10 (1979): 137–54.
Rowland, Christopher, and Christopher R. A. Morray-Jones. *The Mystery of God: Early Jewish Mysticism and the New Testament.* CRINT. Section III, Jewish Traditions in Early Christian Literature 12. Leiden/Boston: Brill, 2009.
Ruckstuhl, Eugen. "Jesus as Gottessohn im Spiegel des markinischen Taufberichts." *Die Mitte des Neuen Testaments: Einheit und Vielfalt neutestamentlicher Theologie: Festschrift für Eduard Schweizer zum siebzigsten Geburtstag.* Edited by Ulrich Luz and Hans Weder. Göttingen: Vandenhoeck & Ruprecht, 1983.
Sabbé, Maurice. "La redaction du récit de la Transfiguration." Pages 65–100 in *La Venue du Messie.* Edited by Edouard Massaux. RechBib 6. Leuven: Leuven University Press, 1962.
Sahlin, Harald. "Die Perikope vom gerasenischen Besessenen und der Plan des Markusevangeliums." *ST* 18 (1964): 159–172.
Samuel, Simon. "The Beginning of Mark: A Colonial/Postcolonial Conundrum." *BibInt* 10 (2002): 405–19.
Samuelsson, Gunnar. *Crucifixion in Antiquity: An Inquiry into the Background and Significance of the New Testament Terminology of Crucifixion.* WUNT 2/310. Tübingen: Mohr Siebeck, 2011.
Sanders, E. P. *Jesus and Judaism.* Philadelphia: Fortress, 1985.
Sasson, Victor. "The Language of Rebellion in Psalm 2 and the Psalter Texts from Deir 'Alla." *AUSS* 24 (1986): 147–154.
Saur, Markus. *Die Königspsalmen: Studien zur Entstehung und Theologie.* BZAW 340. Berlin/New York: de Gruyter, 2004.
Schlatter, Adolf. *Markus: Der Evangelist Für Die Griechen.* 2nd ed. Stuttgart: Calwer, 1984.
Schmidt, Thomas E. "Mark 15:16–32: The Crucifixion Narrative and the Roman Triumphal Procession." *NTS* 41 (1995): 1–18.
Schnabel, Eckhard J. *Mark: An Introduction and Commentary.* TNTC 2. Downers Grove: IVP, 2017.
Schnackenburg, Rudolf. *Gospel According to St John.* London: Burns & Oates, 1982.
Schnackenburg, Rudolf. *Jesus in the Gospels: A Biblical Christology.* Louisville: Westminster John Knox, 1995.
Schneck, Richard. *Isaiah in the Gospel of Mark I-VIII.* BIBAL 1. Vallejo, CA: BIBAL, 1994.

Schneider, Gerhard. "Gab es eine vorsynoptische Szene 'Jesus vor dem Synedrium'?" *NovT* 12 (1970): 22–39.
Schnelle, Udo. "Johannes Und Die Synoptiker." Page 3:1799-1814 in *The Four Gospels 1992: Festschrift Frans Neirynck*. Edited by Frans van Segbroeck. BETL 100. Leuven: Leuven University Press, 1992.
Schnelle, Udo. *Theology of the New Testament*. Translated by M. Eugene Boring. Grand Rapids: Baker Academic, 2009.
Schramm, Brooks. *The Opponents of Third Isaiah: Reconstructing the Cultic History of the Restoration*. JSOTSup 193. Sheffield: Sheffield Academic, 1995.
Schreiber, Johannes. "Die Christologie Des Markusevangeliums: Beobachtungen Zur Theologie Und Komposition Des Zweiten Evangeliums." *ZTK* 58 (1961): 154–83.
Schreiber, Johannes. *Die Markuspassion*. Hamburg: Furche-Verl, 1969.
Schröten, Jutta. *Entstehung, Komposition Und Wirkungsgeschichte Des 118. Psalms*. BBB 95. Weinheim: Beltz Athenäum, 1995.
Schweizer, Eduard. *Das Evangelium Nach Markus*. Texte zum Neuen Testament 11. Göttingen: Vandenhoeck & Ruprecht, 1967.
Schweizer, Eduard. *The Good News According to Mark*. Richmond: John Knox, 1970.
Scott, M. Philip. "Chiastic Structure: A Key to the Interpretation of Mark's Gospel." *BTB* 15 (1985): 17–26.
Scott, Samuel Parsons. "The Digest or Pandects—Book XLVIII. Title IV: On the Julian Law Relating to the Crime of Lesse Majesty." *The Civil Law, Including the Twelve Tables, the Institutes of Gaius, the Rules of Ulpian, the Opinions of Paulus, the Enactments of Justinian, and the Constitutions of Leo; Vol. XI*. Cincinnati: The Central Trust Company, 1932.
Segal, Alan F. *Two Powers in Heaven: Early Rabbinic Reports about Christianity and Gnosticism*. SJLA 25. Leiden: Brill, 1977.
Segal, Michael. "Who Is the 'Son of God' in 4Q246? An Overlooked Example of Early Biblical Interpretation." *DSD* 21 (2014): 289–312.
Selderhuis, H. J., ed. *Psalms 1-72*. RCSOT 7. Downers Grove: IVP Academic, 2015.
Senior, Donald. *The Passion of Jesus in the Gospel of Mark*. The Passion Series 2. Wilmington, DE: Glazier, 1984.
Seow, C. L. *Daniel*. Louisville, KY: Westminster John Knox, 2003.
Shepherd, Tom. "The Narrative Function of Markan Intercalation." *NTS* 41 (1995): 522–40.
Sherwin-White, A. N. *Roman Society and Roman Law in the New Testament*. Grand Rapids: Baker, 1981.
Shiner, Whitney T. "Applause and Applause Lines in the Gospel of Mark." Pages 129–44 in *Rhetorics and Hermeneutics: Wilhelm Wuellner and His Influence*. Edited by James D. Hester and David Hester. Emory Studies in Early Christianity 9. New York: T&T Clark, 2004.
Shiner, Whitney T. "The Ambiguous Pronouncement of the Centurion and the Shrouding of Meaning in Mark." *JSNT* 22 (2000): 3–22.
Shiner, Whitney T. *Proclaiming the Gospel: First-Century Performance of Mark*. Harrisburg, PA: Trinity Press International, 2003.
Shively, Elizabeth E. *Apocalyptic Imagination in the Gospel of Mark: The Literary and Theological Role of Mark 3:22-30*. BNZW 189. Berlin/New York: De Gruyter, 2012.
Shively, Elizabeth E. "Purification of the Body and the Reign of God in the Gospel of Mark." *JTS* 71 (2020): 62–89.

Signoret, J. P., B. A. Baldwin, and D Fraser. "The Behaviour of Swine." Pages 295–29 in *Behaviour of Domestic Animals*. Edited by E. S. E. Hafez. London: Baillière Tindall, 1975.

Skeat, T. C. "Four Years' Work on the Codex Sinaiticus: Significant Discoveries in Reconditioned MS." Pages 109–21 in *The Collected Biblical Writings of T.C. Skeat*. Edited by J. K. Elliott. Leiden: Brill, 2004.

Slomp, Jan. "Are the Words 'Son of God' in Mark 1.1 Original?" *BT* 28 (1977): 143–50.

Smallwood, E. Mary. *The Jews under Roman Rule: From Pompey to Diocletian: A Study in Political Relations*. SJLA 20. Leiden: Brill, 1981.

Smith, D. Moody. *John*. ANTC. Nashville: Abingdon, 1999.

Smith, Stephen H. *A Lion with Wings: A Narrative-Critical Approach to Mark's Gospel*. Sheffield: Sheffield Academic, 1996.

Smith, Stephen H. "Mark 3,1-6: Form, Redaction and Community Function." *Bib* 75 (1994): 153–74.

Smith, Steve. "The Use of Criteria: A Proposal from Relevance Theory." Pages 142–54 in *Methodology in the Use of the Old Testament in the New: Context and Criteria*. Edited by David Allen and Steve Smith. LNTS 597. London/New York: T&T Clark, 2020

Snodgrass, Klyne R. "Streams of Tradition Emerging from Isaiah 40:1-5 and Their Adaptation in the New Testament." *JSNT* 2 (1980): 24–45.

Snodgrass, Klyne R. *The Parable of the Wicked Tenants: An Inquiry into Parable Interpretation*. WUNT 27. Tübingen: Mohr Siebeck, 1983.

Snodgrass, Klyne R. "Recent Research on the Parable of the Wicked Tenants: An Assessment." *BBR* 8 (1998): 187–215.

Snodgrass, Klyne R. *Stories with Intent*. 2nd ed. Grand Rapids: Eerdmans, 2018.

Soards, Marion L. "Tradition, Composition, and Theology in Luke's Account of Jesus Before Herod Antipas." *Bib* (1985): 344–64.

Sorensen, Eric. *Possession and Exorcism in the New Testament and Early Christianity*. WUNT 2/157. Tübingen: Mohr Siebeck, 2002.

Spurgeon, C. H. *The Metropolitan Tabernacle Pulpit: Containing Sermons Preached and Revised*. 56 vols Pasadena, Texas: Pilgrim, 1973.

Stählin, Gustav. *Die Apostelgeschichte*. Göttingen: Vandenhoeck & Ruprecht, 1968.

Standaert, Benoît. *Évangile selon Marc: commentaire*. 3 vols EBib 61. Pendé: J. Gabalda, 2010.

Stanton, Graham. *Jesus and Gospel*. Cambridge/New York: Cambridge University Press, 2004.

Stec, David M. *The Targum of Psalms: Translated with a Critical Introduction, Apparatus, and Notes*. Vol. 16 of *Aramaic Bible*. London: T&T Clark, 2004.

Steck, O. H. *Israel Und Das Gewaltsame Geschick Der Propheten: Untersuchungen Zur Überlieferung Des DeuteronomistischenGeschichtsbildes Im Alten Testament, Spätjudentum Und Urchristentum*. WMANT 23. Neukirchen-Vluyn: Neukirchener Verlag, 1967.

Stegner, William Richard. *Narrative Theology in Early Jewish Christianity*. Louisville: Westminster John Knox, 1989.

Stegner, William Richard. "The Use of Scripture in Two Narratives of Early Jewish Christianity (Matthew 4.1-11; Mark 9.2-8)." Pages 98–120 in *Early Christian Interpretation of the Scriptures of Israel: Investigations and Proposals*. Edited by Craig A. Evans and James A. Sanders. JSNTSup 148. Sheffield: Sheffield Academic, 1997.

Stegner, William Richard. "Wilderness and Testing in the Scrolls and in Matthew 4:1-11." *BR* 12 (1967): 18–27.

Steichele, Hans-Jörg. *Der leidende Sohn Gottes: eine Untersuchung einiger alttestamentlicher Motive in der Christologie des Markusevangeliums: zugleich ein Beitrag zur Erhellung des überlieferungsgeschichtlichen Zusammenhangs zwischen Altem und Neuem Testament.* Münchener Universitätsschriften 14. Regensburg: Pustet, 1980.

Stein, Robert H. *Mark.* Grand Rapids: Baker Academic, 2008.

Stern, David. "Jesus' Parables from the Perspective of Rabbinic Literature." Pages 42–80 in *Parable and Story in Judaism and Christianity.* Edited by Clemens Thoma, Michael Wyschogrod, American Jewish Congress, and Theologische Fakultät Luzern (Switzerland). Studies in Judaism and Christianity. New York: Paulist, 1989.

Stern, David. *Parables in Midrash: Narrative and Exegesis in Rabbinic Literature.* Cambridge: Harvard University Press, 1991.

Stern, David. "The Rabbinic Parable and the Narrative of Interpretation." Pages 78–95 in *The Midrashic Imagination: Jewish Exegesis, Thought, Andhistory.* Edited by Michael A. Fishbane. Albany: State University of New York Press, 1993.

Stern, Frank. *A Rabbi Looks at Jesus' Parables.* Lanham, MD: Rowman & Littlefield, 2006.

Stokes, Ryan E. "The Throne Visions of Daniel 7, 1 Enoch 14 and the Qumran Book of Giants (4Q530): An Analysis of Their Literary Relationship." *DSD* 15 (2008): 340–58.

Stone, Michael E. *Fourth Ezra: A Commentary on the Books of Fourth Ezra.* Fortress, 1990.

Stone, Michael E., and Matthias Henze, eds. *4 Ezra and 2 Baruch: Translations, Introductions, and Notes.* Minneapolis: Fortress, 2013.

Stonehouse, N. B. *The Witness of Matthew and Mark to Christ.* 2nd ed. Grand Rapids: Eerdmans, 1958.

Straub, Jürgen. "Temporale Orientierung und narrative Kompetenz." Pages 15–44 in *Geschichtsbewusstsein: psychologische Grundlagen, Entwicklungskonzepte, empirische Befunde.* Edited by Jörn Rüsen. Köln: Böhlau, 2001.

Strauss, David Friedrich. *The Life of Jesus: Critically Examined.* Edited by Peter C. Hodgson Translated by George Eliot. Lives of Jesus Series. Philadelphia: Fortress, 1972.

Strothmann, Meret Bochum. "Augustus." *Brill's New Pauly Encyclopedia of the Ancient World* 2:363–75.

Stuckenbruck, Loren T. "The Building Blocks for Enoch as the Son of Man in the Early Enoch Tradition." Pages 315–28 in *Parables of Enoch: A Paradigm Shift.* Edited by James H. Charlesworth and Darrell L. Bock. JCTCRSS 11. London: T&T Clark, 2013.

Stuhlmacher, Peter. *Das paulinische Evangelium.* FRLANT 95. Göttingen: Vandenhoeck & Ruprecht, 1968.

Suhl, Alfred. *Die Funktion der alttestamentlichen Zitate und Anspielungen im Markusevangelium.* Gütersloh: G. Mohn, 1965.

Sweat, Laura C. *The Theological Role of Paradox in the Gospel of Mark.* LNTS 492. London/New York: Bloomsbury, 2013.

Swete, Henry Barclay. *The Gospel According to St Mark: The Greek Text with Introduction, Notes and Indices.* 3rd ed. London: Macmillan, 1909.

Syme, Ronald. "Imperator Caesar: A Study in Nomenclature." Pages 40–59 in *Augustus.* Edited by J. C. Edmondson. Edinburgh Readings on the Ancient World. Edinburgh: Edinburgh University Press, 2009.

Talbert, Charles H. *What Is a Gospel? The Genre of the Canonical Gospels.* Philadelphia: Fortress, 1977.

Tannehill, Robert C. "Tension in Synoptic Sayings and Stories." *Int* 34 (1980): 138–50.

Tannehill, Robert C. "The Disciples in Mark: The Function of a Narrative Role." *JR* 57 (1977): 386–405.

Tannehill, Robert C. "The Gospel of Mark as Narrative Christology." *Semeia* 16 (1979): 57–95.
Taylor, Joan E. "Pontius Pilate and the Imperial Cult in Roman Judaea." *NTS* 52 (2006): 555–82.
Taylor, Lily Ross. *The Divinity of the Roman Emperor*. New York: Arno, 1975.
Taylor, N. H. "Herodians and Pharisees: The Historical and Political Context of Mark 3:6; 8:15; 12:13-17." *Neot* 34 (2000): 299–310.
Taylor, Vincent. *The Gospel According to St. Mark: The Greek Text with Introd., Notes, and Indexes*. London: Macmillan, 1959.
Telford, William R. *The Theology of the Gospel of Mark*. New Testament Theology. Cambridge/New York: Cambridge University Press, 1999.
Terrien, Samuel L. *The Psalms: Strophic Structure and Theological Commentary*. Grand Rapids: Eerdmans, 2003.
Thatcher, Tom. "I Have Conquered the World." Pages 140–63 in *Empire in the New Testament*. Edited by Stanley E. Porter and Cynthia Long Westfall. MNTSS 10. Eugene, Or: Pickwick, 2011.
Theisohn, Johannes. *Der auserwählte Richter: Untersuchungen z. traditionsgeschichtl. Ort d. Menschensohngestalt d. Bilderreden d. Äthiopischen Henoch*. SUNT 12. Göttingen: Vandenhoeck und Ruprecht, 1975.
Theissen, Gerd. *The Gospels in Context: Social and Political History in the Synoptic Tradition*. Minneapolis: Fortress Press, 1991.
Theissen, Gerd. *The Miracle Stories of the Early Christian Tradition*. Translated by John Riches. Philadelphia: Fortress, 1983.
Theodore of Mopsuestia. *Commentary on Psalms 1–81*. Translated by Robert C. Hill. WGRW 5. Atlanta, GA: SBL Press, 2006.
Theodoret of Cyrus, Gerard H. Ettlinger, and Adrien C. Cyrus. *Eranistes: Eranistes*. Baltimore: Catholic University of America Press, 2003.
Theophylact. *The Explanation of the Holy Gospel According to Mark*. Translated by Fr. Christopher Stade. Blessed Theophylact's Explanation of the New Testament 2. House Springs, MO: Chrysostom, 2008.
Tigchelaar, Eibert J. C. *Prophets of Old and the Day of the End: Zechariah, the Book of Watchers, and Apocalyptic*. OTS 35. Leiden/New York: Brill, 1996.
Tolbert, Mary Ann. *Sowing the Gospel: Mark's World in Literary-Historical Perspective*. Minneapolis: Fortress, 1989.
Tolmie, Francois. *Narratology and Biblical Narratives: A Practical Guide*. San Francisco: International Scholars, 1999.
Torrey, R. A. *The Treasury of Scripture Knowledge*. Peabody, MA: Hendrickson, 2019.
Toynbee, J. M. C. *Death and Burial in the Roman World*. Aspects of Greek and Roman Life. Ithaca, NY: Cornell University Press, 1971.
Trapp, John. *A Commentary on the Old and New Testaments*. Edited by Hugh Martin. Eureka: Tanski, 1997.
Trocmé, Etienne. *L'Evangile selon Saint Marc*. CNT 2. Genève: Labor et Fides, 2000.
Trocmé, Etienne. *The Formation of the Gospel According to Mark*. Philadelphia: Westminster, 1975.
Trotter, Jonathan R. "The Tradition of Throne Vision in the Second Temple Period: Daniel 7:9-10, 1 Enoch 14:18-23, and the Book of Giants (4Q530)." *RevQ* 25 (2012): 451–66.
Turner, C. H. "Marcan Usage: Notes, Critical and Exegetical, on the Second Gospel IV: Parenthetical Clauses in Mark." *JTS* 26 (1925): 145–56.

Turner, C. H. "Text of Mark 1." *JTS* 28 (1927): 150–58.
Turner, C. H. "Ο Υιος Μου Ο Αγαπητος." *JTS* 27 (1926): 113–29.
Twelftree, Graham H. *In the Name of Jesus: Exorcism among Early Christians*. Grand Rapids: Baker Academic, 2007.
Twelftree, Graham H. *Jesus the Exorcist: A Contribution to the Study of the Historical Jesus*. WUNT 2/54. Tübingen: Mohr Siebeck, 1993.
Ulansey, David. "The Heavenly Veil Torn: Mark's Cosmic Inclusio." *JBL* 110 (1991): 123–25.
Van Eck, Ernst. "A Narratological Analysis of Mark 12:1-12: The Plot of the Gospel of Mark in a Nutshell." *HTS* 45 (1989): 778–800.
Van Henten, Jan Willem. "The First Testing of Jesus: A Rereading of Mark 1.12-13." *NTS* 45 (1999): 349–66.
Van Iersel, B. M. F. *'Der Sohn' in Den Synoptischen Jesusworten: Christusbezeichnung Der Gemeinde Oder Selbstbezeichnung Jesu?* NovTSup 3. Leiden: Brill, 1961.
Van Iersel, B. M. F. "Locality, Structure, and Meaning in Mark." *LB* 53 (1983): 45–54.
Van Iersel, B. M. F. "Concentric Structures in Mark: 1:14-3:35 (4:1) With Some Observations on Method." *BibInt* 3 (1995): 75–98.
Van Iersel, B. M. F. *Mark: A Reader-Response Commentary*. JSNTSup 164. Sheffield: Sheffield Academic, 1998.
Várhelyi, Zsuzsanna. "Imperial Cult, Roman." *The Oxford Encyclopedia of Ancient Greece and Rome* 4:54–57.
de Vaux, Roland. *Les Sacrifices de l'Ancien Testament*. CahRB 1. Paris: J. Gabalda, 1964.
Vermès, Géza. *Scripture and Tradition in Judaism: Haggadic Studies*. Leiden: Brill, 1961.
Versnel, H. S. *Triumphus: An Inquiry into the Origin, Development and Meaning of the Roman Triumph*. Leiden: Brill, 1970.
Vielhauer, Philipp. "Erwägungen zur Christologie des Markusevangeliums." Pages 199–214 in *Aufsätze zum Neuen Testament*. Munich: Kaiser, 1965.
Walahfrid Strabo, Nicholas, Pablo de Santa Maria, Mathias Döring, François Feuardent, Jean Dadré, and Jacques de Cuilly. *Bibliorum sacrorum cum glossa ordinaria*. Venice: Unknown, 1603.
Wallace-Hadrill, Andrew. *Augustan Rome*. 2nd ed. New York: Bloomsbury Academic, 2018.
Wallace-Hadrill, Andrew. *Rome's Cultural Revolution*. New York: Cambridge University Press, 2008.
Wasserman, Tommy. "The 'Son of God' Was in the Beginning (Mark 1:1)." *JTS* 62 (2011): 20–50.
Watson, George Ronald. *The Roman Soldier*. Aspects of Greek and Roman Life. London: Thames & Hudson, 1969.
Watts, James W. "Psalm 2 In the Context of Biblical Theology." *HBT* 12 (1990): 73–91.
Watts, John D. W. *Isaiah 34-66*. WBC 25. Waco: Word, 1987.
Watts, Richard J. *The Pragmalinguistic Analysis of Narrative Texts: Narrative Co-Operation in Charles Dickens's "Hard Times."* Studies and Texts in English. Tübingen: G. Narr, 1981.
Watts, Rikk. "Mark." *Commentary on the New Testament Use of the Old Testament*. Edited by G. K. Beale and D. A. Carson. Grand Rapids: Baker, 2007.
Watts, Rikk. "The Psalms in Mark's Gospel." Pages 25–45 in *The Psalms in the New Testament*. Edited by Steve Moyise and Maarten J. J. Menken. NTSI. London: T&T Clark, 2004.
Watts, Rikk. *Isaiah's New Exodus and Mark*. WUNT 2/88. Tübingen: Mohr Siebeck, 1997.

Weeden, Theodore J. *Mark—Traditions in Conflict*. Philadelphia: Fortress, 1979.
Weeden, Theodore J. "The Heresy That Necessitated Mark's Gospel." *ZNW* 59 (1979): 145–58.
Weinstock, Stefan. *Divus Julius*. Oxford: Clarendon, 1971.
Weiser, Artur. *The Psalms: A Commentary*. OTL. Philadelphia: Westminster, 1962.
Weiss, Bernhard. *Biblical Theology of the New Testament*. Translated by David Eaton and James E. Duguid. 2 vols Edinburgh: T&T Clark, 1882.
Wellhausen, Julius. *Das Evangelium Marci*. Berlin: Reimer, 1903.
Wengst, Klaus. *Pax Romana: And the Peace of Jesus Christ*. Translated by John Bowden. Philadelphia: Fortress, 1987.
Weren, Wim J. C. "Psalm 2 in Luke-Acts: An Intertextual Study." Pages 189–204 in *Intertextuality in Biblical Writings: Essays in Honour of Bas van Iersel*. Edited by J. Draisma. Leuven: Peeters, 1989.
Weren, Wim J. C. "The Use of Isaiah 5,1-7 in the Parable of the Tenants (Mark 12,1-12; Matthew 21,33-46)." *Bib* 79 (1998): 1–26.
Wesley, John. *Wesley's Notes on the Bible*. Edited by G. Roger Schoenhals. Grand Rapids: Francis Asbury, 1987.
Westermann, Claus. *Isaiah 40–66: A Commentary*. Translated by D. M. G. Stalker. OTL. Philadelphia: Westminster, 1969.
Whybray, R. N. *Isaiah 40-66*. NCB. Grand Rapids: Eerdmans, 1981.
Winn, Adam. "Resisting Honor: The Markan Secrecy Motif and Roman Political Ideology." *JBL* 133 (2014): 583–601.
Winn, Adam. *The Purpose of Mark's Gospel: An Early Christian Response to Roman Imperial Propaganda*. WUNT 2/245. Tübingen: Mohr Siebeck, 2008.
Winn, Adam. "Tyrant or Servant?: Political Ideology and Mark 10.42-45." *JSNT* 36 (2014): 325–52.
Winter, Bruce W. *Divine Honours for the Caesars: The First Christians' Responses*. Grand Rapids: Eerdmans, 2015.
Winterbottom, Michael, and D. A. Russell, eds. *Ancient Literary Criticism: The Principal Texts in New Translations*. Oxford: Clarendon Press, 1972.
Witherington, Ben. *The Gospel of Mark: A Socio-Rhetorical Commentary*. Grand Rapids: Eerdmans, 2001.
Wittgenstein, Ludwig. *Philosophical Investigations*. 3rd ed. New York: Macmillan, 1971.
Wong, Suk Kwan. *Allegorical Spectrum of the Parables of Jesus*. Eugene, OR: Wipf & Stock, 2017.
Wood, J. Edwin. "Isaac Typology in the New Testament." *NTS* 14 (1968): 583–89.
Wrede, William. *The Messianic Secret*. Translated by J. C. G. Grieg. Cambridge: J. Clarke, 1971. Translation of *Das Messiasgeheimnis in den Evangelien. Zugleich ein Beitrag zum Verständnis des Markusevangeliums*. Göttingen: Vandenhoeck & Ruprecht, 1901.
Wright, George Al. "Markan Intercalations: A Study in the Plot of the Gospel." Ph.D. diss, Southern Baptist Theological Seminary, 1985.
Wright, N. T. "Son of God and Christian Origins." Pages 118–34 in *Son of God: Divine Sonship in Jewish and Christian Antiquity*. Edited by Garrick V. Allen, Kai Akagi, Paul Sloan, and Madhavi Nevader. University Park, PA: Eisenbrauns, 2019.
Wright, Robert B., ed. *The Psalms of Solomon: A Critical Edition of the Greek Text*. JCTCRSS 1. New York: T&T Clark, 2007.
Zahn, Theodor. *Das Evangelium des Matthäus*. Wuppertal: R. Brockhaus, 1984.
Zanker, Paul. *The Power of Images in the Age of Augustus*. Jerome Lectures 16th ser. Ann Arbor: University of Michigan Press, 1988.

Zeichman, Christopher B. *The Roman Army and the New Testament*. Lanham, MD: Lexington Books/Fortress Academic, 2018.
Zenger, Erich. "The Composition and Theology of the Fifth Book of Psalms, Psalms 107-145." *JSOT* 23 (1998): 77–102.
Zenger, Erich, and Frank-Lothar Hossfeld. *Psalms 3*. Hermeneia. Philadelphia: Fortress, 2011.
Zimmermann, Johannes. "Observations on 4Q246—The 'Son of God.'" Pages 175–90 in *Qumran-Messianism: Studies on the Messianic Expectations in the Dead Sea Scrolls*. Edited by James H. Charlesworth, Hermann Lichtenberger, and Gerbern S. Oegema. Tübingen: Mohr Siebeck, 1998.

Index of References

Hebrew Bible/Old Testament

Genesis
1:1	57
6:2, 4	171
7:11	62, 80
14:18-22	99
22	133
22:1	60–1
26:24	65
38	140–41
37–50	141

Exodus
4:22	33–4, 57, 69, 147
4:22-23	61
10:21-23	158
14–15	102
19:16-20	112
19:18	121
19, 24, 32	111
20:18	121
23:20	57
24	109–10, 113, 115–16
24:1-18	110
24:10	111
24:16	110
24:17	121
28:9-12, 17, 21	132
34:29	110, 112
39:6-7, 14	132

Leviticus
4:5	57
11:7	102

Numbers
12:7	65
24:14	135
24:16	99
24:17	125
32:33-42	95
32:19, 32	96
34:15	96
35:14	96

Deuteronomy
1:31	61, 69
3:20	96
4:10	111
4:30	135
4:36	121
4:41, 46	96
5:2	111
6:4	160
8	72–3
8:1-16	71
8:3	72
9:8	111
14:1	119, 171
14:8	102
18:15	107, 125
18:16	111
32	72
32:10-11	72
32:20	135
32:32	130

Joshua
1:2, 7, 13	65
1:15	96
4:6-7	132
13:8	96
18:7	96
20:8	96
21:36	96
22:4, 7, 11	96
22:24	90

Judges
5:17	96

9:7-20	132	18:36	65
10:8	96	18:43-45	111
11:12	90	19:1-13	111
13:5-7	88	19:10	131
		19:11-13	111
1 Samuel		20:35-43	132
2:10	57	22:19	25
12:3	57		
24:6	57	*2 Kings*	
25	140	1:8	98–9
31:7	161	2:8	111
31:9	96	3:13	90
		7:9	57
2 Samuel		14:8-10	132
1:14, 20	57	15:29	95
4:10, 20	57	23	140
5:11	96		
7	6, 31, 43	*1 Chronicles*	
7:4-29	24	6:63	96
7:10b-16	31	10:9	57
7:11-16	33–4, 99	12:38	96
7:12	39	17:4	65
7:12-14	42, 145	17:13	27
7:12-16	33	22:10	27
7:14	7, 25–7, 31, 33–5, 42, 57, 89, 98–100, 145	28:6	27
		2 Chronicles	
12:1-14	132	5:10	111
12:7	132	16:10	131
14:1-17	132	24:20-22	131
16:10	90	35:21	90
18:19-31	57	36:5	65
19:23	90	36:15	131
22:51	57	36:15-16	131
23:1-2	59		
24:5-7	96	*Esther*	
		1:6	121
1 Kings		8:15	121
1:42	57		
5:1-12	96	*Nehemiah*	
7:13, 40-45	96	9:26	131
8:9	111		
8:25	25	*Psalms*	
9:11-14, 27	96	1	31
10:11, 22	96	1–2	31, 49
13	140	2	*passim*
17	111	2:1	30, 40, 50, 75, 136
17:18	90	2:1-2	27–31, 35, 37, 38–41, 44–8, 51,
18:4, 12-13	131		

Index of References

		73, 75, 84–5, 91–3, 97–8, 101, 104, 136–37, 148–49, 174	2:11	37, 46, 50–1, 173–74
			2:12	30, 75
			3:4	108
2:1-3		27, 46, 137, 156	8:4	120
2:1-12		46, 128–29, 75, 166	15:1	108
2:2		29–30, 38–42, 44, 57, 74–6, 78, 92–3, 123, 137, 145, 147, 148–50, 172, 174	17:51 LXX	57
			21:1 LXX	158
			21:8 LXX	41
			31:14	25
			34:16 LXX	41
2:3		47	39:10	57
2:4		40–1, 47–8	43:3	108
2:4-5		75	45:5	99
2:5		28, 30, 44, 47, 137	46	25
2:6		25, 29, 40, 42, 48–51, 75, 109, 147, 150, 155–56	48	25, 77
			48:1	108
			48:2	108, 116
2:6-7		27–9, 31, 37, 40, 44, 69	48:5	25
			65:7-8	102
2:6-8		137	67:12	57
2:6-9		47, 136	68:8 LXX	102
2:7		4–8, 10, 14, 16, 23, 25–7, 29, 31–4, 36, 39, 40, 42–4, 50, 52–3, 57, 60, 63–8, 70, 73–4, 78–9, 81, 83–4, 89, 91, 98–100, 104–05, 107–09, 122, 124–25, 134, 136, 142, 145, 147, 150, 159, 172–75, 177–78	68:15	108
			68:16-17	111, 116
			68:21 LXX	158
			68:22 LXX	160
			70:19	99
			72:1	25
			76	25
			77:23	62, 80
			78:54	108
			80:8-16	130
			81:6	99
			84	25
2:7-8		21, 34, 46, 50, 135, 172, 175, 178	87:1	108
			87:3-6	25
2:7-9		44, 50–1, 75–6, 124, 173	88:19 LXX	88
			88:20 LXX	68
2:8		28, 30, 34, 44, 46, 50–1, 77, 145, 147, 172–73	88:21 LXX	89
			88:39, 51 LXX	57
			89	33–4, 88
2:8-9		27–9, 37, 45, 50–1	89:4	65, 136
2:8-12		74	89:21-22	65
2:9		28, 44, 50–1, 74–8	89:26-27	7, 43, 89, 98
2:9-12		137	89:27-28	25, 27, 35, 73
2:10		28, 30, 40, 75, 77, 147		
			89:28	26, 34
2:10-11		51	90 LXX	72
2:10-12		45, 47, 47	90:10–13 LXX	71

90:1	99	5:1-2 LXX	131
91	72–3	5:5 LXX	131
91:10-13	71	5:1-7	130, 132
91:4, 11-12	72	6:1	25
95:2	57	11	30, 33, 62, 73–4,
97	112		76–8, 126, 128–29,
97:1-3	111, 116		132
97:1-4	116	11:1-2	59
97:1-6	116	11:2	33, 59, 62, 74–7
97:3	121	11:1-9	73
99:1-5	108, 116	11:1-10	65
99:9	108	11:4	32–3, 44, 74–8
104:32	121	11:6-9	33, 73–5, 77
105:23	68	11:9	108–09
106:11	99	11:12	33, 75
106:19	111	24:18	62
109:1 LXX	146	24:21-22	86
110	36, 42	24:23	109, 116
110:1	34, 42, 50, 120, 124,	25:6-7	109
	146–47, 148, 156	27:2-7	130
110:2	109	27:13	108
110:2-3	25	32:15	59
110:4	42	37:35	65
117 LXX	137	40	57, 74
117:22 LXX	132, 135	40:3	57
117:22-23 LXX	132, 138	40:1-5	57
117:25 LXX	135	40:9	57, 113
117:26 LXX	135	40:10, 26, 29, 31	59
118	136	41:8	65
118:22	135–36	41:27	57
121:1-2	136	42	30, 65, 74, 76,
123:1	25		78
131:10 LXX	57	42:1	5, 34, 59, 60, 62–8,
132:11	25		73–6, 78, 107, 125,
132:11-18	109		134, 147
144:5	121	42:1-7	65
145:13	32, 122	42:6	76
146:6-8	96–7	42:13	65, 78
146:10	108, 116	44:3	59
152:4	88–9	45:24	59
153:3	88–9	48:9-10	65
		48:20	65
Proverbs		49	30, 74, 76, 78
4:1	68		128–31
		49:6	65, 76, 95
Isaiah		49:6-8	76
2:2	112, 135	49:23	78
2:2-3	109	49:24-25	86

50:2	59	1:26-28	116–18
52:7	57, 109, 116, 136, 147	17:3-21	132
		17:22-24	109
52:13	34, 111	19:1-14	132
54:11-13	132	19:10-14	130
55:13	39	20:33	109, 116
56:7	108	20:40	108–09, 116
57:13	108	21:1-5	132
56–66	103	21:15, 20, 33	118
60:6	57	24:3-14	132
61:1	57, 59, 62	27:24	65
61:1-2	96–7	28:14	108
63:1, 15	59	34:23-24	59, 65
63:8	69, 171	34:23-31	109
63:10-14	59	36:25-27	59
63:11–19	62	36:33-36	59
63:19 LXX	80	40:2	113
65	103	40:3	118
65:3 LXX	102	45:8	95
65:1-7	100, 103		
65:1-7 LXX	102	*Daniel*	
65:11, 25	108	2:34-35	136
66:20	108	2:44	122
		3:93 LXX	99
Jeremiah		4:2, 17, 34 LXX	99
2:2	61	4:3	32, 122
2:21	130	4:34	32
2:30	131	5:18 LXX	99
7:25-26	131	7	105, 113, 119, 121–23, 125
12:10	130		
8:19	108, 116		
20:2	131	7:9	114–15, 117–19, 124
20:15	57		
30:24	135	7:9-10	116
31:9	61, 69	7:9-14	105, 116–25
31:20	57, 69	7:13	114, 116, 119–24, 136
31:23	108		
33:21, 22, 26	65	7:13-14	114, 124, 146–48
35:4	131	7:14	32, 34
35:15	65	7:27	32
38:20 LXX	61	8:16	113
		9:11	65
Lamentations		9:16, 20	108
4:1-2	132	10:1-11	123
		10:5-6	114, 118
Ezekiel		10:6	119, 124
1:1	62	10:14	135
1:26	111	12:3	114

Hosea

1:1	57
1:10	69
10:1	130
11:1	57, 61, 69
11:10	69
14:8	90

Joel

2:1	108
2:1-2, 10, 30-31	158
2:28-29	59
2:32	57
3:17	108

Amos

1:5, 8	25
3:7	131
8:9-10	158
9:11	31

Obadiah

16	108

Micah

4:6f.	109, 116
5:2-4	109

Nahum

1:15	57
3:3	118

Zephaniah

3:11	3:11

Haggai

2:23	65

Zechariah

1:6	131
3:8	65
4:7	136
8:3	108
9:6	132
13:2	86
14:8-11	109, 116

Malachi

3:1	57
3:22 LXX	58–9
3:22-23 LXX	111–12
3:23 MT	59
4:4	111

New Testament

Matthew

2:2	150–51
2:16	68
3:1-12	58
3:9	132
3:13–4:13	71
3:17	37, 43–4
4:1-11	37
4:3	132
4:4, 6	72
4:8	113
4:11	72
4:25	94–5
7:9	132
8:28-34	100
8:29	84
11:2	96
11:3	59
11:5	96
11:14	58
12:14	93, 149
12:18	64
12:22-30	86
13:43	114
14:33	165
17:1	113
17:2	110, 118
17:3	111
17:5	37, 44, 107
17:10	58
17:10-12	112
17:18	68
19:28	95, 122
21:5	151
21:9	59, 135
21:15	68, 132, 149
21:33-44	132
21:37	133
21:39	131
22:15	93
23:34, 37	131
23:39	59

25:34, 40	151	1:11	1–2, 4, 6, 7–8, 10, 14, 16, 23, 37, 43–4, 53, 60–3, 65–7, 70–1, 73–4, 78–9, 81, 83–4, 87, 90–1, 97–8, 105, 107–08, 125, 129, 131, 133–34, 137, 142, 145, 159, 172, 177
26–27	93		
26:3	38, 137		
26:3-4	37, 41, 92, 149		
26:57	37, 92, 137, 149		
26:64	144		
27:1	137		
27:1-2, 7	149		
27:1, 7, 17, 27	37, 92		
27:11, 29, 37, 42	150	1:12	87
27:17, 22	150	1:12-13	71–3, 85
27:37	155	1:12-15	70, 73, 87
27:40	159	1:13	73, 97
27:37-54	37	1:14	74
27:51	80	1:14-15	74, 85, 87, 134
27:51-54	161, 174	1:15	74
27:43	165	1:16-20	87
27:54	165, 170	1:16–3:12	90–1, 106
28:3	114	1:20	73
28:11-12	137	1:21-23	87
28:12	37, 92, 149	1:21-28	87, 89, 104
28:16-20	108	1:21-45	91
		1:23-27	85, 94, 97–9
		1:24	83–4, 100, 104
Mark		1:24-25	89, 99
1:1	1, 14, 53–6, 58–60, 74, 84, 97–8, 145, 152, 161, 166, 179	1:29	73
		1:30-3	94
1:1-3	55	1:32-34	90
1:1-11	106	1:32-35	99
1:1-15	59, 74	1:36	73
1:1–3:12	98	1:39	90, 94
1:1–8:29	6	1:40-45	94
1:2-3	57–8	2:1-12	94
1:4-8	58	2:6	138
1:5	94	2:6-7	90
1:6	58	2:10	1
1:7	59, 86, 100	2:16	73, 90, 138
1:8	59, 87	2:18	90, 138
1:9	59–60, 80	2:19	73
1:9-11	4, 54, 58, 60, 72, 126, 134	2:23–3:6	90
		2:24	138
1:9-13	72–3	2:25	73
1:9-15	70, 74	2:28	1
1:10	59, 62, 64, 67, 87	3:1-5	94
1:10-11	73–4, 79–80, 85, 89, 104, 158, 161, 173, 178	3:4	93
		3:6	73, 91, 93, 98, 104, 137–38, 148
1:10-13	33, 75–6, 86–7, 103	3:6-11	90
1:10-15	85, 89	3:7	73

3:7-12	87, 90–1, 93, 96–8, 104	8:31	1, 106, 118, 132, 138, 141, 178
3:7-8	93–4	8:38	1, 73, 106, 119, 121, 125
3:10	94		
3:11	2, 14, 83–4, 90–1, 97, 99–100, 104, 145, 172, 178	9:1	106, 119, 125, 132
		9:2	108, 119
		9:2-3	114
3:11-12	85, 87, 89, 94	9:3	115, 118–20
3:13	106	9:2-8	105, 106–13, 115–17, 119, 125–27
3:13-19	94–5		
3:14	73		
3:16	80	9:4	111
3:22-27	104	9:7	1, 6, 7, 10, 14, 16, 23, 37, 44, 67, 78–9, 81, 83–4, 105–08, 125–27, 129, 131, 133–34, 137, 142, 172
3:22-30	85, 106		
3:24-26	85		
3:27	100		
3:28-30	86		
4:22	179		
4:35-41	106	9:8	73
4:36	73	9:9	1, 119, 126, 178
5:1	98	9:11	58
5:1-20	85, 87, 89, 98, 100–04	9:11-13	112
		9:12	1, 112
5:1-43	106	9:14	138
5:6	99	9:31	1, 138, 141, 178
5:7	2, 14, 83–4, 87, 98–100, 104, 172, 178	10:2	138
		10:33	1
		10:33-34	133, 138, 141, 178
5:8-13	99	10:45	1
5:10	99	11:1-11	135
5:18	73	11:9	59
5:20	95	11:9-10	135
5:24	73	11:11	73
5:33	160	11:18, 27	138
5:40	73	11:27-28	134
6:1-6	106	11:27–12:12	135
6:30-56	106	11:28	131–32
7:1, 5	138	11:33	134
7:24-30	106	12:1	130–31
7:31	95	12:1-9	132
8:1	138	12:1-12	129, 137–38, 140–42
8:1-10, 22-26	106		
8:10	73	12:6	2, 14, 131, 133–36, 142, 178
8:11-13	106		
8:11, 15	138	12:6-8	138
8:27–9:1	112	12:7-8	135
8:29	106, 125	12:9	131, 135
8:30	106	12:10-11	132, 135–36
8:30–16:8	6	12:12	131, 138

Index of References

12:13	138	15:38-39	79–80, 158, 161, 172–73, 178
12:14, 32	160		
12:38	138	15:39	1–2, 4, 6, 8–10, 16, 21, 78, 98, 108, 126, 137, 143–44, 148, 158–75, 178
13:26	1, 119, 121		
14:14	73		
14:17	73		
14:28	178	15:40-41	161
14:33	112	15:42-47	161
14:41	1	16:5	114
14:43	138	16:5-7	178
14:53	138, 149		
14:55	149	Luke	
14:55-60	144	1:17	58
14:58	157	1:32-33	6
14:60-62	149	1:32-35	33, 37, 42–3, 99–100
14:61	1–2, 6, 14, 137, 143, 145, 149–50, 152, 156, 172, 178	1:35	89
		1:68	144
		2:43	68
14:61-62	4, 120, 144, 148, 157, 174	3:1-20	58
		3:15-16	59
		3:21–4:13	71
14:62	98, 121, 146–47	3:22	37, 43–4, 63, 80, 133
14:67	73		
14:70	160	4:1-13	37
15:1	38, 73, 92, 137–38, 148–49, 152, 157	4:4, 10-11	72
		4:18-19	96
15:1-5	149	4:34	84, 89
15:1-15	148, 150	4:41	84, 89
15:2	149–50, 157	6:17	94
15:2-5	152	7:19-20	59
15:2, 9, 12	150–51	7:22	96
15:7	73	8:26-39	100
15:15	152	8:28	84
15:16-20	153–55, 160	8:51, 54	68
15:16-32	152	9:28	113
15:16-40	126	9:29	118
15:18	151	9:30	111
15:22	138	9:35	37, 44, 67–8, 107
15:26	49, 151, 155, 157	9:42	68
15:29	157	11:47, 49	131
15:29-30	160	13:34	131
15:31	73, 157, 160	13:35	59
15:32	150–52, 156	16:14	41
15:33	158	19:38	59, 135, 151
15:33-39	157–58, 161	20:9-18	132
15:34-36	160	20:13	133
15:36	80	20:15	131
15:37	80	22:28-30	95
15:37-39	2		

22:63–23:43	37, 149	7:37	125
22:66	137	7:56	62, 80
22:67–23:39	40	10:11	62, 80
22:70	40, 144	13:22–23, 30, 33	39
23:2	152	13:27	37, 40
23:2, 3, 37, 38	40	13:27-28	39
23:2, 37	150	13:32-33	39
23:3	150	13:33	37, 40, 52, 178
23:5, 13, 14, 35	40	14:15	97
23:13	38, 41		
23:16	40	Romans	
23:35	40–1	1:2-4	6
23:38	155	1:3-4	37, 42–3, 52
23:45	80	1:25	125
23:47	161, 171	9:5	144
24:4	114		
		1 Corinthians	
John		2:3	37
1:29-34	44	15:26, 45, 52	135
1:29-49	43		
1:32-34	44	2 Corinthians	
1:34	37, 43	1:3	144
1:41	37, 44	7:15	37
1:49	37, 44, 151	11:31	144
1:51	62, 80		
4:46-53	68	Ephesians	
6:14, 35	59	1:3	144
12:13	59, 135, 151	2:20	133
12:15	151	6:5	37
18:28–19:30	152		
19:3, 12, 14, 15, 19, 21	150	Philippians	
19:12	152	2:9-11	108
19:19	155	2:12	37
19:20	138		
19:21	150	1 Timothy	
20:12	114	3:16	108
Acts		2 Timothy	
3:13, 26	68	3:1	135
4:5	37–8, 40, 137		
4:11	133, 136	Hebrews	
4:24	97	1:2	135
4:24-28	48, 92	1:3	42
4:24-29	38–9, 47, 93	1:3-5	147
4:25-26	37	1:3-12	6
4:25-28	40, 51, 136	1:5	37, 42, 50, 52
4:25-29	73, 149	1:5-14	108
4:25-30	65	1:7, 13	50
4:27, 30	68	5:5	37, 52

5:5-6	147	20:1-3	86
5:5-8	42	21:10	113
10:37	59		
13:12	138	**Apocrypha**	

James		Baruch	
5:3	135	5:5-7	57
		22:1	62

1 Peter		Epistle of Jeremiah	
1:5, 20	135	1:23	118
2:4-8	133		

2 Peter		1 Esdras	
1:17	37, 108	1:49	41
1:18	108	2:3	99
3:3	135	4:9	116
		8:56	118

1 John		2 Esdras	
2:18	135	13–14	29
3:8	83		

Jude		Judith	
18	135	1:17-29	116

Revelation		1 Maccabees	
1:13-15	119, 124	4:46	59
1:13-16	114, 123, 126	6:39	118
1:18	45	14:41	59
2:16	33, 74–5, 77		
2:26-27	44–5, 74–5, 77, 123	2 Maccabees	
2:26-28	37	2:4-8	113–14
3:5	114	3:31	99
3:21	44	10:1-8	95
4:1	62, 80		
4:4	114	Sirach	
5:5-6	45	4:10	171
7:13-14	114	36:10	95
11:12	113	36:11	69
11:15	37, 44, 51, 73	41:8	99
11:18	37, 45, 73	48:9-10	59
11:19	62, 80	48:10	95
12:5	37, 44	48:24	57
14:14	114		
17:18	37, 44, 73	Tobit	
19:11	33, 62, 74–5, 80	13:11	109, 116
19:11-19	77		
19:14	114	Wisdom of Solomon	
19:15	33, 37, 44, 74–5, 78	1:1	35
19:19	37, 44, 73–5, 78	2:13	65

2:18	35, 171	48:8-10	30, 76, 122, 147
4:18	35	49:1, 3	33, 75
5:5	35	49:2	30, 77
6:1	35	49:2, 4	75
18:13	69	49:3	59, 76-7
		50:4	30

Old Testament Pseudepigrapha

		50:4-5	75
		51:3	146-47
Apocalypse of Abraham		52:4	122, 147
12	113	52:6	122
19:4	62	53:6	122
		54:3-5	86
Apocalypse of Zephaniah		55:4	86, 122, 146-47
3	113	60:2	122
		61:8	146-47
Assumption of Moses		62:2	59, 122, 146-47
10:1	86	62:2-7	146
		62:3, 5	122
2 Baruch		62:3-7	147
13:1	113	62:15	114
40:1-4	109	69:28	86
51:1-3	114	69:29	146-47
73:6	73	71:1-10	116
		90:20-27	116
1 Enoch		106:2-6	114
6-11	115		
10:4	86	*2 Enoch*	
13:8	113	22:8-10	114
14	115, 116	29:3	116
14:8	117		
14:18	115	*Ezekiel the Tragedian*	
14:18-23	115-18, 121	68-69	111, 116
14:20	114-15, 117-18		
18:6	113	*4 Ezra*	
18:6-16	113	2:39-40	121
18:8	109, 111, 116	7:28-29	29, 35
22:1	113	7:97	114
24:2-25:6	109, 116	9:38-10:27	144
25:1	113	10:25	114
25:3	116	12:32	59, 123
32:2	113	13	109, 146
45:3	122, 146-47	13:1-13	123
46:1	122, 146-47	13:3-6	114
47:3	122	13:6	113
48-49	65	13:10	33, 75
48-50	30, 52, 70, 74	13:10-28	74
48:2	122, 120	13:26	123
48:3-7	146-47	13:31-37	28-9, 69, 75, 77, 114, 123
48:4-7	75-6		

13:32	35	17:37	59
13:35-36	156	17:46	28
13:37	35, 78	18:4	69
13:38	33, 75, 78		
13:52	29	*Sibylline Oracles*	
13:53	35	2:170-176	95
14:9	29, 35	3:652	75
		3:652-654	30
Joseph and Aseneth		3:652-656	28
14:2	80	3:652-670	77
		3:652-795	74
Jubilees		3:360-665	75
1:12	131	3:663-664	28
1:17-29	109	3:663-665	30
1:24-25, 28	69	3:669-670	30
2:20	69	3:669-371	75
19:29	69	3:670	28
		3:702	69
Liber antiquitatum biblicarum		3:716-720	109, 116
(Pseudo-Philo)		3:788-795	33, 73, 75, 77
59:2	88–9		
59:4	72		
60:1-3	89	*Testament of Benjamin*	
		9:2	125
Lives of the Prophets			
Passim	131	*Testament of Dan*	
		5:10-11	86
Odes of Solomon		*Testament of Joseph*	
36:3	3	19:1-7	95
Psalms of Solomon		*Testament of Judah*	
11:1-2, 4-6	57	24:2	59, 62, 80
13:9	69	24:3	69
17	27, 29, 33, 52, 70, 74, 76-7, 136	25:3	86
17:1	28	*Testament of Levi*	
17:3	28	2:5	113
17:12	28	2:6	62, 80
17:21	29, 65, 75	5:1	62, 80
17:21-25	76	18:6	62, 80
17:22-24	28	18:8	69
17:23-24	69, 74, 78	18:11	59
17:23-51	109	18:11-12	86
17:24	33		
17:26	33, 76	*Testament of Reuben*	
17:26-32	95	6:10-12	86
17:30-32	28		
17:32	29, 33	*Testament of Zebulun*	
17:35-36	33, 76, 78	9:8	86

Testament of Abraham
A 12:5   114
A 12:3-5   117

Testament of Moses
10:1-5   57

Dead Sea Scrolls

CD (Damascus Document)
7:20   59
19:10-11   59

1QS (Rule of the Community)
1:11   125
8:13-14   57
9:10-11   59, 125, 145

1Q28a (1QSa) *(Rule of the Congregation)*
1:1   135
2:10-12   6
2:11-12   28, 31, 33, 35, 52, 69, 125

1Q28b (1QSb) *(Rule of the Blessings)*
5:20   59

1QM (War Scroll)
1:16   89
3:5   89
5:1   59
6:6   89
13:2-6   89

1Q30 (Liturgical Text A?)
Frag. 12   89

1QpHab (Pesher to Habakkuk)
2:5-6   135
2:9   131
7:5   131
9:6   135

4Q161 (4QpIsa^a) *(Isaiah Pesher^a)*
in toto   59
Col. 3, frag. 7.26   32

4Q174 (4QFlor) *(Florilegium)*
in toto   6, 31, 33, 39, 43, 136, 145
1:10-14   7
1:11–2:6   31, 42–3
1:15, 19   135
1:18-19   28, 39, 69, 73
1:18–2:2   84, 86, 101

4Q175 (4QTest) *(Testimonia)*
1:5-8   125

4Q176 (4QTanḥ) *(Tanḥumim)*
in toto   57

4Q213^a(4QLevi^a Ar) *(Aramaic Levi^a)*
in toto   57

4Q246 (Aramaic Apocalypse)
in toto   32, 42, 122, 146
1:9–2:1   28, 35, 52, 69
I:9–2:9   33, 100
2:1   32, 99
2:5   32, 122
2:6   32
2:9   32, 122

4Q252 (4QcommGen A) *(Commentary on Genesis A)*
5:1-4   31
5:3   59

4Q369 (4QPEnosh?) *(Prayer of Enoch ?)*
2:1-8   34
2:1-10   57–8
2:6   35

4Q500 (4QpapBened) *(Benediction)*
in toto   130

4Q504 (4QDibHam^a) *(Words of the Luminaries^a)*
3:5-6   69

4Q521 (Messianic Apocalypse)
2:5-8	96
2:6	59

4Q558 (4QVision^b ar)
2:4-5	59

11Q5 (11QPs^a) (Psalms^a)
28:11	88

11Q11 (11QapocrPs) (Apocryphal Psalms)
2:2-3	72
5:4-13	72

11Q13 (11QMelch) (Melchizedek)
2:11-13, 24-25	86
2:17-18	125

Josephus

Antiquities of the Jews
6.157, 165	88
8.13	111
8.68, 177, 185	118
10.38	131
11.133	95
13.9	95
13.50	96
14.36	150
15.195-201	167
15.331-41	167
15.363-64	167
15.373	150
17:254	96
18.1	152
25.292-98	167

Jewish War
1.14	150
1.63	95
1.391-95	167
1.403	167
1.404-06, 408-15	167
2.8	152
2.43	96
4.3	153
5.272	132
6.316	169

Philo

Against Flaccus
2:40	152
6:36-39	153

On the Cherubim
1:22	118

On the Decalogue
1:54	118

On the Life of Moses
1:155-58	111

On Rewards and Punishments
87-90	73

Who Is the Heir?
1:224	118

Targumic Texts

Targum Exodus
28:14, 16	132

Targum Isaiah
28:16	136
41:8-9	64–5
42:1	64
42:1-4	59
43:1	64
43:10	64–5
44:1-2	64
52:13	65
53:5	144
65:3	102

Targum Onqelos
Gen 49:24	132

Targum Psalms
91:2-8	72
118:22	132, 136

Targum Pseudo-Jonathan
Deut 30:4	58

Targum Zechariah
4:7	136
6:12-13	136
10:4	136

Mishnah

Berakot
7:3	144

'Ohalot
17-18	102

Pesaḥim 10:6	136

Soṭah
9:15	58

Babylonian Talmud

Baba Batra
75b	89

Baba Qamma
7:7	102

Berakot
7b	35, 84
10	74
10a	35, 84
56a	136

'Erubin
43a-b	58

Ḥagigah
14a-b	124

Megillah
19b	111

Pesaḥim
119a	136

Sanhedrin
38b	124
65b	102
96b	124
98a	124

Sukkah
52a	28, 34–5, 52, 69–70, 145

Zebaḥim
102a	111

Jerusalem Talmud

Berakot
2:3	136
5:5a	144

Sanhedrin
2b:1	144

Tosefta

Sukkah
3:2	136

Midrash and Other Rabbinic Works

Midrash Psalms
2.2, 4	35, 84
2.9	35
3.2	35, 74, 84
26.6	136
72:2	124
92.10	35, 84
118.12	35, 84
118:20	135
118:21	135
118.22	136

Midrash Proverbs
19:21	130

Genesis Rabbah
55.6	111

Exodus Rabbah
2:6	111
15:26	124
20:9	132
30:17	130
40:2	111
46:2	132

Leviticus Rabbah
27:11   35, 84
37:4   136

Deuteronomy
  Rabbah
2.7   111
3.17   111–12

Numbers Rabbah
19:8   86

Esther Rabbah
7:10   132, 135
7:23   35, 84

Lamentations Rabbah
4:1   132

Mekilta
167   111

Mekilta de Rabbi Simeon ben
  Yoḥai
7   35, 84

Pesiqta de Rab Kahana
4:7   86
17:5; 27:5   136

Pesiqta Rabbati
4.2   111
35:3   58
36   86
36:1; 51:7   136

Pirqe Rabbi Eliezer
24   135
43   58

Sipra on Leviticus
263   86

Sipre on Deuteronomy
312   130

Tanḥuma A
  Numbers
10.1-2   111

Tanḥuma B
  Genesis
2.24   35, 84

Tanḥuma B
  Leviticus
7:6   130
8.18   35, 84

Classical and Early Christian Writings

1 Clement
36   47, 50, 147
36:4   50
59:2-4   68

1 Apocalypse of John
17:10   80

Ambrose
  De Spiritu Sancto
  2.6.57   1
  Exposition of the Christian Faith
  1.10.67   3
  Enarrationes in XII Psalmos
    Davidicos
  45.2   126

Apocalypse of Peter
15   108

Aristotle
  Ethica nicomachea
  3.2.1112a13   12
  6.2.1139a23-24 12
  6.13.1144b27 12
  Poetics
  1.1452a22-29 170
  Rhetoric
  3.1414b   53

Athanasius
  Apologia secunda
  2.20   47
  Orationes contra Arianos
  2.20.52   50
  4.24   50
  Epistulae festales
  11   46–8, 93, 149

Homily on Matthew 21:2
8.3-4   46

Augustine
Confessions
10.8.14   12
Contra Faustum Manichaeum
12.43   47, 50, 173
13.7   46, 51, 149
De consensus evangelistarum
2.4   47-8, 51
3.16.53   47, 149
20.57   171
De fide rerum quae non videntur
7   47, 50, 173
De sermon Domini in monte
21.72   47, 149
Enarrationes in Psalmos
2   46
2.3   48
2.7-8   51
46.4   156
47.5   47-8, 51
Epistulae
93.3.9   46-7, 51
169   3
185.5.19   47, 51
In Evangelium Johannis tractatus
115, 117   47-8, 50-1, 155, 173
Post collationem adversus Donatistas
5.19   46
Quaestiones in evangelium Matthaei
43   3
Sermones
28   126
218.5   48, 51, 155-56

Basil
Contra Eunomium
2.15   58

Barnabas
6:2; 16:5   133
12:10   3

Bede
Expositio in Marcum
1.4   58

15.26   47, 49, 155-56
15.39   171
Homiliae
1.1   58

Cassiodorus
Commentarii in Psalmos
2   49, 147, 155
15, 20, 46   156

Cicero
De invention rhetorica
2.17.53   151
De legibus
2.22.57   103
De oratore
2.78.315   61
3.50.196   161
Epistulae ad Atticum
12.45.3   163
13.28.3   163
In Verrum
2.5.168   154
Orator ad M. Brutum
50.168   161
63.214-19   161
Pro Rabirio Perduellionis Reo
3.10   154
4.12   154
5.15-16   154

Clement of Alexandria
Paedagogus
1.6.25   4, 63

Cyril of Jerusalem
Catecheses
10.1   50
12.18   47, 50, 173
14.13   47, 49, 143, 173-74

Cyprian
Ad Quirinum testimonia adversus Judaeos
2.29   47, 50

Didache
9:2   65

9:2-3	68	*Gospel of the Ebionites*	
10:2-3	68	Frg. 4	63

Didymus of Alexandria
Fragmenta in Psalmos
2.8   51

Gospel of Thomas
65   133
66   132

Digesta
1.18.8-9   152
48.4.1   151

Gregory of Nazianzus
Orationes
30.9   50

Dio Cassius
Hist.
40.18   169
43.45.3   163
44.6.4   163
47.18.4   163
56.27   151
62.4.3   153
64.20-21   153

Gregory of Nyssa
Contra Eudomium libri duodecim
9.4   47
11.3   47, 50

Gregory Thaumaturgus
Homiliae quatuor
IV   3

Dio Chrysostom
Orationes
4.67-70   154

Hilary of Poitiers
De Trinitate
11.18   63
11.37   105, 108
Commentary on Matthew
17.2   126
33.7   171

Diodore of Tarsus
Commentarii in Psalmos
2   45–6
2.1-2   47, 149

Hippolytus
Against the Jews
2.5   47

Diognetus
8:9, 11   68
9:1   68

Discourse on the Holy Theophany
106   3

On Genesis
49.5   46, 149

Eusebius
Commenarius in Evangelium Lucam
9   108, 126
Commentarius in Psalmos
2   147
2.2   46, 149
Historia ecclesiastica
1.3.6   46
2.15.1-2   18
3.8.11   46–7, 50–1, 173
3.39.15   11
6.14.6-7   18
6.25.5   18

Homer
Illiad
18.478-608   140
Odyssey
8   140–41
14.7   101

Horace
Odes
1.12.47   163

Irenaeus
Ad. Haer.
3.1.2	18
3.16.7	3
3.17.1	3
4.21	47, 50, 173
5.33.3	73

Epideixis tou apostolikou kerygmatos
74	46

Jerome
Commentariorum in Matthaeum
3.17	126
27.54	171

Commentarioli in Psalmos
2	50

De viris illustribus
8	18

John Chrysostom
Ad Theodorum lapsum
1.11	108

Catechesis ad illuminandos
1.4	47, 50, 173

Homilia in Matthaeum
29:19	46

Homiliae in Matthaeum
36	45–6, 149
86	92–3, 149
90	93, 149

John of Damascus
Or. Trans.
2	108

Justin
Apologia i
40	45–6, 49, 84–5, 147

Dialogus cum Tryphone
76.1	3
88.8	4, 63
100	3
103.6	4, 63
106	18
122	47, 136, 173
126	136

Lucian
How to Write History
53	53

Pro imaginibus
4	161

Martyrdom of Polycarp
14:1, 3	68
20:1	68

Methodius
Symposium
8.9	63

Origen
Commentarii in evangelium Joannis
1.14	58
1.32	63
6.23	47–8
28.12	92–3, 149

Commentarii in evangelium Matthaei
12.1	46, 149
12.31	106
12.43	126
13.9	46–8, 149
130	47–8, 155

Exegetica in Psalmos
2.9	51

Contra Celsum
2.4	16
2.65	126

De principiis
3.3	46, 149

Homiliae in Psalmos
2.1-2	41, 92, 149

Paulus
Sententiae
5.21.3	151

Petronius
Satyricon
53.3	151

Pliny the Elder
Naturalis historia
2.93-94	163

Pliny the Younger
Epistulae
10.30.1	152
10.97.1	152

Plutarch
Aemilius Paullus
34.4	153

Caesar
2	154
67.2	163

De recta ratione audiendi
41d	161

Polycarp
Philippians
2.1	51

Pseudo-Cyprian
De duobus montibus Sina et Sion
9.1-2	49, 155

Pseudo-Jerome
Comm. Matt.
27.54	171

Quintilian
Declamationes
274	154

Institutio oratoria
5.13.42	161
8.5.2-3, 13-14	161
9.3.34	80, 173
12.9.8	161

Seneca the Elder
Controversiae
7.4.10	161

Seneca the Younger
De beneficiis
3.26	151

Epistulae morales
108.8-9	161

Suetonius
Gaius Caligula
19.3	153

Divus Julius
88	163

Nero
25	153

Tiberius
17	153
58	151

Tacitus
Annales
1.23.4	168
1.24.3	168
1.39	169
1.72-73	151
3.49	168

Dialogus de oratoribus
20, 22	161

Tertullian
Adversus Marcionem
3.20	47, 50, 173
3.22	46, 149
4.25	47, 50, 173
4.39	46–7, 50, 149, 173
4.42	41, 46, 149
5.3, 4, 17	46, 149
5.3-4	47–8
5.17	47, 50, 173
5.27	47

Apologeticus
16.8	169

De resurrection carnis
20	46

Theodore of Mopsuestia
Comm. Ps.
2.6	50
2.9	51

Theodoret of Cyrus
Commentarii in Psalmos
2.1-2	41, 46–7, 92, 149
2.9	47

Epistulae
146	46–7, 50, 173

Hist. eccl.
1.3 50

Theophylact
Enarrationes in Marcum
1.1 2, 16
15.39 171

Virgil
Aeneid
6.791-98 169

Index of Modern Authors

Abrahams, I. 144, 181
Achtemeier, P. J. 6, 181
Adams, A. W. 55
Adams, E. 121
Alexander, L. 11-2, 19
Alford, H. 92
Alkier, S. 11, 15-6, 134
Allen, D. 17, 156
Allen, G. 123
Allison, Jr., D. C. 20, 41-2, 58, 92-3, 96, 109, 111-12, 126-27, 131, 158, 179
Alonso Schökel, L. 26
Alt, A. 25
Alter, R. 14-5
Ando, C. 165
Annen, F. 100-03
Atkinson, K. 28-9, 76
Attridge, H. W. 42, 166
Aune, D. E. 12, 19, 45, 119
Austin, J. L. 64

Bächli, O. 90
Bal, M. 13-5, 61, 107, 138, 140
Barker, J. W. J. 179
Barrett, C. K. 38, 44
Barton, C. A. 154
Bates, M. W. 42-3
Bauckham, R. 73, 116, 136
Bauman, R. A. 154
Beard, M. 166-67
Becker, E-M. 179
Becking, B. 26
Berlin, A. 25-6
Bernett, M. 165, 167
Best, E. 11, 79
Betz, H. D. 6
Bieler, L. 5
Black, C. C. 56, 58, 60, 62-3, 79, 87, 90-2, 94-5, 97, 105-07, 113, 131, 149, 152, 160, 173

Black, M. 129-30, 132, 146
Blackburn, B. 6
Blenkinsopp, J. 62
Blinzler, J. 152
Boccaccini, G. 146
Bock, D. L. 30, 38, 59, 89, 95, 99, 100, 107, 144, 148, 153
Bond, H. K. 12, 179
Borges, J. L. 140
Boring, M. E. 2-3, 8, 10, 13, 18, 41, 54, 56, 58, 62, 64, 71, 79, 80, 85-7, 90, 92, 106, 113-14, 125, 131, 133-34, 138, 149, 158
Bosworth, D. A. 140-41
Botner, M. 4-5, 15, 35, 54-6, 59, 64-5, 71-2, 88-9, 133-35, 145-46, 178
Bousset, W. 1, 5, 7, 9, 16, 64, 66-70, 143, 159, 162-63
Bovon, F. 33, 41, 99
Božović, N. 172
Brand, C. E. 168
Braumann, G. 149
Brenner-Idan, A. 121
Bretscher, P. G. 61, 66
Brettler, M. Z. 25-6
Briggs, C. A. 24
Briggs, E. G. 24
Broadhead, E. K. 3
Brooke, G. J. 31, 130
Brooks, P. 102, 140
Brown, J. K. 17, 70, 156
Brown, R. E. 18, 42, 44, 92, 144, 149, 151-52
Bruce, F. F. 43-4
Bryan, C. 12, 18, 57
Buitenwerf, R. 30
Bultmann, R. 3, 5, 19, 43-4, 109, 155
Burdon, C. 101
Burkett, D. 113
Burkill, T. A. 91
Burridge, R. A. 12, 19

Buse, I. 62, 80

Cahill, M. 53
Caird, G. B. 45, 105
Calvin, J. 27, 155, 170–71
Camery-Hoggatt, J. 151–52
Campbell, C. R. 60,
Campbell, J. B. 100, 168–69
Caneday, A. B. 71, 79–80
Caragounis, C. C. 120
Carey, Holly J. 17, 156
Carlson, R. A. 111
Carlston, C. E. 106
Carniti, C. 26
Carroll, J. T. 40–1
Carter, W. 101
Casey, M. 124
Catchpole, D. R. 145
Chapman, D. W. 151, 154
Charlesworth, J. H. 7, 27, 29, 89
Chatman, S. B. 13, 61
Chevallier, M-A. 76–7
Chilton, B. D. 64, 109
Chilton,C.W. 151
Cho, B. 146
Chronis, H. L. 10, 158
Clifford, R. J. 25, 36
Cockerill, G. L. 42
Coggins, R. J. 29
Cole, R. L. 24–6
Coleridge, S. T. 172
Collins, A. Y. 1, 6–9, 12, 15, 23–6, 29, 35, 54, 56, 58–9, 62–4, 69, 71–2, 77, 79–80, 84–5, 90–1, 94, 101, 106–07, 110, 113, 118–20, 123, 133–34, 138, 144, 150–51, 159, 161–62, 164–65, 175
Collins, J. J. 7, 24–7, 29–33, 35, 69, 99–100, 114, 120–23
Colwell, E. C. 162
Conzelmann, H. 38
Cooke, G. 25
Cotter, D. 140
Craigie, P. C. 24–5
Cranfield, C. E. B. 18, 60, 67, 84, 91, 95, 111, 113, 131, 137, 170
Cross, F. M. 32
Crossan, J. D. 133
Croy, N. C. 54

Cullmann, O. 2, 5, 7, 10, 63, 67
Culpepper, R. A. 109

Dahood, M. J. 24–5, 72
Dällenbach, L. 138, 140
Dalman, G. H. 66–70
Davies, J. 113, 115
Davies, W. D. 41, 92, 112, 126, 131
Davis, P. G. 10, 158
Day, J. 26
Deissmann, G. A. 9, 15, 56, 163
Deppe, D. B. 13, 79, 80
Derrett, J. D. M. 101–03, 130
Dewey, J. 12–4, 54, 138
Dibelius, M. 38, 48–9
Doble, P. 38–40
von Dobschütz, E. 13
Dobson, B. 168
Dodd, C. H. 41–2, 44
Donahue, J. R. 18, 62, 87, 91–3, 98, 106, 110, 113, 131, 133, 138
Donaldson, T. L. 106, 108–09, 111–13, 115
Dormandy, R. 101
Dormeyer, D. 12, 58, 133
Dowd, S. E. 11, 160
Draisma, S. 40
Drury, J. 130
Duling, D. C. 43
Dunn, J. D. G. 2–3, 7, 42, 59, 106, 114
Dupont, F. 154

Eaton, J. H. 24–5, 72
Eco, U. 11, 13–6, 88, 157, 169
Edwards, J. R. 13, 62, 79, 149
Egger, W. 91, 94
Ehrman, B. D. 54–5
Elliott, J. K. 54–5
Engnell, I. 26
Ernst, J. 94
Evans, C. A. 9, 18, 27, 29, 32, 34, 56, 79, 107, 109–11, 113–14, 118, 130, 132–33, 136, 144–45, 148–50, 153, 163, 169

Ferda, T. S. 32, 41–2, 48, 92, 99, 155, 156
Ferguson, A. 58
Fischel, H. A. 131
Fitzmyer, J. A. 32–3, 38, 58, 89, 99
Flusser, D. 32
Focant, C. 63, 79, 95, 131–33, 137

Index of Modern Authors

Förster, N. 155
Fowler, R. M. 151–52, 160
France, R. T. 79, 84, 86, 88, 90, 99, 106, 112, 125, 131–33, 137–38
Frankfort, H. 25
Frei, H. W. 12–4, 18, 25, 55, 130
Fuller, R. H. 7, 67
Funk, R. W. 71

Galinsky, K. 56, 163, 165–66, 168
Gamel, B. K. 3, 9–10, 158–63, 172
García Martínez, F. 32, 96
Garland, D. E. 126
Garrett, S. R. 72
Gathercole, S. J. 59
Genest, H. 79
Gerhardsson, B. 70–1
Gero, S. 29
Gibson, J. B. 71
Gide, A. 138
Gill, J. 64, 170
Globe, A. 54–5
Gnilka, J. 10, 54, 58, 60, 63, 85–6, 90, 94, 102, 107, 109–10, 125, 131–33, 145, 147, 149–50, 153, 158
Goldingay, J. 24, 72, 102–03, 115, 121
Goldsmith, D. 31
Goodacre, M. S. 160
Gordon, R. 34, 165
Gould, E. P. 4, 162
Grant, M. 168
Green, J. B. 33, 40, 99
Grotius, H. 154, 170
Grundmann, W. 18, 58, 94, 133, 155, 158
Grünebaum, E. 145
Guelich, R. A. 56–7, 59, 62, 90–1, 94–5, 102
Gundry, R. H. 18, 41, 62–4, 79, 88, 90, 92–3, 106–07, 150–51, 153
Gunkel, H. 23–4, 26
Gurtner, D. 80, 158

Haenchen, E. 38, 43–4, 155
Hahn, F. 2, 7
Ḥakham, ʿA. 125
Hare, D. R. A. 91
Harner, P. B. 162
Hartman, L. 91
Hartman, L. F. 114, 121
Harvey, W. J. 61

Hatina, T. R. 58, 109
Hays, R. B. 7, 11, 16–17, 19–20, 23, 27, 44, 57–8, 63, 66, 109, 126, 131, 133, 172
Head, P. 1, 54
Heil, J. P. 61, 66–7, 71, 93, 110–11
Hengel, M. 7, 9, 18–9, 36, 43, 132, 146, 154, 162–63
Henry, M. 64, 170–71
Hollander, J. 17
Holtzmann, H. J. 4
Hooker, M. D. 1, 3, 6, 54, 61, 71, 79, 86–92, 94–5, 105–06, 112–14, 118, 120, 133, 158–59, 161
Horsley, R. A. 160
Horstmann, M. 108
Hossfeld, F-L. 24–6, 36, 84, 122
Hovde, C. F. 20
Huizenga, L. A. 11, 15, 66–7
Hultgren, A. J. 130, 132–33
Humphrey, R. L. 14
Incigneri, B. J. 18

Iverson, K. R. 133, 160–61

Jackson, H. M. 79–80, 172
Janse, S. 26–7, 29–33, 35, 37–9, 41, 43, 74, 76–7, 80, 99, 107
Jefferson, A. 140–41
Jeremias, J. 63–4, 66–8, 70, 88, 108–09, 129–30, 132–33
Jervell, J. 38–9
Jipp, J. W. 42–3
Johnson, E. S. 160–61, 168
Johnson, L. T. 40
Johnson, N. C. 33–4, 42–3
de Jong, I. J. F. 138, 140–41
Juel, D. 5–7, 38, 62–3, 65–8, 79–80, 144, 151–52, 160
Jülicher, A. 130

Kazmierski, C. R. 2, 90, 93, 133
Keaveney, A. 151
Keck, L. E. 2, 6, 5, 74, 90–1, 94
Kee, H. C. 18, 26, 43–4, 88, 90, 94, 99, 108–09, 111, 113–15, 123, 125–26, 131
Keel, O. 26
Keener, C. S. 43
Kempthorne, R. 144
Kennedy, D. 100

Kennedy, J. 20
Kenyon, F. G. 55
Kermode, F. 11, 19, 57
Kertelge, K. 102
Kim, S. 6, 124–25, 148
Kim, T. H. 9, 164–65
Kingsbury, J. D. 3, 6, 10–11, 35, 54, 58, 60–2, 93, 106, 143, 145, 159
Kister, M. 7
Klauck, H-J. 130, 133
Kloppenborg, J. S. 63, 130
Klostermann, E. 48, 94
Knibb, M. A. 29
Koch, D-A. 6, 90, 99
Koester, C. R. 42, 45
Koester, H. 18
Kohler, K. 145
Kramer, W. R. 39
Kristeva, J. 16
Kugel, J. 33
Kuhn, H-W. 155
Kuhn, K. A. 32
Kuhn, K. G. 35
Kümmel, W. G. 18, 36
Kvanvig, H. 146

La Gioia, F. 91, 97
Lane, W. L. 54, 63, 79, 94
à Lapide, C. C. 155, 171
Larsen, M. D. C. 12
Lau, M. 101
Lausberg, H. 80
Lee, A. H. I. 32
Lee, S. S. 111–12
Légasse, S. 3, 60, 63, 84, 87–8, 93–4, 102, 131–33
Leim, J. E. 15
Lentzen-Deis, F. 79
Levenson, J. D. 112
Levinsohn, S. H. 60
Lewis, C. S. 14–5
Lightfoot, R. H. 53–4
Lindars, B. 3, 36, 38, 63
Lohmeyer, E. 58, 60, 62, 64, 67, 108, 159
Long, T. G. 126
Longenecker, B. W. 6
Lorein, G. W. 136
Lövestam, E. 35, 73–4, 133, 135, 144
Lowe, M. F. 133

Lüdemann, G. 38
Lührmann, D. 88, 149
Lust, J. 84
Luz, U. 6

Macaskill, G. 115
MacIntyre, A. 12, 15
Maclear, G. F. 162
Madden, J. A. 151
Magnus, A. 2, 155, 171
Maier, P. L. 155
Malbon, E. S. 8, 10, 12–4, 56, 60–1, 79, 83–5, 90, 113
Maldonado, J. de. 171
Marcus, J. 7, 19, 23, 31, 34–5, 54, 57–60, 62–4, 74, 79–80, 85–95, 97, 99–102, 105–12. 125–26, 131–34, 136, 138, 144–45, 150–51, 153–56, 158–59, 170
Marshall, I. H. 38, 67–8
Martin, R P. 6
Masson, C. 105
Matera, F. J. 3, 53–4, 79, 84, 88, 95, 133, 135, 145, 149–52, 155, 158
Mauser, U. 20, 58, 71
Mays, J. L. 24
McCann, Jr., J. C. 24–5
Meeks, W A. 111
Meggitt, J. J. 153, 165
Melville, H. 19–20
Mercier, R. 43
Mettinger, T. N. D. 25
Metzger, B. M. 29, 54–5
Meyer, H. A. W. 87–8, 91, 94, 105, 115, 162
Michaels, J. R. 44
Michel, O. 108
Michie, D. 11–2, 138
Milgrom, J. 31
Milik, J. T. 32
Millar, F. 18
Miller, S. R. 121
Mitchell, D. C. 24–5, 72
Moj, M. 13
Moloney, F. J. 12, 19, 53, 91–2, 95, 107, 111–12, 114
Montgomery, J. A. 121
de Moor, J. C. 130, 132–33
Moore, S. D. 11
Moscicke, H. M. 101–02
Moss, C. R. 114

Index of Modern Authors

Motyer, S. 79–80
Moule, C. F. D. 2, 6–7
Mowinckel, S. 24
Müller, U. B. 108
Murgatroyd, P. 140
Myers, C. 14, 101, 160

Nelles, W. 139–40
Nickelsburg, G. W. E. 29–30, 76, 122–23, 146
Noegel, S. P. 96
Nolan, B. M. 41, 92
Nolland, J. 41
Noreña, C. F. 165
North, J. 165–67
Novakovic, L. 96
Novenson, M. V. 56, 88

O'Brien, K. S. 133, 135, 137–38, 145
Oden, T. C. 18
Oegema, G. S. 31, 99
Oldenhage, T. 133
Otto, E. 25
Overstreet, L. R. 151–52
Owen, J. 64

Parker, D. C. 55
Peddinghaus, C. D. 155
Peppard, M. 3, 9, 23, 56, 162–66, 168
Perrin, N. 6, 147
Pesch, R. 18, 38–9, 54, 62–3, 67, 84–6, 88, 90–5, 105–10, 112, 119, 125–26, 129, 131–34, 138, 144, 149, 151, 153
Pierce, C. S. 11
Plummer, A. 162
Poirier, J. C. 109
Pomykala, K. 29
Poole, M. 170
Poorthuis, M. 36
Powell, M. A. 11, 13, 62
Price, S. R. F. 163, 165–67

von Rad, G. 25, 27
Reimarus, H. S. 4–6, 64, 70
Rengstorf, K. H. 108
Reploh, K-G. 94
Resseguie, J. L. 61
Reynolds, B. E. 115
Rhoads, D. M. 11–2, 138

Richardson, A. 71–2, 168
Ricoeur, P. 12–3, 19, 169
Ridderbos, H. N. 43–4
Riesenfeld, H. 108
Rinon, Y. 141
Roberts, J. J. M. 24, 59
Roskam, H. N. 18
Ron, M. 140
Ross, A. P. 24
Rouwhorst, G. 36
Rowe, C. K.. 11, 15, 20, 61
Rowe, R. D. 7
Rowland, C. 114, 116–17, 119
Russell, D. A. 53

Sabbé, M. 113
Sahlin, H. 102
Samuelsson, G. 154
Sanders, E. P. 151
Sasson, V. 84
Saur, M. 25
Schmidt, K. L. 94
Schmidt, T. E. 151, 155–56
Schnabel, E. J. 151
Schnackenburg, R. 10, 43
Schneider, G. 149
Schnelle, U. 13, 179
Schramm, B. 102
Schreiber, J. 5
Schröten, J. 136
Schweizer, E. 63, 79, 88, 91, 94–5, 107, 112, 114
Scott, S. P. 151
Segal, A. F. 124
Segal, M. 32, 122
Senior, D. 144
Seow, C. L. 114, 120
Shepherd, T. 113
Sherwin-White, A. N. 149, 151–52
Shiner, W. T. 160–62
Shively, E. E. 12, 85–6, 90, 100–01
Skeat, T. C. 55
Slomp, J. 54
Smallwood, E. M. 18, 150, 167
Smith, D. E. 53
Smith, D. M. 43–4
Smith, S. H. 11
Smith, S. 17, 156
Smith-Christopher, D. L. 115

Snodgrass, K. R. 57, 129–33, 135, 137
Soards, M. L. 38, 92
Sorensen, E. 85–6
Spurgeon, C. H. 64
van Staalduine-Sulman, E. 136
Stählin, G. 38
Standaert, B. 58, 60, 84, 90–1, 93, 99–102, 132–33
Stec, D. M. 72, 131
Steck, O. H. 131
Stegner, W. R. 70–1, 113
Steichele, H-J. 2, 6–7, 34, 62–3, 68, 107, 125
Stein, R. H. 79, 91, 99, 102
Stern, D. 132
Stern, F. 133
Stokes, R. E. 115
Stone, M. E. 29, 123
Stonehouse, N. B. 60
Straub, J. 12
Strauss, D. F. 109
Strothmann, M. B. 164
Stuckenbruck, L. T. 76, 115
Stuhlmacher, P. 57
Sweat, L. C. 160
Swete, H. B.. 151–52, 159, 162
Syme, R. 168

Talbert, C. H. 4, 12
Tannehill, R. C. 173
Taylor, J. E. 167
Taylor, L. R. 163–64, 168
Taylor, V. 18, 60, 62–3, 88, 91–2, 94, 99–100, 106, 109, 126, 144–45, 150–52, 159, 170
Telford, W. R. 3
Terrien, S. L. 24
Thatcher, T. 154
Theisohn, J. 146
Theissen, G. 18, 85, 97, 101, 103
Tigchelaar, E. J. C. 115
Torrey, R. A. 155
Trapp, J. 155
Trocmé, E. 3, 84, 88, 107, 131–32
Trotter, J. R. 115

Turner, C. H. 55, 58
Twelftree, G. H. 85–6, 88, 101

Ulansey, D. 14, 79–80

Van Eck, E. 138
Van Iersel, B. M. F. ' 11, 13, 35–6, 38–40, 85
Várhelyi, Z. 163–64
de Vaux, R. 103
Versnel, H. S. 153
Vielhauer, P. 63, 108

Wallace-Hadrill, A. 166
Wasserman, T. 54–5
Watson, G. R. 168
Watts, J. W. 102
Watts, J. D. 36
Watts, R. 7, 16, 20, 27, 54, 57, 60, 62–4, 86, 100–02, 107, 110–12, 114, 118, 130–31, 133, 136–37,
Weeden, T. J. 5–6, 106
Weinstock, S. 163–64
Weiser, A. 26
Weiss, B. 4
Wellhausen, J. 4
Wengst, K. 100–01
Weren, W. J. C. 40–1, 49, 130
Westermann, C. 102
Whybray, R. N. 102
Wilke, C. 145
Winn, A. 3, 9–10, 56, 163
Winter, B. W. 9, 53, 152, 163–65, 167
Winterbottom, M. 53
Witherington, B. 19, 100
Wittgenstein, L. 88, 117
Wong, S. K. 130
Wood, J. E. 18, 150, 167
Wrede, W. 4–5, 88
Wright, N. T. 7
Wright, R. B. 28, 74

Zahn, T. 170
Zanker, P. 165
Zenger, E. 24–6, 36, 72, 84, 112, 136
Zimmermann, J. 99, 133

www.ingramcontent.com/pod-product-compliance
Lightning Source LLC
Chambersburg PA
CBHW071934240426
43668CB00038B/1678